23/12/71

AUTHOR	CLASS No.
RALEIGH, Sir W.	930
TITLE *History of the World.*	BOOK No.
	57202460

D1626115

The History of the World

By C. A. Patrides

The Phoenix and the Ladder:
The Rise and Decline of the Christian View of History
Milton's 'Lycidas' (editor)
Milton's Epic Poetry (editor)
Approaches to 'Paradise Lost' (editor)
Milton and the Christian Tradition
The Cambridge Platonists (editor)

The title page of *The History of the World* (1614) engraved
by Renold Elstracke from a design by Ralegh (see p. xv)

Sir Walter Ralegh

THE HISTORY
OF THE
WORLD

Edited by

C. A. Patrides

Macmillan

First published 1971 *by*
THE MACMILLAN PRESS LTD
London and Basingstoke
Associated companies in New York Toronto
Dublin Melbourne Johannesburg and Madras

SBN 333 01837 0

Printed in Great Britain by
R. & R. CLARK LTD
Edinburgh

For the Fryes: Roland, Jean, and Roland Jr.

ἡ ἀγάπη οὐ ζητεῖ ἑαυτῆς

Contents

To the Reader   xi
A Note on the Frontispiece   xv
Ralegh and The History of the World:
    An Introduction   I
A Note on Method   41

THE HISTORY OF THE WORLD

The Preface   45

Book I. From the Creation vnto Abraham

*Ch. I.   Of the Creation, and Preseruation of the World   85
*Ch. II.   Of mans estate in his first Creation, and of Gods rest 119
*Ch. III.   Of the place of Paradise   131
*Ch. IV.   Of the two chiefe Trees in the Garden of Paradise   134
*Ch. V.   Of diuers memorable things betweene the fall of
               Adam, and the floud of *Noah*   143
*Ch. VI.   Of idolatrous corruptions ... and of the Reliques of
               Truth touching these ancient times ...   146
 Ch. VII.   Of *Noahs* Floud   154
 Ch. VIII.   Of the first planting of Nations after the floud ...   155
*Ch. IX.   Of the beginning and establishment of Gouerne-
               ment   156
 Ch. X.   Of *Nimrod, Belvs*, and *Ninvs* ...   165
*Ch. XI.   Of *Zoroaster* ... and of the diuers kinds of Magicke   165
*Ch. XII.   Of the memorable buildings of *Ninvs*, and of his
               wife *Semiramis* ...   169

Book II. From the birth of Abraham to the destruction of the Temple of Salomon

*Ch. I.   Of the time of the birth of *Abraham* ...   179
 Ch. II.   Of the Kings of Ægypt ...   179

* The asterisk designates chapters which — in addition to the Preface — are reprinted here in part or in whole.

*Ch. III.   Of the delivery of Israel out of Ægypt   180
*Ch. IV.   Of the iournying of the Israelites . . . with a discourse
                   of Lawes   184
*Ch. V.   The Storie of the Israelites . . . to the death of *Moses*   200
   Ch. VI.   Of the Nations with whom the Israelites had deal-
                   ing . . .   202
   Ch. VII.   Of the Tribes of Israel . . .   202
   Ch. VIII.   Of the Kingdome of Phœnicia   202
   Ch. IX.   Of the Tribe of *Ephraim* . . .   202
   Ch. X.   Of the memorable places of *Dan, Simeon, Ivda,
                   Rvben* . . .   203
   Ch. XI.   The Historie of the Syrians . . .   203
   Ch. XII.   Of the Tribe of *Beniamin* . . .   203
*Ch. XIII.   Of the memorable thinges . . . to the Warre of
                   Troy . . .   203
   Ch. XIV.   Of the Warre of Troy   209
   Ch. XV.   Of *Sampson, Eli,* and *Samvel*   210
   Ch. XVI.   Of *Savl*   210
   Ch. XVII.   Of *David*   210
   Ch. XVIII. Of *Salomon*   210
*Ch. XIX.   Of *Salomons* Successors . . .   210
   Ch. XX.   Of *Iehoram* . . . and *Ahazia*   212
*Ch. XXI.   Of *Athalia* . . .   212
   Ch. XXII.   Of *Ioas* . . . [and] the building of Carthage   217
   Ch. XXIII. Of *Vzzia*   217
   Ch. XXIV.   Of the Antiquities of Italie, and foundation of
                   Rome . . .   217
   Ch. XXV.   Of *Ezekia* . . .   218
   Ch. XXVI.   Of the Kings that raigned in Ægypt . .   218
   Ch. XXVII. Of *Manasse(s)* . . .   218
   Ch. XXVIII. Of the times . . . to the destruction of Ierusalem   218

Book III. From the destruction of Ierusalem to the time of Philip of Macedon

*Ch. I.   Of the time . . . [to] the fall of the Assyrian Empire   221
   Ch. II.   Of the originall . . . of the Persians   222
   Ch. III.   Of *Cyrvs*   222
   Ch. IV.   The estate of things . . . to the Raigne of *Darivs*   222
   Ch. V.   Of *Darius* . . .   222
*Ch. VI.   Of *Xerxes*   222
   Ch. VII.   Of things . . . to the beginning of the Peloponnesian
                   [War]   232
   Ch. VIII.   Of the Peloponnesian Warre   233
   Ch. IX.   Of matters concurring with the Peloponnesian
                   Warre . . .   233
   Ch. X.   Of the expedition of *Cyrvs* the younger   233

Ch. XI.   Of the affaires of Greece ... [under] the Lacedæ-
                 monians   233
*Ch. XII.   Of the flourishing estate of Thebes ...   233

Book IV. From the raigne of Philip of Macedon,
to ... Antigonvs

Ch. I.   Of *Philip* ...   243
*Ch. II.   Of *Alexander* the Great   243
Ch. III.   The raigne of *Aridævs*   320
Ch. IV.   Of the great Lordship which *Antigonvs* got in Asia   320
*Ch. V.   Of the great ciuill Warre betweene *Alexanders* Cap-
                 taines ...   320
Ch. VI.   Of the warres betweene ... *Alexanders* Princes ...   320
Ch. VII.   The growth of Rome: and setling of the Easterne
                 Kingdomes   321

Book V. From the setled rule of Alexanders Successors
in the East, vntil the Romans, preuailing ouer all,
made Conquest of Asia and Macedon

*Ch. I.   Of the first Punick Warre   325
*Ch. II.   Of diuers actions passing betweene the first and
                 second Punick Warres   350
Ch. III.   Of the second Punick Warre   368
Ch. IV.   Of *Philip* the Father of *Persevs* ...   369
Ch. V.   The Warres of the Romans with *Antiochvs* ...   369
*Ch. VI.   The second Macedonian Warre   369

A Dictionary of Names   399
A Bibliographical Note   417

To the Reader

SIR WALTER RALEGH never ceases to fascinate. But the recognition traditionally extended to him depends largely on information obtained from secondary sources. Widely known, he is as widely unread. His life is re-written with increasing frequency,[1] yet his major work, *The History of the World*, is not readily accessible. Perhaps its size defeats even the most determined reader. The last edition of the work in 1829 covers six volumes of nearly 3,000 pages, and intimidates no less than do the humble anthologies which, like the most recent one (published as long ago as 1917), provide us with a few 'literary' passages torn from their context. To make matters worse, Ralegh's thesis – the assured vision of a divinely-sanctioned order within the historical process – is at best an oddity, at worst an embarrassment.

Uncertain as I am of the value of secondary sources, I have tried to provide extracts from *The History of the World* which are far less than the original work yet much more than the 'occasional pieces of gorgeous prose' provided in antho-

[1] The best biography written in the previous century was by William Stebbing (1891, reissued in 1899); the best in ours is by Edward Thompson (1935). Other ventures published since 1900 include the performances I. A. Taylor (1902), Henry David Thoreau (1st ed., 1905), M. D. Haywood (1913), M. A. S. Hume (1926, but first published in 1897), Milton Waldman (1928, reissued in 1950), D. B. Chidsey (1931), Eric Ecclestone (1941), H. R. Williamson (1951), Sir Philip Magnus (1952, reset with minor changes in 1956), P. E. Edwards (1953), Willard Wallace (1959), Margaret Irwin (1960), A. L. Rowse (1962), N. L. Williams (1962), J. H. Adamson and H. F. Folland (1969), *et al*. Several biographies are addressed to the very young: Geoffrey Trease, *Fortune, my Foe* (1949); Charles Norman, *The Shepherd of the Ocean* (1952); and Henrietta Buckmaster, *Walter Raleigh: Man of Two Worlds* (1964).

logies. But certain as I am of the need to demonstrate the impressive unity of Ralegh's work, I have repeatedly avoided disregarding his context (see 'A Note on Method', below, pp. 41–2). Moreover, I have not included chapters and sections simply because they are generally held to be of sufficient literary merit; indeed, I have often reprinted pages where Ralegh obviously nods, for even apparently dull paragraphs tend in their passage through the flowing narrative to be transported to higher regions. In this manner I have endeavoured to relate the particular to the general, even as I have attempted to demonstrate Ralegh's overall conception through representative selections from all the five books of *The History of the World*.

I venture no apologies for Ralegh's thesis because none is needed. Its oddities cannot be denied, much less its embarrassments. But as they are oddities and embarrassments which elicited the enthusiastic response of our predecessors at least to the end of the seventeenth century, they can be disregarded only if we are prepared to confine ourselves to our own age.

This edition aims to acquaint ourselves once more with *The History of the World* and thereby better to understand Ralegh. But I also thought it particularly useful to provide students of the late sixteenth and early seventeenth centuries with a work whose Preface is 'the culminating document of Renaissance historiography in England',[1] whose opening chapters are the best single collection of the age's most sacrosanct verities, and whose five books are jointly the finest assertion of the view of history that leads from the Elizabethan history plays including Shakespeare's, to the performance of Milton in his *History of Britain* no less than in *Paradise Lost*. When all is said, however, I wished to provide the text to one of the most popular works of the seventeenth century and the principal labour of the period's most widely venerated hero.

[1] Lily B. Campbell, *Shakespeare's 'Histories': Mirrors of Elizabethan Policy* (San Marino, Calif., 1947) p. 79. Cf. F. P. Wilson, *Shakespearian and Other Studies* (Oxford, 1969) p. 6, and M. M. Reese, *The Cease of Majesty* (1961) p. 16: 'The divergent ideas about history current in the sixteenth century were magnificently reconciled at its close in Raleigh's *History*'.

The text is reprinted from the authoritative first edition of
1614. The authority of the first edition has been established
by Racin (see below, p. 418). Its obvious misprints are here
corrected, and its flamboyant typography selectively tempered. I have used the copy which is now in the British
Museum (C.38.i.10) but which Ralegh had presented to
Princess Elizabeth, the eldest daughter of King James and
sister to Prince Henry, for whom the *History* was intended.
The copy is still magnificently preserved despite its remarkable fortunes. It is known to have been in the possession of
Princess Elizabeth when she accompanied her husband
Frederick the Elector Palatine to Prague where she was
eventually crowned Queen of Bohemia (1619). On their
flight from Prague in November 1620, however, the copy
passed into the hands of a member of the conquering Spanish
armies. In 1648, when the city was recaptured by the Swedes,
the copy was recovered by a German who presented it to
Elizabeth's son John Philip Frederick.[1]

My indebtedness to many scholars is acknowledged with
pleasure. The sage counsel of Professor Pierre Lefranc of the
Université Laval has repeatedly illumined my darkness; and
if on occasion I was obliged to disagree with his authoritative
conclusions, I hope he will not misconstrue my stubbornness
as a sign of ingratitude. I am no less indebted to Professor
G. E. Aylmer of the University of York, who placed his
formidable knowledge at my disposal and wisely advised me
to include several sections which I was prepared to overlook;
to Professor F. Smith Fussner of Reed College, who en-
couraged me precisely when his authoritative judgement was
most needed; to Professor John Racin, Jr., of West Virginia
University – himself now at work on an edition of Ralegh's
Preface – who generously corrected a number of my errors;
and to Professors Ernest A. Strathmann of Pomona College
and Elkin C. Wilson of New York University, and Dr
Frances A. Yates of the Warburg Institute, who responded
with alacrity to my requests for their assistance. Like all

[1] W. B. Rye, *England as seen by Foreigners* (1865) p. 222; *Catalogue of
Books in the Library of the British Museum printed* ... *to the year 1640*
(1884) II 820.

students of Ralegh, I benefited greatly from Miss Agnes M. C. Latham's discriminating editions of his *Poems* (1951) and *Selected Prose and Poetry* (1965). Additionally, I am deeply grateful to Mr C. B. L. Barr of the York Minster Library, who lent me his extensive knowledge of Latin on two occasions; to Mr P. N. Furbank, who welcomed the present edition on behalf of Macmillan's and patiently advised me on a number of details; to Mr T. M. Farmiloe, who supervised my pages for the press; to Mr Denis Cahill, who improved the manuscript in several important respects; and to Mr Malcolm Harrison, who designed the jacket.

I should finally like to express my gratitude to the Trustees of the British Museum for their kind permission to reproduce Ralegh's title page and to reprint the selections chosen, and to the staff of the Reading Room for their courteous assistance.

Langwith College,   C. A. P.
University of York,
21 April 1971

A Note on the Frontispiece

THE frontispiece reproduced here from the first edition of *The History of the World* (1614) was engraved by Renold Elstracke from a design by Ralegh. It has been called 'the most elaborate of its kind known in English bibliography'.[1]

The design is a visual interpretation of Cicero's celebrated 'definition' in *De oratore*: 'Historia vero testis temporum, lux veritatis, vita memoriae, magistra vitae, nuntia vetustatis.'[2] Cicero's five phrases are inscribed on the two columns which flank Experience, on the gown of History who supports the earth in her hands and tramples on Death and Oblivion, and on the two columns which flank Truth. In the upper part of the design, the earth (with interesting details of Adam and Eve at the moment of disobedience, and ships at war in the Atlantic) is further flanked by two representations of Fame – good and ill – whose conflict is resolved by the omniscient eye of Providence which gazes downwardly into the composition and outwardly into the historical process.

The implications of the design are stated in the explanatory verses supplied by Ben Jonson and based on the Ciceronian dictum. His poem was originally printed facing the title page:

[1] William Stebbing, *Sir Walter Ralegh* (Oxford, 1891) p. 276.
[2] *De Oratore*, II ix 36 – which in the Loeb Classical Library translation (by E. W. Sutton, 1942) reads: 'History ... bears witness to the passing of the ages, sheds light upon reality, gives life to recollection and guidance to human existence, and brings tidings of ancient days'! Ben Jonson, in the poem quoted here, is more precise and less prolix.

THE MINDE OF
THE FRONT

From Death *and darke* Obliuion (*neere the same*)
The Mistresse of Mans life, *graue Historie,*
Raising the World *to good, or* Euill *fame,*
Doth vindicate it to Æternitie.

High Prouidence *would so: that nor the good*
Might be defrauded, nor the Great secur'd,
But both might know their wayes are *vnderstood,*
And the reward, and punishment assur'd.

This makes, that lighted by the beamie hand
Of Truth, which searcheth the most hidden springs,
And guided by Experience, *whose streight wand*
Doth mete, whose Line *doth sound the depth of things:*

Shee chearefully supporteth what shee reares;
Assisted by no strengths, but are her owne,
Some note of which each varied Pillar *beares,*
By which as proper titles shee is knowne,

Times witnesse, Herald of Antiquitie,
The light of Truth, and life of Memorie.

Ralegh and
The History of the World:
An Introduction

> *Think now*
> *History has many cunning passages, contrived corridors*
> *And issues . . .*
>
> T. S. ELIOT, Gerontion

I

Is it unreasonable to wonder whether Ralegh ever existed? Even the spelling of his name varies more spectacularly than that of any other Elizabethan,[1] which may well be symbolic of the confluence of fact and fiction in nearly all reports of his divers activities. According to a celebrated story first told by Thomas Fuller, Ralegh gained access to the court of Elizabeth in or about 1582 by means of a gesture which may not be true but is certainly characteristic:

> *Captain Raleigh* coming out of *Ireland* to the *English Court* in good habit (his Cloaths being then a considerable part of his estate) found the Queen

---

[1] The authoritative conclusion is that the proper spelling is *Ralegh* (see T. N. Brushfield, 'Ralegh Miscellanea', *Transactions of the Devonshire Association for the Advancement of Science, Literature, and Art*, XLI [1909] 179–214). However, an alarming number of variants (listed by W. M. Wallace, *Sir Walter Raleigh* [Princeton, 1959] p. 319) extend throughout the seventeenth century. As A. L. Rowse drily notes (*Ralegh and the Throckmortons* [1962] p. 160), even Sir Arthur Throckmorton could not make up his mind how to spell his brother-in-law's name; he often settled on 'Raelly'.

walking, till meeting with a *Plashy place*, she seemed to scruple going thereon. Presently *Raleigh* cast and spred his new Plush Cloak on the ground, whereon the Queen trod gently, rewarding him afterwards with many *Suits*, for his so free and seasonable tender of so fair *a foot Cloath*.[1]

Ralegh was then probably twenty-nine years old.[2] When at the end of his life on 29 October 1618 he ascended the scaffold in Old Palace Yard, Westminster, it is reported in one of the many surviving accounts that

putting off his doublet, and gowne, he desired the headsman to shew him the Axe, which not being suddenly granted unto him, he said I prithee, let me see it, dost thou thinke that I am afraid of it, so it being given unto him, he felt along upon the edge of it, and smiling, spake unto M. Sheriffe saying, this is a sharpe medecine, but it is a physician that will cure all diseases.[3]

The 'truth' of either story is of slight consequence, for the better part of Ralegh's career is far stranger than fiction.

'He had in the outward man', we are told, 'a good presence, in a handsome and well compacted person, a strong naturall wit, and a better Judgement, with a bould and plausible tongue, where he could set out his parts to the best advantage.'[4] The outward appearance was wedded to an excellent

[1] *The History of the Worthies of England* (1662), 'Devon-shire', p. 262. Several scholars think the story has 'the ring of truth' (M. C. Bradbrook, *The School of Night* [Cambridge, 1936] p. 31 ; W. M. Wallace, *Sir Walter Raleigh* [Princeton, 1959]; *et al.*). It is interestingly supported by Walter Oakeshott, *The Queen and the Poet* (1960) pp. 22 f.

[2] The year of Ralegh's birth, often said to be 1552, has lately been revised to 1554 (see Agnes M. C. Latham, 'A Birth-date for Sir Walter Ralegh', *Études Anglaises*, ix [1956] 243–5). On his respectable social origins consult A. L. Rowse, *Ralegh and the Throckmortons* (1962) pp. 129 ff.

[3] Sir Thomas Overbury, *The Arraignment and Conviction of S*[r] *Walter Rawleigh* (1648) p. 34. The 'most complete and detailed version' supplied by R. H. Bowers, 'Raleigh's Last Speech: the "Elms" Document', *Review of English Studies*, n.s., II (1951) 209–16, is substantially different. But see John Pory's report to Sir Dudley Carleton (31 Oct 1618), in William S. Powell, 'John Pory on the Death of Sir Walter Raleigh', *The William and Mary Quarterly*, 3rd series, ix (1952) 532–8; and Chamberlain's letter to Carleton (same date), in *The Letters of John Chamberlain*, ed. Norman E. McClure (Philadelphia, 1939) II 175 ff., and *The Chamberlain Letters*, ed. Elizabeth M. Thomson (1966) pp. 199 ff.

[4] Sir Robert Naunton, 'Rauleigh', in *Fragmenta Regalia* (1641) p. 34. The statement is repeated *verbatim* by William Winstanley, *England's Worthies* (1660) p. 252, and quoted by Anthony à Wood, *Athenæ Oxonienses* (1691) I 371.

mind, for Ralegh had an enthusiasm for learning which in time placed him among the most extravagantly 'universal' men of the English Renaissance. Posterity, awe-stricken, confessed with David Lloyd in 1665 that

> so contemplative he was, that you would think he was not active; so active, that you would say he was not prudent. A great Soldier, and yet an excellent Courtier: an accomplished Gallant, and yet a bookish man; a man that seemed born for any thing he undertook.[1]

Ralegh pursued so many activities that he cannot be confined within any single category. 'Authors are perplex'd', reported Anthony à Wood, 'under what topick to place him, whether of Statesman, Seaman, Souldier, Chymist, or Chronologer; for in all these he did excell.'[2] Yet even this list hardly exhausts Ralegh's variegated activities. He was also historian, philosopher, and theologian. He was a poet whose verses have been enthusiastically described as 'extraordinary by any standards' – though Aubrey's judgement is perhaps nearer the mark ('He was somtimes a Poet, not often').[3] Moreover, he pursued commercial enterprises which enriched his country if not himself; he was a noted patron of literature and the

---

[1] *The States-men and Favourites of England* (1665) p. 487. Even the dramatist John Ford – not otherwise enthusiastic about Ralegh – conceded that he was 'stored with the best of Natures furniture' (below, p. 13, n. 2).

[2] *Athenæ Oxonienses* (1691) 1 371; the statement is borrowed from John Shirley, *The Life of the Valiant & Learned Sir Walter Raleigh* (1677) p. 242; cf. Fuller (as above, p. 2, n. 1) p. 261. But the further report that Ralegh was 'a great Chymist' (John Aubrey, *Brief Lives*, ed. O. L. Dick, 2nd ed. [1950] p. 254) must needs be qualified in the light of J. W. Shirley's study, 'The Scientific Experiments of Sir Walter Ralegh, the Wizard Earl, and the Three Magi in the Tower, 1603–1617', *Ambix*, IV (1949) 52–66.

[3] *Brief Lives*, ed. O. L. Dick, 2nd ed. (1950) p. 260. The enthusiastic description is by M. C. Bradbrook, *The School of Night* (Cambridge, 1936) p. 87. Ralegh's contemporaries judged his poetry as 'most loftie, insolent, and passionate' (George Puttenham [?], *The Arte of English Poesie*, ed. G. D. Willock and Alice Walker [Cambridge, 1936] p. 63), or as 'the most passionate among vs to bewaile and bemoane the perplexities of Loue' (Francis Meres, *Palladis Tamia* [1598] p. 284). The most balanced modern estimate is by Peter Ure, 'The Poetry of Sir Walter Ralegh', *Review of English Literature*, I (1960) iii 19–29; see also Pierre Lefranc, *Sir Walter Ralegh écrivain* (Paris, 1968) ch. xiv (i). The surviving 'books' of *The Ocean to Scinthia* appear to be fragments of an incomplete work; see A. M. Buchan, 'Ralegh's *Cynthia* – Facts or Legend', *Modern Language Quarterly*, I (1940) 461–74.

sciences; he designed ships; and he was a politician distinguished for his remarkably liberal tendencies.[1] We are also
assured that he was 'a pioneer in naval medicine, dietetics, and
hygiene'.[2] As Aubrey said, 'He was no Slug'.[3]

Ralegh crossed the trajectories of nearly every Elizabethan
and Jacobean personality of major stature. As Sidney's acquaintance he penned one of the most noteworthy tributes
to the 'Scipio, Cicero and Petrarch of our time'.[4] He countered
Marlowe's 'smooth song' of 'The Passionate Shepherd to his
Love' with the sombre lyric of 'The Nymph's Reply to the
Shepherd' – and was in time to share with him the widespread
disapprobation of their 'atheism'.[5] His friendship with
Spenser is immortalised in 'Colin Clouts Come Home
Againe', even as he was the recipient of the letter which
expounds Spenser's 'whole intention' in The Faerie Queene.[6]

[1] In 1593, in his capacity as Member of Parliament, he pleaded for the
toleration of extreme Protestants in 'a liberal-minded, independent speech'
(J. E. Neale, Elizabeth I and her Parliaments 1584–1601 [1957] pp. 288 f.).
See further W. K. Jordan, The Development of Religious Toleration in England
(1932) I 214–18.

[2] Christopher Hill, Intellectual Origins of the English Revolution (Oxford,
1965) p. 145.

[3] Brief Lives, ed. O. L. Dick, 2nd ed. (1950) p. 254. I suppose I should
mention that Ralegh also made tobacco fashionable. Not everyone was later
to approve of his smoking, King James least of all! 'He was too guilty', said
Winstanley severely, 'of occasioning the mode of his vanity' (England's
Worthies [1660] p. 259).

[4] An Epitaph vpon the right Honourable sir Philip Sidney, l. 58 (in
Poems, ed. Agnes M. C. Latham [1951] p. 7).

[5] The quoted phrase is Izaac Walton's (The Compleat Angler, 4th ed.
[1668] p. 76 [ch. iv]), who entitled the poems 'The Milk-maids Song' and
'The Milk-maids Mothers Answer'; the titles given above are from their joint
publication in Englands Helicon (1600). On Marlowe's connection with
Ralegh's 'little academe' consult Eleanor G. Clark, Ralegh and Marlowe
(1941, repr. 1965) Pt II. On Ralegh's 'atheism' see Agnes M. C. Latham,
Sir Walter Ralegh (1965) pp. 31 ff.; Willard M. Wallace, Sir Walter
Raleigh (Princeton, 1959) pp. 76 ff.; George T. Buckley, Atheism in the
English Renaissance (Chicago, 1932) ch. xi; and esp. Ernest A. Strathmann,
Sir Walter Ralegh: A Study in Elizabethan Skepticism (1951) ch. ii–iii, and
G. B. Harrison, ed., Willobie his Avisa (1926) pp. 205 ff. See below also,
p. 20.

[6] See the commentary on 'Colin Clouts Come Home Againe' in the
Variorum edition of The Minor Poems (Baltimore, 1943) pp. 447 ff.; also
S. Meyer, An Interpretation of Edmund Spenser's 'Colin Clout' (Cork, 1969)

His other friends included the historian Camden and possibly the poet Chapman, the geographer Hakluyt as well as the mathematicians John Dee and Thomas Hariot, and Henry Percy the 'Wizard Earl' of Northumberland.[1] Ben Jonson also emerges in Ralegh's life, first as tutor to young Wat Ralegh and later as author of the verses on the emblematic frontispiece of *The History of the World* (above, p. xvi). It may be that Shakespeare likewise put in a brief appearance,[2] and so – all too tangentially – did John Donne.[3] In all,

---

ch. vi, A. L. Rowse, *Ralegh and the Throckmortons* (1962) pp. 150 ff., and Walter Oakeshott, *The Queen and the Poet* (1960) Pt 1, ch. iii. It is also said that *The Faerie Queene* (III v, and IV vii) sets forth the relations between Ralegh (Timias) and Queen Elizabeth (Belphoebe); see esp. Kathrine Koller, 'Spenser and Ralegh', *ELH: Journal of English Literary History*, 1 (1934) 37–60.

[1] See Chapman's verses on Ralegh as the 'heroike Author' of the 1595 expedition to Guiana, in 'De Guiana, Carmen Epicum' (*The Poems of George Chapman*, ed. Phyllis B. Bartlett [1941] pp. 353–7). On Hakluyt, Hariot, *et al.*, but esp. on the 'Wizard Earl' who necessarily forms the starting-point for any account of the rise of natural philosophy in England, see Eleanor G. Clark, *Ralegh and Marlowe* (1941) ch. xiv–xv, and particularly Robert H. Kargon, *Atomism in England from Hariot to Newton* (Oxford, 1966). See also A. C. Crombie *et al.*, 'Thomas Harriot: An Original Practitioner in the Scientific Art', *Times Literary Supplement*, 23 Oct 1969 (pp. 1237–8).

[2] Armado in *Love's Labour's Lost* appears to be a caricature of Ralegh (a conjecture most categorically affirmed by Walter Oakeshott, *The Queen and the Poet* [1960] ch. iv). The identification hinges on the nature of 'the School of Night', on which see Ernest A. Strathmann, *Sir Walter Ralegh* (1951) pp. 262–71, and his article in *Modern Language Notes*, LVI (1949) 176–86. Cf. M. C. Bradbrook, *The School of Night: A Study of the Literary Relationships of Sir Walter Ralegh* (Cambridge, 1936) esp. pp. 154 ff., and Frances A. Yates, *A Study of 'Love's Labour's Lost'* (Cambridge, 1936). The never-ending search for the 'real' Shakespeare has inevitably included his identification with Ralegh – as by Henry Pemberton, Jr, *Shakespeare and Sir Walter Ralegh* (Philadelphia, 1914). Finally, Paulette Michel-Michot has argued the improbable thesis of 'Sir Walter Raleigh as a Source for the Character of Iago', *English Studies*, L (1969) 85–9.

[3] Donne was one of the 'gentlemen voluntaries' during the raid on Cadiz mounted by Essex and Ralegh in 1596 (see Edward Le Comte, *Grace to a Witty Sinner: A Life of Donne* [1956] pp. 28 ff.); the epigrams he penned on the occasion are edited by H. J. C. Grierson, *The Poems of John Donne* (Oxford, 1912) I 75–76; II 59. Moreover, Anne Donne's sister was married to Sir Nicholas Carew (born Throckmorton), brother to Ralegh's wife. Donne's only surviving comment on *The History of the World* is adverse:

Ralegh's position as the Queen's 'favourite' — literally and metaphorically — placed him at the very centre of life in Elizabethan England, even though his actual authority was never very substantial and declined altogether after his clandestine marriage to Elizabeth Throckmorton.[1] But initially the Queen appears to have appreciated the talents of her favourite, to the utter frustration of other courtiers: 'she tooke him for a kind of Oracle, which netled them all'.[2] When he complained that

> Fortune hath taken the away my loue
> my liues soule and my soules heauen above
> fortune hath taken the away my princess
> my only light and my true fancies mistres

— she would promptly answer:

> Ah silly pugge wert thou so sore afraid,
> mourne not (my Wat) nor be thou so dismaid,
> it passeth fickle fortunes powere and skill,
> to force my harte to thinke thee any ill ...[3]

Yet so unable was Ralegh patiently to bear the vicissitudes of the royal favours — 'Shee is gonn, Shee is lost! Shee is fovnd, she is ever faire!' — that when upon his marriage she left on a progress without him, he wrote to Secretary Cecil in the full expectation that his letter would be perused by royal eyes:

'Why was Sir Walter Ralegh thought the fittest Man to write the History of these Times?' (*apud* Edward Thompson, *Sir Walter Ralegh* [1935] p. 239).

[1] The accounts of Ralegh's marriage by Camden (*The Historie of ... Elizabeth*, tr. R. Norton [1630] IV 74), Anthony à Wood (*Athenæ Oxonienses* [1691] I 370), *et al.*, should be read in the light of the study by A. L. Rowse, *Ralegh and the Throckmortons* (1962) ch. viii *et seq.* See also Walter Oakeshott, *The Queen and the Poet* (1960) Pt I, ch. ii.

[2] Sir Robert Naunton, *Fragmenta Regalia* (1641) p. 35. The statement also appears in Winstanley, *England's Worthies* (1660) p. 253, and Anthony à Wood, *Athenæ Oxonienses* (1691) I 371.

[3] The Queen's poem was discovered only recently; it is quoted, together with Ralegh's lines, from the texts provided by L. G. Black, 'A Lost Poem by Queen Elizabeth I', *Times Literary Supplement*, 23 May 1968 (p. 535). The two poems, like the Marlowe–Ralegh exchanges noted earlier, form part of the vogue discussed by E. F. Hart, 'The Answer-Poem of the Early Seventeenth Century', *Review of English Studies*, n.s., VII (1956) 19–29. Some of the answers to Ralegh's *The Lie* are reprinted in *Poems*, ed. Agnes Latham (1951) pp. 135 ff.

My heart was never broken till this day, that I hear the Queen goes away so far off. . . . I that was wont to behold her riding like *Alexander*, hunting like *Diana*, walking like *Venus*, the gentle wind blowing her fair hair about her pure cheeks, like a nymph; sometime sitting in the shade like a Goddess; sometime singing like an angel; sometime playing like *Orpheus*. Behold the sorrow of this world! Once amiss, hath bereaved me of all. . . .[1]

In words as in deeds, the Elizabethans tended to exuberance.

Sir Walter's rhetoric may have moved the royal heart but did not touch the 'netled' courtiers. Deeply envied and feared for 'that awfulness and ascendancy in his Aspect over other mortalls', he generated mistrust far beyond the circle of courtiers; repeatedly denounced for his 'bloody pride', he became – as a follower of Essex phrased it – 'the best-hated man of the world, in Court, city and country'.[2] In time he was undone by two 'friends': Sir Robert Cecil, who undermined him in the eyes of King James;[3] and Sir Francis Bacon, who provided the legal basis – such as it was – for his execution in 1618.[4]

II

Ralegh at the end of his life described himself as 'A Seafaring man, a Souldior and a Courtier'.[5] The estimate is, I think,

[1] *The 11th: and last booke of the Ocean to Scinthia*, l. 493 (in *Poems*, ed. Agnes Latham [1951] p. 42), and Edward Edwards, *The Life of Sir Walter Ralegh* (1868) ii: *Letters of Sir Walter Ralegh*, pp. 51–2; respectively.

[2] The first phrase is by Aubrey (*Brief Lives*, ed. O. L. Dick, 2nd ed. [1950] p. 257); the second is from a ballad (quoted by Margaret Irwin, *That Great Lucifer* [1962] p. 170, *et al.*). Cf. Aubrey (as before) p. 254: 'his *naeve* [flaw or blemish] was that he was damnable proud'. But as we are justly reminded, 'There is no incident on record which exemplifies his damnable pride' (N. L. Williams, *Sir Walter Raleigh* [1962, repr. 1965] pp. 88–9).

[3] See *The Secret Correspondence of Sir Robert Cecil with James VI, King of Scotland*, ed. Sir David Dalrymple, Lord Hailes (1766), and the account by P. M. Handover, *The Second Cecil* (1959) pp. 277 ff.

[4] The official *apologia*, issued at the express command of James I, was *A Declaration of the Demeanor and Cariage of Sir Walter Raleigh* (1618); it is reprinted by Vincent T. Harlow, *Ralegh's Last Voyage* (1932) pp. 335–56. Agnes Latham attributes the work to Bacon (*Essays and Studies*, n.s., iv [1951] 94); but R. H. Bowers considers it 'more likely' that Bacon 'edited a draft drawn up by a member of his legal staff' (as in the next note, p. 209).

[5] R. H. Bowers (ed.), 'Ralegh's Last Speech: The "Elms" Document', *Review of English Studies*, n.s., ii (1951) 215.

significant in that the common denominator of all three
offices is the service of England. True, Ralegh asserted in
one of his poems that he sought new worlds 'for golde, for
prayse, for glory'.[1] Yet his passionate championship of the
colonisation of America, joined to his extraordinary zeal in
mounting and leading expeditions across the Atlantic, must
be seen as major contributions to those momentous enterprises which in time were translated into the fact of the
British Empire.[2]

Ralegh was by no means the only Elizabethan to be
obsessed with the colonisation of the new world. The challenge attracted a host of his contemporaries once they were
stirred by Sir Humphrey Gilbert's planting of the first
English colony in North America in 1583, or roused by
Hakluyt's endless propaganda in favour of the imperial idea.
But Ralegh remains instrumental because as Gilbert's half-
brother he was directly involved in the exploit of 1583 and,
on Gilbert's death, inherited his patent; while through the
dedication of Hakluyt's propaganda to him he was publicly
identified with all aspects of the American enterprise.[3] Above
all, it was generally if erroneously assumed that he enjoyed
the confidence of his remarkable Queen, now said to be 'very
famous and admirable' even in distant Guiana where she was
known – so Ralegh tactfully reported – as 'Ezrabeta Cassipuna
Aquerewana, which is as much as Elizabeth, the great

[1] *The 11th: and last booke of the Ocean to Scinthia*, l. 61 (in *Poems*, ed.
Agnes Latham [1951] p. 27). Jonson is also said to have remarked that 'S^r
W. Raughlye esteemed more of fame than conscience' (*Ben Jonson*, ed. C. H.
Herford and Percy Simpson [Oxford, 1925] 1 138). Some authority on
conscience!

[2] The epic story is related by A. L. Rowse, *The Elizabethans and America*
(1959) esp. ch. iii, and most fully by David B. Quinn, *Raleigh and the British
Empire* (1947). Cf. Lacey B. Smith, *The Elizabethan Epic* (1966) esp. pp.
215–33. The colonisation of Ireland (in which Ralegh also figured) was
'intertwined' with that of America, according to D. B. Quinn, *The Elizabethans and the Irish* (Ithaca, N.Y., 1966) esp. ch. ix. Consult also Sir John
Pope Hennessy, *Sir Walter Ralegh and Ireland* (1883).

[3] Ralegh was the recipient not only of Hakluyt's labours but of countless
other works as well. A typical performance is John Case (?), *The Praise
of Musicke* (Oxford, 1586); several others are cited by Christopher Hill,
Intellectual Origins of the English Revolution (Oxford, 1965) ch. iv,
passim.

princesse or greatest commaunder'.[1] Chapman inevitably broke into song:

> Guiana, whose rich feet are mines of golde,
> Whose forehead knockes against the roofe of Starres,
> Stands on her tip-toes at faire England looking,
> Kissing her hand, bowing her mightie breast,
> And euery signe of all submission making,
> To be her sister, and the daughter both
> Of our most sacred Maide.
> ('De Guiana, Carmen Epicum', ll. 18–24)

At the accession of James I, however, Ralegh's fortunes declined disastrously. For he was then brought to trial, and sentenced to death.

The charge was no less astonishing than the procedure at his trial. Arrested on 'evidence' which was not produced until some months later and then withdrawn, he was accused of being an agent of Spain! According to the indictment, 'he did conspire and goe about to deprive the King of his government, and to raise up sedition within the Realme, to alter Religion, and to bring in the Romish Superstition, and to procure forraigne enemies to invade the Kingdomes'.[2] The trial, held on 17 November 1603, has been described as 'criminal procedure seen at its worst', 'an outrage'.[3] Not only was the evidence lacking, but the Attorney-General, Sir Edward Coke – the glory of English law, and its shame – behaved in a manner hardly calculated to instil faith in justice. An eyewitness, Sir Thomas Overbury (whose murder

[1] The Discoverie of the large, rich, and bewtifvl Empire of Gviana (1596) p. 7.

[2] Sir Thomas Overbury, The Arraignment and Conviction of Sr Walter Rawleigh (1648) p. 2. Cf. Winstanley's manifestly prejudiced account in England's Worthies (1660) p. 253.

[3] Sir John Macdonell, Historical Trials (Oxford, 1927) ch. ix and H. R. Trevor-Roper, Historical Essays (1951) p. 105, respectively. See also Sir Harry L. Stephen, 'The Trial of Sir Walter Raleigh', Transactions of the Royal Historical Society, 4th series, II (1919) 172–87; Charles Williams, James I (1934) pp. 270 ff.; and Bruce Williamson, Sir Walter Ralegh and his Trial (1936). The full proceedings of the trial are in John Shirley (above, p. 3, n. 2), pp. 67–170, as well as in Ralegh, Works (Oxford, 1829) I 649–690, and David Jardine, Criminal Trials (1832) I 400–52; extracts are given by Catherine Drinker Bowen, The Lion and the Throne (1957) ch. xv-xvii, and N. L. Williams, Sir Walter Rcleigh (1962) pp. 186–216.

ten years later became the other great scandal of the reign of
James I), marked the Attorney-General's 'vehement words'
and added that everyone present 'wished that hee had not
behaved himself so violently and bitterly'.[1] Even Secretary
Cecil decided openly to appear scandalised – as he might well
have been, considering that later he himself was to be in the
pay of the King of Spain![2] However, neither Cecil nor the
Attorney-General need be singled out for condemnation,
just as James I does not merit our partisan denunciations as
an 'uncouth, uncivilised, yet cunning and learned monster
from a Northern fairy-tale'![3] For Ralegh's contemporaries
the attempts of King James to seek accommodation with Spain
automatically meant the immediate removal of all representa-
tives of Elizabeth's consistently anti-Spanish policy. In short,
as Aubrey remarked sometime later, Ralegh 'fell a Sacrifice to
Spanish Politicks'.[4]

The condemned man's last thoughts were for his wife. 'My
love I send you', he wrote, 'that you may keepe it when I am
dead; and my councell, that you may remember it when I am
noe more. . . .'[5] Elizabeth Ralegh in turn appealed to their
'friend' Cecil. Always wont to consult him in 'hast and
skrebbling' – and consistently alarming spelling – she would
plead: 'For God sake, let me heer from you the trewth; for
I am much trobled'.[6] Presently she wrote: 'If the greved teares
of an unfortunat woman may resevef ani fafor, or the un-

---

[1] *The Arraignment and Conviction of S*r *Walter Rawleigh* (1648) pp. 4, 5.
Even Coke's widow was sceptical! She said on his death: 'We shall never see
his like again – praises be to God!' (S. E. Thorne, *Sir Edward Coke* [1957]
p. 4; *apud* Christopher Hill, *Intellectual Origins of the English Revolution*
[Oxford, 1965] p. 225).

[2] See Sir John Digby's despatch to King James on 9 Sep 1613 concerning
Cecil's acceptance of an annual pension from Spain of 4,000 crowns, later
raised to 6,000 (in S. R. Gardiner, *History of England* . . . 1603–1616
[1863] II 357 f.). The scandalous practice involved others as well; see G. E.
Aylmer, *The Struggle for the Constitution* (1963) p. 32.

[3] Margaret Irwin, *That Great Lucifer* (1962) p. 160.

[4] *Brief Lives*, ed. O. L. Dick, 2nd ed. (1950) p. 260. The same point is
made by John Shirley (above, p. 3, n. 2), pp. 216–17.

[5] December 1603: in *Letters of Sir Walter Ralegh*, ed. Edward Edwards
(1868) p. 284. It is said that on the night before his execution Ralegh also
composed 'The Passionate Mans Pilgrimage' (in *Poems*, ed. Agnes Latham
[1951] pp. 49–51).   [6] Sep 1597; in *Letters*, p. 403.

spekeabell sorros of my ded hart may resevef ani cumfort, then let my sorros cum before you. ... I am not abell, I protest befor God, to stand on my trembling leges.'¹

But the sentence of death was not carried out. King James relented at the last possible moment, less because he was inclined to exercise the royal prerogative of mercy and more because he was impressed by the outcry over the conduct of Ralegh's trial. The prisoner was therefore conveyed to the Tower where he was to remain for nearly thirteen years, from 16 December 1603 to 19 March 1616.

Ralegh was throughout this period 'civilly dead'. To the mounting irritation of the King, however, he did not behave as if he was. He addressed a series of petitions to every person of influence. He secured the Queen's intercession and, more important still, he befriended the 'rising sun' of the Jacobean court, the gifted heir to the throne Prince Henry. He even wrote and published *The History of the World* (1614) which despite its initial anonymity was known to have been authored by Ralegh. But as one of his contemporaries observed, 'Sir *Walter Rawleigh* was one that it seemes fortune had picked out of purpose, of whom to make an example, and to use as her Tennis-Ball, thereby to shew what she could do'.² Prince Henry, the 'greatest hope' that Ralegh had for his eventual release, died after a brief illness on 6 November 1612 – 'how and by what means', it was rumoured, 'is suspected by all'.³ The King himself was so far from pleased with *The History of the World* that he suppressed it 'for divers exceptions, but specially for beeing too sawcie in censuring princes'.⁴ Worse,

¹ 18 (?) Nov 1603; in *Letters*, p. 407.

² Sir Robert Naunton, *Fragmenta Regalia* (1641) p. 33; reiterated with some slight variations by Winstanley, *England's Worthies* (1660) pp. 250–51, and Anthony à Wood, *Athenæ Oxonienses* (1691) 1 369.

³ The first phrase is from Chamberlain's letter of 12 Nov 1612 (in *The Letters of John Chamberlain*, ed. Norman E. McClure [Philadelphia, 1939] 1 389, and *The Chamberlain Letters*, ed. Elizabeth M. Thomson [1966] p. 195); the rumour is reported by Carew Ralegh, *A Brief Relation of Sr. Walter Raleghs Troubles* (1669) p. 8. See also Ralegh's elegy on the dead Prince (in *Poems*, ed. Agnes Latham [1951] p. 52). Their friendship is placed within a larger context by Elkin C. Wilson, *Prince Henry and English Literature* (Ithaca, N.Y., 1946) esp. pp. 142–4.

⁴ John Chamberlain to Sir Dudley Carleton, 5 Jan 1615 (in the editions cited in the previous note: McClure, 1 568, and Thomson, p. 195).

Spain's formidable ambassador Sarmiento (later Count of
Condomar) insinuated his way into the King's confidence, so
that when Ralegh was released from prison to mount another
expedition to Guiana, some details of his preparations were
immediately transmitted to Spain.

The inevitable disaster encompassed many individuals besides Ralegh. Young Wat Ralegh died during an engagement
with the Spaniards, a leading member of the expedition committed suicide, the men dispersed. The grief-stricken Ralegh
in a moving letter to his wife reported their shattering loss.
'My braynes', he wrote, 'are broken.' He added: 'Comfort
your hart (deerest BESSE), I shall sorrow for us bothe. I shall
sorrow the lesse, because I have not longe to sorrowe, because
not longe to live. . . .'[1] He was arrested some time after his
return to England. A half-hearted attempt to escape abroad
proved abortive owing to betrayal.[2] There was no trial. A
hearing convened on 28 October 1618 decided – reputedly
at Bacon's intervention – that the sentence of death passed
on Ralegh fifteen years earlier could now be carried out. One
of the further charges presently added was Ralegh's violation
of Spanish territory. The inconsistency was ironic in the
extreme. It was most forcefully stated by his nephew:
'*Ralegh* was condemned for being a friend to the Spanyard,
and lost his life for being their utter enemie'.[3]

III

Ralegh's execution on the day following the hearing, on
29 October 1618, relieved King James of the last visible
reminder of the Elizabethan age. But in fact Ralegh in

---

[1] 22 Mar 1618; in *Letters of Sir Walter Ralegh*, ed. Edward Edwards
(1868) p. 359.

[2] The culprit was his custodian Sir Lewis Stukeley. As Chamberlain
reported on 4 Dec 1618 (in the editions just cited: McClure, II 191, and
Thomson, p. 203): 'He is now most commonly knowne and called by the
name of Sir Judas Stukeley'.

[3] Carew Ralegh, *A Brief Relation of S^r. Walter Raleghs Troubles* (1669)
p. 9. For excerpts from the hearing consult N. L. Williams, *Sir Walter
Raleigh* (1962) pp. 264–6. All the relevant material has been collected by
Vincent T. Harlow, *Ralegh's Last Voyage* (1932).

death posed a far greater threat than he ever did when alive. As a modern historian remarks, 'The ghost of Ralegh pursued the House of Stuart to the scaffold'.[1]

The judgement sounds extravagant, and invites scepticism. Yet it is well to recall the widespread persuasion that (as John Pory reported within two days of Ralegh's execution) 'his death will doe more hurte to the faction that sought it, then ever his life could have done'.[2] It was a persuasion compounded of several factors: the outrage over the injustice meted to Ralegh at the trial of 1603, the sympathy generated by his long years of imprisonment, the general approbation extended to *The History of the World*, the shock which followed rumours that his last expedition had been foredoomed, the popular outcry over the inconsistent charges which led to his execution, and the deep impression made by his courage on the scaffold. But in the end the historical facts of Ralegh's life proved less important than the interpretation gradually imposed on them. Given the mounting opposition to King James, Ralegh was presently canonised as the principal martyr of royal authoritarianism, repression and injustice. In a typical outburst, Francis Osborne used Ralegh to denounce the court of 'our Espaniolised English':

> as the foolish Idolaters were wont to Sacrifice the choycest of their Children to the Devill, the common enemy of Humanity; so our King gave up this incomparable jewel to the will of this Monster in Ambition, under the pretence of an superannuated Transgression; Contrary to the opinion of the most honest sort of Gown-men.[3]

In like manner, Sir John Eliot's celebration of the sufferings of 'our *Raleigh*' was a pointed affirmation that his courage 'chang'd the affection of his enemies, & turn'd their ioy

[1] G. M. Trevelyan, *History of England*, 3rd ed. (1945) p. 388.

[2] 31 Oct 1618; in W. S. Powell, 'John Pory on the Death of Sir Walter Raleigh', *The William and Mary Quarterly*, 3rd series, ix (1952) 537. The exceptions to this attitude include the unforgiving view of the dramatist John Ford who moralised Ralegh's execution as a warning to anyone who likewise leans 'too credulously to his owne strength' (see the edition of Ford's comments by George F. Reinecke, in *English Language Notes*, vi [1969] 252–54). It may not be irrelevant that Sir John Popham, who as Lord Chief Justice presided at Ralegh's trial in 1603, was Ford's great-uncle.

[3] *Historical Memoires on the Reigns of Queen Elizabeth and King James* (1658) ii 16–17 and 19.

to sorrow, & all men else it fill'd wth admiration'.[1] Even more explicitly, Sir Anthony Weldon in a scurrilous pamphlet praised Ralegh 'whose least part was of more worth then the whole race of the best of the Scots Nation', firmly denounced James as 'the Fountain of all our late Afflictions and miseries', and for good measure described Scotland as 'a nasty barren Country (rather a Dunghill then a Kingdome)'.[2] So drastically was Ralegh made to conform to republican sentiment that a widely circulated report even claimed that upon the death of Elizabeth he had planned to 'sett up a Commonwealth'.[3]

It is of course pointless to insist that Ralegh was not a republican, however opposed he may have been to the abuses of the royal prerogatives under James.[4] The emerging new order required a symbol, and Ralegh appeared ideally suited for transubstantiation. His popularity thus guaranteed, any number of books were promptly attributed to his pen,[5] even as several others expressly invoked his ghost. When 'A.B.' decided to provide a translation of Leonardus Lessius' *De providentia numinis* (1613), he thought it wise to rename the work *Rawleigh his Ghost* (1631). As he explained:

> I am the more easily perswaded, that the very Name of him (by way of this feigned Apparition, and the like answerable Title of the Translatiõ) may beget in many an earnest desire of perusing this Booke; and so become the more profitable. . . .[6]

---

[1] *The Monarchie of Man*, ed. A. B. Grosart (1879) II 158–59. Ralegh's execution had been witnessed by Eliot as well as by two other future spokesmen for the New Order, John Pym and John Hampden.

[2] *A Cat may look upon a King* (1652) pp. 2, 42–3 and 67–8.

[3] Aubrey, *Brief Lives*, ed. O. L. Dick, 2nd ed. (1950) p. 257. Ralegh's transformation into a Puritan hero has elicited a flamboyant paragraph from H. R. Trevor-Roper, 'The Last Elizabethan: Sir Walter Raleigh', in *Historical Essays* (1951) pp. 106–7. But I would rather commend the brief account by Sir Charles Firth, *Essays Historical & Literary* (Oxford, 1938) p. 53, and especially the substantial exposition by Christopher Hill, *Intellectual Origins of the English Revolution* (Oxford, 1965) ch. iv.

[4] On the limits of Ralegh's opposition, consult Hill (as in the previous note) pp. 150 ff.   [5] See the list provided by Hill, pp. 204 ff.

[6] 'The Translatovr to the Reader', *Rawleigh his Ghost* (St Omer, 1631). Other writers who laboured under the influence of Ralegh's ghost included William Baldwin (1620?) and Thomas Scott (1626). Consult the full list provided by T. N. Brushfield, *A Bibliography of Sir Walter Ralegh*, 2nd rev. ed. (Exeter, 1908) Pt xx.

The popularity of Ralegh's own great work, *The History of the World*, would under the circumstances appear to have been inevitable. Yet its ten editions and several reprints during the seventeenth century[1] cannot be attributed exclusively to the fame of its author. The decisive factors were rather the comprehensive vision of the historical process and the lucid and sustained prose which together produced a unified work of literature.

IV

The History of the World has been termed 'the first serious attempt in England, and one of the first in modern Europe, at a history the scope of which should be universal in both time and space'.[2] In fact, however, its general framework is not in the least original; it belongs to the tradition of Christian historiography which reaches its terminal point some fifty years later in *Paradise Lost*.[3] Ralegh's prose work and Milton's poem are the two greatest formulations in English of the mode of thinking which over the centuries interpreted history as a progressive manifestation of the divine purpose in a linear movement extending from the

[1] The first edition of 1614 was followed by another in 1617 and one each in 1621, 1628, 1634, 1652, 1666, 1671, 1677 and 1687. Ralegh's name, with an engraved portrait by Simon Passe, first appeared in 1617. See the full details in Brushfield (as in the previous note), Pts x–xi, but as amended by John Racin, Jr., 'The Early Editions of Ralegh's *History of the World*', *Studies in Bibliography*, XVII (1964) 199–209.

[2] Newman T. Reed, 'The Philosophical Background of Sir Walter Ralegh's *History of the World*', *Northwestern University Summaries of Dissertations*, II (1934) 12. With even greater enthusiasm Margaret Irwin calls Ralegh's work 'more vast in its conception than any man had ever dared attempt' (*That Great Lucifer* [1962] p. 219). Earlier in the nineteenth century, William Oldys rather hysterically described it as 'that ocean of history, wherein he has outdone all that went before him, and given such lights to futurity as must ever be grateful' (Ralegh, *Works* [Oxford, 1829] I 448).

[3] C. A. Patrides, *Milton and the Christian Tradition* (Oxford, 1966) ch. viii, ' "Ascending by Degrees Magnificent": The Christian View of History'. The chapter is an abridgement of the larger study cited in the next note.

creation to the Last Judgement.[1] The interpretation origi-
nated with the great prophets who looked on history as the
arena wherein God acts in judgement or in mercy. Once
extended by St Paul and accepted by the early apologists,
the theory was further developed by Eusebius of Caesarea
who argued that the Christian faith was established even
before the creation of the world. But the most influential
formulation was ventured by St Augustine who in *De
civitate Dei* maintained that all events are inexorably pro-
gressing towards their final consummation in God. Subsequent commentators were even more insistently bent on
imposing order on historical events, and often co-ordinated
history in terms of Four Monarchies or Six Ages. The links
forged through the centuries involve any number of works
written or compiled, but the principal performances remain
the *Historia sacra* of Paulus Orosius, the *Historia ecclesiastica
gentis anglorum* of St Bede, the *Chronica* of Otto of Freising,
the colossal *Speculum historiale* of Vincent of Beauvais, and
the composite *Flores historiarum* of Roger of Wendover which
was continued along drastically original lines in the *Chronica
maiora* of Matthew Paris. The advent of Protestantism did
not terminate the tradition; quite the contrary, since Luther
himself provided an outline of historical events in terms of
the Six Ages, Melanchthon lent his assistance to a similar
performance by Johann Carion, Sleidanus wrote the enor-
mously popular *De quatuor summis imperiis*, and a legion of
minor writers promptly fell in step. In England, Ralegh's
own endeavour had been preceded by attempts like Holin-
shed's *Chronicles* (1577), Lodowick Lloyd's *The Consent of
Time* (1590), John More's *Table from the Beginning of the
World* (1593), William Perkins's *Specimen digesti* (1598),
and Anthony Munday's *Briefe Chronicle* (1611), and was to
be followed by works like Henry Isaacson's *Saturni ephe-
merides* (1633), James Ussher's *Annals* (1650–54), William
Howell's *Institution of General History* (1661), and Robert

---

[1] The full details of this interpretation – upon which my summary here
draws – are available in my study *The Phoenix and the Ladder: The Rise and
Decline of the Christian View of History* (Berkeley and Los Angeles, 1964).
See also ' "The Bloody and Cruell Turke": The Background of a Renaissance Commonplace', *Studies in the Renaissance*, x (1963) 126–35.

Baillie's *Operis historici* (1668). The common denominator
of these works is their linear conception of history from the
creation, and their insistent proclamation that history is a
record of divine mercies and judgements.

Ralegh's celebrated Preface to *The History of the World* is
a lucid testimony to his espousal of the commonly-accepted
providential theory of history.[1] Known in time as 'A Pre-
monition to Princes', the Preface asserts that '*Events* are
always seated in the inaccessible Light of Gods high
Providence'. The quoted statement is not Ralegh's; it is
borrowed from Sir William Sanderson's restatement of
Ralegh's thesis in 1656, precisely because Sanderson was
favourably disposed to Ralegh the historian even while he
was militantly opposed to Ralegh the political figure. 'The
Scales of Gods Providence', continued the impressed
Sanderson, 'are never at rest, always moving; now up, now
down; to humble, and to exalt.' He went on:

> Reade but the story of some Centuries of our *Christian* world, abreviated
> in the *Preface* of Sir *Walter Ralegh's* History: How long was it, that
> wickedness had leave to lord it? With what strength of policy, the Tyrants
> of each time, sold themselves to settle the work of sin? And though in the
> period of that portion of time (compared with everlasting) and of our
> neighbour-affairs, (with the succeeds of the vast Universe) In these (I say)
> he religiously observes (perchance in some) the most notorious impieties
> punished and revenged....[2]

Significantly, while Ralegh during the trial of 1603 was
censured for his alleged 'heathenish, blasphemous, athe-
istical, and profane opinions', in 1618 he was assured by

[1] On the wide dissemination of this theory, consult especially Herschel
Baker, *The Wars of Truth* (1952) ch. i (iv), and *The Race of Time* (Toronto,
1967) ch. i; Lily B. Campbell, *Shakespeare's 'Histories': Mirrors of Eliza-
bethan Policy* (San Marino, Calif., 1947); Leonard F. Dean, *Tudor Theories
of History Writing*, University of Michigan Contributions in Modern
Philology, No. 1 (1947); F. Smith Fussner, *The Historical Revolution:
English Historical Writing and Thought 1580–1640* (1962); E. M. W.
Tillyard, *Shakespeare's History Plays* (1944); and my own studies cited in
the previous note. See further William Haller, *Foxe's Book of Martyrs and the
Elect Nation* (1963), and T. D. Kendrick, *British Antiquity* (1950). The
concern with history in dramatic literature is surveyed by Irving Ribner,
The English History Play in the Age of Shakespeare (Princeton, 1957).

[2] *A Compleat History of the Lives and Reigns of Mary Queen of Scotland,
and of her Son and Successor, James* (1656) pp. 281, 282.

SWR B

Sir Edward Montague, the Lord Chief Justice: 'Your faith
hath heretofore been questioned, but I am satisfied you are a
good Christian, for your book, which is an admirable work,
doth testify as much'.[1]

But if both friends and enemies understood the general
import of Ralegh's work and responded with enthusiasm,
King James, as we have seen, thought that Ralegh had been
'too sawcie in censuring princes'. The royal displeasure may
appear singularly odd since Ralegh had simply restated
widely-accepted assumptions. But however enthusiastic the
common reception of the 'lessons' repeatedly drawn from
history, monarchs were always concerned lest the fondness
for 'parallelism' should lead to treasonous equations of the
past with the present. Their concern was not imaginary.
Thomas Heywood in 1612 explicitly observed that 'If wee
present a forreigne History, the subiect is so intended, that
in the liues of *Romans*, *Grecians*, or others, either the vertues
of our Country-men are extolled, or their vices reproued'.[2]
We have indeed ample evidence to substantiate the inclination of the Elizabethans and Jacobeans to discern contemporary references in works of history[3] no less than in
dramatic literature.[4] Under the circumstances it is not
surprising that both Elizabeth and James restricted the activities of historians considerably, and sometimes decisively.[5]

[1] David Jardine, *Criminal Trials* (1832) 1 450 and 501.

[2] *An Apology for Actors* (1612) sig. F3[v]. The ultimate appeal of Heywood's
'parallelism' is to the work which had conditioned a generation of readers,
Plutarch's *Parallel Lives*.

[3] See particularly Herschel Baker, *The Race of Time* (Toronto, 1967) pp.
28–34. Milton in his *History of Britain* likewise affirmed a parallel between
the period after the Roman conquest and his own age; see the account by
William R. Parker, *Milton* (Oxford, 1968) 1 331 ff.

[4] Two examples may suffice. Act V of *Gorboduc* has been called 'no more
than a tract for the times on the subject of the succession, containing a palpable
attack on Mary's title' (J. E. Neale, *Queen Elizabeth* [1934, repr. 1967] p.
200). Again, Jonson's *Catiline* has been described as 'a commentary on the
private and public affairs closest to Jonson and his country' (B. N. De Luna,
Jonson's Romish Plot [Oxford, 1967]). But see also the thorough study by
David Bevington, *Tudor Drama and Politics: A Critical Approach to Topical
Meaning* (Cambridge, Mass., 1968).

[5] See Sir Charles Firth, *Essays Historical & Literary* (Oxford, 1938) pp.
55 ff., and Christopher Hill, *Intellectual Origins of the English Revolution*
(Oxford, 1965) pp. 177 f.

Hardly unaware of these developments, Ralegh in his Preface piously disclaimed any interest in reproaching the present through the past, but wittily proceeded to leave the question wide open:

> It is enough for me (being in that state I am) to write of the eldest times: wherein also why may it not be said, that in speaking of the past, I point at the present, and taxe the vices of those that are yet lyuing, in their persons that are long since dead; and haue it laid to my charge. But this I cannot helpe, though innocent. And certainely if there be any, that finding themselues spotted like the Tigers of old time, shall finde fault with me for painting them ouer a new; they shall therein accuse themselues iustly, and me falsly. (below, p. 80)

The reaction of one spotted tiger we know! King James suppressed Ralegh's work not only because it was said to censure princes but especially because it appeared to be a veiled denunciation of his reign. Part of the 'evidence' consisted of Ralegh's several comparisons of the early seventeenth century with the expired glories of the Elizabethan age.[1] But even more crucial was his unremitting series of 'parallels' – some intentional, some accidentally relevant – for instance the portrait of the irresolute King Rehoboam who was 'transported by his familiars and fauourites', and especially the account of the great Queen Semiramis and her incompetent successor Ninias ('esteemed no man of war at all, but altogether feminine, and subjected to ease and delicacy'). King James knew well enough whom Ninias was supposed to represent![2]

[1] A number of the relevant passages are interestingly juxtaposed by A. L. Rowse, *Ralegh and the Throckmortons* (1962) pp. 263 f.

[2] On Rehoboam, see *HW*, II xix 1 (in the 1614 ed., p. 505); on Ninias, see below, p. 179. James's acceptance of his portrayal in Ninias is endorsed by J. I. McCollum, 'Ralegh's *History of the World*', *The Carrell*, v (1964) 5; William Oldys, in Ralegh's *Works* (Oxford, 1829) I 464; Rowse (as in the previous note) p. 268; William Stebbing, *Sir Walter Ralegh* (Oxford, 1891) p. 280; Edward Thompson, *Sir Walter Ralegh* (1935) p. 238; *et al.* It may be noted that while Elizabeth was variously designated as Astraea, Cynthia, Deborah, Judith, etc. (cf. Elkin C. Wilson, *England's Eliza* [Cambridge, Mass., 1939], and Frances A. Yates in *Journal of the Warburg and Courtauld Institutes*, x [1947] 27–82), there is evidently no allusion to her as Semiramis. But Ralegh's context would seem to point to her just the same.

V

The providential theory of history espoused in the Preface to *The History of the World* extends well into the work itself.[1] But Ralegh's concern is not merely to affirm that history is a record of divine judgements. His principal aim is to assert the unity of historical events by an emphasis on the order pervading their entire course since the creation of the world. True, the fundamental assumptions of the Christian faith do not appear to concern him; his vision is obviously not Christocentric, and the Last Judgement – so common an element in other universal histories – is not accommodated within his scheme. One is tempted to conclude that Ralegh was not 'orthodox' but (as we have been told often enough) a thoroughgoing sceptic, perhaps even an 'atheist', and at any rate not 'a religious person'.

Ralegh's reputed 'atheism' need not detain us long since it is refuted in chapter after chapter of *The History of the World*.[2] At the same time, however, some readers are still of the opinion that 'it cannot be urged that Ralegh was in any profound sense a religious person'; his religion was rather 'a habit of thought than an ecstatic union with the Deity', 'there was so much more of speculation than of faith in his attitude'.[3] But must one subordinate reason to faith, or experience ecstasy, before he can be called religious?

1 See below, pp. 157 f., 200 ff., 210 ff., 216 f., 253, 256, etc.

2 Cf. J. Beau, 'La Religion de Sir Walter Ralegh', *Revue anglo-américaine*, xi (1934) 410–22. The Renaissance meaning of 'atheism' is now obsolete; in modern terminology it may well be called 'higher criticism' (C. F. Tucker Brooke, *Essays on Shakespeare and other Elizabethans* [1948] pp. 141 f.).

3 Milton Waldman, *Sir Walter Raleigh* (1928, 1950) p. 90. Pierre Lefranc, in *Sir Walter Ralegh écrivain* (Paris, 1968), is more precise: 'Ni sur la grâce, ni sur la prédestination, ni sur l'élection, ni sur la justification par la foi ou par les œuvres, *The History* n'apporte en effet la moindre clarté. On n'y aperçoit pas non plus la moindre trace d'une dévotion au Christ, ni l'expression d'un sens intime du péché, ni même ce minimum fonda-mental de conscience religieuse qui se traduisait couramment à l'époque par une méditation sur la Chute. A la place de ce qui devrait constituer le centre solide et vivant de la foi de Ralegh, il est donc impossible d'apercevoir autre chose qu'un vide' (p. 473). The extent of my own disagreement is evident throughout these pages.

The student of Ralegh's thought is constantly subjected to similarly odd assumptions which yield equally odd conclusions. He is justly alarmed by the sharply divergent views propounded in recent years. Should he accept one historian's opposition between 'orthodoxy' and 'scepticism'?[1] Should he assent to the emphasis which a scholar places on orthodoxy at the expense of the sceptical strain?[2] Should he agree with another historian who pursues Ralegh's 'scepticism' all too relentlessly?[3] Threatened as we are by ever more exaggerated readings of the inquiring mind of Ralegh, we would be well advised to remember the relative nature of the terms at our disposal. 'His scepticism', we have been wisely reminded, 'was academic – and, by Montaigne's standards, shallow.'[4]

'Orthodoxy' is likewise relative. *The History of the World*, judged in the light of Christian theology, can only be found wanting; but judged in the light of Christian historiography – its natural milieu – it will be discovered to conform to the patterns of thought already established by tradition. Ralegh's vision may not extend to the end of history but there was adequate precedent in the equally restricted conception of Eusebius. The Last Judgement must in any case be regarded as inevitable once we are given the pattern of history's linear progress so strenuously insisted upon by Ralegh, and especially the division of history into Four Monarchies which he so firmly asserts in the final pages.[5] By the same token, *The History of the World* while not Christocentric is resolutely *theo*centric – precisely the burden of the traditional universal history! However, it would be foolish to deny that Ralegh's silences on Christ or the Last Judgement are in

---

[1] 'Ralegh was never an orthodox Christian. The whole turn of Ralegh's mind and temper was sceptical' (A. L. Rowse, *Ralegh and the Throckmortons* [1962] p. 268).

[2] Ernest A. Strathmann, *Sir Walter Ralegh: A Study in Elizabethan Skepticism* (1951), claims that as time passed orthodoxy gained the upper hand.

[3] Christopher Hill, *Intellectual Origins of the English Revolution* (1965) ch. iv. Hill, of course, disagrees with Strathmann's thesis ('hardly proven').

[4] F. Smith Fussner, *The Historical Revolution* (1962) p. 192.

[5] See below, p. 394. Ralegh's adherence to the concept of the Four Monarchies is even more clearly affirmed in the 'exquisite Abstract' of his work published later as *Tvbvs Historicvs: An Historical Perspective* (1636).

themselves most eloquent. Indeed, it was noted at the time of his execution that 'he spake not one word of Christ, but of the great and incomprehensible God', which a wit promptly saw as evidence that Ralegh was 'an a-christ, not an atheist'.[1] This is as much as to say that Ralegh was by nature non-devotional. His place in the manifestation of the religious impulse in seventeenth-century England is not with Herbert or Crashaw but with Milton or the Cambridge Platonists. So far indeed, he is entirely 'modern'.

But was Ralegh 'modern' in the historiographical sense as well? Matthew Arnold thought him, on the contrary, quite 'ancient', which is to say obsolete,[2] largely because he accepted the Bible as an authority of unquestionable validity. If we are also shocked by Ralegh's uncritical attitude to the Bible, it should be held in mind that his behaviour is fully representative of his age. Well aware that 'divine testimonies doe not perswade all naturall men to those things, to which their owne reason cannot reach', he was also convinced that 'both the truth and antiquitie of the bookes of God finde no companions equall, either in age or authority'.[3] Ralegh may often permit his Icarian reason to rise into perilous domains but in the end circumscribes it within the bounds of Scriptural authority.

Equally representative of his age is the attitude he displays towards authorities other than the Bible. Like most historians of his own day, he invokes authorities to establish the consensus of opinion; and where he finds them in disagreement, he simply selects the interpretation most suitable to his particular purposes.[4] In this respect the first four

[1] Aubrey, *Brief Lives*, ed. O. L. Dick, 2nd ed. (1950) p. 259.

[2] Arnold's conclusion was inevitable since he measured Ralegh against Thucydides! (*On the Modern Element in Literature* [1857], in *On the Classical Tradition*, ed. R. H. Super [Ann Arbor, 1960] pp. 26–8).

[3] *HW*, I vii 1 (in the 1614 ed., p. 98), and I viii 2 (p. 130), respectively. See below, pp. 134 ff., 198 ff., and consult further E. A. Strathmann, *Sir Walter Ralegh* (1951) pp. 132 ff. Ralegh's loyalty to the Bible obliged him to accept a chronology which placed the world's creation in the year 4031 B.C. His conclusion is not unlike that of his contemporaries, as I have argued in 'Renaissance Estimates of the Year of Creation', *Huntingdon Library Quarterly* XXVI (1963) 315–22. Cf. Strathmann, pp. 197–218.

[4] On Ralegh's method as 'the approved method of writing ancient history', see esp. F. Smith Fussner, *The Historical Revolution* (1962) pp. 202 ff.

chapters of *The History of the World* are of fundamental importance, for Ralegh's treatment of the vast commentaries on Genesis sets the tone of the entire work as he moves through them without pausing to consider their relative merits.[1] His attitude to individual writers is similarly uncritical. Marsilio Ficino, for instance, is repeatedly cited as an authority on morality and religion, but we may well doubt whether Ralegh was even aware of his importance as a Platonist.[2]

But this is not to say that *The History of the World* is merely a composite work based on an uncritical accumulation of authorities. The evidence on hand supports neither Aubrey's belief that Ralegh had simply 'compiled' his work, nor Ben Jonson's claim that 'The best wits of England were Employed for making of his historie'.[3] Ralegh was by nature 'an undefatigable reader': even before his imprisonment, we are told, he never embarked on the high seas but 'he carried always a Trunke of Bookes along with him'.[4] Once in prison he naturally depended on the assistance of friends and acquaintances for the provision of 'old books, or any manuscrips, wherin I cann read any of our written antiquites'.[5] The research and the writing were almost entirely his own. The research itself yielded no mean contributions in several

[1] The commentators on Genesis who provided the raw material of Ralegh's opening chapters include Cardinal Cajetan, Joannes Mercerus, Bento Pereira, Andrew Willet, *et al*. See the studies by Arnold Williams, below, p. 418.

[2] Sears Jayne, 'Ficino and the Platonism of the English Renaissance', *Comparative Literature*, IV (1952) esp. p. 218.

[3] Aubrey, *Brief Lives*, ed. O. L. Dick, 2nd ed. (1950) p. 258, and *Ben Jonson*, ed. C. H. Herford and Percy Simpson (Oxford, 1925) I 138. Jonson also remarked that he 'himself had written a peice to him of ye punick warre which he altered and set in his booke'. On the part in question (*HW*, v i-iii), see Sir Charles Firth, *Essays Historical & Literary* (Oxford, 1938) pp. 37 f.

[4] Winstanley, *England's Worthies* (1660) p. 252, and Aubrey (as in the previous note) p. 254, respectively. Winstanley is quoting Naunton's report that Ralegh was 'an indefalliable reader' (*Fragmenta Regalia* [1641] p. 34).

[5] From Ralegh's letter to Sir Robert Cotton requesting several books which are expressly named (*Letters*, ed. Edward Edwards [1868] p. 322). It should be noted that Ralegh was totally dependent on his knowledge of Latin since he knew very little Greek and no Hebrew (cf. below, p. 79).

spheres.[1] The translation of his raw material into the prose of his great *History* demonstrates how disinclined he was slavishly to imitate the sources consulted, for the information available to him was constantly modified and adapted to the purposes of his overall design.[2] The celebrated digression on 'conjectures' is in this respect not irrelevant (below, pp. 212 ff.). Ralegh's apparent credulity is repeatedly qualified even through mere phrases, witness the opening clause of the following sentence:

> if we may beleeue *Herodotus*, the Armie of *Xerxes*, being reviewed at *Thermopylæ*, consisted of fiue millions, two hundred eightie three thousand two hundred twenty men – (III vi 2)

– besides, adds Ralegh dismissively, 'besides Laundresses, Harlots, and Horses . . .'.

But the total control which Ralegh exercised over *The History of the World* is nowhere more clearly evident than in the unity he imposed on its various parts.

VI

The History of the World was never completed. Ralegh wrote and published only Part One whose narrative ends abruptly in 168 B.C., with a page or two added on the rising Roman Empire; and despite reports that he had also written a second part which he then destroyed,[3] we may rest assured

---

[1] On Ralegh's contributions to cartography and geographical literature, for instance, consult R. A. Skelton, 'Ralegh as a Geographer', *Virginia Magazine of History and Biography*, LXXI (1963) 131–49.

[2] The discovery of the working papers for *The History of the World* – first announced by W. F. Oakeshott in *The Times* of 29 Nov 1952 – confirms that Ralegh had complete control over his work. See also the astonishing range of the books he collected, in Walter Oakeshott, 'Sir Walter Ralegh's Library', *The Library*, 5th series, XXIII (1968) 285–327. Ralegh's procedure has been demonstrated in some detail with reference to his treatment of the history of ancient Persia; see M. Aryanpur-Kashani, 'Sir Walter Raleigh's *Historie of the World* and Persia', *Dissertation Abstracts*, XX (1959) 2274 [University of Colorado].

[3] Thus Aubrey, *Brief Lives*, ed. O. L. Dick, 2nd ed. (1950), p. 259, and Winstanley, *England's Worthies* (1660) pp. 256 f. Notwithstanding Ralegh's own statement (below, pp. 396-7), it was claimed that he cast Part Two into

that the work was simply abandoned. But critics are generally agreed that Ralegh's *History* is as unaffected by its incompleteness as is *The Faerie Queene*.

Yet *The History of the World* would appear to lack unity. David Hume was perhaps the first – though certainly not the last – to differentiate sharply between the 'Jewish and Rabbinical learning' in Books I–II, and 'the Greek and Roman story' of Books III–V.[1] The distinction is now widely accepted as self-evident: nearly all scholars respond to Ralegh's work much the same way that Henry James reacted to George Eliot's *Daniel Deronda* ('all the Jewish burden of the story tended to weary me'). The most crucial argument involves the claim that in the *History* 'the theological system which dominates the first part is much less in evidence in the second'. 'Ralegh's providential interpretation of events is commonest', we are told, 'when he is following the Bible'; but 'when he follows secular sources, he is more apt to offer human causes'. 'His precepts looked back', writes another scholar, 'his practice looked forward. In precept he stressed the role of God as a cause, but in practice he pursued the secondary causes of accident and motive.'[2] Lately, it has even been suggested that Ralegh was 'on the side of the Moderns against the Ancients':

Ralegh's importance is that he employed a secular and critical approach to the study of world history which was in very large part a study of Biblical history; and that he did this in English, in a work which was a best-seller. So he contributed, perhaps more than has been recognized, to that

---

the fire either because of his disillusionment over Prince Henry's death, or else because Part One sold 'very slowly at first'! Later, Ralegh was also held responsible for *An Introduction to a Breviary of the History of England* (1693) which focuses on William the Conqueror but was to have been carried to the reign of Elizabeth I. On this work see the biographies of Ralegh by Edward Edwards (1868) pp. 513 ff., and William Stebbing (1891) pp. 271 f.

[1] *History of England* (Boston, 1868) IV 377. The sentiment is as often quoted as endorsed – e.g. by Willard M. Wallace, *Sir Walter Raleigh* (Princeton, 1959) p. 245, *et al.*

[2] *Seriatim*: Sir Charles Firth, *Essays Historical & Literary* (Oxford, 1938) p. 49; Leonard F. Dean, *Tudor Theories of History Writing*, University of Michigan Contributions in Modern Philology, No. 1 (1947) pp. 17 ff.; and J. R. Hale, 'Introduction' to *The Evolution of British Historiography* (1967) p. 14.

segregation of the spiritual from the secular which was the achievement of the seventeenth century.[1]

So much for the claims of our scholars. Let's now look at Ralegh's work.

The precise way that Books I–II could be said to prepare for 'the Greek and Roman story' in Books III–V will be suggested later; here we may usefully remind ourselves that the opening books contain something more than 'Jewish and Rabbinical learning'. They also contain a host of mythological references and any number of quotations from authors of every age to the Renaissance. These references and quotations jointly testify to one 'truth' in particular, that within the historical process mankind forms an interdependent entity, a spiritual unity. Ralegh details his conviction in divers ways. There is the premeditated fusion of pagan myths and Christian verities until the suggestiveness of the first yields to the certainty of the second. There is the patient exposition of the series of events which led from the creation of Adam to the rise of individual tribes and finally nations. There are the incessant reminders that the history of nations is coeval. In the following quotations – all of which are opening sentences of sections in Book II – Ralegh's immediate interest is to co-ordinate his chronological framework but he simultaneously endeavours to consolidate the various families of men into a unity:

And in this age of the World, and while *Moses* yet liued, *Deucalion* raigned in *Thessalie*, *Crotopus* then ruling the *Argiues* ...   (ii vi 5)

Neare the beginning of *Salomons* raigne, *Agelaus* the third of the *Heraclidæ* in *Corinth*; *Labotes* in *Lacedæmon*; and soone after *Syluius Alba* the fourth of the *Syluij*, swaied those Kingdomes: *Laoesthethes* then gouerning *Assyria*: *Agastus* and *Archippus* the second and third Princes after *Codrus*, ruling the *Athenians*. ...   (ii xviii 6)

The first yeare of *Manasses* was the last of *Romulus*. ...   (ii xxvii 6)

There liued with *Ioas*, *Mezades* and *Diognetus* in *Athens*: *Eudemus* and *Aristomides* in *Corinth*: about which time *Agrippa Syluius*, and after him *Syluius Alladius*, were Kings of the *Albans* in *Italie*. *Ocrazapeo*, commonly called *Anacyndaraxes*, the thirtie seuenth King succeeding vnto *Ophratanes*, began his raigne ouer the *Assyrians*, about the eighteenth yeare of *Ioas*,

---

[1] Christopher Hill, *Intellectual Origins of the English Revolution* (Oxford, 1965) pp. 187–88. Hill's enlistment of Ralegh among the Moderns is ventured on p. 183.

which lasted fortie two yeares. In the sixteenth of *Ioas, Cephrenes,* the fourth from *Sesac,* succeeded vnto *Cheops* in the Kingdome of *Ægypt,* and held it fiftie yeares. . . .   (II xxii 6)

When all is said, however, the cardinal way Ralegh asserts the unity of mankind is through the providential theory of history.

The theory of providential causation espoused in *The History of the World* is not a conclusion which Ralegh attained late in life. In 1591 – which is to say over twenty years before the publication of the *History* – he had related the engagement between the *Revenge* and the Spanish fleet in purely secular terms, but in the end ascribed the final destruction of the enemy to the intercession of God:

> Thus it hath pleased God to fight for vs, & to defend the iustice of our cause, against the ambicious & bloody pretenses of the Spaniard, who seeking to deuour all nations, are themselues deuoured. A manifest testimonie how uniust & displeasing, their attempts are in the sight of God, who hath pleased to witnes by the successe of their affaires his mislike of their bloudy and iniurious designes, purposed & practised against all Christian Princes, ouer whom they seeke vnlawfull and vngodly rule and Empery.[1]

This astonishing claim is certainly not warranted by Ralegh's rousing narrative of mere men at war. It therefore surprises, perhaps even it shocks – yet one may well ask whether Ralegh had not actually intended the reader to be surprised, even to be shocked. The theory of providential causation is after all not a readily apparent 'fact'; it is a mystery which defies comprehension. 'We oft doubt', says the Chorus in *Samson Agonistes,* 'What th' unsearchable dispose / Of highest wisdom brings about'; 'Oft he seems to hide his face, / But unexpectedly returns'.[2] It may well be, I suggest, that Ralegh's assertion of divine intervention in the fight between the *Revenge* and the Spanish fleet is not in the least gratuitous; he meant it because he planned it. Significantly, the role played by purely 'human causes' is not denied; it is simply placed within the larger context of supernatural causation.

---

[1] *A Report of the trvth of the fight about the Iles of Açores, this last sommer, betwixt the Reuenge, one of her Maiesties shippes, and an Armada of the King of Spaine* (1591) sig. C3.

[2] *Samson Agonistes,* ll. 1745–50.

But we prefer explicit assertions, whether of God's total subordination of the created order to his omnipotent purposes, or man's unobstructed pursuit of his own destiny. We incline favourably to the deployment of terms like predestination or free will, oblivious of the fact that these are not merely philosophical concepts but states of experience beyond definition. It is not as if we have not been warned against over-simplifications in Christian theology and in all great literature! The classical concept of *moira* is instructive, for we could mistake it for 'fate', perhaps even for predestination: the Delphic oracle spoke, *therefore* Oedipus acted as he did. But a man forewarned of his destiny who nevertheless thoughtlessly kills an elderly man and foolishly marries a woman twice his age without ever pausing to reflect on the past, is surely 'fated' so long as we take 'fate' to mean the destiny of man as it has been predicted by the gods but is enforced by the individual himself. Christian thinkers arrived at an identical balance. St Paul exhorted the faithful to 'work out *your own* salvation with fear and trembling; for *it is* God which worketh in you both to will and to do of his good pleasure' (Phil. 2:12 f.). In the Johannine Apocalypse the Lamb is reported as saying, 'Behold, I stand at the door, and knock: *if* any man hear my voice, *and* open the door, I *will* come in to him, and will sup with him, and he with me' (Rev. 3:20). The same balance controls St Augustine's brilliant 'inconsistency' in upholding man's free will at one moment and denying it the next, no sooner asserting that our salvation is both 'from the will of man and from the mercy of God' than adding that 'the whole process is credited to God, who both prepareth the will to receive divine aid and aideth the will which has been thus prepared'.[1] During the controversies ushered in by the Reformation the balance was upset, as Protestants charged that Catholics made free will 'the absolute Lord of its own actions', and Catholics charged that Protestants 'leaue vs as a stone or blocke to be moued by God onely'.[2]

---

[1] *Enchiridion*, XXXII (*Library of Christian Classics*, VII [1955] 358).
[2] George Downame, *Papa Antichristus* (1620), tr. Richard Baxter in *The Safe Religion* (1657) p. 389, and Robert Parsons, S.J., *Trial of Spirits* (Douai?, 1620) p. 17, respectively.

But the principal thinkers of that turbulent era never really abandoned the traditional 'inconsistency' of the Bible and St Augustine. There was Luther, beguiled into dazzling contradictions as he defended the folly of his God against the wisdom of Erasmus. There was even Arminius, widely maligned as *Pelagius redivivus*, who unhesitatingly asserted that God's grace 'goes before, accompanies, and follows', 'excites, assists, operates' whatever we do. There was Hugo Grotius, never in doubt that man possesses free will ('not an errour of *Pelagius*, but Catholick sense'), yet as convinced that grace does not depend on man's free will because 'Grace worketh how far, and how much it pleaseth'. Similarly, John Donne was assured not only that the will of man is 'but Gods agent', but also that 'neither God nor man determine mans will . . . but they condetermine it'. The same 'inconsistency' appears in Shakespeare's plays, manifesting itself at one end of the pendulum's swing in Cassius' statement that the fault is not in our stars but in ourselves, and in the other in Florizel's words in *The Winter's Tale* that we are 'the slaves of chance'.[1] Yet occasionally the pendulum stands still over statements like Hamlet's:

> There's a divinity that shapes our ends,
> Rough-hew them how we will.
>
> (v ii 10–11)

Hamlet's 'fate' is the universal concept of *moira* which attributes primacy to God yet senses that somehow man's faculties and godlike reason must hew – perhaps only rough-hew – his own destiny. Human experience confirms that the course of our lives must be attributed to 'human causes', but it confirms also belief in supernatural causation, even in the unexpected intervention of God 'to fight for

[1] On Luther see esp. B. A. Gerrish, *Grace and Reason* (Oxford, 1962). My other quotations are, *seriatim*, from Arminius, *Works*, tr. James Nichols (1825–75) ii 700; Grotius, *Choice Discourses*, tr. Clement Barksdale (1658), Appendix: p. 105; and Donne, *Sermons*, ed. E. M. Simpson and G. R. Potter (Berkeley, 1953–62) ix 75, and *Essays in Divinity*, ed. E. M. Simpson (Oxford, 1952) p. 80. Shakespeare's 'inconsistent' passages on free will are collected by Roland M. Frye, *Shakespeare and Christian Doctrine* (Princeton, 1963) pp. 157–65.

vs' – as Ralegh said of the destruction of the Spanish – '&
to defend the iustice of our cause'.[1]

Ralegh's account of the fight of the *Revenge* in 1591
asserts providential causation abruptly, unexpectedly, well
past the half-way mark of the narrative. Another work, the
popular *Instructions to his Son*, has a different strategy: the
worldly wisdom of its early sections may appear to be 'coldly
prudential', even 'calculating', but it terminates in the firm
proclamation of the final chapter, 'Let God be thy protector
and director in all thy Actions'. In Ralegh's words,

> Serve God, let him be the Author of all thy actions, commend al thy
> endevours to him that must either wither or prosper them, please him
> with praire, lest if he frowne, he confound all thy fortunes and labors like
> drops of Rayne on the sandy grounde.[2]

The History of the World deploys an entirely different strategy
again. The providential control of history is asserted neither
at the half-way mark nor at the end; it is on the contrary
proclaimed with appropriate magniloquence at the outset,
in both the Preface and the opening lines of the main text
(below, pp. 48 ff., and 85). The tactic carries a number
of implications which do not appear to have been appreciated
fully.

The Preface and the opening chapters jointly maintain
several things at once. They assert providential causation in
a particular way, by means of precise 'examples'. But the
examples are *not* drawn from biblical history; on the contrary
they are first drawn from the history of England, France and
Spain – what we persist in calling 'secular' history – and only
thereafter confirmed through any number of analogous precedents culled from the Scriptures. In other words, Ralegh
serves notice at the very outset of *The History of the World*
that historical events since the creation are indivisible; they
may *not* be sundered into 'sacred' and 'secular' history, not

---

[1] The preceding paragraph is borrowed from my discussion of Grace in
Milton and the Christian Tradition (Oxford, 1966) pp. 201–2.

[2] *Instrvctions to his Sonne*, 4th ed. (1633) pp. 98–99. The work was first
published posthumously in 1632 and reached a sixth edition within four
years. The tradition it extends is set forth by Agnes M. C. Latham, 'Sir
Walter Ralegh's *Instructions to his Son*', in *Elizabethan and Jacobean Studies
presented to F. P. Wilson*, ed. Herbert Davis and Helen Gardner (Oxford,
1959) pp. 199–218.

even when in pursuit of man's behaviour in history the emphasis appears to be placed on 'the secondary causes of accident and motive'. The point is of fundamental importance since it constitutes the first step in Ralegh's attempts to educate the reader.

The second step is taken almost at the same time. Once Ralegh in the Preface has surveyed the history of England and other nations, he advances to the opening chapters, which cumulatively invoke the Bible as their principal authority. A multitude of other authorities are also cited, but they are consistently cited with approval only where they endorse the claims of the Bible. Ralegh's method is displayed not only in the opening chapters, however, but throughout the better part of Books I and II. As we are made constantly aware of his ambition to look on events from both the human and the divine standpoints, so we are also invited to observe his consistent allocation of primacy to God. In his own words on a particular occasion,

> though (speaking humanely) the beginning of Empire may be ascribed to reason and necessitie; yet it was God himselfe that first kindled this light in the minds of men.... (below, p. 157)

The statement could be made to appear merely gratuitous so long as we are prepared to ignore either the emphasis placed earlier on the omnipotence of God, or the insistence on the subservience of the created order to its Creator, or the intricate balance maintained between divine foreknowledge and man's free will. All other events are similarly qualified. Details set forth in nominally secular terms ('speaking humanly') are sooner or later qualified by Ralegh's metaphysical claims. Lest the reader tends to overlook the sacred framework, Ralegh intervenes with either an immediate judgement or an evaluation which concludes the given chapter. Immediate judgements abound. While reciting the deeds of Abimelech, for instance, Ralegh pauses to promote a specific event into a general principle:

> All other passions and affections by which the soules of men are tormented, are by their contraries oftentimes resisted or qualified. But ambition, which begetteth euery vice, and is it selfe the childe and darling of *Satan*, looketh only towards the ends by it selfe set downe, forgetting nothing (how fearefull and inhumane soeuer) which may serue it: remembring

> nothing, whatsoeuer iustice, pietie, right or religion can offer and alleadge on the contrary.... (II xiii 7)

Again, the reign of King Amaziah affords Ralegh the opportunity to castigate a particular form of pride – 'a foolish and a wretched pride, wherwith men being transported, can ill endure to ascribe vnto God the honour of those actions, in which it hath pleased him to vse their owne industrie, courage, or foresight' – and to commend the 'heroism' involved in acknowledging God's assistance:

> so farre from weaknesse is the nature of such thanksgiuing, that it may well be called the height of magnanimitie; no vertue being so truly heroicall, as that by which the spirit of a man aduanceth it selfe with confidence of acceptation, vnto the loue of God. (II xxxii 8)

The narration of 'the Greek and Roman story' is similarly oriented. In the battle of Salamis – a nominally 'secular' event (below, pp. 224 ff.) – Ralegh's metaphysical claims are advanced during the evaluation of the character of Xerxes at the end of the same chapter (pp. 231 ff.). The Persian defeat, it is implicitly asserted, was the direct result of the tyrannical rule of Xerxes – which is to say that God once again deployed secondary causes as instruments of his justice, in this instance the Greeks to defeat the Persians. It is not without significance that as much is maintained in the prolonged chapters devoted to the rise of the Athenian Empire, its destruction by Sparta, and the subordination of all the Greeks to the Macedonians. The common denominator of all these phases of Greek history is the usurpation of sovereignty by force and the consequent divine punishment. Just as Athens deprived her colonies of their freedom, so Sparta imposed her tyrannical authority on Athens – and so, in turn, both were overcome by the Macedonians:

> two people [who] deserued best the plague of tyrannie, hauing first giuen occasion thereunto, by their great ambition, which wearied and weakened all the Countrie by perpetuall Warre. (III viii 1)

Here the alert reader recalls numerous formulations of the same general principle in the 'Jewish' books, for instance:

> Neither was it *Ierusalem* alone that hath so oftentimes beene beaten downe and made desolate, but all the great Cities of the world haue with their inhabitants, in seuerall times and ages, suffered the same shipwracke. And it hath beene Gods iust will, to the end that others might take

warning, if they would, not onely to punish the impietie of men, by famine, by the sword, by fire, and by slauerie; but hee hath reuenged himselfe of the very places they possest; of the wals and buildings, yea of the soyle and the beasts that fedde thereon.   (ii xii 3)

Much later, in Ralegh's account of Alexander the Great, we read again of 'the infinite spirit of the *Vniuersall*, piercing, mouing, and gouerning all thinges' (below, p. 253). Finally, a few pages from the end, the advent of the Roman Empire is prefaced with the ominous remark,

Now began the *Romans* to swell with the pride of their fortune; and to looke tyrannically vpon those that had beene vnmannerly toward them before. . . .   (below, p. 396)

The History of the World is constructed as a series of inter-locked parallel movements orchestrated by God but per-formed by man himself.

Ralegh's own exposition, then, appears not to support the alleged severance of his work into two disconnected parts. The reader who reaches 'the Greek and Roman story' in Book III is already sufficiently educated to read a nominally secular history in the terms dictated by Ralegh. For by then the method has been demonstrated repeatedly; the principal authority has been proclaimed in no uncertain terms; secular sources have been made to bow before the Bible; the sacred framework of universal history has been firmly established; and 'human causes' have been relentlessly subordinated to providential causation.

Ralegh himself was able to survive in the midst of apparent 'contraditions', for he possessed that distinctly Renaissance gift which was a 'capacity to live and think upon many different levels'.[1] But realistic as he was, he knew that the reader – however well 'trained' to read history *sub specie aeternitatis* – was all too often bound to extricate secular events from their divine context. Hence the warning in the Preface that it is a 'monstrous' impiety to confound God and Nature – primary and secondary causes – or the insistence that God intervenes not as a *deus ex machina* but 'by the

[1] See, respectively, F. P. Wilson, *Elizabethan and Jacobean* (Oxford, 1945) pp. 12 f., and M. C. Bradbrook, *The School of Night* (Cambridge, 1936) pp. 43 ff.

medium of mens affections, and naturall appetites'.[1] Hence also the constant reminders of providential causation in the last three Books,[2] and hence too the emphasis so often placed on the inadequacy of explaining human affairs through a consideration of secondary causes only.[3] True, the burden of Ralegh's observations frequently appears to be on the pragmatic at the expense of the moral; worse, Machiavelli often seems to rear his head, as in the long digression on tyranny (below, pp. 351 ff.). But the reader who is mindful of the framework erected in Books I and II will observe that the pragmatic is circumscribed by the moral, even as he will conclude that the long shadow cast by Machiavelli cannot by itself achieve Ralegh's conversion into a representative of 'free inquiry'.[4] Upon consideration even the numerous 'digressions' will emerge as indispensable amendments to Ralegh's central design. I am aware of the claim that

> Some of his digressions, such as those on the location of the earthly paradise, or on free will and predestination, are academic discussions apart from the general movement of the *History*. His most significant digressions are those dealing with political theory; they show, however, the same confusion which has been noted in the whole plan for the work.[5]

---

[1] *HW*, Preface (below, pp. 74 ff.), and II v 10 (in the 1614 ed., p. 309).

[2] In Book V, for instance, the fall of the Roman Empire is expressly attributed not so much to external enemies – 'rude *Barbarians*' – as to internal 'affections' directed by God. Ralegh's constant effort to balance free will and predestination is again patently clear: 'vnto all Dominions God hath set their periods: Who, though he hath giuen vnto Man the knowledge of those waies, by which Kingdomes rise and fall; yet hath left him subject vnto the affections, which draw on these fatall changes, in their times appointed' (v iii 13).   [3] Cf. E. A. Strathmann, *Sir Walter Ralegh* (1951) pp. 112 f.

[4] As Christopher Hill claims in *Intellectual Origins of the English Revolution* (Oxford, 1965) pp. 180–92. But on Machiavelli's influence on Ralegh's works other than the *History*, see Nadja Kempner, *Raleghs staatstheoretische Schriften: die Einführung des Machiavellismus in England* (Leipzig, 1928); Mario Praz, 'Un machiavellico inglese: Sir Walter Raleigh', *La Cultura*, VIII (1929) 16–27; and Vincent Luciani, 'Ralegh's *Discourse of War* and Machiavelli's *Discorsi*', *Modern Philology*, XLVI (1948) 122–31. Cf. Strathmann (previous note) pp. 161–71. The relevant passages are collected in Pierre Lefranc's *Sir Walter Ralegh écrivain* (Paris, 1968) App. G.

[5] N. T. Reed (as before, p. 15, note 2) p. 15. The digressions named are reprinted below, on the location of Eden, pp. 131 f.; on free will and predestination, pp. 115 f., 129 f.; and on political theory, pp. 156 f., 184 ff., ff., etc. But see also Ralegh's own observations on 'digressions', in historiography and in life (below, pp. 78 f.)

But even a minimum of reflection will establish that Ralegh's 'digressions' are as relevant to *The History of the World* as Milton's are to *Lycidas*. The digression on the location of Eden, for instance, is intended not so much to demonstrate the range of Ralegh's scholarship as to teach a method of approach to contradictory sources. The digression on free will and predestination is of capital importance in a work which has already proposed to explore the conduct of man within a sacred context, thereby to exhibit (as Milton phrased it on a parallel occasion) 'supernal Grace contending / With sinfulness of Man'.[1] The digressions of political theory, finally, should hardly surprise us in a work of history. It were indeed very odd had they been missing!

Ralegh's method in *The History of the World* is not dissimilar to the method of his friend Spenser in *The Faerie Queene* or of Milton in *Paradise Lost*. Their scope is of equally epic proportions, and equally encyclopaedic; their aim is alike to teach by example ('so much more profitable and gratious'); and their assumptions are ultimately grounded upon the Scriptures and built with the materials of tradition. Moreover, each attempted to train his reader responsibly to study 'the whole book of sanctity and virtue'.

VII

Ralegh's style is sometimes said to possess 'a dignity and majesty unequalled save in the writings of the greatest masters of the English language'.[2] Normally, however, praise is reserved for his 'fitful splendor', for those 'occasional pieces of gorgeous prose' which like the famous peroration on Death (below, p. 396) dispose many readers to use phrases such as 'the most beautiful passage of prose' in English literature.[3] But the praise of isolated

---

[1] *Paradise Lost*, XI 359–60.

[2] Eric Ecclestone, *Sir Walter Ralegh* (Harmondsworth, Middx., 1941) p. 90.

[3] *Seriatim*: J. R. Hale, 'Introduction' to *The Evolution of British Historiography* (1967) p. 19; W. M. Wallace, *Sir Walter Raleigh* (Princeton, 1959) p. 247; and Milton Waldman, *Sir Walter Raleigh* (1928; 1950) p. 31.

passages is as meaningless as the claim that Ralegh's prose is 'unequalled'. Far more enlightening, I should think, are the attempts to contrast the style of Ralegh's letters with the 'formal prose' of *The History of the World*,[1] or to compare the clarity of his prose with the practice of his contemporaries:

> no Elizabethan is less affected, or freer from intolerable divagations and toilsome 'Asiatic' circumlocutions. Ralegh's final judgement on Epaminondas has often been praised. It is unsurpassed for conciseness, is epigrammatic without being false, packed without being obscure. . . .[2]

Even more instructive, however, is the demonstration of the unity which links the divers 'pieces of gorgeous prose'.

We have already noted that the unity of Ralegh's subject is centred on the providential theory of history, even as the unity of his method is the gradual education of the reader to recognise the constant presence of God within the historical process. Concurrently, however, there is a unity of style — subdued where he discusses the information provided by his sources, solemn where he ponders questions of general principle, assured where he proclaims the authority of the Bible, spirited where he describes the clash of mighty armies, eloquent where he recites the achievements of great men, vehement where he portrays evil in action, serene where he posits the intervention of God. The unity of Ralegh's style must be attributed, I think, to his successful modulation of an infinitely varied tone. Different subjects have different cadences, and in each case, once the cumulative effect is achieved, the measure alters in accord with the new theme. Thus Jupiter's wondrous sexual exploits are boomed forth through an overwhelming roll-call of the women he 'rauished, betrayed, stole away, and tooke by strong hand':

> *Niobe, Laodemia,* and *Alcema* the wife of *Amphitryon,* by whom he had *Pelasgus, Sarpedon, Argus,* and *Hercules*: by *Taygete* he had *Taygetus,* of

---

[1] C. F. Tucker Brooke, *Essays on Shakespeare and other Elizabethans* (New Haven, 1948) pp. 131 f.

[2] 'Sir Walter Ralegh's Prose', *The Times Literary Supplement,* 31 Jan 1935 (p. 54); on Epaminondas, see below, pp. 236 ff. A. L. Rowse militantly observes that Ralegh's *History* is 'far more readable than the prose-works of Donne or Lancelot Andrewes, now so adventitiously fashionable' (*Ralegh and the Throckmortons* [1962] pp. 264–5). Its style is analysed by Pierre Lefranc, *Sir Walter Raleigh écrivain* (Paris, 1968) ch. xiv (ii).

whom the mountaine *Taygetus* tooke name, with another sonne called
Saon, of whom *Sauona*: by *Antiope* he had *Amphion* and *Zetus*: by *Læda*,
Castor & *Pollux*, *Helen* & *Clytemnestra*: by *Danaë Perseus*: by *Iordana
Deucalion*: by *Charme* (the daughter of *Eubulus*) *Britomartis*, by *Pro-
togenia* he had *Athlius* the father of *Endymion.* . . . (1 vi 5)

— and so on. We are of course reminded of Milton, not only
in the similarity of their magniloquent voices but in the
equally implicit moral judgement.

The influence of Ralegh on Milton is beyond dispute.[1]
As we have been told repeatedly, Milton even adapted
Ralegh's wording on two occasions. One is Ralegh's pre-
fatory sonnet to *The Faerie Queene* ('Methought I saw the
graue where Laura lay') which was obviously recollected by
Milton in Sonnet XXIII ('Methought I saw my late
espoused saint'). The other occasion involves the exotic
lines of *Paradise Lost* on

> Rich *Mexico* the seat of *Mo[n]tezume*,
> And *Cusco* in *Peru*, the richer seat
> Of *Atabalipa*, and yet unspoil'd
> *Guiana*, whose great Citie *Geryons* Sons
> Call *El Dorado*:
>
> (XI 407–11)

which echo Ralegh's similarly evocative lines on

> that mighty, rich, and beawtifull Empire of *Guiana*, and of that great
> and Golden City, which the Spaniards call *El Dorado*, and the naturals
> *Manoa*, which Citie was conquered, reedified, and inlarged by a younger
> sonne of *Guianacapa* Emperor of *Peru*, at such time as *Francisco Pazaro*
> and others conquered the said Empire, from his two elder brethren
> *Guascar*, and *Atabalipa*, both them contending for the same, the one
> being fauoured by the *Oreiones* of *Cuzco*, the other by the people of
> *Caximalca.* . . .[2]

---

[1] Edward Thompson much too enthusiastically describes this influence as
'greater, I believe, than that of any other English prose writer' (*Sir Walter
Ralegh* [1935] pp. 236–7).

[2] *The Discoverie of the large, rich, and bewtifvl Empire of Gviana* (1596),
'The Epistle Dedicatorie'. The two passages are quoted frequently, as by
Sir Charles Firth, *Essays Historical & Literary* (Oxford, 1938) p. 52, and the
author of the *TLS* article (above, p. 36, n. 2). Of the items discussed
next, Firth also calls attention to the fig-tree, and M. Weidhorn asserts the
parallel Xerxes = Satan ('Satan's Persian Expedition', *Notes and Queries*, n.s.,
v [1958] 389–92). See further George W. Whiting, *Milton's Literary Milieu*
(Chapel Hill, N.C., 1939) pp. 15–35.

Milton's debt to Ralegh extends also to *The History of the World*, possibly in the kinship which may be said to exist between Milton's Satan and Ralegh's Xerxes (below, pp. 222 ff.) but especially in the description of the Indian figtree (below, pp. 134 ff.) whose leaves are plucked by Milton's Adam and Eve to cover their nakedness:

> The Figtree, not that kind for Fruit renownd,
> But such as at this day to *Indians* known
> In *Malabar* or *Decan* spreads her Armes
> Braunching so broad and long, that in the ground
> The bended Twigs take root, and Daughters grow
> About the Mother Tree, a Pillard shade
> High overarcht, and echoing Walks between;
> There oft the *Indian* Herdsman shunning heate
> Shelters in coole, and tends his pasturing Herds
> At Loopholes cut through thickest shade: Those Leaves
> They gatherd, broad as *Amazonian* Targe,
> And with what skill they had, together sowd. . . .
>
> (IX 1101–12)

Details apart, however, Ralegh's influence on Milton can best be measured in terms of the remarkable tonal range of *The History of the World* which finds its finest counterpart in the equally polyphonic music of *Paradise Lost*. Milton responded to Ralegh because he discerned in him an artist who, like himself, had achieved a style answerable to his great argument.

Milton's contemporaries responded no less enthusiastically. Most readers of the *History* were attracted by Ralegh's espousal of the traditional theory of history – witness in particular the decision of Alexander Ross, a rather fierce guardian of orthodoxy, to attempt both its abridgement and its continuation.[1] But even authorities on historiography praised Ralegh's achievement, for example the scholar Diggory Wheare, whose statement in 1623 coincides with the verdict of his century. 'Of al modern Writers', said

---

[1] Ross's labours (besides his violent attacks on Sir Thomas Browne, Bacon, Harvey, Hobbes, and all followers of Copernicus and Galileo) are: *The Marrow of Historie, or an Epitome of all Historical Passages from the Creation, to the End of the last Macedonian War. First set out at large by Sir Walter Rawleigh* (1650); and *The History of the World: the Second Part, in Six Books: being a Continuation of the famous History of Sir Walter Raleigh . . . deduced to these Later-Times* (1652).

Wheare, 'Sir *Walter Rawleigh* our Country-man deserves the first place.'[1]

The response of republicans was additionally conditioned by their view of Ralegh as a martyr of Stuart tyranny.[2] But Cromwell himself extolled the *History* primarily because it orders divers elements into an impressively unified structure. As he advised his son, 'Recreate yourself with Sir Walter Raughleye's History: it's a body of history, and will add much more to your understanding than fragments of story'.[3] Cromwell had no difficulty, it appears, to wind his way through Ralegh's 'many cunning passages, contrived corridors / And issues . . .'

---

[1] *The Method and Order of Reading* ... *Histories*, tr. Edmund Bohun (1685) p. 41. The treatise was first published in Latin in 1623; Wheare was professor of history at Oxford. Firth (as before), p. 51, quotes other seventeenth-century encomia. Cf. E. A. Strathmann, *Sir Walter Ralegh* (1951) pp. 255 ff.

[2] The legend survived into the Restoration, as in the anonymous *Britannia and Rawleigh*, which attacks the corruptions of the court of Charles II even as it glances meaningfully back upon the noble age best represented by Ralegh. The work is sometimes attributed to Marvell, as by Zera S. Fink, *The Classical Republicans* (Evanston, Ill., 1945) pp. 125 ff.

[3] *The Writings and Speeches of Oliver Cromwell*, ed. Wilbur C. Abbott (Cambridge, Mass., 1939) II 236. The letter is dated 2 Apr 1650.

A Note on Method

THE original spelling has been retained since a modernised version would have altered Ralegh's tone considerably, and perhaps decisively. The modern reader will not encounter difficulties which he cannot expeditiously overcome.

The annotation is limited to essentials. Ralegh's text tempts the enthusiastic scholar to provide laboriously learned footnotes; but I refused to yield as I did not wish to intrude upon his remarkably lucid style. The numerous names he invokes are identified laconically in a discreetly appended Dictionary (below, pp. 399 ff.). The notes confine themselves to the provision of the most essential explanatory information, important cross-references, the identification of quotations in verse, and the translation of passages in Latin which Ralegh failed to translate. I have often borrowed the translations given in *An Abridgment of the History of the World*, edited by Laurence Eachard and published by Ralegh's grandson Philip Ralegh (1700), or in the anthology edited by G. E. Hadow (1917). In identifying quotations I was helped as much by the editions of his poems by J. Hannah (1875) and Agnes M. C. Latham (1951), as by Ralegh's marginal notes.

If nature abhors a vacuum, so does the reader who must cope with passages torn from their context. Here, consequently, the selections chosen are 'placed' within Ralegh's general scheme. Where chapters are omitted, their titles are still retained as a constant reminder of the all-important continuity of the narrative. In a further attempt to demonstrate the nature of this continuity, I have also supplied the titles of all the sections omitted from Book I (pp. 85–175).

The Preface is reprinted in its entirety but for a few pages whose expansive arguments are summarised in the notes.

Book I as the foundation of Ralegh's edifice is represented here with generous selections. While lack of space prevented the accommodation of the lengthy expostulations on the location of the Garden of Eden (Ch. III) and especially the Flood of Noah (Ch. VII), the purpose of the Book – the descent of mankind from Adam to the rise of the Assyrian Empire – is firmly set forth. It is against this background that Ralegh twice forgoes the linear progress of his narrative to expatiate on the rise of Government (Ch. IX) and the divers forms of Magic (Ch. XI).

Books II–III carry the narrative from Abraham to Philip of Macedon. The vast material is by and large not made available here, except for several discourses of variable importance (all in Book II): the account of the miraculous crossing of the Red Sea (Ch. III, §9); the dissertation on Laws in connection with the events at Mt Sinai (Ch. IV, §§4 ff.); two homilies on the presence of God in history (Ch. V, §10, and Ch. XIX, §3); and the 'digression' on conjectures (Ch. XXI, §6). However, on three occasions we revert to the narrative proper: in Book II, for Ralegh's outline of the expedition of the Argonauts (Ch. XIII, §6); and in Book III, for his interpretation of the defeat of Xerxes at Salamis (Ch. VI, §§ 4–11) and the much-praised account of the death of Epaminondas (Ch. XII, §6–7).

Book IV is devoted entirely to the rise and decline of the Macedonian Empire. The core of this Book – the lengthy recital of the achievements of Alexander the Great (Ch. II) – is reprinted here in its entirety, to demonstrate in profuse detail Ralegh's control over a sustained story within the context of his comprehensive design.

Book V begins with a section which is an appendix to the account of Alexander's deeds but also strikes that patriotic note so often sounded in Ralegh's pages. Thereafter we pause again to listen to Ralegh's views on naval warfare (Ch. I, §6) which extend into a later section (Ch. I, §9). The narrative is now well within sight of the acme of the Roman Empire, but here *The History of the World* sweeps to its final three sections which terminate in the celebrated peroration on Death.

THE HISTORY
OF THE WORLD

The Preface

How vnfit, and how vnworthy a choice I haue made of my self, to vndertake a worke of this mixture; mine owne reason, though exceeding weake, hath sufficiently resolued me. For had it beene begotten then with my first dawne of day, when the light of common knowledge began to open it selfe to my yonger yeares: and before any wound receiued, either from Fortune or Time: I might yet well haue doubted, that the darkenesse of Age and Death would haue couered ouer both It and Mee, long before the performance. For, beginning with the Creation: I haue proceeded with the History of the World; and lastly purposed (some few sallies excepted) to confine my discourse, within this our renowned Iland of Great Brittaine. *I confesse that it had better sorted with my dissability, the better part of whose times are runne out in other trauailes; to haue set together (as I could) the vnioynted and scattered frame of our English affaires, than of the vniuersall: in whome had there beene no other defect, (who am all defect) then the time of the day, it were enough; the day of a tempestuous life, drawne on to the very euening ere I began. But those inmost, and soulepeircing wounds, which are euer aking while vncured: with the desire to satisfie those few friends, which I haue tried by the fire of aduerfitie; the former enforcing, the latter perswading; haue caused mee to make my thoughts legible, and my selfe the Subiect of euery opinion wise or weake.*

To the world I present them, to which I am nothing indebted: neither haue others that were, (Fortune changing) sped much better in any age. For, Prosperity and Aduersity haue euer-more tied and vntied vulgar affections. And as we see it in experience, That dogs doe alwaies barke at those they know not; and that it is in their nature to accompany one another in those clamours:

so is it with the inconsiderate multitude. Who, wanting that vertue which wee call Honesty in all men, and that especiall gift of GOD which we call Charity in Christian men; condemne, without hearing; and wound, without offence giuen: led there-vnto by vncertaine report only; which his Maiesty[1] *truly acknow-ledgeth for the Author of all lies.* Blame no man (*saith Siracides*) before thou haue inquired the matter: vnderstand first, and then reforme righteously. *Rumor, res sine teste, sine iudice, maligna, fallax;* Rumour is without witnesse, without iudge, malicious and deceiueable. *This vanity of vulgar opinion it was, that gaue St.* Augustine *Argument to affirme, That he feared the praise of good men, and detested that of the euill. And heerein no man hath giuen a better rule, then this of* Seneca; Conscientiæ satisfaciamus: nihil in famam labo-remus; sequatur vèl mala, dum benè merearis. Let vs satisfie our owne consciences, and not trouble our selues with fame: be it neuer so ill, it is to be despised so we deserue well.

For my selfe, if I haue in any thing serued my Country, and prised it before my priuate: the generall acceptation can yeeld me no other profit at this time, than doth a faire sunshine day to a Sea-man after shipwrack; and the contrary no other harme than an outragious tempest after the port attained. I know that I lost the loue of many, for my fidelity towardes Her, whom I must still honor in the dust; though further than the defence of Her excellent person, I neuer persequuted any man. Of those that did it, and by what deuice they did it: He that is the Supreame Iudge of all the world, hath taken the accompt; so as for this kind of suffering, I must say with Seneca, Mala opinio, benè parta, delectat.[2]

As for other men; if there be any that haue made themselues Fathers of that fame, which hath beene begotten for them: I can neither enuy at such their purchased glory, nor much lament mine owne mishap in that kind; but content myselfe to say with Virgil, Sic vos non vobis,[3] *in many particulars.*

To labour other satisfaction, were an effect of phrenzie, not of hope: seeing it is not Truth, but Opinion, that can trauaile the

---

[1] James I, in his *Daemonologie* (Edinburgh, 1597).
[2] 'An ill reputation is a delight if it be virtuously acquired' (G. E. Hadow, 1917).   [3] 'So you produce for others, not for yourselves' (*id.*).

*world without a passeport. For were it otherwise; and were there
not as many internall formes of the minde, as there are externall
figures of men; there were then some possibility, to perswade by
the mouth of one Aduocate, euen Equity alone.*

*But such is the multiplying and extensiue vertue of dead
Earth, and of that breath-giuing life which GOD hath cast
vpon Slime and Dust: as that among those that were, of whome we
reade and heare, and among those that are, whom we see and
conuerse with; euery one hath receiued a seuerall picture of face,
and euerie one a diuerse picture of minde; euery one a forme apart,
euery one a fancy and cogitation differing: there being nothing
wherein Nature so much triumpheth, as in dissimilitude. From
whence it commeth, that there is found so great diuersity of
opinions; so strong a contrariety of inclinations; so many naturall
and vnnaturall; wise, foolish; manly, and childish affections, and
passions in Mortall Men. For it is not the visible fashion and
shape of plants, and of reasonable Creatures, that makes the
difference, of working in the one, and of condition in the other;
but the forme internall.*

*And though it hath pleased GOD, to reserue the Art of
reading mens thoughts to himselfe: yet, as the fruit tels the name
of the Tree; so doe the outward workes of men (so farre as their
cogitations are acted) giue vs whereof to guesse at the rest. Nay,
it were not hard to expresse the one by the other, very neare the
life: did not craft in many, feare in the most, and the worlds
loue in all, teach euery capacity, according to the compasse it hath,
to qualifie and maske ouer their inward deformities for a time.
Though it be also true,* Nemo potest diu personam ferre fictam:
cito in naturam suam recidunt, quibus veritas non subest.
No man can long continue masked in a counterfeit behauiour:
the thinges that are forced for pretences, hauing no ground of
truth, cannot long dissemble their owne natures. *Neither can
any man (saith* Plutarch*) so change himselfe, but that his heart
may be sometime seene at his tongues end.*

*In this great discord and dissimilitude of reasonable creatures,
if wee direct our selues to the Multitude;* Omnis honestæ
rei malus iudex est vulgus, The common people are euill
Iudges of honest things, *and* whose wisdome (*saith Ecclesiastes*) is to bee despised; *if to the better sort; euery vnderstanding hath a peculiar iudgment, by which it both censureth*

*other men, and valueth it selfe. And therefore vnto mee it will
not seeme strange, though I finde these my worthlesse papers
torne with Rats: seeing the slouthfull Censurers of all ages, haue
not spared to taxe the Reuerend Fathers of the Church, with
Ambition; the seuerest men to themselues, with Hypocrisie; the
greatest louers of Iustice, with Popularity; and those of the
truest valour and fortitude, with vaine-glorie. But of these
natures, which lie in wayt to finde fault, and to turne good into
euill, seeing Salomon complained long since: and that the very
age of the world renders it euery day after other more malitious;
I must leaue the professors to their easie waies of reprehension,
than which there is nothing of more facility.*

*To me it belongs in the first part of this præface, following the
common and approued custome of those who haue left the
memories of time past to after ages; to giue, as neare as I can,
the same right to History which they haue done. Yet seeing
therein I should but borrow other mens wordes; I will not
trouble the Reader with the repetition. True it is, that among
many other benefits, for which it hath beene honored; in this one
it triumpheth ouer all humane knowledge, That it hath giuen vs
life in our vnderstanding, since the world it selfe had life and
beginning, euen to this day; yea it hath triumphed ouer time,
which besides it, nothing but eternity hath triumphed ouer: for
it hath carried our knowledge ouer the vast & deuouring space
of so many thousands of yeares, and giuen so faire and peircing
eies to our minde; that we plainely behould liuing now, as if we
had liued then, that great World,* Magni Dei sapiens opus,
the wise worke (*saith Hermes*) of a great GOD, *as it was then,
when but new to it selfe. By it I say it is, that we liue in the very
time when it was created: we behold how it was gouerned: how
it was couered with waters, and againe repeopled: How Kings
and Kingdomes haue florished and fallen; and for what vertue
and piety GOD made prosperous; and for what vice and defor-
mity he made wretched, both the one and the other. And it is not
the least debt which we owe vnto History, that it hath made vs
acquainted with our dead Ancestors; and, out of the depth and
darkenesse of the earth, deliuered vs their memory and fame.
In a word, wee may gather out of History a policy no lesse wise
than eternall; by the comparison and application of other mens
fore-passed miseries, with our owne like errours and ill deseruings.*

But it is neither of Examples the most liuely instructions, nor the words of the wisest men, nor the terror of future torments, that hath yet so wrought in our blind and stupified mindes; as to make vs remember, That the infinite eye and wisdome of GOD doth peirce through all our pretences; as to make vs remember, That the iustice of GOD doth require none other accuser, than our owne consciences: which neither the false beauty of our apparent actions, nor all the formallitie, which (to pacifie the opinions of men) we put on; can in any, or the least kind, couer from his knowledge. And so much did that Heathen wisdome confesse, no way as yet qualified by the knowledge of a true GOD. If any (*saith Eurypides*) hauing in his life committed wickednesse, thinke he can hide it from the euerlasting gods, he thinkes not well.

To repeat GODS iudgements in particular, vpon those of all degrees, which haue plaied with his mercies; would require a volume apart: for the Sea *of examples hath no bottome. The markes, set on priuate men, are with their bodies cast into the earth; and their fortunes, written onely in the memories of those that liued with them: so as they who succeed, and haue not seene the fall of others, doe not feare their owne faults. GODS iudgments vpon the greater and greatest, haue beene left to posterity; first, by those happy hands which the Holy Ghost hath guided; and secondly, by their vertue, who haue gathered the acts and ends of men, mighty and remarkeable in the world. Now to poynt farre off, and to speake of the conuersion of Angells into Deuills, for Ambition: Or of the greatest and most glorious Kings, who haue gnawne the grasse of the earth with beasts, for pride and ingratitude towards GOD: Or of that wise working of* Pharao, *when he slue the Infants of* Israel, *ere they had recouered their Cradles: Or of the policy of* Iezabel, *in couering the Murder of* Naboth *by a triall of the* Elders, *according to the Law: with many thousands of the like: what were it other, than to make an hopelesse proofe, that farre-off examples would not be left to the same farr-off respects, as heretofore? For who hath not obserued, what labour, practise, perill, bloudshed, and cruelty, the Kings and Princes of the world haue vndergone, exercised, taken on them, and committed; to make them-selues and their issues maisters of the world? And yet hath* Babylon, Persia, Egypt, Syria, Macedon, Carthage, Rome, *and the rest, no*

SWR C

fruit, flower, grasse, nor leafe, springing vpon the face of the Earth, of those seedes: No; their very roots and ruines doe hardly remaine. Omnia quæ manu hominum facta sunt, vel manu hominum euertuntur, vel stando & durando deficiunt: All that the hand of man can make, is either ouerturnd by the hand of man, or at length by standing and continuing consumed. *The reasons of whose ruines, are diuersly giuen by those that ground their opinions on second causes. All Kingdomes and States haue fallen (say the Politicians) by outward and forraine force, or by inward negligence and dissension, or by a third cause arising from both: Others obserue, That the greatest haue sunck downe vnder their owne weight; of which* Liuie *hath a touch:* eo creuit, vt magnitudine laboret sua:[1] *Others, That the diuine prouidence (which* Cratippus *obiected to* Pompey*) hath set downe the date and period of euery estate, before their first foundation and erection. But hereof I will giue my selfe a day ouer to resolue.*

For seeing the first bookes of the following story, haue vndertaken the discourse of the first Kings and Kingdomes: and that it is impossible for the short life of a Preface, to trauaile after and ouer-take farr-off Antiquity, and to iudge of it; I will, for the present, examine what profit hath beene gathered by our owne Kings, and their Neighbour Princes: who hauing beheld, both in diuine and humane letters, the successe of infidelitie, iniustice, and crueltie; haue (notwithstanding) planted after the same patterne.

True it is that the iudgements of all men are not agreeable; nor (which is more strange) the affection of any one man stirred vpp a-like with examples of like nature: But euery one is touched most, with that which most neerely seemeth to touch his owne priuate; Or otherwise best suteth with his apprehension. But the iudgements of GOD are for euer vnchangeable; neither is he wearied by the long processe of time, and wont to giue his blessing in one age, to that which he hath cursed in another. Wherefore those that are wise, or whose wisdome, if it be not great, yet is true and well grounded; will bee able to discerne the bitter fruites of irreligious policie, as well among those examples that are found in ages remoued farr from the present, as in

---

[1] 'it has grown so much that it is burdened with its own greatness' (G. E. Hadow, 1917).

*those of latter times. And that it may no lesse appeare by euident
proofe, than by asseueration, That ill doing hath alwaies beene
attended with ill successe; I will here, by way of preface, runne
ouer some examples, which the worke ensuing hath not reached.*

Among our Kings of the Norman *race, we haue no sooner
passed ouer the violence of the* Norman Conquest, *than we
encounter with a singular and most remarkeable example of Gods
iustice, vpon the children of* Henry *the first. For that King, when
both by force, craft, and crueltie, hee had dispossest, ouer-reacht,
and lastly made blind and destroyed his elder Brother* Robert
Duke of Normandy, *to make his owne sonnes Lords of this
Land:* GOD *cast them all, Male and Female, Nephewes and
Neeces (*Maud *excepted) into the bottome of the Sea, with aboue
a hundred and fiftie others that attended them; whereof a great
many were Noble, and of the King dearely beloued.*

To passe ouer the rest, till we come to Edward *the Second;
it is certain, that after the Murder of that King, the issue of
bloud then made, though it had some times of stay and stopping,
did againe breake out; and that so often, and in such aboundance,
as all our Princes of the Masculine race (very few excepted) died
of the same disease. And although the young yeares of* Edward
*the Third, made his knowledge of that horrible fact no more then
suspitious: yet in that hee afterwards caused his owne Vncle the
Earle of* Kent *to die, for no other offence than the desire of his
Brothers redemption, whome the Earle as then supposed to bee
liuing; (the King making that to be treason in his Uncle, which
was indeed treason in him-selfe, had his Vncles intelligence beene
true) this I say made it manifest, that hee was not ignorant of
what had past, nor greatly desirous to haue had it otherwise;
though he caused* Mortimer *to die for the same.*

This cruelty the secret and vnsearchable iudgement of GOD
reuenged, on the Grand-child of Edward *the Third: and so it
fell out, euen to the last of that Line, that in the second or third
descent they were all buried vnder the ruines of those buildings, of
which the Mortar had beene tempered with innocent bloud. For*
Richard *the second, who saw, both his* Treasurers, *his* Chan-
cellor, *and his* Steward, *with diuers others of his Counsailours,
some of them slaughtered by the people, others in his absence
executed by his enemies; yet hee alwaies tooke him-selfe for
ouer-wise, to bee taught by examples. The Earles of* Huntington

and Kent, Montague *and* Spencer, *who thought them-selues
as great polititians in those daies, as others haue done in these:
hoping to please the King, and to secure them-selues, by the
Murder of* Gloucester; *died soone after, with many other their
adherents, by the like violent hands; and farre more shamefully
then did that Duke. And as for the King him-selfe (who in
regard of many deedes, vnworthy of his Greatnesse, cannot bee
excused, as the disauowing him-selfe by breach of Faith,
Charters, Pardons, and Patents) He was in the Prime of his
youth deposed; and murdered by his Cosen-germane and vassall,*
Henry *of* Lancaster; *afterwards* Henry *the fourth.*

*This King, whose Title was weake, and his obtaining the
Crowne traiterous: who brake Faith with the Lordes at his
landing, protesting to intend only the recouerie of his proper
Inheritance; brake faith with* Richard *himselfe; and brake
Faith with all the Kingdome in Parliament, to whom he swore
that the deposed King should liue. After that he had enioyed this
Realme some few yeares, and in that time had beene set vpon
on all sides by his Subiects, and neuer free from conspiracies and
rebellions: he saw (if Soules immortall see and discerne any
thinges after the bodies death) his Grand-childe* Henrie *the sixt,
and his Sonne the Prince, suddenly, and without mercy, murdered;
the possession of the Crowne (for which he had caused so much
blood to bee powred out) transferred from his race; and by the
Issues of his Enemies worne and enioyed: Enemies, whom by his
owne practise hee supposed, that he had left no lesse powerlesse,
than the succession of the Kingdome questionlesse; by entailing
the same vpon his owne Issues by Parliament. And out of doubt,
humane reason could haue iudged no otherwise, but that these
cautious prouisions of the Father, seconded by the valour and
signall victories of his Sonne* Henry *the fift, had buried the
hopes of euery Competitor, vnder the despaire of al reconquest
and recouery. I say, that humane reason might so haue iudged:
were not this passage of* Casaubon *also true;* Dies, hora,
momentum, euertendis dominationibus sufficit, quæ ada-
mantinis credebantur radicibus esse fundatæ; A day, an
houre, a moment, is enough to ouerturne the things, that
seemed to haue beene founded and rooted in Adamant.

Now for Henrie *the sixt, vpon whom the great storme of
his Grandfathers greeuous faults fell, as it formerly had done*

vpon Richard *the Grand-childe of* Edward: *although he was generally esteemed for a gentle and innocent Prince; yet as he refused the daughter of* Armaignac, *of the House of* Nauarre, *the greatest of the Princes of* France, *to whom hee was affianced (by which match hee might haue defended his Inheritance in* France) *and married the Daughter of* Aniou, *(by which he lost all that hee had in* France) *so as in condiscending to the vnworthy death of his Vnckle of* Glocester, *the maine and strong pillar of the house of* Lancaster; *Hee drew on himselfe and this kingdome the greatest ioynt-losse & dishonor, that euer it sustained since the* Norman *Conquest. Of whom it may truly be said, which a Counsellor of his owne spake of* Henrie *the Third of* France, Q'uil estoit vn fort gentil Prince; mais son reigne est aduenu en vne fort mauuois temps, That he was a very gentle Prince; but his reign happened in a very vnfortunate season.

It is true, that Buckingham *and* Suffolke *were the practisers and contriuers of the Dukes death:* Buckingham *and* Suffolke, *because the Duke gaue instructions to their authority, which otherwise vnder the Queen had bin absolute; the Queene, in respect of her personall wound,* spretæque iniuria formæ, *because* Gloucester *disswaded her marriage. But the fruit was answerable to the seed; the successe to the Counsaile. For after the cutting downe of* Gloucester, Yorke *grew vp so fast, as hee dared to dispute his right, both by arguments and armes; in which quarrell,* Suffolke *and* Buckingham, *with the greatest number of their adherents, were dissolued. And although for his breach of Oath by Sacrament, it pleased God to strike down* Yorke: *yet his sonne the Earle of* March, *following the plaine path which his Father had troden out, despoyled* Henry *the Father, and* Edward, *the sonne, both of their liues and Kingdomes. And what was the end now of that politique* Lady *the* Queene, *other then this, That shee liued to behold the wretched ends of all her partakers: that she liued to looke on, while her Husband the King, and her onely sonne the Prince, were hewen in sunder; while the Crowne was set on his head that did it. Shee liued to see her selfe despoiled of her Estate, and of her moueables: and lastly, her Father, by rendring vp to the Crowne of* France *the Earledome of* Prouence *and other places, for the payment of Fifty thousand crownes for her ransome, to become a*

starke beggar. And this was the end of that subtiltie, which
Siracides *calleth* fine, *but* vnrighteous: *for other fruit hath
it neuer yeelded since the world was.*

And now came it to Edward *the fourths turne (though after
many difficulties) to triumph. For all the Plants of* Lancaster
were rooted vpp; *One onely Earle of* Richmond *excepted:
whome also hee had once bought of the Duke of Britaine, but
could not hold him. And yet was not this of* Edward *such a
plantation, as could any way promise it selfe stability. For this*
Edward *the King (to omit more than many of his other cruelties)
beheld and allowed the slaughter, which* Gloucester, Dorset,
Hastings, *and others, made of* Edward *the Prince in his owne
presence: of which tragicall Actors, there was not one that escaped
the iudgement of* GOD *in the same kinde. And He, which
(besides the execution of his brother of* Clarence, *for none other
offence then hee him-selfe had formed in his owne imagination)
instructed* Gloucester *to kill* Henry *the sixt, his predecessour;
taught him also by the same Art to kill his owne sonnes and
Successors* Edward *and* Richard. For those Kings, which
haue sold the bloud of others at a low rate; haue but made
the Market for their owne enemies, to buy of theirs at the
same price.

To Edward *the fourth succeeded* Richard *the Third, the
greatest Maister in mischeife of all that fore-went him: who
although, for the necessity of his Tragedie, hee had more parts to
play, and more to performe in his owne person, then all the rest;
yet hee so well fitted euery affection that playd with him, as if
each of them had but acted his owne interest. For he wrought so
cunningly vpon the affections of* Hastings, *and* Buckingham,
*enemies to the Queene and to all her kindred: as hee easily
allured them to condiscend, that* Riuers *and* Grey, *the Kings
Maternall Vncle and halfe brother, should (for the first) bee
seuered from him: secondly, hee wrought their consent to haue
them imprisoned, and lastly (for the avoyding of future inconuenience) to haue their heads seuered from their bodies. And
hauing now brought those his chiefe instruments to exercise that
common precept, which the* Deuill *hath written on euery post,
namely, To depresse those whome they had grieued, and to
destroy those whom they had deprest; Hee vrged that argument
so farre and so forcibly; as nothing but the death of the yong*

*king himselfe, and of his brother, could fashion the conclusion.
For hee caused it to be hammered into* Buckinghams *head, That,
whensoeuer the king, or his brother, should haue able yeares to
exercise their power; they would take a most seuere reuenge of
that curelesse wrong, offered to their vncle and brother,* Riuers
and Grey.

But this was not his manner of reasoning with Hastings,
*whose fidelity to his Maisters sonnes was without suspect: and
yet the Diuell, who neuer disswades by impossibility, taught him
to try him. And so hee did. But when hee found by* Gatesby,
*who sounded him, that he was not fordable; He first resolued to
kill him sitting in councell: wherein hauing fayled with his
sword; He set the Hangman vpon him, with a weapon of more
weight. And because nothing else could moue his appetite; He
caused his head to be stricken off, before he eate his dinner. A
greater iudgement of* GOD, *than this vpon* Hastings, *I haue
neuer obserued in any storie. For the selfe same daie that the
Earle* Riuers, Grey, *and others, were (without triall of Law,
or offence giuen) by* Hastings *aduice executed at* Pomfret: *I say*
Hastings *him-selfe in the same daie, and (as I take it) in the
same houre, in the same lawlesse manner had his head stricken
off in the* Tower *of* London. *But* Buckingham *liued a while
longer; and with an eloquent oration perswaded the* Londoners
to elect Richard *for their king. And hauing receiued the Earl-
dome of* Hereford *for reward, besides the high hope of marrying
his daughters to the Kings onely sonne, after many grieuous
vexations of minde, and vnfortunate attempts, being in the end
betrayed and deliuered vp by his trustiest seruant; He had his
head seuered from his body at* Salisbury, *without the trouble of
any of his* Peeres. *And what successe had* Richard *himselfe after
all these mischefes and Murders, policies, and counter-policies to
Christian religion: and after such time, as with a most mercilesse
hand hee had pressed out the breath of his Nephews and Naturall
Lords; other than the prosperity of so short a life, as it tooke end,
ere himselfe could well looke ouer and discerne it? the great
outcrie of innocent bloud, obtayning at* GODS *hands the effusion
of his; who became a spectacle of shame and dishonor, both to his
friends and enemies.*

This cruell King, Henry *the seauenth cut off; and was therein
(no doubt) the immediate instrument of* GODS *iustice. A*

politicke Prince hee was if euer there were any, and who by the ingine of his wisdome, beat downe and ouerturned as many strong oppositions both before and after hee ware the crowne as euer King of England did: I say by his wisdome, because as he euer left the raines of his affections in the hands of his profit, so he alwaies wayed his vndertakings by his abillities, leauing nothing more to hazard than so much as cannot be denied it in all humane actions. Hee had well obserued the proceedings of Loys *the eleuenth, whome hee followed in all that was royall or royal-like, but hee was farre more iust, and begun not their processes whome hee hated or feared by the execution, as* Loys *did.*

Hee could neuer indure any mediation in rewarding his seruants, and therein exceeding wise, for what so euer him-selfe gaue, hee him-selfe receiued backe the thanks and the loue, knowing it well that the affections of men (purchased by nothing so reddely as by benefits) were traynes that better became great Kings, than great subiects. On the contrary, in what so-euer hee greeued his subiects, he wisely put it off on those, that he found fit ministers for such actions. How-so-euer, the taking off, of Stanles *head, who set the Crowne on his, and the death of the young Earle of* Warwick, *sonne to* George D. *of* Clarence, *shews, as the successe also did, that he held somewhat of the errors of his Ancesters, for his possession in the first line ended in his grand children, as that of* Edward *the third and* Henry *the fourth had done.*

Now for King Henry *the eight: if all the pictures and Patternes of a mercilesse Prince were lost in the World, they might all againe be painted to the life, out of the story of this King. For how many seruants did hee aduance in hast (but for what vertue no man could suspect) and with the change of his fancy ruined againe; no man knowing for what offence? To how many others of more desert gaue hee aboundant flowers from whence to gather hony, and in the end of Haruest burnt them in the Hiue? How many wiues did hee cut off, and cast off, as his fancy and affection changed? How many Princes of the bloud (whereof some of them for age could hardly crawle towards the block) with a world of others of all degrees (of whome our common Chronicles haue kept the accompt) did he execute? Yea, in his very death-bed, and when he was at the point to haue giuen his accompt to* GOD *for the aboundance of bloud already spilt: He imprisoned the Duke of* Norfolke *the Father; and executed the Earle of* Surrey *the sonne; the one, whose desernings he knew not how to value, hauing neuer omitted any thing that concerned his owne honour, and the Kings seruice; the other, neuer hauing committed anything worthy of his least displeasure: the one exceeding valiant and aduised; the other, no lesse valiant than learned, and of excellent hope. But besides the sorrowes which hee heaped vpon the Fatherlesse, and widdowes at home: and besides the vaine enterprises abroad, wherein it is thought that hee consumed more Treasure, than all our victorious Kings did in their seuerall Conquests: what causelesse and cruell warres did he make vpon his owne Nephew King* Iames *the fift? What Lawes and Wills did he deuise, to establish this Kingdome in his owne issues? vsing his sharpest weapons to cut off, and cut downe those branches, which sprang from the same roote that him-selfe did. And in the end (notwithstanding these his so many irreligious prouisions) it pleased GOD to take away all his owne, without increase; though, for themselues in their seuerall kindes, all Princes of eminent vertue. For these wordes of* Samuel *to* Agag *King of the* Amalekites, *haue beene verified vpon many others:* As thy sword hath made other women childlesse: so shall thy mother be childlesse among other women. *And that bloud, which the same King* Henry *affirmed, that the cold aire of* Scotland *had frozen vp in the North, GOD hath diffused by the sunshine of his grace: from whence* His Maiesty *now liuing, and long to liue, is descended. Of whome I may say it truely, That if all the malice of the world were infused into one eie: yet could it not discerne in His life, euen to this daie, any one of those foule spots, by which the Consciences of all the forenamed* Princes *(in effect) haue beene defiled; nor any droppe of that innocent bloud on the sword of his iustice, with which the most that fore-went him, haue stayned both their hands and fame. And for this Crowne of* England; *it may truely be avowed, That he hath receiued it euen from the hand of GOD, and hath stayed the time of putting it on, howsoeuer he were prouoked to hasten it: That Hee neuer tooke reuenge of any man, that sought to put him beside it: That Hee refused the assistance of Her enemies, that wore it long, with as great glory as euer* Princesse *did, That* His Maiesty *entred not by a breach, nor by bloud; but by the Ordinary gate, which his owne right set open; and into which, by a generall loue and Obedience, Hee was receiued. And howsoeuer* His Maiesties *præceding title to this Kingdome, was preferred by many Princes (witnesse the Treaty at* Cambray *in the yeare,* 1559) *yet hee neuer pleased to dispute it, during the life of that renowned* Lady, *his Prædecessor; no, notwithstanding the iniury of not being declared Heire, in all the time of Her long reigne.*

Neither ought wee to forget, or neglect our thankefulnesse to GOD *for the vniting of the Northerne parts of Brittany to the South, to wit of Scotland to England, which though they were seuered but by small brookes and bancks, yet by reason of the long continewed warre, and the cruelties exercised vpon each other, in the affection of the Nations, they were infinitly seuered. This I say is not the least of Gods blessings which* His Maiesty *hath brought with him vnto this Land: No, put all our petty greeuances together, and heap them vp to their hight, they wil appeare but as a Mole-hil, compared with the Mountaine of this concord. And if all the Historiens since then; haue acknowledged the vniting of the Red-Rose, and the White, for the greatest happinesse, (Christian Religion excepted) that euer this Kingdome receiued from* GOD, *certainely the peace betweene the two Lions of gold and gules, and the making them one, doth by many degrees exceed the former; for by it, besides the sparing of our british bloud, heretofore and during the difference so often & aboundantly shed, the state of England is more assured, the Kingdom more inabled to recouer her auntient honor and rights, and by it made more inuincible, than by all our former alliances, practices, policies and conquests. It is true that hereof we do not yet finde the effect. But had the Duke of Parma in the yeare* 1588, *ioyned the army which hee commanded, with that of Spaine, and landed it on the south coast; and had his Maiesty at the same time declared himselfe against vs in the north, it is easie to diuine what had become of the liberty of England, certainely we would then without murmur haue bought this vnion at a farre greater prise than it hath since cost vs.*

It is true, that there was neuer any Common-weale or Kingdome in the world, wherein no man had cause to lament. Kings liue in the world and not aboue it. They are not infinite to examine euery mans cause, or to releiue euery mans wants. And yet, in the latter, (though to his owne preiudice) His Maiesty *hath had more compassion of other mens necessities, than of his owne Coffers. Of whome it may be said, as of* Salomon, Dedit Deus Salomoni latitudinem Cordis:[1] *Which if other men doe not vnderstand with* Pineda, *to be meant by* Liberality, *but by* Latitude of knowledge; *yet may it bee better spoken of* His Maiesty, *than of any King that euer* England *had; who as well in Diuine, as Humane vnderstanding, hath exceeded all that fore-went him, by many degrees.*

I could say much more of the Kings Maiesty, *without flatterie: did I not feare the imputation of presumption, and withall suspect, that it might befall these papers of mine, (though the losse were little) as it did the Pictures of* Queene Elizabeth, *made by vnskilfull and common Painters; which by her owne Commandement, were knockt in peeces and cast into the fire. For ill* Artists, *in setting out the beauty of the externall: and weake writers, in describing the vertues of the internall; doe often leaue to posterity, of well-formed faces a deformed memory; and of the most perfect and Princely mindes, a most defectiue repræsentation. It may suffice, and there needes no other discourse; if the honest* Reader *but compare the cruell and turbulent passages of our former Kings, and of other their Neighbour-Princes (of whome for that purpose I haue inserted this breife discourse) with* His Maiesties *temperate, revengelesse, and liberall disposition: I say, that if the honest* Reader *weigh them iustly, and with an euen hand: and withall, but bestow euery deformed child on his true* Parent; *He shall find, that there is no man which hath so iust cause to complaine, as the King him-selfe hath.*

Now as we haue told the successe of the trumperies and cruelties of our owne Kings, and other great personages: so we finde, that GOD *is euery where the same* GOD. *And as it pleased him to punish the vsurpation, and vnnaturall cruelty of* Henry *the first, and of our third* Edward, *in their Children for many generations: so dealt* He *with the sonnes of* Loys Debonaire, *the sonne of* Charles *the great, or* Charlemain. *For after such time as* Debonaire *of* France, *had torne out the eies of* Bernard *his Nephew, the sonne of* Pepin, *the eldest sonne of* Charlemain, *and heire of the Empire, and then caused him to die in prison, as did our* Henry *to* Robert *his elder brother: there followed nothing but murders vpon murders, poysonings, imprisonments,*

[1] I Kings 4.29: 'God gave Solomon ... largeness of heart'.

and ciuill warre; till the whole race of that famous Emperour was extinguished. . . .[1]

Let vs now see if GOD *be not the same* GOD *in* Spaine, *as in* England *and* France. *Towards whome we wil looke no further backe than to* Don Pedro *of* Castile: *in respect of which Prince, all the Tyrants of* Sicil, *our* Richard *the third, and the great* Euan Vasilowich *of* Moscouia, *were but pettie ones: this* Castilian, *of all Christian and Heathen Kings, hauing beene the most mercilesse. For besides those of his owne bloud and Nobility which hee caused to bee slaine in his owne Court and Chamber, as* Sancho Ruis *the great Maister of* Calatraua, Ruis Gonsales, Alphonso Tello, *and* Don Iohn *of* Arragon, *whome he cutt in peeces and cast into the streets, denying him Christian buriall: I say besides these, and the slaughter of* Gomes Manriques, Diego Peres, Alphonso Gomes, *and the great commander of* Gastile; *Hee made away the two Infants of* Arragon *his Cosen-germans, his brother* Don Frederick, Don Iohn de la Cerde, Albuquerques, Nugnes de Guzman, Cornel, Cabrera, Tenorio, Mendes de Toledo, Guttiere *his great Treasurer, and all his Kindred, and a world of others. Neither did he spare his two youngest brothers, innocent Princes: whome after hee had kept in close prison from their Cradles, till one of them had liued sixteene yeares, and the other, foureteene; hee murdered them there. Nay hee spared not his Mother, nor his wife the Lady* Blanch *of* Bourbon. *Lastly as he caused the Arch-bishop of* Toledo, *and the Deane, to bee killed of purpose to enioy their treasures: so did he put to death* Mahomet Aben Alhamar *King of* Barbarie, *with seauen and thirty of his Nobilitie; that came vnto him for succour, with a great summe of mony, to leuy (by his fauour) some companies of souldiers to returne withall. Yea he would needs assist the Hangman with his owne hand, in the execution of the old King; insomuch as Pope* Vrban *declared him an enemie both to* GOD *and* Man. *But what was his end? Hauing beene formerly beaten out of his Kingdome, and re-established by the valour of the* English Nation, *led by the famous Duke of* Lancaster: *He was stabbed to death by his younger Brother the Earle of* Astramara, *who dispossest all his Children of their inheritance; which, but for*

---

[1] Nearly three folio pages are here omitted; they set forth in some detail the fortunes of Louis I le Débonnaire, Francis I, and their successors.

*the Fathers iniustice and cruelty, had neuer beene in danger of
any such thing. . . .*[1]

*Oh by what plots, by what forswearings, betrayings, oppressions,
imprisonments, tortures, poysonings, and vnder what
reasons of State, and politique subteltie, haue these forenamed
Kings, both strangers, and of our owne Nation, pulled the
vengeance of GOD vpon them-selues, vpon theirs, and vpon their
prudent ministers! and in the end haue brought those things to
passe for their enemies, and seene an effect so directly contrarie to
all their owne counsailes and cruelties; as the one could neuer
haue hoped for them-selues; and the other neuer haue succeeded;
if no such opposition had euer beene made. GOD hath said it
and performed it euer:* Perdam sapientiam sapientum, I will
destroy the wisdome of the wise.

*But what of all this? and to what end doe we lay before the
eies of the liuing, the fal and fortunes of the dead: seeing the
world is the same that it hath bin; and the children of the
present time, wil stil obey their parents? It is in the present
time, that all the wits of the world are exercised. To hold the
times we haue, we hold all things lawfull: and either we hope
to hold them for euer; or at least we hope, that there is nothing
after them to bee hoped for. For as wee are content to forget our
owne experience, and to counterfeit the ignorance of our owne
knowledge, in all things that concerne our selues; or perswade
our selues, that GOD hath giuen vs letters patents*[2] *to pursue
all our irreligious affections, with a* non obstante: *so wee
neither looke behind vs what hath beene, nor before vs what
shall bee. It is true, that the quantitie which wee haue, is of the
body: wee are by it ioyned to the earth: we are compounded of
earth; and wee inhabit it. The Heauens are high, farr off
and vnsearcheable: wee haue sense and feeling of corporal
things; and of eternall grace, but by reuelation. No meruaile then
that our thoughts are also earthlie: and it is lesse to bee wondred
at, that the words of worthlesse men cannot cleanse them; seeing*

[1] Over three folio pages are here omitted; they set forth in some detail the
fortunes of Ferdinand V of Aragon and Castile, Charles V, and Philip II.

[2] *Litteræ patentes:* documents issued by a person in authority conferring
some right or privilege; they usually included a clause whose first two words,
non obstante (notwithstanding), indicated that all statutes to the contrary were
superseded.

their doctrine and instruction, whose vnderstanding the Holy Ghost vouchsafed to inhabite, haue not performed it. For as the Prophet Esai *cryed out long agone,* Lord, who hath be-leeued our reports? *And out of doubt, as* Esai *complained then for him selfe and others: so are they lesse beleeued, euery day after other. For although Religion, and the truth thereof, bee in euery mans mouth, yea in the discourse of euery woman, who for the greatest number are but* Idolls *of vanitie: what is it other than an vniuersall dissimulation? Wee professe that wee know* GOD: *but by workes we deny him. For Beatitude doth not consist in the knowledge of diuine things, but in a diuine life: for the Deuills know them better than men.* Beatitudo non est diuinorum cognitio, sed vita diuina. *And certainly there is nothing more to bee admired, and more to bee lamented, than the priuat contention, the passionate dispute, the personall hatred, and the perpetuall warre, massacres, and murders, for Religion among* Christians: *the discourse whereof hath so occupied the World, as it hath well neare driuen the practise thereof out of the world. Who would not soone resolue, that tooke knowledge but of the religious disputations among men, and not of their liues which dispute, that there were no other thing in their desires, than the purchase of Heauen; and that the World it selfe were but vsed as it ought, and as an Inne or place, wherein to repose our selues in passing on towards our celestiall habitation? when on the contrary, besides the discourse & outward profession, the soule hath nothing but hypocrisie. Wee are all (in effect) become* Comædians *in religion: and while we act in gesture and voice, diuine vertues, in all the course of our liues wee renounce our Persons, and the parts wee play. For Charitie, Iustice, and Truth, haue but their being* in termes, *like the Philosophers* Materia prima.

Neither is it that wisdome, which Salomon *defineth to be the* Schoole-Mistresse of the knowledge of God, *that hath valuation in the world: it is enough that we giue it our good word; but the same which is altogether exercised in the seruice of the World, as the gathering of riches cheifly; by which we purchase and obtaine honour, with the many respects which attend it.*

These indeed bee the markes, which (when wee haue bent our consciences to the highest) wee all shoote at. For the obtayning

*whereof it is true, that the care is our owne; the care our owne in
this life, the perill our owne in the future: and yet when we
haue gathered the greatest aboundance, wee our selues enioy no
more thereof, than so much as belongs to one man. For the rest;
Hee that had the greatest wisdome, and the greatest ability that
euer man had, hath told vs that this is the vse:* When goods
increase (*saith Salomon*) they also increase that eat them;
and what good commeth to the Owners, but the beholding
thereof with their eyes? *As for those that deuour the rest, and
follow vs in faire weather: they againe forsake vs in the first
tempest of misfortune, and steere away before the Sea and Winde;
leauing vs to the malice of our destinies. Of these, among a
thousand examples, I will take but one out of Maister* Dannet,
and vse his owne words: Whilest the Emperour *Charles* the
fift, after the resignation of his Estates, stayed at Vlushing
for winde, to carrie him his last iournie into Spaine; Hee
conferred on a time with *Seldius*, his brother *Ferdinands*
Embassadour, till the deepe of the night. And when *Seldius*
should depart: the Emperour calling for some of his seruants
and no bodie answering him (for those that attended vpon
him, were some gone to their lodgings, and all the rest a
sleepe) the Emperour tooke vp the candle him-selfe, and
went before *Seldius* to light him downe the staires; and so
did, notwithstanding all the resistance that *Seldius* could
make. And when Hee was come to the staires foot, He said
thus vnto him: *Seldius*, remember this of *Charles* the Emperour, when hee shalbe dead and gone, That Him, whome
thou hast knowne in thy time enuironed with so many
mighty Armies, and Guards of souldiors, thou hast also
seene alone, abandoned, and forsaken, yea euen of his
owne domesticall seruants, &c. I acknowledge this change
of Fortune to proceed from the mighty hand of *GOD*;
which I will by no meanes goe about to withstand.

*But you will say that there are some things else; and of greater
regard than the former. The first, is the reuerend respect that is
held of great men, and the Honour done vnto them by all sorts
of people. And it is true indeed: prouided, that an inward loue
for their iustice and piety, accompany the outward worship
giuen to their places and power; without which what is the
applause of the Multitude, but as the outcrie of an Heard of*

Animals, *who without the knowledge of any true cause, please them-selues with the noyse they make?* For *seeing it is a thing exceeding rare, to distinguish Vertue and Fortune: the most impious (if prosperous) haue euer beene applauded; the most vertuous (if vnprosperous) haue euer beene despised. For as Fortunes man rides the Horse, so Fortune her-selfe rides the* Man. *Who, when hee is descended and on foote: the Man taken from his Beast, and Fortune from the Man; a base groome beates the one, and a bitter contempt spurnes at the other, with equall libertie.*

The second, is the greatning of our posterity, and the contemplation of their glory whome wee leaue behind vs. Certainly, of those which conceiue that their soules departed take any comfort therein, it may truly be said of them, which Lactantius *spake of certaine Heathen Philosophers,* quod sapientes sunt in re stulta.[1] *For when our spirits immortall shalbe once seperate from our mortall bodies, and disposed by* GOD: *there remaineth in them no other ioy of their posterity which succeed, than there doth of pride in that stone, which sleepeth in the Wall of a Kings Palace; nor any other sorrow for their pouertie, than there doth of shame in that, which beareth vp a Beggars cotage.* Nesciunt mortui, etiam sancti, quid agunt viui etiam eorum filij quia animæ mortuorum rebus viuentium non intersunt. The dead though holy, know nothing of the liuing, no, not of their owne children: for the soules of those departed, are not conuerstant with their affaires that remaine. *And if wee doubt of Saint* Augustine, wee cannot of Iob; *who tells vs,* That wee know not if our sonnes shalbe honorable: neither shall wee vnderstand concerning them, whether they shalbe of low degree. *Which* Ecclesiastes *also confermeth:* Man walketh in a shadow, and disquieteth him-selfe in vaine: hee heapeth vp riches, and cannot tell who shall gather them. The liuing (*saith hee*) know that they shall die, but the dead know nothing at all; for who can shew vnto man, what shalbe after him vnder the Sunne? *Hee therefore accompted it among the rest of worldly vanities, to labour and trauaile in the world; not knowing after death, whether a foole or a wise man should enioy the fruits thereof:* which made mee

[1] 'they are Wise in a foolish thing' (trans. Laurence Eachard/Philip Ralegh, 1700).

(saith hee) endeauour euen to abhorre mine owne labour. *And what can other men hope, whose blessed or sorrowfull estates after death GOD hath reserued? mans knowledge lying but in his hope; seeing the Prophet Esai confesseth of the elect, That Abraham is ignorant of vs, and Israel knowes vs not. But hereof wee are assured, that the long and darke night of death: (of whose following day we shall neuer behold the dawne, till his returne that hath triumphed ouer it) shall couer vs ouer, till the world bee no more. After which, and when wee shall againe receiue Organs glorified and incorruptible, the feats of Angelicall affections: in so great admiration shall the soules of the blessed bee exercised, as they cannot admit the mixture of any second or lesse ioy; nor any returne of foregone and mortall affection, towards friends, kindred, or children. Of whome whether wee shall retaine any particular knowledge, or in any sort distinguish them: no man can assure vs; and the wisest men doubt. But on the contrary; If a diuine life retaine any of those faculties, which the soule exercised in a mortall body; wee shall not at that time so diuide the ioyes of Heauen, as to cast any part thereof on the memory of their felicities which remaine in the World. No; bee their estates greater than euer the World gaue, wee shall (by the difference knowne vnto vs) euen detest their consideration. And whatsoeuer comfort shall remaine of all forepast, the same will consist in the charitie, which we exercised liuing: and in that Pietie, Iustice, and firme Faith, for which it pleased the infinite mercy of GOD to accept of vs, and receiue vs. Shall we therefore value honour and riches at nothing? and neglect them, as vnnecessarie and vaine? certainlie no. For that infinite wisdome of GOD, which hath distinguished his Angells by degrees: which hath giuen greater and lesse light, and beautie, to Heauenly bodies: which hath made differences betweene beasts and birds: created the Eagle and the flie, the Cedar and the Shrub: and among stones, giuen the fairest tincture to the Rubie, and the quickest light to the Diamond; hath also ordained Kings, Dukes or Leaders of the people, Magistrates, Iudges, and other degrees among men. And as honour is left to posteritie, for a marke and ensigne of the vertue and vnderstanding of their Ancestors: so, seeing Siracides preferreth Death before Beggerie: and that titles, without proportionable estates, fall vnder the miserable succour of other mens pittie; I accompt it foolishnesse*

*to condemne such a care: Prouided, that worldly goods bee well
gotten, and that wee raise not our owne buildings out of other
mens ruines.* For as Plato *doth first preferre the perfection of
bodilie health; secondly, the forme and beautie; and thirdly,*
Diuitias nulla fraude quæsitas:[1] *so Hieremie cries,* Woe vnto
them that erect their houses by vnrighteousnesse, and their
chambers without equitie: *and Esai the same,* Woe to those
that spoyle and were not spoyled. *And it was out of the true
wisdome of* Salomon, *that hee commandeth vs,* not to drinke
the wine of violence; not to lie in wait for bloud; and not to
swallow them vp aliue, whose riches wee couet: for such are
the wayes (*saith hee*) of euery one that is greedy of gaine.

*And if wee could affoord our selues but so much leisure as to
consider, That hee which hath most in the world, hath, in
respect of the world, nothing in it: and that he which hath the
longest time lent him to liue in it, hath yet no proportion at all
therein, setting it either by that which is past when wee were not,
or by that time which is to come in which wee shall abide for
euer: I say, if both, to wit our proportion in the world, and our
time in the world, differ not much from that which is nothing;
it is not out of any excellency of vnderstanding, that wee so much
prise the one, which hath (in effect) no being: and so much neglect
the other, which hath no ending: coueting those mortall things of
the world, as if our soules were therein immortall, and neglecting
those things which are immortall, as if our selues after the world
were but mortall.*

*But let euery man value his owne wisdome, as hee pleaseth.
Let the Rich man thinke all fooles, that cannot equall his
aboundance; the Reuenger esteeme all negligent, that haue not
troden downe their opposites; the Politician, all grosse, that cannot merchandize their faith: Yet when wee once come in sight
of the Port of death, to which all winds driue vs; and when by
letting fall that fatall Anchor, which can neuer be weighed
againe, the Nauigation of this life takes end: Then it is I say,
that our owne cogitations (those sad and seuere cogitations,
formerly beaten from vs by our Health and Felicitie) returne
againe, and pay vs to the vttermost for all the pleasing passages
of our liues past. It is then that wee crie out to* GOD *for mercie;
then, when our selues can no longer exercise cruelty towards others:*

[1] 'Riches acquired without guile' (G. E. Hadow, 1917).

and it is onely then, that wee are strucken through the soule with this terrible sentence, That GOD will not be mockt. *For if according to Saint* Peter, The *righteous scarcely bee saued:* and that GOD *spared not his Ángells: where shall those appeare, who, hauing serued their appetites all their liues, presume to thinke, that the seuere commandements of the All-powerfull* GOD *were giuen but in sport; and that the short breath, which wee draw when death presseth vs, if wee can but fashion it to the sound of* Mercy *(without any kinde of satisfaction or amends) is sufficient?* O quam multi, *saith a reuerend Father,* Cum hac spe ad eternos labores & bella descendunt:[1] *I confesse that it is a great comfort to our friends, to haue it said, that wee ended well: for wee all desire (as* Balaam *did) to die the death of the righteous. But what shall wee call a disesteeming, an apposing, or (indeed) a mocking of* GOD; *if those men doe not appose him, disesteeme him, and mocke him, that thinke it enough for* GOD, *to aske him forgiuenesse at leisure, with the remainder and last drawing of a malitious breath? For what doe they other-wise, that die this kinde of well-dying, but say vnto* GOD *as followeth? Wee beseech thee O* GOD, *that all the falshoods, forswearings, and treacheries of our liues past, may be pleasing vnto thee; that thou wilt for our sakes (that haue had no leisure to doe anything for thine) change thy nature (though impossible) and forget to bee a iust* GOD; *that thou wilt loue iniuries and oppressions, call ambition wisdome, and charity foolishnesse. For I shall præiudice my sonne (which I am resolued not to doe) if I make restitution; and confesse my selfe to haue beene vniust (which I am too proud to doe) if I deliuer the oppressed. Certainly, these wise worldlings haue either found out a new* GOD; *or haue made One: and in all likelihood such a Leaden One, as* Lewis *the eleuenth ware in his Cappe; which, when he had caused any that he feared, or hated, to be killed, hee would take it from his head and kisse it: beseeching it to pardon him this one euill act more, and it should be the last, which, (as at other times) hee did; when by the practise of a* Cardinall *and a falsified Sacrament, he caused the Earle of* Armagnack *to bee stabbed to death; mockeries indeed fit to be vsed towards a Leaden, but not towards the euer-liuing* GOD.

[1] 'O how many ... descend to Eternal Torments and Sorrows with this Hope!' (trans. Laurence Eachard/Philip Ralegh, 1700).

*But of this composition are all the deuout louers of the world,
that they feare all that is durelesse and ridiculous: they feare the
plots and practises of their opposites, and their very whisperings:
they feare the opinions of men which beat but vpon shadowes:
they flatter and forsake the prosperous and vnprosperous, bee
they friends or Kings: yea they diue vnder water, like Ducks,
at euery pebble stone, that's but throwne towards them by a
powerfull hand: and on the contrary, they shew an obstinate and
Giant-like valour, against the terrible iudgements of the All-
powerfull GOD: yea they shew themselues gods against GOD,
and slaues towards men; towards men whose bodies and consciences are alike rotten.*

*Now for the rest: If wee truly examine the difference of both
conditions; to wit of the rich and mighty, whome wee call
fortunate; and of the poore and oppressed, whome we account
wretched: wee shall finde the happinesse of the one, and the
miserable estate of the other, so tied by GOD to the very instant,
and both so subiect to interchange (witnesse the suddaine downefall of the greatest Princes, and the speedy vprising of the
meanest persons) as the one hath nothing so certaine, whereof to
boast; nor the other so vncertaine, whereof to bewaile it selfe.
For there is no man so assured of his honour, of his riches,
health, or life; but that hee may be depriued of either or all, the
very next houre or day to come.* Quid vesper vehat, incertum
est, What the euening will bring with it, it is vncertaine.
And yet yee cannot tell (*saith Saint Iames*) what shalbe to
morrow. To day he is set up, and to morrow hee shall not
bee found; for hee is turned into dust, and his purpose
perisheth. *And although the aire which compasseth aduersitie,
be very obscure: yet therein wee better discerne GOD, than in
that shinning light which enuironeth worldly glorie; through
which, for the clearenesse thereof, there is no vanitie which
escapeth our sight. And let aduersitie seeme what it will; to
happie men, ridiculous, who make them-selues merrie at other
mens misfortunes; and to those vnder the* crosse, *greiuous: yet
this is true, That for all that is past, to the very instant, the
portions remainning are equall to either. For bee it that wee haue
liued many yeares,* and (*according to Salomon*) in them all wee
haue reioyced; *or bee it that wee haue measured the same length
of daies, and therein haue euer-more sorrowed: yet looking backe*

from our present being, we find both the one and the other, to wit, the ioy and the woe, sayled out of sight; and death, which doth pursue vs and hold vs in chace, from our infancie, hath gathered it. Quicquid ætatis retro est, mors tenet: What-so-euer of our age is past, death holds it. *So as who-so-euer hee bee, to whome Fortune hath beene a seruant, and the Time a friend: let him but take the accompt of his memory (for wee haue no other keeper of our pleasures past) and truelie examine what it hath reserued, either of beauty and youth, or foregone delights; what it hath saued, that it might last, of his dearest affections, or of what euer else the amorous Spring-time gaue his thoughts of contentment, then vnualuable; and hee shall finde that all the art which his elder yeares haue, can draw no other vapour out of these dissolutions, than heauie, secret, and sad sighes. Hee shall finde nothing remaining, but those sorrowes, which grow vp after our fast-springing youth; ouer-take it, when it is at a stand; and ouer-top it vtterly, when it beginnes to wither: in so much as looking backe from the very instant time, and from our now being; the poore, diseased, and captiue creature, hath as little sence of all his former miseries and paines; as hee, that is most blest in common opinion, hath of his fore-passed pleasures and delights. For what-so-euer is cast behind vs, is iust nothing: and what is to come, deceiptfull hope hath it.* Omnia quæ euentura sunt, incerto iacent.[1] *Onely those few black Swannes I must except: who hauing had the grace to value wordly vanities at no more than their owne price; doe, by retayning the comfortable memorie of a well-acted life, behold death without dread, and the graue without feare; and embrace both, as necessary guides to endlesse glorie.*

For my selfe, this is my consolation, and all that I can offer to others, that the sorrowes of this life, are but of two sorts: whereof the one hath respect to GOD; *the other, to the World. In the first wee complaine to* GOD *against our selues, for our offences against him; and confesse,* Et tu iustus es in omnibus quæ venerunt super nos, And thou O Lord art iust in all that hath befallen vs. *In the second wee complaine to our selues against* GOD: *as if hee had done vs wrong, either in not giuing vs worldly goods and honours, answering our appetites: or for taking them againe from vs, hauing had them; forgetting*

[1] 'All things in the future are uncertain' (G. E. Hadow, 1917).

that humble and iust acknowledgment of Iob, The Lord hath giuen, and the Lord hath taken. *To the first of which Saint* Paul *hath promised blessednesse; to the second, death. And out of doubt hee is either a foole or vngratefull to* GOD, *or both, that doth not acknowledge, how meane so-euer his estate bee, that the same is yet farre greater, than that which* GOD *oweth him: or doth not acknowledge, how sharpe so-euer his afflictions bee, that the same are yet farre lesse, than those which are due vnto him. And if an Heathen wise man*[1] *call the aduersities of the world but* tributa viuendi, *the tributes of liuing: a wise Christian man ought to know them, and beare them, but as the tributes of offending. He ought to beare them man-like, and resoluedly;* & *not as those whining souldiors doe,* qui gementes sequuntur imperatorē.[2]

For seeing God, who is the Author of all our tragedies, hath written out for vs, and appointed vs all the parts we are to play: and hath not, in their distribution, beene partiall to the most mighty Princes of the world; That gaue vnto Darius *the part of the greatest Emperour, and the part of the most miserable begger, a begger begging water of an Enemie, to quench the great drought of death; That appointed* Baiazet *to play the* Gran Signior *of the* Turkes *in the morning, and in the same day the* Footstoole *of* Tamerlane (*both which parts* Valerian *had also playd, beeing taken by* Sapores) *that made* Bellisarius *play the most victorious Captaine, and lastly the part of a blinde begger; of which examples many thousands may be produced: why should other men, who are but as the least wormes, complaine of wrongs? Certainly there is no other account to be made of this ridiculous world, than to resolue, That the change of fortune on the great Theater, is but as the change of garments on the lesse. For when on the one and the other, euery man weares but his owne skin; the Players are all alike. Now if any man, out of weaknes, prise the passages of this world otherwise (for saith* Petrarch, Magni ingenij est reuocare mentem a sensibus[3]) *it is by reason of that vnhappie fantasie of ours, which forgeth in the braines of Man all the miseries (the*

---

[1] Seneca.

[2] 'who follow their general with lamentations' (G. E. Hadow, 1917).

[3] 'It is a Point of great Wit, to call the Mind from the Senses' (trans. Laurence Eachard/Philip Ralegh, 1700).

corporall excepted) *whereunto hee is subiect: Therein it is, that Misfortune and Aduersitie worke all that they worke. For seeing Death, in the end of the Play, takes from all, whatsoeuer Fortune or Force takes from any one: it were a foolish madnes in the shipwracke of worldly things, where all sinkes but the Sorrow, to saue it. That were, as* Seneca *saith,* Fortunæ succumbere, quod tristius est omni fato, to fall vnder Fortune, of all other the most miserable destinie.

But it is now time to sound a retrait; and to desire to be excused of this long pursuit: and withall, that the good intent, which hath moued me to draw the picture of time past (*which we call* Historie) *in so large a table, may also be accepted in place of a better reason.*

The examples of diuine prouidence, euery where found (*the first diuine Histories being nothing else but a continuation of such examples*) *haue perswaded me to fetch my beginning from the beginning of all things; to wit,* Creation. *For though these two glorious actions of the Almightie be so neare, and* (*as it were*) *linked together, that the one necessarily implyeth the other:* Creation, *inferring* Prouidence: (*for what Father forsaketh the child that he hath begotten?*) *and* Prouidence *presupposing* Creation: *Yet many of those that haue seemed to excell in worldly wisedome, haue gone about to disioyne this coherence; the* Epicure *denying both Creation & Prouidence, but granting that the world had a beginning; the* Aristotelian *granting Prouidence, but denying both the Creation and the Beginning.*

Now although this doctrine of Faith, touching the Creation in time (*for* by Faith we vnderstand, that the world was made by the word of God) *be too weighty a work for* Aristotles *rotten ground to beare vp, vpon which he hath* (*not with-standing*) *founded the Defences & Fortresses of all his* Verball Doctrine: *Yet that the necessitie of infinite power, and the worlds beginning, and the impossibility of the contrary euen in the iudgement of Naturall reason, wherein hee beleeued, had not better informed him; it is greatly to bee maruailed at. And it is no lesse strange, that those men which are desirous of knowledge* (*seing* Aristotle *hath fayled in this maine poynt; and taught litle other than* termes *in the rest*) *haue so retrencht their mindes from the following and ouertaking of truth, and so absolutely subiected them-selues to the law of those Philosophicall principles; as all contrary kinde of teaching, in the search of causes, they haue condemned either for phantasticall, or curious. But doth it follow, that the positions of Heathen Philosophers, are vndoubted grounds and principles indeed, because so called? Or that* ipsi dixerunt, *doth make them to bee such? certainly no. But this is true, That where naturall reason hath built any thing so strong against it selfe, as the same reason can hardly assaile it, much lesse batter it downe: the same in euery question of Nature, and finite power, may bee approued for a fundamentall law of humane knowledg. For saith* Charron *in his Booke of wisdome,* Tout proposition humane a autant d'authoritè que l'autre, si la raison n'on fait la difference; Euery humane proposition hath equall authoritie, if reason make not the difference, *the rest being but the fables of principles. But hereof how shall the vpright and vnpartiall iudgment of man giue a sentence, where opposition and examination are not admitted to giue in euidence? And to this purpose it was well said of* Lactantius, Sapientiam sibi adimunt, qui sine vllo iudicio inuenta maiorum probant, & ab aliis pecudum more ducuntur: They neglect their owne wisdome, who without any iudgment approue the iuuention of those that fore-went them; and suffer them-selues, after the manner of Beasts, to bee led by them. *By the aduantage of which slouth and dullnesse, ignorance is now become so powerfull a Tyrant: as it hath set true Philosophie, Phisick, and Diuinity, in a Pillory; and written ouer the first,* Contra negantem Principia; *ouer the second,* Vertus specifica; *and ouer the third,* Ecclesia Romana.

But for my selfe, I shall neuer bee perswaded, that GOD hath shut up all light of Learning within the lanthorne of Aristotles *braines: or that it was euer said vnto him, as vnto* Esdras, Accendam in Corde tuo Lucernam intellectus: *that GOD hath giuen inuention but to the Heathen; and that they onely haue invaded Nature, and found the strength and bottome thereof; the same nature hauing consumed all her store, and left nothing of price to after-ages. That these and these bee the causes of these and these effects, Time hath taught vs; and not reason: and so hath experience, without Art. The Cheese-wife knoweth it as well as the Philosopher, that sowre Runnet doth coagulate her milke into a curde. But if wee aske a reason of this cause, why the sowrenesse doth it? whereby it doth it? and the manner*

*how? I thinke that there is nothing to bee found in vulgar
Philosophie, to satisfie this and many other like vulgar questions.
But man, to couer his ignorance in the least things, who cannot
giue a true reason for the Grasse vnder his feete, why it should
bee greener rather then red, or of any other colour; that could
neuer yet discouer the way and reason of Natures working, in
those which are farre lesse noble creatures than him-selfe; who
is farre more Noble than the Heauens them-selues:* Man (*saith
Salomon*) that can hardly discerne the things that are vpon
the Earth, and with great labour finde out the things that
are before vs; *that hath so short a time in the world, as hee
no sooner beginnes to learne, than to die; that hath in his memory
but borrowed knowledge; in his vnderstanding, nothing trulie;
that is ignorant of the Essence of his owne soule, and which the
wisest of the Naturalists (if* Aristotle *bee hee) could neuer so
much as define, but by the Action and effect, telling vs what it
workes (which all men know as well as hee) but not what it is,
which neither hee, nor any else, doth know, but GOD that
created it;* (for though I were perfect, yet I know not my
soule, *saith* Iob). *Man I say, that is but an Idiot in the next
cause of his owne life, and in the cause of all the actions of his
life: will (notwithstanding) examine the art of GOD in creating
the World; of GOD who (saith Iob)* is so excellent as wee
knowe him not; *and examine the beginning of the worke,
which had end before Man-kind had a beginning of being. Hee
will disable GODS power to make a world, without matter to
make it of. He will rather giue the mothes of the Aire for a cause;
cast the worke on necessity or chance; bestow the honour thereof
on Nature; make two powers, the one to be the Author of the*
Matter, *the other of the* Forme; *and lastly, for want of a
worke-man, haue it Eternall: which latter opinion* Aristotle, *to
make him-selfe the Author of a new Doctrine, brought into the
World: and his Sectatours*[1] *haue mainetained it;* parati ac
coniurati, quos sequuntur, Philosophorum animis inuictis
opiniones tueri.[2] *For* Hermes, *who liued at once with, or soone
after,* Moses, Zoroaster, Musæus, Orpheus, Linus, Anaximenes, Anaxagoras, Empedocles, Melissus, Pherecydes,

[1] Sectaries, followers.
[2] 'prepared and united to defend with invincible spirit the opinions of the
philosophers whom we follow'.

Thales, Cleanthes, Pythagoras, Plato, *and many others* (*whose opinions are exquisitely gathered by* Steuchius Eugubinus[1]) *found in the necessitie of inuincible reason,* One eternal and infinite Being, *to be the Parent of the vniuersall.* Horum omnium sententia quamuis sit incerta, eodem tamen spectat, vt Prouidentiam vnam esse consentiant: siue enim Natura, siue Æther, siue Ratio, siue mens, siue fatalis necessitas, siue diuina Lex; idem esse quod a nobis dicitur Deus: All these mens opinions (*saith Lactantius*) though vncertaine, come to this; That they agree vpon one Prouidence; whether the same bee Nature, or light, or Reason, or vnderstanding, or destinie, or diuine ordinance; that it is the same which we call *GOD. Certainely, as all the Riuers in the world, though they haue diuers risings, and diuers runnings; though they some times hide them-selues for a while vnder ground, and seeme to be lost in Sea-like Lakes; doe at last finde, and fall into the great* Ocean: *so after all the searches that humaine capacitie hath; and after all Philosophicall contemplation and curiositie; in the necessitie of this infinite power, all the reason of man ends and dissolues it selfe....*[2]

Now for Nature; *As by the ambiguity of this name, the schoole of* Aristotle *hath both commended many errours vnto vs, and sought also thereby to obscure the glory of the high Moderator of all things, shining in the Creation, and in the gouerning of the World: so if the best definition bee taken out of the second of* Aristotles phisicks, *or primo de* Cælo, *or out of the fifth of his* Metaphysicks; *I say that the best is but nominall, and seruing onely to difference the beginning of Naturall motion, from Artificiall: which yet the* Academicks *open better, when they call it* A Seminary strength, infused into matter by the Soule of the World: *who giue the first place to* Prouidence, *the*

---

[1] Agostino Steuco, the Italian scholar whose eclectic treatise *De perenni philosophia* (1540) argued the agreement between Christian theology and the thinkers here enumerated by Ralegh; see further C. B. Schmitt, 'Perennial Philosophy: From Agostino Steuco to Leibniz', *Journal of the History of Ideas,* xxvii (1966) 505–32. The tradition reaches back to the Italian Neoplatonists, and ahead to Henry More and Cudworth; see my edition of *The Cambridge Platonists* (London, 1969, and Cambridge, Mass., 1970) pp. 6–7.

[2] About five folio pages are here omitted; they argue further against theories which in any way tend to qualify the world's creation out of nothing.

second to Fate, *and but the third to* Nature. Prouidentia (*by which they vnderstand GOD*) dux & caput; Fatum, medium ex prouidentia prodiens; Natura postremum. *But bee it what hee will, or bee it any of these (GOD excepted) or participating of all: yet that it hath choice or vnderstanding (both which are necessarily in the cause of all things) no man hath avowed. For this is vnanswerable of* Lactantius: Is autem facit aliquid, qui aut voluntatem faciendi habet, aut scientiam; Hee onely can bee said to bee the doer of a thing, that hath either will or knowledge in the doing it.

But the will and science of Nature, are in these words truely exprest by Ficinus: Potest vbique Natura, vel per diuersa media, vel ex diuersis materijs, diuersa facere: sublata vero mediorum materiarumque diuersitate, vel vnicum vel similimum operatur, neque potest quando adest materia non operari; It is the power of Nature by diuersity of meanes, or out of diuersity of matter, to produce diuers things: but taking away the diuersity of meanes, and the diuersity of matter, it then workes but one or the like worke; neither can it but worke, matter beeing present. *Now if* Nature *made choyce of diuersity of matter, to worke all these variable workes of Heauen and Earth; it had then both vnderstanding and will; it had counsaile to beginne; reason to dispose; vertue and know-ledge to finish; and power to gouerne: without which, all things had beene but one and the same: all of the matter of Heauen; or all of the matter of Earth. And if we grant* Nature *this will, and this vnderstanding, this counsaile, reason, and power:* Cur Natura potius, quã Deus nominetur? *Why should we then call such a cause rather Nature, than God? God, of whom all men haue notion, and giue the first and highest place to Diuine power:* Omnes homines notionem deorum habent, omnesque summum locum diuino cuidam numini assignant. *And this I say in short; that it is a true effect of true reason in man (were there no authority more binding than reason) to acknowledge and adore the first and most sublime power.* Vera Philosophia, est ascensus ab his quæ fluunt, & oriuntur, & occidunt, ad ea quæ vere sunt, & semper eadem: *True Philosophy, is an ascending from the things which flow, and rise, and fall, to the things that are for euer the same.*

For the rest; I do also account it not the meanest, but an impiety monstrous, to confound God and Nature: be it but in tearmes. For it is God, that only disposeth of all things according to his owne will; and maketh of one Earth, Vessels *of* honor and dishonor. *It is Nature that can dispose of nothing, but according to the will of the matter wherein it worketh. It is God, that commandeth all: It is Nature that is obedient to all. It is God that doth good vnto all, knowing and louing the good he doth: It is Nature, that secondarily doth also good, but it neither knoweth nor loueth the good it doth. It is God, that hath all things in himselfe: Nature, nothing in it selfe. It is God, which is the Father, and hath begotten all things: It is Nature, which is begotten by all things; in which it liueth and laboureth; for by it selfe it existeth not. For shall we say, that it is out of affection to the earth, that heauy things fall towards it? Shall we call it Reason, which doth conduct euery Riuer into the salt Sea? Shall we tearme it knowledge in fire, that makes it to consume combustible matter? If it be Affection, Reason, and Knowledge in these: by the same Affection, Reason, and knowledge it is, that Nature worketh. And therfore seeing all things work as they do, (call it by* form, *by* Nature, *or by what you please) yet because they work by an impulsion, which they cannot resist; or by a faculty, infused by the supremest power: we are neither to wonder at, nor to worship, the faculty that worketh, nor the Creature wherein it worketh. But herein lies the wonder: & to him is the worship due, who hath created such a Nature in things, & such a faculty, as neither knowing it selfe, the matter wherein it worketh, nor the vertue and power which it hath; doth yet work all things to their last and vttermost perfection. And therefore euery reasonable man, taking to himselfe for a ground that which is granted by all Antiquity, and by al men truly learned that euer the world had; to wit; That there is a power infinit, and eternall, (which also necessity doth proue vnto vs, without the helpe of Faith; and Reason, without the force of Authoritie) all things doe as easily follow which haue beene diliuered by diuine letters, as the waters of a running Riuer doe successiuely pursue each other from the first fountaines.*

This much I say it is, that Reason it selfe hath taught vs: and this is the beginning of knowledge. Sapientia præcedit, Religio sequitur: quia prius est Deum scire, consequens colere; *Sapience goes before, Religion followes: because it is first to know God, and then to worship him. This Sapience* Plato *calleth,* absoluti boni scientiam, *The science of the absolute good: and another,* scientiam rerum primarum, sempiternarum, perpetuarum. *For Faith (saith* Isidore) *is not extorted by violence; but by reason and examples perswaded:* fides nequaquam vi extorquetur; sed ratione & exemplis suadetur. *I confesse it, that to inquire further, as of the essence of God, of his power, of his Art, and by what meane He created the world: Or of his secret iudgment, and the causes; is not an effect of Reason:* Sed cum ratione insaniunt, *but they grow mad with reason, that inquire after it. For as it is no shame nor dishonor (saith a French Author)* de faire arrest au but qu'on nasceu surpasser, *For a man to rest himselfe there, where he finds it impossible to passe on further: so whatsoeuer is beyond, and out of the reach of true reason, It acknowledgeth it to be so; as vnderstanding it selfe not to be infinite, but according to the Name and Nature it hath, to be a Teacher, that best knowes the end of his own Art. For seeing both Reason and Necessity teach vs (Reason, which is* pars diuini spiritus in corpus humanũ mersi) *that the world was made by a power infinite; and yet how it was made, it cannot teach vs: and seeing the same Reason and Necessity make vs know, that the same infinit power is euery wher in the world; and yet how euery where, it cãnot informe vs: our beleefe hereof is not weakned, but greatly strengthned, by our ignorance; because it is the same Reason that tels vs, That such a Nature cannot be said to be God, that can be in all conceiued by man.*

I haue beene already euer long, to make any large discourse either of the parts of the following Story, or in mine owne excuse: especially in the excuse of this or that passage; seeing the whole is exceeding weake and defectiue. Among the grosest, the vnsutable diuision of the bookes, I could not know how to excuse, had I not been directed to inlarge the building after the foundation was laid, and the first part finished. All men know that there is no great Art in the deuiding euenly of those things, which are subiect to number and measure. For the rest, it sutes well enough with a great many Bookes of this age, which speake to much, and yet say little; Ipsi nobis furto subducimur, *We are stollen away from our selues, setting a high price on all that is our owne. But hereof, though a late good Writer, make complaint, yet shall it not lay hold on me, because I beleeue as he doth; that who so thinkes him-selfe the wisest man, is but a poore and miserable ignorant. Those that are the best men of war, against all the vanities and fooleries of the World, doe alwaies keepe the strongest guards against themselues, to defend them from them-selues, from selfe loue, selfe estimation, and selfe opinion.*

Generally concerning the order of the worke, I haue onely taken counsaile from the Argument. For of the Assyrians, *which after the downefall of* Babel *take vp the first part, and were the first great Kings of the World, there came little to the view of posterity: some few enterprises, greater in fame than faith, of* Ninus *and* Semiramis *excepted.*

It was the story of the Hebrewes, *of all before the* Olympiads, *that ouercame the consuming disease of time; and preserued it selfe, from the very cradle and beginning to this day: and yet not so entire, but that the large discourses thereof (to which in many Scriptures wee are referred) are no where found. The Fragments of other Stories, with the actions of those Kings and Princes which shot vp here and there in the same time, I am driuen to relate by way of digression: of which we may say with* Virgil.

Apparent rari nantes in gurgite vasto;
They appeare here and there floting in the great gulfe of time.[1]

To the same first Ages do belong the report of many Inuentions therein found, and from them deriued to vs; though most of the Authors Names, haue perished in so long a Nauigation: For those Ages had their Lawes; they had diuersity of Gouernment; they had Kingly rule; Nobilitie, Pollicie in warre; Nauigation; and all, or the most of needfull Trades. To speake therefore of these (seeing in a generall Historie we should haue left a great deale of Nakednesse, by their omission) it cannot properly bee called a digression. True it is that I haue also made many others: which if they shall be layd to my charge, I must cast the fault into the great heape of humane error. For seeing wee digresse in all the wayes of our liues: yea seeing the life of man is nothing else but digression; I may the better bee excused, in writing their liues and actions. I am not altogether ignorant in the Lawes of Historie, *and of the Kindes.*

[1] *Aeneid,* I 118.

The same hath beene taught by many; but by no man better, and with greater breuity, than by that excellent learned Gentleman Sir Francis Bacon. *Christian Lawes are also taught vs by the Prophets and Apostles; and euery day preacht vnto vs. But wee still make large digressions: yea the teachers themselues do not (in all) keepe the path which they poynt out to others.*

For the rest; after such time as the Persians *had wrested the Empire from the* Chaldæans, *and had raised a great Monarchie, producing Actions of more importance than were else-where to be found: it was agreeable to the Order of Story, to attend this Empire; whilest it so florished, that the affaires of the nations adioyning had reference there-vnto. The like obseruance was to bee vsed towards the fortunes of* Greece, *when they againe began to get ground vpon the* Persians, *as also towards the affaires of* Rome, *when the* Romans *grew more mighty than the* Greekes.

As for the Medes, *the* Macedonians, *the* Sicilians, *the* Carthaginians, *and other* Nations, *who resisted the beginnings of the former Empires, and afterwards became but parts of their composition and enlargement: it seemed best to remember what was knowne of them from ther seuerall beginnings, in such times and places, as they in their flourishing estates opposed those Monarchies; which in the end swallowed them vp. And herein I haue followed the best Geographers: who seldome giue names to those small brookes, whereof many, ioyned together, make great Riuers; till such time as they become united, and runne in a maine streame to the Ocean* Sea. *If the Phrase be weake, and the Stile not euery-where like it selfe: the first, shewes their legitimation and true Parent; the second, will excuse it selfe vpon the Variety of Matter. For* Virgill, *who wrote his* Eclogues, gracili auena,[1] *vsed stronger pipes when he sounded the warres of* Aeneas. *It may also bee layd to my charge that I vse diuers* Hebrew *words in my first booke, and else where: in which language others may thinke, and I my-selfe acknowledge it, that I am altogether ignorant: but it is true, that some of them I finde in* Montanus; *others in lattaine Carecter in* S. Senensis, *and of the rest I haue borrowed the interpretation of some of my learned friends. But say I had been beholding to neither, yet were it not to bee wondred at hauing had an eleuen yeares leasure,*

---

[1] 'with slender pipe'.

to attaine the knowledge of that, or of any other tongue; How-so-euer, I know that it will bee said by many, That I might haue beene more pleasing to the Reader, if I had written the Story of mine owne times; hauing been permitted to draw water as neare the Well-head as another. To this I answere, that who-so-euer in writing a moderne Historie, shall follow truth too neare the heeles, it may happily strike out his teeth. There is no Mistresse or Guide, that hath led her followers and seruants into greater miseries. He that goes after her too farre off, looseth her sight, and looseth him-selfe: and hee that walkes after her at a midle distance; I know not whether I should call that kind of course Temper or Basenesse. It is true, that I neuer trauailed after mens opinions, when I might haue made the best vse of them: and I haue now too few daies remayning, to imitate those, that either out of extreame ambition, or extreame cowardise, or both, doe yet, (when death hath them on his shoulders) flatter the world, betweene the bed and the graue. It is enough for me (being in that state I am) to write of the eldest times: wherein also why may it not be said, that in speaking of the past, I point at the present, and taxe the vices of those that are yet lyuing, in their persons that are long since dead; and haue it laid to my charge. But this I cannot helpe, though innocent. And certainely if there be any, that finding themselues spotted like the Tigers of old time, shall finde fault with me for painting them ouer a new; they shall therein accuse themselues iustly, and me falsly.

For I protest before the Maiesty of GOD, That I malice no man vnder the Sunne. Impossible I know it is to please all: seeing few or none are so pleased with themselues, or so assured of themselues, by reason of their subiection to their priuate passions; but that they seeme diuerse persons in one and the same day. Seneca hath said it, and so doe I: Vnus mihi pro populo erat:[1] and to the same effect Epicurus, Hoc ego non multis sed tibi;[2] or (as it hath since lamentably fallen out) I may borrow the resolution of an ancient Philosopher, Satis est vnus, Satis est nullus.[3] For it was for the seruice of that inestimable Prince Henry, the successiue hope, and one of the greatest of the

[1] 'One is to me instead of All' (trans. Laurence Eachard/Philip Ralegh, 1700).

[2] "This I intend, not for the multitude, but for you' (G. E. Hadow, 1917).

[3] 'One is enough, None is enough' (Eachard/Ralegh).

Christian World, that I vndertooke this Worke. It pleased him to peruse some part thereof, and to pardon what was amisse. It is now left to the world without a Maister: from which all that is presented, hath receiued both blows & thanks. Eadem probamus, eadem reprehendimus: hic exitus est omnis iudicij, in quo lis secundum plures datur.[1] *But these discourses are idle. I know that as the charitable will iudge charitably: so against those,* qui gloriantur in malitia,[2] *my present aduersitie hath disarmed mee. I am on the ground already; and therefore haue not farre to fall: and for rysing againe, as in the Naturall priuation their is no recession to habit; so is it seldome seene in the priuation politique. I doe therefore for-beare to stile my* Readers Gentle, Courteous, *and* Friendly, *thereby to beg their good opinions, or to promise a second and third volume (which I also intend) if the first receiue grace and good acceptance. For that which is already done, may be thought enough; and too much: and it is certaine, let vs claw the Reader with neuer so many courteous phrases; yet shall we euer-more be thought fooles, that write foolishly. For conclusion; all the hope I haue lies in this, That I haue already found more vngentle and vncurteous Readers of my Loue towards them, and well-deseruing of them, than euer I shall doe againe. For had it beene otherwise, I should hardly haue had this leisure, to haue made myselfe a foole in print.*

---

[1] 'For we approve and reprehend the same things. And this is the End of every Judgment, when the Controversie is committed to many' (Eachard/ Ralegh).
[2] 'who exult in ill-will'.

SWR D

THE FIRST PART
OF THE HISTORIE
OF THE WORLD:

Intreating of the Beginning,
and first ages of the same,
from the Creation vnto
Abraham.

THE FIRST BOOKE.

Ch. I. *Of the Creation, and Preseruation of the World*

§1. *That the inuisible God is seene in his Creatures.*

God, whome the wisest men acknowledge to be a power vneffable, and vertue infinite, a light by abundant claritie inuisible, an vnderstanding which it selfe can onely comprehend, an essence eternall and spirituall, of absolute purenesse and simplicitie, was and is pleased to make himselfe knowne by the worke of the World: in the wonderfull magnitude whereof, (all which he imbraceth, filleth, and sustaineth) we behold the image of that glorie, which cannot bee measured, and withall that one, and yet vniuersall nature, which cannot be defined. In the glorious lights of heauen, we perceiue a shadow of his diuine countenance, in his mercifull prouision for all that liue, his manifold goodness: and lastly, in creating and making existent the world vniuersall by the absolute art of his owne word, his power and almightinesse, which power, light, vertue, wisedome, and goodnesse, being all but attributes of one simple essence, and one God, wee in all admire, and in part discerne *per speculum creaturarum*, that is, in the disposition, order, and varietie of celestiall and terrestriall bodies: terrestriall, in their strange and manifold diuersities; celestiall, in their beautie and magnitude; which in their continuall and contrarie motions, are neither repugnant, intermixt, nor confounded. By these potent effects we approch to the knowledge of the omnipotent cause, and by these motions their Almightie mouer.

In these more then wonderfull workes, God (saith *Hugo*) speaketh vnto man, and it is true, that these be those discourses of God, whose effects all that liue witnesse in themselues; the sensible, in their sensible natures; the reasonable, in their reasonable soules: for according to *S. Gregorie, Omnis homo eo ipso quòd rationalis conditus est, ex ipsa ratione, illum qui se condidit, Deum esse colligere debet:* Euery man, in that he is reasonable, out of the same reason may know, that he which made him is God. This God all men behold (saith *Iob*) which is according to the *Fathers*, *Dominationem illius conspicere in creaturis, to discerne him in his prouidence by his creatures.* That God hath beene otherwise seene, to wit, with corporall eyes, exceedeth the small proportion of my vnderstanding, grounded on these places of *S. Iohn*, and *S. Paul*, Yee haue not heard his voice at any time, neither haue yee seene his shape. And againe, Whom neuer man saw, nor can see.

And this I am sure agreeth with the nature of Gods simplicitie, of which *S. Augustine, Ipsa enim natura, vel substantia, vel quolibet alio nomine appellandum est, idipsum quod Deus est, corporaliter videri non potest*, That nature, or that substance, or by whatsoeuer name that is to be called which is God, whatsoeuer that bee, the same cannot be corporally perceiued. And of this opinion were *Origen, Cyrill, Chrysostome, Gregorie Nazianzenus, Hierome, Augustine, Gregorie* the Great, *Euaristus, Alcuinus, Dionisius Areopagita, Aquinas*, and all others of authoritie. But by his owne word, and by this visible world, is God perceiued of men, which is also the vnderstood language of the Almightie, vouchsafed to all his creatures, whose Hieroglyphical Characters, are the vnnumbred Starres, the Sunne, and Moone, written on these large volumes of the firmament: written also on the earth and the seas, by the letters of all those liuing creatures, and plants, which inhabit and reside therein. Therefore said that learned *Cusanus, Mundus vniuersus nihil aliud est, quàm Deus explicatus*, The world vniuersall is nothing else but God exprest. And the inuisible things of God (saith St. *Paul*) are seene by creation of the world, being considered in his creatures. Of all which there was no other cause preceding then his owne will, no other matter then his owne power, no other workeman then his owne word, no other consideration then his owne infinite goodnesse. The example and patterne of these his creatures, as he beheld the same in all eternitie in the abundance of his owne loue, so was it at length in the most wise order, by his vnchanged will mooued, by his high wisedome disposed, and by his almightie power perfected, and made visible. And therefore (saith *Mirandula*) wee ought to loue God *Ex fide, & ex effectibus*, (that is) both perswaded by his word; and by the effects of the worlds creation: *Neque enim qui causa caret, ex causa & origine sciri, cognoscique potest, sed vel ex rerum, quæ factæ sunt, quæque fiunt & gubernantur obseruatione & collatione, vel ex ipsius Dei verbo*: For he of whome there is no higher cause, cannot bee knowne by any knowledge of cause or beginning, (saith *Montanus*) but either by the obseruing and conferring of things, which he hath, or doth create and gouerne, or else by the word of God himselfe.

§2. *That the wisest of the Heathen, whose authoritie is not to be despised, haue acknowledged the world to haue beene created by GOD.*

This work, and creation of the world, did most of the ancient and learned Philosophers acknowledge, though by diuers termes, and in a different maner exprest, I meane all those who are entitled by *S. Augustine, Summi Philosophi,* Philosophers of highest iudgement and vnderstanding. *Mercurius Trismegistus* calleth God, *Principium vniuersorum,* The originall of the vniuersall: to whome he giueth also the attributes of *Mens, natura, actus, necessitas, finis, & renouatio.* And wherein he truly, with S[t]. *Paul,* casteth vpon God all power; confessing also, that the world was made by Gods almighty word, and not by hands: *verbo, non manibus, fabricatus est mundus. Zoroaster* (whom *Heraclitus* followed in opinion) tooke the word *fire* to expresse God by (as in *Deuteronomy* and in S[t]. *Paul* it is vsed) *Omnia ex vno igne genita sunt, All things* (saith he) *are caused or produced out of one fire.*

So did *Orpheus* plainely teach, that the world had beginnings in time, from the will of the most high God; whose remarkeable wordes are thus conuerted. *Cùm abscondisset omnia* Ivpiter *summus, deinde in lumen gratum emisit, ex sacro corde operans cogitata & mirabilia*: Of which I conceiue this sense; *When great* Ivpiter *had hidden all things in himselfe, working out of the loue of his sacred heart, he sent thence* or brought forth *into gratefull light, the admirable workes which he had forethought.*

Pindarus the Poet, and one of the wisest, acknowledged also one God, the most high, to be the Father and Creator of all things; *Vnus Deus Pater Creator summus*. *Plato* calleth God the cause and originall, the nature and reason of the vniuersall, *totius rerum natura, causa, & origo Deus*. But hereof more at large hereafter.

Now although the curiosity of some men haue found it superfluous, to remember the opinions of Philosophers, in matters of Diuinity: (it being true that the Scripture hath not want of any forraine testimony) yet as the *Fathers* with others excellently learned are my examples herein; so S^t. *Paul* himselfe did not despise, but thought it lawfull, and profitable, to remember whatsoeuer he found agreable to the word of God, among the Heathen, that he might thereby take from them all escape by way of ignorance, God rendring vengeance to them, that know him not: as in his Epistle to *Titus* he citeth *Epimenides* against the *Cretians*, and to the *Corinthians, Menander*, and in the seuenteenth of the *Acts, Aratus, &c.* for Truth (saith S^t. *Ambrose*) by whomsoeuer vttered, is of the holy Ghost; *Veritas à quocunque dicatur, à spiritu sancto est:* and lastly let those kinde of men learne this rule. *Quæ sacris seruiunt, prophana nòn sunt, Nothing is prophane that serueth to the vse of holy things.*

§3. *Of the meaning of* In Principio. *Genes.* 1.1.

This visible world of which *Moses* writeth, God created in the beginning, or first of all: in which (saith *Tertullian*) things beganne to bee. This word *beginning* (in which the *Hebrewes* seeke some hidden mysterie, and which in the *Iewes Targum* is conuerted by the word *Sapientia*) cannot be referred to succession of time, nor to order, as some men haue conceiued, both which are subsequent: but only to creation then. For before that beginning, there was neither primary matter to bee informed, nor forme to informe, nor any being, but the eternall. Nature was not, nor the next parent of time begotten, time properly and naturally taken; for if God had but disposed of matter already in being, then as the word *beginning* could not bee referred to all things, so must it follow, that the institution of matter proceeded from a greater power then that of God. And by what name shall we then call such a one (saith *Lactantius*) as exceedeth God in potency: for it is an act of more excellency to make, then to dispose of things made: whereupon it may be concluded, that matter could not be before this beginning: except we faine a double creation, or allow of two powers, and both infinite, the impossibility whereof scorneth defence. *Nàm impossibile plura esse infinita: quoniàm alterum esset in altero finitum, There cannot be more infinites then one; for one of them would limit the other.*

§4.   *Of the meaning of the words Heauen and Earth. Genes.* 1.1.

The vniuersall matter of the world (which *Moyses* comprehendeth vnder the names of *Heauen and Earth*) is by diuers diuersly vnderstood: for there are that conceiue, that by those wordes, was meant the first matter, as the *Peripatetikes* vnderstand it, to which S^t. *Augustine* and *Isidore* seeme to adhere. *Fecisti mundum* (saith S^t. Augustine) *de materia informi, quam fecisti de nulla re, penè nullam rem*: (that is) *Thou hast made the world of a matter without forme: which matter thou madest of nothing, and being made, it was little other then nothing.*

But this potentiall and imaginary *materia prima* cannot exist without forme. *Peter Lombard, the Schoole-men, Beda, Lyranus, Comestor, Tostatus* and others, affirme, that it pleased God first of all to create the Empyrean Heauen: which at the succeeding instant (saith *Beda* and *Strabo*) hee filled with *Angels*. This Empyrean Heauen *Steuchius Eugubinus* calleth *Diuine claritie, and vncreated:* an errour, for which he is sharply charged by *Pererius*, though (as I conceiue) he rather failed in the subsequent, when he made it to be a place and the seate of Angels, and iust Soules, then in the former affirmation: for of the first, That God liueth in eternall light, it is written; *My soule praise thou the Lord, that couereth himselfe with light:* and in the Reuelation, *And the City hath no neede of Sunne, neither of the Moone to shine in it: for the glory of God did light it.* And herein also *Iohn*

Mercer vpon *Genesis* differeth not in opinion from *Eugubinus:* for as by heauen created in the beginning, was not meant the inuisible or supercelestiall, so in his iudgement, because it was in all eternity the glorious seate of God himselfe, it was not necessary to be created; *Quem mundum super-cœlestem meo iudicio creari* (saith Mercer) *non erat necesse.*

But as *Moses* forbare to speake of Angels, and of things inuisible, and incorporate, for the weakenesse of their capacities, whom he then cared to informe of those things, which were more manifest, (to wit) that God did not only by a strong hand deliuer them from the bondage of *Ægypt,* according to his promise made to their forefathers: but also that he created, and was the sole cause of this aspectable, and perceiueable Vniuersal; so on the other side I dare not thinke, that any supercelestiall Heauen, or whatsoeuer else (not himselfe) was increate and eternal: and as for the place of God before the world created, the finite wisedome of mortall men hath no perception of it, neither can it limit the seate of infinite power, no more then infinite power it selfe can be limited: for his place is in himselfe, whom no magnitude else can containe: *How great is the house of God* (saith Baruch) *how large is the place of his possessions; it is great, and hath no end, it is high and vnmeasurable.*

But leauing multiplicity of opinion, it is more probable and allowed, that by the wordes *Heauen and Earth,* was meant the solid matter and substance, aswell of all the Heauens, and Orbes supernall, as of the Globe of the Earth and Waters, which couered it ouer, (to wit) that very matter of all things, *materia, Chaos, possibilitas, siue posse fieri.* Which matter (saith *Caluin*) was so called, *quòd totius mundi semen fuerit; Because it was the seede of the Vniuersall,* an opinion of ancient Philosophers long before.

§5. *That the substance of the waters, as mixt in the body of the earth, is by* Moses *vnderstood in the word Earth: and that the Earth, by the attributes of vnformed and voide, is described as the Chaos of the ancient Heathen.*

Moses first nameth Heauen and Earth (putting waters but in the third place) as comprehending waters in the word

Earth, but afterward hee nameth them apart, when God by his spirit beganne to distinguish the confused Masse, and (as *Basil* saith) *præparare naturam aquæ ad fæcunditatem vitalem*; *to prepare the nature of water to a vitall fruitfulnesse.*

For vnder the word *Heauen*, was the matter of all heauenly bodies, and natures exprest: and by the name of *Earth and Waters*, all was meant, whatsoeuer is vnder the Moone, and subiect to alteration. Corrupt seedes bring forth corrupt plants; to which the pure heauens are not subiect, though subiect to perishing. *They shall perish* (saith Dauid) and *the heauens shall vanish away like smoke* saith *Esay.* Neither were the waters the matter of Earth: for it is written, *Let the waters vnder the heauens be gathered into one place, and let the dry land appeare*: which proueth that the dry land was mixt and couered with the waters, and not yet distinguished; but no way, that the waters were the matter or seede of the Earth, much lesse of the Vniuersall. *Initio tu Domine terram fundasti, Thou, O Lord, in the beginning hast founded the Earth*: and againe, *The Earth was couered with the Deepe* (meaning with waters) *as with a garment*, saith *Dauid.* And if by naturall arguments it may bee proued, that water by condensation may become earth, the same reason teacheth vs also, that earth rarified may become water: water, aire: aire, fire; and so on the contrary, *Deus ignis substantiam per aerem in aquam conuertit, God turneth the substance of fire, by aire, into water.* For the Heauens and the Earth remained in the same state, in which they were created, as touching their substance, though there was afterwards added multiplicitie of perfection, in respect of beauty and ornament. *Cælum verò & terra in statu creationis remanserunt, quantum ad substantiam, licèt multiplex perfectio decoris & ornatus eis postmodùm superaddita est.* And the word which the Hebrewes call *Maim*, is not to be vnderstood according to the Latine translation simply, and as specificall water; but the same more properly signifieth liquor. For (according to *Montanus*) *Est autem Maim liquor geminus, & huic nomen propter verborum penuriam, Latina lingua plurale numero aquas fecit. For Maim* (saith he) *is a double liquor*, (that is, of diuers natures) *and this name or word the Latines wanting a voice to expresse it, call it in the Plural, Aquas, Waters.*

This Masse, or indigested matter, or Chaos created in the beginning was without forme, that is, without the proper forme, which it afterwards acquired, when the Spirit of God had separated the Earth, and digested it from the waters: *And the earth was voide:* that is, not producing any creatures, or adorned with any plants, fruits, or flowers. But after *the Spirit of God had moued vpon the waters,* and wrought this indigested matter into that forme, which it now retayneth, then did *the earth budde forth the hearbe, which seedeth seede, & the fruitfull tree according to his kinde, and God saw that it was good;* which attribute was not giuen to the Earth, while it was confused, nor to the Heauens, before they had motion, and adornement. *God saw that it was good;* that is, made perfect: for perfection is that, to which nothing is wanting. *Et perfecti Dei perfecta sunt opera, The workes of the perfect God, are perfect.*

From this lumpe of imperfect matter had the ancient Poets their inuention of *Demogorgon:* *Hesiodvs* and *Anaxagoras* the knowledge of that Chaos, of which *Ouid:*

> *Ante mare, & terras, & (quod tegit omnia) cælum,*
> *Vnus erat toto naturæ vultus in Orbe,*
> *Quen dixere Chaos, rudis indigestaque moles.*

> Before the Sea and Land was made, and Heauen, that all doth hide,
> In all the world one only face of nature did abide:
> Which Chaos hight, a huge rude heape.[1]

§6. *How it is to be vnderstood that the Spirit of God moued vpon the waters, and that this is not to be searched curiously.*

After the creation of Heauen and Earth, then voide and without forme, the Spirit of God moued vpon the waters. The *Seuenty Interpreters* vse the word *super-ferebatur,* moued vpon or ouer: *incubabat,* or *fouebat* (saith *Hierome*) out of *Basil*; and *Basil* out of a Syrian Doctor; *Equidem non meam tibi, sed viri cuiusdam Syri sententiam recensebo* (saith

---

[1] Metrical translations are normally provided by Ralegh himself. Here we have one of the few exceptions, for the translation is borrowed from Arthur Golding, *The xv Bookes of P. Ouidius Naso, entytuled Mᵗamorphosis* (1567) 1 5–8.

Basil) which wordes *incubare* or *fouere* importing warmth, hatching, or quickning, haue a speciall liking. *Verbum translatum est ab auibus pullitiei suæ incubantibus, quàmuis spirituali, & planè inenarrabili, non autèm corporali modo*; *The word is taken of birds hatching their yong, not corporally, but in a spirituall and vnexpressible manner.*

Some of the Hebrewes conuert it to this effect, *Spiritus Dei volitabat, The Spirit of God did flutter*: the Chaldæan Paraphrast in this sense, *ventus à conspectu Dei sufflabat*, or as other vnderstand the Chaldæan, *flabat, pellebat, remouebat: the winde from the face of God did blow vnder, driue, or remoue*, or *did blow vpon*, according to the 147. *Psalme. He caused his winde to blow, and the waters increase: but there was yet no winde nor exhalation: Arias Montanus* in these wordes, *Et spiritus Elohim Merachefet, id est, effitacitèr motitans, confouens, ac agitans super factes gemini liquoris; The Spirit of God effectually and often mouing, keeping warme, and cherishing, quickning and stirring vpon the face of this double liquor.* For he maketh foure originals, whereof three are agents, and the last passiue and materiall, to wit, *causa*, which is the diuine goodnesse, *Iehi*, which is, *fiat, siue erit, let it be*, or *it shall be. Quæ vox verbo Dei prima prolata fuit: which voice* (saith he) *was the first that was vttered by the word of God.* The third *Spiritus Elohim, the Spirit of God, id est, vis quædam diuina, agilis ac præsens per omnia pertingens, omnia complens*, that is, *a certaine diuine power, or strength euery where, actiue and extending, and stretching through all, filling and finishing all things.* The fourth he calleth *Maim, id est, materies ad omnem rem conficiendam habilis; matter apt to become euerything.* For my selfe I am resolued (*Cùm Deus sit superrationale omni ratione, Seeing God is in all reason aboue reason*) that although the effects which follow his wonderfull wayes of working, may in a measure be perceiued by mans vnderstanding, yet the manner and first operation of his diuine power cannot bee conceiued by any minde, or spirit, compassed with a mortall body. *Animalis homo quæ Dei sunt non percipit: For my thoughts* (saith the Lord in *Esay*) *are not your thoughts, neither are your wayes my wayes.* And as the world hath not knowne God himselfe: so are his wayes (according to S^t. *Paul*) *past finding out. O righteous*

Father, the world hath not knowne thee, saith *Christ.* And therefore, whether that motion, vitality and operation, were by incubation, or how else, the manner is only knowne to God, *quemodo in omnibus sit rebus, vel per essentiam, vel per potentiam, intellectus noster non capit;* For how God (saith S^t. *Augustine,* speaking of his Vbiquitie) *is in all things, either by essence, presence, or power, our vnderstanding cannot comprehend. Nihil inter Deum hominem que distaret, si consilia, & dispositiones illius maiestatis æternæ, cogitatio assequeretur humana: There would be no difference betweene God and Man, if mans vnderstanding could conceiue the counsels and disposing of that eternall Maiesty;* and therefore to be ouer-curious in searching how the all-powerful Word of God wrought in the creation of the world, or his all-piercing and operatiue Spirit distinguishing, gaue forme to the matter of the Vniuersall, is a labour and search like vnto his, who not contented with a knowne and safe foord, will presume to passe ouer the greatest Riuer in all parts, where hee is ignorant of their depths: for so doth the one loose his life, and the other his vnderstanding. We behold the Sunne, and enioy his light, as long as we looke towards it, but tenderly, and circumspectly: we warme our selues safely, while wee stand neare the fire; but if we seeke to outface the one, or enter into the other, we forthwith become blinde or burnt.

But to eschew curiosity: this is true, that the English word (moued) is most proper and significant: for of motion proceedeth all production, and all whatsoeuer is effected. And this omnipotent Spirit of God, which may indeede bee truely called *Principium motus,* and with *Mirandula, vis causæ efficientis, The force of the efficient cause,* S^t. *Augustine* sometimes taketh for the holy Ghost; sometime for a winde or breath, *sub nomine spiritus, vnder the name of a spirit,* which is sometimes so taken; or for *virtualis creatura, for a created virtuality: Tertullian* and *Theodoret* call it also a breath or winde: *Mercurius* nameth it *Spiritum tenuem intelligibilem, a pure or thinne intelligible spirit:* Anaxagoras, *mentem:* Tostatvs, *voluntatem & mentem Dei, The will and minde of God;* which *Mens,* Plato *in Timæo,* maketh *animam mundi, The soule of the world:* and in his sixt Booke *de Republica* he calleth it *the law of Heauen;* in his Epistles, the *leader of things to come, and the presence of things past.* But as *Cyprian* wrote of the Incarnation of Christ our Sauiour, *Mens deficit, vox silet, & non mea tantùm, sed etiàm Angelorum*: *My minde faileth, my voice is silent, and not mine only, but euen the voice of Angels*: so may all men else say in the vnderstanding, and vtterance of the wayes and workes of the Creation; for to him (saith *Nazianzenus*) there is not one substance by which he is, and an other, by which he can, *Sed consubstantiale illi est quicquid eius est, & quicquid est, Whatsoeuer attribute of him there is, and whatsoeuer he is, it is the very same substance that himselfe is.*

But the Spirit of God which moued vpon the waters, cannot be taken for a breath or winde, nor for any other creature, separate from the infinite actiue power of God, which then formed and distinguished, and which now sustaineth, and giueth continuance to the Vniuersall. For the Spirit of the Lord filleth all the world; and the same is it, *which maintayneth all things*, saith *Salomon*. *If thou send forth thy Spirit* (saith *David*) *they are created*: And *Gregorie, Deus suo præsentiali esse, dat omnibus rebus esse, ita quòd, si se rebus subtraheret, sicut de nihilo facta sunt omnia, sic in nihilum defluerent vniuersa*; *God giueth being to all things, by being present with all things, so as, if he should withdraw himselfe from them, then as of nothing the world was made, it would againe fall away, and vanish into nothing.* And this working of Gods Spirit in all things, *Virgil* hath exprest excellently.

> *Principio cœlum ac terras, camposque liquentes,*
> *Lucentemque globum Lunæ, Titaniaque astra,*
> *Spiritus intus alit: totamque infusa per artus,*
> *Mens agitat molem, & magno se corpore miscet.*

> The heauen, the earth, and all the liquid mayne,
> The Moones bright Globe, and Starres Titanian,
> A Spirit within maintaines: and their whole Masse,
> A Minde, which through each part infus'd doth passe,
> Fashions, and workes, and wholly doth transpierce
> All this great body of the Vniuerse.[1]

And this was the same Spirit, which moued in the Vniuersall, and thereby both distinguished and adorned it. *His Spirit hath garnished the heauens*, saith *Iob*. So then the

[1] *Aeneid,* vi 724–27.

Spirit of God moued vpon the waters, and created in them
their spirituality, and naturall motion; motion brought forth
heat; and heat rarifaction, and subtility of parts. By this
Spirit, (which gaue heat and motion, and thereby, operation
to euery nature, while it moued vpon the waters, which were
in one indigested lumpe, and Chaos, disposed to all formes
alike) was begotten aire: an element, superior, as lighter
then the waters, through whose vast, open, subtile, dia-
phanicke, or transparent body, the light afterwards created
might easily transpierce: light, for the excellency thereof,
being the first creature which God called good, whose
creation immediately followed. This Spirit *Chrysostome*
calleth a vitall Operation, *aquis à Deo insitam, ex qua aquæ
non solùm motionem, sed & vim procreandi animalia habuerint.*
He calleth it *a vitall Operation giuen by God vnto the waters,
whereby the waters had not only motion, but also power to
procreate or bring forth liuing creatures.*

§7. *Of the light created, as the materiall substance of the Sunne:
and of the nature of it, and difficulty of knowledge of it:
and of the excellency and vse of it: and of motion, and heat
annexed vnto it.*

These waters were afterwards congregated, and called the
Sea: and this light afterwards (in the fourth day) gathered
and vnited, and called the Sunne, the Organ, and instrument
of created light. For this first and dispersed light did not (as
I conceiue) distinguish the night from the day, but with a
reference to the Sunnes creation, and the vniting of the
dispersed light therein. This is proued by these wordes, *Let
there be lights in the firmament, to separate the day from the
night:* which lights in the firmament of heauen were also
made for signes, and for seasons, and for dayes, and for
yeares, implying a motion instantly to follow, by which dayes
and yeares are distinguished; after which succeeded Time,
or together with which, that Time (which was the measure
of motion) began. For that space of the first three dayes
which preceded the Suns creation, or formall perfection,
when as yet there was not any motion to be measured, and

the day named in the fift verse, was but such a space, as afterwards by the Sunnes motion made a ciuill or naturall day. And as Waters were the matter of aire, of the firmament, and of the lower and vpper waters, and of the seas, and creatures therein: Earth, the matter of Beasts, plants, minerals, and mans body: so may light (for expression sake) be called the Chaos, or materiall substance of the Sunne, and other lights of heauen. Howbeit neither the Sunne, nor any thing sensible, is that light it selfe, *quæ causa est lucidorum, which is the cause that things are lightsome* (though it make it selfe and all things else visible) but a body most illightned, which illuminateth the Moone, by whom the neighbouring Region (which the Greekes call *Æther*, the place of the supposed Element of fire) is affected and qualified, and by it all bodies liuing in this our aire. For this light *Auicenna* calleth *vehiculum & fomentum omnium cælestium virtutum, & impressionum: the conducter, and preseruer, or nourisher of all celestiall vertues and impressions*, nothing descending of heauenly influences, but by the *medium*, or meanes of light. *Aristotle* calleth light, a quality, inherent, or cleauing to a Diaphanous body, *Lumen est qualitas inhærens Diaphano:* but this may be better auouched of the heat, which it transporteth and bringeth with it, or conducteth: which heat (say the Platonicks) *abeunte lumine residet in subiecto, the light being departed doth reside in the subiect*, as warmth in the aire, though the same be depriued of light. This light *Plotinus* and all the *Academikes* make incorporall, and so doth *Montanus, Cui nec duritia resistit, nec spatium: Which neither hardnesse resisteth, nor space leaueth.*

Aristole findeth corporalitie in the beames of light; but it is but by way of repetition of other mens opinions, saith *Picolomineus, Democritus, Leucippus*, and *Epicurus*, giue materiality to light it selfe, but improperly: for it passeth at an instant, from the heauen to the earth, nor is it resisted by any hardnesse, because it pierceth through the solid body of glasse, or other Cristalline matter; and whereas it is withstood by vncleane and vnpure earthy substances, lesse hard and more easie to inuade then the former, the same is, *Quòd obstaculum naturâ terreum atque sordidum, non capit candidam luminis puritatem: Because an obstacle, by nature, earthy and foule, doth not receiue the pure clearnesse of light*: alluding to that most diuine light, which onely shineth on those mindes, which are purged from all worldly drosse, and humane vncleannesse.

But of this created light, there is no agreement in opinion: neither doe I maruaile at it, for it cannot be found either in the Fathers, Philosophers, or Schoole-men, or other ancient or latter Writers, that any of them vnderstood either it or themselues therein: all men (to cast off ignorance) haue disputed hereof, but there is no man that hath beene taught thereby. *Thomas Aquinas* (not inferiour to any in wit) as he hath shewed little strength of argument in refuting the opinions of *Beda, Hugo, Lombard, Lyranus,* and others: so is his owne iudgement herein, as weake as any mans; and most of the Schoole-men were rather curious in the nature of termes, and more subtile in distinguishing vpon the parts of doctrine already laid downe, then discouerers of any thing hidden, either in Philosophie or Diuinity: of whome it may be truly said, *Nihil sapientiæ odiosius acumine nimio: Nothing is more odious to true wisdome, then too acute sharpnesse.* Neither hath the length of time, and the search of many learned men, (which the same time hath brought forth and deuoured) resolued vs, whether this light be substantiall, corporall, or incorporall: Corporall they say it cannot be, because then it could neither pierce the aire, nor those hard, solid, and Diaphanous bodies, which it doth, and yet euery day we see the aire illighted: incorporall it cannot be, because it is sensible: sensible it is, because it sometime affecteth the sight of the eye with offence, and therefore by most of the Fathers so esteemed: others say (as *Patricius*) that it cannot be matter, because no forme so excellent as it selfe to informe it: neither can it be any accident, which is not separable without the destruction of the subiect: for light being taken from the Sunne, the Sunne is no more the Sunne in existence. Secondly, if light were proceeding from matter and forme, then either, or both must be one of these, Lucide or bright, darke or opake, Diaphanous or transparent; but darkenesse cannot be parent of light; and things Diaphanous (being neither light, nor darkenesse, but capable of either) cannot be the cause of either, and therefore must the matter, or forme, or both, be Lucide and shining. Lucide and shining obtayne their so being of the light, and therefore, if we deriue this being of light from a former, then would the progresse goe on infinitely, and against nature; and therefore he concludeth that light in the Sunne hath his being primarily, and immediately of it selfe, and is therefore the Sunnes forme, and the forme of all Lucide and shining bodies: but what is taught hereby, let others iudge.

But in my vnderstanding, *lumen*, (which may be Englished by the word Shine) is an intentionall Species of that, which may be Englished by Light, and so, this shining which proceedeth from the Sunne, or other lights of heauen, or from any other light, is an image, or intentionall Species thereof; and an intentionall Species may be vnderstood by the example of a redde, or greene colour, occasioned by the shining of the Sunne through redde or greene glasse: for then wee perceiue the same colour cast vpon any thing opposite: which rednesse or other colour we call the *intentionall Species* of the colour in that glasse. And againe, as this light, touching his simple nature, is no way yet vnderstood: so it is disputed, whether this light first created be the same, which the Sunne inholdeth and casteth forth, or whether it had continuance any longer, then till the Sunnes creation.

But by the most wise and vnchanged order, which God obserued in the worke of the world, I gather, that the light, in the first day created, was the substance of the Sunne: for *Moses* repeateth twise the maine parts of the vniuersall; first, as they were created in matter; secondly, as they were adorned with forme: first, naming the Heauens, the Earth, the Waters, all confused, and afterward, the Waters congregated, the Earth made dry land, and the Heauens distinguished from both, and beautified. And therefore the Earth, as it was earth, before it was vncouered, and before it was called, *Arida*, or dry land; and the Waters were waters, before they were congregated and called the Sea, though neither of them perfect, or inriched with their vertuall formes: so the Sunne, although it had not his formall perfection, his circle, beauty, and bounded magnitude, till the fourth day, yet was the substance thereof in the first day (vnder the name of Light) created; and this light formerly dispersed, was in the same fourth day vnited and set in the firmament of Heauen: for to Light created in the first day God gaue no proper place or fixation, and therefore the effects named by *Anticipation*, (which was to separate day from night) were precisely performed, after this light was congregated and had obtained life and motion. Neither did the wisedome of God finde cause why it should moue (by which motion dayes and nights are distinguished) till then: because there was not yet any creature produced, to which, by mouing, the Sunne might giue light, heat, and operation.

But after the Earth (distinguished from waters) beganne to budde forth the budde of the hearbe, &c. God caused the Sunne to moue, and (by interchange of time) to visite euery part of the inferiour world; by his heate to stirre vp the fire of generation, and to giue actiuity to the seedes of all natures: For as a King, which commandeth some goodly building to bee erected, doth accommodate the same to that vse and end, to which it was ordayned; so it pleased God (saith *Procopius*) to command the light to be; which by his all-powerfull word he approued, and approuing it disposed thereof, to the vse and comfort of his future creatures.

But in that it pleased God to aske of *Iob*, *by what way is the light parted, and where is the way where light dwelleth*; we thereby know, that the nature thereof falleth not vnder mans vnderstanding; and therefore let it suffice, that by Gods grace we enioy the effects thereof. *For this light is of the treasure of God* (saith *Esdras*.) *And those which inhabite the heauens, doe only know the essence thereof. Nihil ignotum in cælo, nihil notum in terra, Nothing vnknowne in heauen, nothing perfectly knowne on earth. Res veræ sunt in mundo inuisibili, in mundo visibili vmbræ rerum: Things themselues are in the inuisible world, in the world visible but their shadowes;* Surely if this light be not spirituall, yet it approcheth nearest vnto spirituality; and if it haue any corporality, then of all other the most subtile and pure; for howsoeuer, it is of all things seen, the most beautifull, and of the swiftest motion, of all other the most necessary and beneficiall. For it ministreth to men and other creatures all celestiall influences; it dissipateth those sadde thoughts and sorrowes, which the darkenesse both begetteth and maintaineth; it discouereth vnto vs the glorious workes of God, and carrieth vp with an Angelicall swiftnesse our eyes vnto heauen, that by the sight thereof, our mindes being informed of his visible meruailes, may continually trauaile to surmount these perceiued heauens, and to finde out their omnipotent cause and Creatour. *Cognitio non quiescit in rebus creatis; Our knowledge doth not quiet it selfe in things created. Et ipsa lux facit, vt cætera mundi membra digna sint laudibus, cùm suam bonitatem & decorem omnibus communicet, It is the light,* (saith S^t. *Ambrose*) *that maketh the other part of the world so worthy of praise, seeing that it selfe communicateth its goodnesse and beauty vnto all:* of which *Ouid* out of *Orpheus*:

> *Ille ego sum, qui longum metior annum,*
> *Omnia qui video, per quem videt omnia mundus,*
> *Mundi oculus.*

> The world discernes it selfe, while I the world behold,
> By me the longest yeares, and other times are told,
> I the worlds eye.[1]

Lastly, if we may behold in any creature any one sparke of that eternall fire, or any farre-off-dawning of Gods glorious brightnesse, the same in the beauty, motion, and vertue of this light may be perceiued. Therefore was God called *lux ipsa*, and the light by *Hermes* named *lux sancta*, and *Christ* our Sauiour said to bee *that light which lighteneth euery man that commeth into the world.* Yet in respect of Gods incomprehensible sublimitie, and puritie, this is also true, that God is neither a minde, nor a Spirit of the nature of other Spirits, nor a light, such as can be discerned. *Deus profectò non mens est, at verò vt sit mens causa est; nèc spiritus, sed causa qua spiritus extat; nec lumen, sed causa qua lumen existit. God* (saith *Hermes* in *Pœmandro*) *certainely is not a minde, but the cause, that the minde hath his being; nor spirit, but the cause by which euery spirit is; nor light, but the cause by which the light existeth.*

So then the *Masse* and *Chaos* being first created, void, darke, and unformed, was by the operatiue Spirit of God pierced and quickned, and the Waters hauing now receiued

[1] *Metamorphoses,* IV 226–28.

Spirit and motion, resolued their thinner parts into aire, which God illightned, the Earth also by being contignat, and mixt with waters (participating the same diuine vertue) brought forth the budde of the hearbe that seedeth seede, &c. and for a meane and organ, by which this operatiue vertue might be continued, God appointed the light to be vnited, and gaue it also motion and heat, which heat caused a continuance of those seuerall *species*, which the Earth (being made fruitfull by the Spirit) produced, and with motion begat the time, and times succeeding.

§8. *Of the firmament, and of the waters aboue the firmament; and whether there by any cristalline heauen, or any* primum mobile.

§9. *A conclusion repeating the summe of the workes in the Creation, which are reduced to three heads: The creation of matter, The forming of it, The finishing of it.*

To conclude, it may bee gathered out of the first Chapter of *Genesis*, that this was the order of the most wise GOD in the beginning, and when there was no other nature, or being, but Gods incomprehensible eternitie. First, he created the matter of all things: and in the first three daies he distinguished and gaue to euery nature his proper forme; the forme of leuitie to that which ascended, to that which descended, the forme of grauitie: for he separated light from darkenesse, deuided waters from waters, and gathered the waters vnder the firmament into one place. In the last three dayes, God adorned, beautified, and replenished the world: he set in the firmament of Heauen, the Sunne, Moone, and Starres; filled the Earth with Beasts, the Aire with Fowle, and the Sea with Fish, giuing to all, that haue life, a power generatiue, thereby to continue their Species and kindes; to creatures vegetatiue and growing, their seedes in themselues; for *he created all things, that they might haue their being: and the generations of the world are preserued.*

§10. *That nature is no* Principium per se; *nor forme the giuer of being*: *and of our ignorance, how second causes should haue any proportion with their effects.*

And for this working power, which we call Nature, the beginning of motion and rest, according to *Aristotle*, the same is nothing else, but the strength and faculty, which God hath infused into euery creature, hauing no other selfe-ability, then a Clocke, after it is wound vp by a mans hand, hath. These therefore that attribute vnto this facultie, any first or sole power, haue therein no other vnderstanding, then such a one hath, who looking into the sterne of a shippe, and finding it guided by the helme and rudder, doth ascribe some absolute vertue to the peece of wood, without all consideration of the hand, that guides it, or of the iudgement, which also directeth and commandeth that hand; forgetting in this and in all else, that by the vertue of the first act, all Agents worke whatsoeuer they worke: *Virtute primi actus agunt agentia omnia quicquid agunt:* for as the minde of man seeth by the Organ of the eye, heareth by the eares, and maketh choise by the will: and therefore we attribute sight to the eye, and hearing to the eares, &c. and yet it is the minde only, that giueth abilitie, life, and motion to all these his instruments and Organs; so God worketh by Angels, by the Sunne, by the Starres, by Nature, or infused properies, and by men, as by seuerall organs, seuerall effects; all second causes whatsoeuer being but instruments, conduits, and pipes, which carry and disperse what they haue receiued from the head and fountaine of the Vniuersall. For as it is Gods infinite power, and euery-where-presence (compassing, embracing, and piercing all things) that giueth to the Sunne power to draw vp vapours, to vapours to be made cloudes, cloudes to contayne raine, and raine to fall: so all second and instrumentall causes, together with Nature it selfe, without that operatiue facultie which God gaue them, would become altogether silent, vertuelesse, and dead: of which excellently *Orphevs; Per te virescunt omnia, All things by thee spring forth in youthfull greene.* I enforce not these things, thereby to annihilate those variable vertues, which God hath giuen to his creatures,

animate and inanimate, to heauenly and earthly bodies, &c.
for all his workes in their vertues praise him: but of the
manner how God worketh in them, or they in or with each
other, which the Heathen Philosophers, and those that
follow them, haue taken on them to teach: I say there is not
any one among them, nor any one among vs, that could
euer yet conceiue it, or expresse it, euer enrich his owne
vnderstanding with any certaine truth, or euer edifie others
(not foolish by selfe-flatterie) therein. For (saith *Lactantius*,
speaking of the wisedome of the Philosophers) *si facultas
inueniendæ veritatis huic studio subiaceret; aliquandò esset
inuenta; cùm verò tot temporibus, tot ingenijs in eius inquisitione
contritis, non sit comprehensa, apparet nullam ibi esse sapientiam,
If in this studie* (saith he) *were meanes to finde out the truth, it
had ere this beene found out: but seeing it is not yet comprehended,
after that so much time, and so many wits haue beene worne out
in the inquirie of it, it appeareth, that there is no wisedome there
to be had. Nàm side vna re præcisa scientia haberetur, omnium
rerum scientia necessariò haberetur, If the precise knowledge of
any one thing were to be had, it should necessarily follow, that
the knowledge of all things were to be had.* And as the Philosophers were ignorant in nature, and the wayes of her
working: so were they more curious, then knowing, in
their first matter and Physicall forme. For if their first
matter had any being, it were not then the first matter: for,
as it is the first matter, it hath only a power of being, which
it altogether leaueth, when it doth subsist. And seeing it is
neither a substance perfect, nor a substance inchoate, or in
the way of perfection, how any other substance should
thence take concrescence, it hath not beene taught; neither
are these formes (saith a learned Authour) any thing, *si
ex ea exprimantur potentia, quæ nihil est.* Againe, how this
first matter should be *subiectum formarum,* and passiue,
which is vnderstood to precede the forme, it is hard to
conceiue: for to make forme which is the cause, to be
subsequent to the thing caused (to wit, to the first matter)
is contrary to all reason, diuine and humane: only it may be
said, that originally there is no other difference betweene
matter and forme, then betweene heat and fire, of which the
one cannot subsist without the other, but in a kind of

rationall consideration. Leauing therefore these riddles to their louers, who by certaine scholasticall distinctions wrest and peruert the truth of all things, and by which *Aristotle* hath laboured to proue a false eternitie of the world, I thinke it farre safer to affirme with S^t. *Avgvstine, That all species and kinds are from God, from whom, whatsoeuer is naturall, proceedeth, of what kinde or estimation soeuer, from whence are the seedes of all formes, and the formes of all seedes and their motions. . . .*

§ 11. *Of Fate*; *and that the Starres haue great influence*: *and that their operations may diuersly be preuented or furthered.*

And, as of Nature, such is the dispute and contention concerning Fate or Destinie, of which the opinions of those learned men that haue written thereof, may be safely receiued, had they not thereunto annexed and fastened an ineuitable necessity, and made it more generall, and vniuersally powerfull then it is, by giuing it dominion ouer the minde of man, and ouer his will; which *Ouid* and *Iuuenal.*

> *Ratio satum vintere nulla valet.*
> *Seruis regna dabunt, captiuis Fata triumphos,*
>
> Gainst Fate no counsell can preuaile.
> Kingdomes to flaues, by Destinie,
> To Captiues triumphs giuen be.[1]

An errour of the *Chaldæans*, and after them of the Stoicks, the Pharisees, Priscillianists, the Bardisanists, and others, as *Basil, Augustine,* and *Thomas* haue obserued: but, that Fate is an obedience of second causes to the first, was well conceiued of *Hermes,* and *Apuleius* the Platonist. *Plotinus* out of the Astronomers calleth it a disposition from the acts of celestiall Orbes, vnchangeably working in inferiour bodies, the same being also true enough, in respect of all those things, which a rationall minde doth not order nor direct. *Ptolomie, Seneca, Democritus, Epicurus, Chrysippus, Empedocles,* and the *Stoicks,* some of them more largely, others more strictly, ascribe to Fate a binding and ineuitable necessity, and that it is the same which is spoken and

[1] Ovid, *Tristia* III vi 18; Juvenal, VII 201.

determined by God (*quod de vnoquoque nostrûm fatus est Deus*) and the definite lot of all liuing. And certainely it cannot be doubted, but the Starres are instruments of farre greater vse, then to giue an obscure light, and for men to gaze on after Sunne set: it being manifest, that the diuersity of seasons, the Winters, and Sommers, more hot and cold, are not so vncertained by the Sunne and Moone alone, who alway keep one and the same course, but that the Starres haue also their working therein.

And if we cannot deny, but that God hath giuen vertues to springs, and fountaines, to cold earth, to plants and stones, Minerals, and to the excrementall parts of the basest liuing creatures, why should wee robbe the beautifull Starres of their working powers? for seeing they are many in number and of eminent beauty and magnitude, we may not thinke, that in the treasury of his wisedome who is infinite, there can be wanting (euen for euery starre) a peculiar vertue and operation; as euery hearbe, plant, fruit, and flower, adorning the face of the Earth hath the like. For as these were not created to beautifie the earth alone, and to couer and shadow her dusty face, but otherwise for the vse of man and beast, to feede them and cure them: so were not those vncountable glorious bodies set in the firmament, to no other end, then to adorne it, but for instruments and organs of his diuine prouidence, so farre as it hath pleased his iust will to determine. *Origen* vpon this place of *Genesis, Let there be light in the firmament, &c.* affirmeth that the Starres are not causes (meaning perchance binding causes) but are as open bookes, wherein are contained and set downe all things whatsoeuer to come; but not to be read by the eyes of humane wisedome: which latter part I beleeue well, and this saying of *Syracides* withall. *That there are hidde yet greater things then these be, and we haue seene but a few of his workes.* And though, for the capacitie of men, we know somewhat, yet in the true and vttermost vertues of hearbs and plants, which our selues sow and set, and which grow vnder our feete, we are in effect ignorant; much more in the powers and working of celestiall bodies: for *hardly* (saith *Salomon*) *can we discerne the things that are vpon the earth, and with great labour finde we out those things that are before vs: who can then, inuestigate the things that are in heauen? Multum est de rebus cœlestibus aliquid cognoscere: It is much to know a little of heauenly things.* But in this question of Fate, the middle course is to be followed, that as with the Heathen we doe not binde God to his creatures, in this supposed necessity of destinie, so on the contrary we doe not robbe those beautifull creatures of their powers and offices. For had any of these second causes despoiled God of his prerogatiue, or had God himselfe constrained the minde and will of man to impious acts by any celestiall inforcements, then sure the impious excuse of some were iustifiable; of whom S^t. *Avgvstine. Impiâ peruersitate in malis factis rectissimè reprehendendis ingerunt accusandum potiùs auctorem syderum, quàm commissorem scelerum. Where we reprehend them of euill deedes, they againe with wicked peruersenesse vrge, that rather the Authour and Creatour of the Starres, then the doer of the euill is to be accused.*

But that the Starres and other celestiall bodies incline the will by mediation of the sensitiue appetite, which is also stirred by the constitution and complexion, it cannot be doubted. *Corpora cœlestia* (saith *Damascene*) *constituunt in nobis habitus, complexiones, & dispositiones, The heauenly bodies* (saith he) *make in vs habits, complexions, and dispositions*: for the body (though *Galen* inforce it further) hath vndoubtedly a kinde of drawing after it the affections of the minde, especially bodies strong in humour, and mindes weake in vertues: for those of cholericke complexion are subiect to anger, and the furious effects thereof; by which they suffer themselues to be transported, where the minde hath not reason to remember, that passions ought to be her vassailes, not her Masters. And that they wholly direct the reasonlesse minde I am resolued: For all those which were created mortall, as birds, beasts, and the like are left to their naturall appetites, ouer all which, celestiall bodies (as instruments and executioners of Gods prouidence) haue absolute dominion. What we should iudge of men, who little differ from beasts, I cannot tell: for as he that contendeth against those inforcements, may easily master or resist them: so whosoeuer shall neglect the remedies by vertue and pietie prepared, putteth himselfe altogether vnder the power of his sensuall appetite; *Vincitur fatum si resistas, vincit si contempseris: Fate will be ouercome, if thou resist it, if thou neglect, it conquereth.*

But that either the Starres or the Sunne haue any power ouer the mindes of men immediately, it is absurd to thinke, other then as aforesaid, as the same by the bodies temper may be effected. *Lumen solis ad generationem sensibilium corporum confert, & ad vitam ipsam mouet, & nutrit, & auget, & perficit: The light of the Sunne* (saith Saint *Avgvstine*) *helpeth the generation of sensible bodies, moueth them to life, and nourisheth, augmenteth, and perfecteth them:* yet still as a Minister, not as a Master: *Bonus quidem est Sol, in ministerio, non imperio; The Sunne is good to serue, not to sway* (saith S^t. *Ambrose.*) And S^t. *Avgvstine: Deus regit inferiora corpora per superiora; God ruleth the bodies below by those aboue,* but he auoucheth not that superiour bodies haue rule ouer mens minds, which are incorporeall.

But howsoeuer we are by the Starres inclined at our birth, yet there are many things both in nature and art, that encounter the same, and weaken their operation: and *Aristotle* himselfe confesseth, that the heauens doe not alwaies worke their effects in inferiour bodies, no more then the signes of raine and wind doe alwaies come to passe. And it is diuers times seene, that paternall vertue and vice hath his counter-working to these inclinations. *Est in Iuuencis patrum virtus*; *In the young off-spring the fathers vertue is,* and so the contrary, *patrum vitia:* and herein also there is often found an enterchange; the Sonnes of vertuous men, by an ill constellation become inclinable to vice, and of vitious men, to vertue.

Egregia est soboles, scelerato nata parente.

A worthy sonne is borne of a wicked father.

But there is nothing (after Gods reserued power) that so much setteth this art of influence out of square and rule, as education doth: for there are none in the world so wickedly inclined, but that a religious instruction and bringing vp may fashion anew, and reforme them; nor any so well disposed, whom (the raines being let loose) the continuall fellowship and familiaritie, and the examples of dissolute men may not corrupt and deforme. Vessels will euer retaine

a sauour of their first liquor: it being equally difficult either
to cleanse the minde once corrupted, or to extinguish the
sweet sauour of vertue first receiued, when the minde was
yet tender, open, and easily seasoned; but where a fauour-
able constellation (allowing that the Starres incline the will)
and a vertuous education doe happily arriue, or the contrarie
in both, thereby it is that men are found so exceeding
vertuous or vitious, heauen and earth (as it were) running
together, and agreeing in one: for as the seedes of vertue
may by the art and husbandry of Christian counsaile produce
better and more beautifull fruit, then the strength of selfe
nature and kinde could haue yeelded them; so the plants
apt to grow wild, and to change themselues into weedes, by
being set in a soile sutable, and like themselues, are made
more vnsauory and filled with poyson. It was therefore truly
affirmed, *Sapiens adiuuabit opus astrorum, quemadmodùm
agricola terræ naturam*; *A wise man assisteth the worke of the
Starres, as the husbandman helpeth the nature of the soile.*
And *Ptolomie* himselfe confesseth thus much, *Sapiens, &
omnia sapientis medici dominabuntur astris, A wise man, and
the ominous art of a wise Physitian shall preuaile against the
starres.* Lastly, we ought all to know, that God created the
starres, as he did the rest of the Vniuersall, whose influences
may be called his reserued and vnwritten lawes. But let vs
consider how they binde: euen as the lawes of men doe; for
although the Kings and Princes of the world haue by their
lawes decreed, that a theefe and a murderer shall suffer
death; and though their ordinances are daylie by Iudges
and Magistrates (the Starres of Kings) executed accordingly,
yet these lawes doe not depriue Kings of their naturall or
religious compassion, or binde them without prerogatiue, to
such a seuere execution, as that there should be nothing left
of libertie to iudgement, power, or conscience: the Law in
his owne nature being no other then a deafe Tyrant. But
seeing that it is otherwise, and that Princes (who ought to
imitate God in all they can) doe sometimes for causes to
themselues knowne, and by mediation, pardon offences both
against others and themselues, it were then impious to take
that power and libertie from God himselfe, which his
Substitutes enioy; God being mercy, goodnesse, and charitie

it selfe. Otherwise that example of prayer by our Sauiour taught, *And let vs not be ledde vnto temptation, but deliuer vs from euill*, had beene no other but an expense of wordes and time; but that God (which only knoweth the operation of his owne creatures truly) hath assured vs, that there is no inclination or temperature so forcible, which our humble prayers and desires may not make frustrate, and breake asunder: for were it (as the Stoicks conceiue) that Fate or Destinie, though depending vpon eternall power, yet being once ordered and disposed, had such a connexion and immutable dependencie, that God himselfe should in a kinde haue shut vp himselfe therein. *How miserable then were the condition of men* (saith St. *Avgvstine*) *left altogether without hope.*

And if this strength of the Starres were so transfer'd, as that God had quitted vnto them all dominion ouer his creatures; be he Pagan or Christian that so beleeueth, the only true God of the one, and the imaginarie Gods of the other would thereby be despoiled of all worship, reuerence, or respect.

And certainely, God which hath promised vs the reward of well-doing, which Christ himselfe claimed at the hands of the Father (*I haue finished the worke which thou gauest me to doe.*) And the same God, who hath threatned vnto vs the sorrow and torment of offences, could not contrary to his mercifull nature, be so vniust, as to bind vs ineuitably to the destinies, or influences of the Starres, or subiect our soules to any imposed necessitie. But it was well said of *Plotinus*, that the starres were significant, but not efficient, giuing them yet something lesse then their due: and therefore as I doe not consent with those, who would make those glorious creatures of God vertuelesse: so I thinke that we derogate from his eternall and absolute power and prouidence, to ascribe to them the same dominion ouer our immortall soules, which they haue ouer all bodily substances, and perishable natures: for the soules of men, louing and fearing God, receiue influence from that diuine light it selfe, whereof the Sunnes claritie, and that of the Starres is by *Plato* called but a shadow. *Lumen est vmbra Dei, & Deus est lumen luminis, Light is the shadow of Gods brightnesse, who is the light of light.* But to end this question, because this Destinie, together with Prouidence, Prescience, and Predestination are often confounded, I thinke it not impertinent to touch the difference in a word or two, for euery man hath not obserued it, though all learned men haue.

§12. *Of Prescience.*

Prescience, or fore-knowledge (which the Greekes call *Prognosis*, the Latines *præcognitio*, or *præscientia*) considered in order and nature (if we may speake of God after the manner of men) goeth before Prouidence: for God fore-knew all things, before he had created them, or before they had being to be cared for; and Prescience is no other then an infallible fore-knowledge. For whatsoeuer our selues fore-know, except the same be to succeede accordingly, it cannot be true that we fore-know it. But this Prescience of God (as it is Prescience only) is not the cause of any thing futurely succeeding: neither doth Gods fore-knowledge impose any necessity, or binde. For in that we fore-know that the Sunne will rise, and set; that all men borne in the world shall die againe; that after Winter, the Spring shall come; after the Spring Sommer and Haruest, and that according to the seuerall seedes that we sow, we shall reape seuerall sorts of graine, yet is not our fore-knowledge the cause of this, or any of these: neither doth the knowledge in vs binde or constraine the Sunne to rise and set, or men to die; for the causes (as men perswade themselues) are otherwise manifest and knowne to all. *The eye of man* (saith *Boetivs*) *beholdeth those things subiect to sense, as they are; the eye seeth that such a beast is a horse, it seeth men, trees, and houses, &c. but our seeing of them (as they are) is not the cause of their so being, for such they be in their owne natures.* And againe out of the same Authour. *Diuina prouidentia rebus generandis non imponit necessitatem, quià si omnia euenirent ex necessitate, præmia bonorum, & pœna malorum periret, Diuine prouidence* (saith he) *imposeth no necessity vpon things that are to exist, for if all came to passe of necessity, there should neither be reward of good, nor punishment of euill.*

§13. *Of Prouidence.*

Now Prouidence (which the Greekes call *Pronoia*) is an intellectuall knowledge, both fore-seeing, caring for, and ordering all things, and doth not only behold all past, all present, and all to come, but is the cause of their so being, which Prescience (simply taken) is not: and therefore Prouidence by the Philosophers (saith S^t. *Augustine*) is deuided into Memorie, Knowledge, and Care: Memorie of the past, Knowledge of the present, and Care of the future; and we our selues account such a man for prouident, as, remembring things past, and obseruing things present, can by iudgement, and comparing the one with the other, prouide for the future, and times succeeding. That such a thing there is as Prouidence, the Scriptures euerywhere teach vs, *Moses* in many places, the Prophets in their prædictions: Christ himselfe and his Apostles assure vs hereof; and, besides the Scriptures, *Hermes*, *Orpheus*, *Euripides*, *Pythagoras*, *Plato*, *Plotinus*, and (in effect) all learned men acknowledge the Prouidence of God: yea the Turks themselues are so confident therein, as they refuse not to accompanie and visit each other, in the most pestilent diseases, nor shunne any perill whatsoeuer, though death therein doe manifestly present it selfe.

The places of Scripture prouing Prouidence, are so many, both in generall and particular, as I shall neede to repeate but a few of them in this place. *Sing vnto God* (saith *David*) *which couereth the heauens with cloudes, and prepareth raine for the earth, and maketh the grasse to grow vpon the mountaines, which giueth to beasts their foode, and feedeth the young Rauen that cries: all these waite vpon thee, that thou maiest giue them foode in due season. And thou shalt drinke of the riuer Cheareth* (saith God to *Eliah*) *and I haue commanded the Rauens to feede thee there. Behold the Fowles of the aire, they sow not, nor reape, and yet your heauenly Father feedeth them: againe, are not two sparrowes sold for a farthing? and one of them shall not fall on the ground without your Father: yea all the haires of your head are numbred.* And S^t. *Peter, Cast all your care on him, for he careth for you; And his iudgements are written* (saith *David*).

God therefore, who is euery where present, *who filleth the heauens and the earth, whose eyes are vpon the righteous, and his countenance against them that doe euill,* was therefore by *Orpheus* called *oculus infinitus, an infinite eye,* beholding all things, and cannot therefore be esteemed as an idle looker on, as if he had transferred his power to any other: for it is contrary to his owne word. *Gloriam meam alteri non dabo: I will not giue my glorie to another.* No man commandeth in the Kings presence, but by the Kings direction; but God is euery where present, and King of Kings. The example of Gods vniuersall prouidence is seene in his creatures. The Father prouideth for his children: beasts and birds and all liuings for their young ones. If prouidence be found in second Fathers, much more in the first and Vniuersall: and if there be a naturall louing care in men, and beasts, much more in God, who hath formed this nature, and whose diuine loue was the beginning, and is the bond of the Vniuersall. *Amor diuinus rerum omnium est principium, & vinculum vniuersi* (saith *Plato.*) *Amor Dei est nodus perpetuus, mundi copula, partiumque eius immobile sustentaculum, ac vniuersæ machinæ fundamentum, The loue of God is the perpetuall knot, and linke or chaine of the world, and the immoueable piller of euery part thereof, and the Basis and foundation of the vniuersall.* God therefore who could onely be the cause of all, can onely prouide for all, and sustaine all; so as to absolute power; to euery-where presence; to perfect goodnesse; to pure and diuine loue; this attribute and transcendent habilitie of Prouidence is only proper and belonging.

§14. *Of Predestination.*

Now for Predestination; we can difference it no otherwise, from Prouidence and Prescience, then in this, that Prescience only fore-seeth: Prouidence fore-seeth and careth for, and hath respect to all creatures, euen from the brightest Angels of heauen, to the vnworthiest wormes of the earth, and Predestination (as it is vsed specially by Diuines) is only of men, and yet not of all to men belonging, but of their saluation properly, in the common vse of Diuines, or perdition, as some haue vsed it. Yet *Peter Lombard*, *Thomas*, *Bernensis Theologus*, and others, take the word Predestination more strictly, and for a preparation to felicitie: diuers of the Fathers take it more largely somtimes: among whom S[t]. *Augustine* speaking of two Citties, and two societies, vseth these wordes, *Quarum est vna, quæ prædestinata est in æternum regnare cum Deo, altera æternum supplicium subire cum Diabolo, Whereof one is it, which is predestinated to raigne for euer with God, but the other is to vndergoe euerlasting torment with the Deuill:* for according to *Nonivs Marcellvs, destinare est præpare*; and of the same opinion are many Protestant writers, as *Caluin, Beza, Buchanus, Danæus*, and such like: and as for the manifold questions hereof arising, I leaue them to the Diuines; and why it hath pleased God to create some vessels of honour, and some of dishonour, I will answere with *Gregorie*, who saith, *Qui in factis Dei rationem non videt, infirmitatem suam considerans, cur non videat, rationem videt: He that seeth no reason in the actions of God, by consideration of his owne infirmitie perceiueth the reason of his blindnesse.* And againe with S[t]. *Avgvstine, Occulta esse causa potest, iniusta esse non potest: Hidden the cause of his Predestination may be, vniust it cannot be.*

§15. *Of Fortune: and of the reason of some things that seeme to be by fortune, and against reason and prouidence.*

Lastly, seeing Destinie or Necessitie is subsequent to Gods prouidence, and seeing that the Starres haue no other dominion, then is before spoken, and that Nature is nothing, but as *Plato* calleth it, *Dei artem, vel artificiosum Dei Organum, The art, or artificiall Organ of God*: and *Cvsanvs, Diuini præcepti instrumentum, The instrument of the diuine precept*, we may then with better reason reiect that kinde of Idolatrie, or God of fooles, called *Fortune* or Chance: a Goddesse, the most reuerenced, and the most reuiled of all other, but not ancient; for *Homer* maketh her the Daughter of *Oceanus*, as *Pausanias* witnesseth in his *Messeniacks*. The Greekes call her τύχην signifying a relatiue being, or betiding, so as before *Homers* time this great Ladie was scarce heard off, and *Hesiodus*, who hath taught the birth and beginning of all these counterfait Gods, hath not a word of *Fortune:* yet afterward shee grew so great and omnipotent, as from Kings and Kingdomes, to beggers and cottages, shee ordered all things, resisting the wisedome of the wisest, by making the possessor thereof miserable: valuing the folly of the most foolish by making their successe prosperous, insomuch as the actions of men were said to be but the sports of Fortune, and the variable accidents happening in mens liues, but her pastimes: of which *Palladius*, *Vita hominum ludus fortunæ est*, *The life of man is the play of Fortune*; and because it often falleth out, that enterprises guided by ill counsels haue equall successe to those by the best iudgment conducted, therefore had Fortune the same external figure with Sapience: whereof *Athenæus*.

> *Longissimè à Sapientia Fors dissidet,*
> *Sed multa perficit tamen simillima.*

> From wisedome Fortune differs farre,
> And yet in workes most like they are.[1]

But I will forbeare to be curious in that, which (as it is commonly vnderstood) is nothing else but a power imaginarie, to which the successe of humane actions and endeuours were for their varietie ascribed; for when a manifest cause could not bee giuen, then was it attributed to Fortune, as if there were no cause of those things, of which most men are ignorant, contrary to this true ground of *Plato: Nihil est ortum sub Sole, cuius causa legitima non præcesserit, Nothing euer came to passe vnder the Sunne, of which there was not a iust preceding cause.* But *Aquinas* hath herein answered in one destination, whatsoeuer may be obiected; for many things there are (saith he) which happen *besides the intention of the inferiour, but not besides the intention of the superiour: Præter intentionem inferioris, sed non præter intentionem superioris,* (to wit) the ordinance of God; and therefore (saith *Melanchton*) *Quod Poetæ fortunam, nos Deum appellamus, Whom the Poets call Fortune, we know to be God,* and that this is true, the

---

[1] Only fragments of the plays of Athenaeus survive, often in the form of quotations (as in Aristotle's *Nicomachean Ethics*, vi ii 6 and iv 5).

Scripture in many places teacheth vs, as in the law of murder. *He that smiteth a man, and he die, shall die the death, and if a man hath not laid waite, but God hath offered him into his hands, then I will appoint thee a place whither he shall flee.* Now where the Scripture hath these wordes, *God hath offered him into his hands,* we say, if he hurt him by Chance, and in *Deuteronomie* the nineteenth, where the slipping of an Axe from the helue, whereby an other is slaine, was the worke of God himselfe, we in our phrase attribute this accident to Chance or Fortune: and in the *Prouerbs* the sixteenth, *The lot is cast into the lap, but the whole disposition thereof is of the Lord:* so as that which seemeth most casuall and subiect to Fortune, is yet disposed by the ordinance of God, as all things else; and hereof the wiser sort, and the best learned of the Philosophers were not ignorant, as *Cicero* witnesseth for them, gathering the opinion of *Aristotle* and his sectators, with those of *Plato*, and the *Academikes* to this effect, That the same power which they called *animam mundi, the soule of the world,* was no other then that incomprehensible wisedome, which we expresse by the name of God, gouerning euery being aswell in heauen as in earth; to which wisedome and power they sometime gaue the title of necessitie or Fate, because it bindeth by ineuitable ordinance: sometime, the stile of Fortune, because of many effects there appeare vnto vs no certaine causes. To this effect speaketh S^t. *Augustine* in his questions vpon *Genesis* the first Booke: the same hath *Seneca* in his fourth of *Benefits*; which was also the doctrine of the Stoicks, of which sect hee was: *For whatsoeuer* (saith hee) *thou callest God, be it Nature, Fate, or Fortune, all are but one and the same, differenced by diuers termes, according as he vseth, and exerciseth his power diuersly.*

But it may be obiected, that if Fortune and Chaunce were not sometimes the causes of good and euill in men, but an idle voice, whereby we expresse successe, how comes it then, that so many worthy and wise men depend vpon so many vnworthy and emptie-headed fooles; that riches and honour are giuen to externall men, and without kernell: and so many learned, vertuous, and valiant men weare out their liues in poore and deiected estates. In a word there is no other inferiour, or apparent cause, beside the partialitie of mans affection, but the fashioning and not fashioning of our selues according to the nature of the time wherein we liue, for whosoeuer is most able, and best sufficient to discerne, and hath withall an honest and open heart and louing truth, if Princes, or those that gouerne, endure no other discourse then their owne flatteries, then I say such an one, whose vertue and courage forbiddeth him to be base and a dissembler, shall euermore hang vnder the wheele, which kinde of deseruing well and receiuing ill, wee alwaies falsly charge Fortune withall. For whosoeuer shall tell any great man or Magistrates, that he is not iust, the Generall of an Armie, that he is not valiant, and great Ladies that they are not faire, shall neuer be made a Counseller, a Captaine, or a Courtier. Neither is it sufficient to be wise with a wise Prince, valiant with a valiant, and iust with him that is iust, for such a one hath no estate in his prosperitie; but he must also change with the successour, if he be of contrary qualities, saile with the tide of the time, and alter forme and condition, as the Estate or the Estates Master changeth: Otherwise how were it possible, that the most base men, and separate from all imitable qualities, could so often attaine to honour and riches, but by such an obseruant slauish course? These men hauing nothing else to value themselues by, but a counterfait kinde of wondring at other men, and by making them beleeue that all their vices are vertues, and all their dustie actions cristalline, haue yet in all ages prospered equally with the most vertuous, if not exceeded them. For according to *Menander, Omnis insipiens arrogantia & plausibus capitur, Euery foole is wonne with his owne pride and others flattering applause:* so as whosoeuer will liue altogether out of himselfe, and studie other mens humours, and obserue them, shall neuer be vnfortunate; and on the contrary, that man which prizeth truth and vertue (except the season wherein he liueth be of all these, and of all sorts of goodnesse fruitfull) shall neuer prosper by the possession or profession thereof. It is also a token of a worldly wise man, not to warre or contend in vaine against the nature of times wherein he liueth: for such a one is often the authour of his owne miserie, but best it were to follow the aduise, which the

Pope gaue the Bishops of that age, out of *Ouid*, while the Arian Heresie raged:

Dùm furor in cursu est, currenti cede furori.

While furie gallops on the way,
Let no man furies gallop stay.[1]

And if *Cicero* (then whom that world begat not a man of more reputed iudgement) had followed the counsaile of his brother *Qvintvs*, *Potuisset* (saith *Petrarch*) *in lectulo suo mori, potuisset integro cadauere sepeliri, He might then haue died the death of nature, and beene with an vntorne and vndisseuered body buried*; for as *Petrarch* in the same place noteth: *Quid stultius quàm desperantem (præsertim de effectu) litibus perpetuis implicari, What more foolish then for him that despaires, especially of the effect, to be entangled with endlesse contentions?* Whosoeuer therefore will set before him *Machiauels two markes to shoote at* (to wit) riches, and glorie, must set on and take off a backe of yron to a weake wooden bow, that it may fit both the strong and the feeble: for as he, that first deuised to adde sailes to rowing vessels, did either so proportion them, as being fastened aloft, and towards the head of his Mast, he might abide all windes and stormes, or else he sometime or other perished by his owne inuention: so that man which prizeth vertue for it selfe, and cannot endure to hoise and strike his sailes, as the diuers natures of calmes and stormes require, must cut his sailes, and his cloth, of meane length and breadth, and content himselfe with a slow and sure nauigation, (to wit) a meane and free estate. But of this dispute of Fortune, and the rest, or of whatsoeuer Lords or Gods, imaginarie powers, or causes, the wit (or rather foolishnesse) of man hath found out: let vs resolue with S[t]. *Paul*, who hath taught vs, that there is *but one God, the Father, of whom are all things, and we in him, and one Lord, Iesus Christ, by whom are all things, and we by him*; there are diuersities of operations, but God is the same which worketh all in all.

---

[1] *Remedia amoris,* 119.

Ch. II. *Of mans estate in his first Creation, and of Gods rest*

§1. *Of the Image of God, according to which man was first created.*

The creation of all other creatures being finished, the heauens adorned, and the earth replenished, GOD said, *Let vs make man in our owne Image, according to our likenesse.*

Man is the last and most admirable of Gods workes to vs knowne, *ingens miraculum homo, man is the greatest wonder* (saith *Plato* out of *Mercvrivs:*) *Naturæ ardentissimæ artificium, The artificiall worke of the most ardent or fire-like nature* (as saith *Zoroaster*) though the same be meant, not for any excellencie externall, but in respect of his internall forme, both in the nature, qualities, and other attributes thereof: in nature, because it hath an essence immortall, and spirituall; in qualities, because the same was by God created holy and righteous in truth; in other attributes, because Man was made Lord of the world, and of the creatures therein.

> *Sanctius his animal mentisque capacius altæ*
> *Deerat adhuc: & quod dominari in cætera posset,*
> *Natus homo est.*

> More holy then the rest, and vnderstanding more
> A liuing creature wants, to rule all made before,
> So man beganne to be.[1]

Of this Image and similitude of God, there is much dispute among the Fathers, Schoole-men, and late Writers: Some of the Fathers conceiue, that man was made after the Image of God, in respect chiefly of Empire and dominion, as S[t]. *Chrysostome, Ambrose,* and some others: which S[t]. *Ambrose* denyeth to the woman in these wordes, *Vt sicut Deus vnus, ab eo fieret homo vnus, & quomodò ex Deo vno omnia, ità ex vno homine omne genus esset super faciem totius terræ: Vnus igitur vnum fecit, qui vnitatis eius haberet imaginem,*

[1] Ovid, *Metamorphoses,* 1 76–78.

That as God is one, one man might be made by him, and that in what manner all things are of one God, likewise of one man the whole kinde should be vpon the face of the whole earth: Therefore he being one made one, that should haue the Image of his vnitie. But whereas it is gathered out of the following wordes of the same Verse, that man was after the image of God in respect of rule and power, it is written *Dominamini* in the plurall number, *and let them rule ouer the fish of the Sea, &c.* and therefore cannot the woman be excluded. Others conceiue, that man is said to be after the image of God in respect of his immortall soule only, because as God is inuisible, so the soule of man is inuisible, as God is immortall and incorporall, so is the soule of man immortall and incorporall; and as there is but one God which gouerneth the world, so but one soule which gouerneth the body of man; and as God is wholly in euery part of the world, so is the soule of man wholly in euery part of the body: *Anima est tota in toto, & tota in qualibet parte, The soule is wholly in the whole body, and wholly in euery part thereof*, according to *Aristotle*; though *Chalcidius*, and other learned men denie that doctrine; which that it is otherwise then potentially true, all the *Aristotelians* in the world shall neuer proue. These and the like arguments doe the *Iewes* make (saith *Tostatus*) and these resemblances, betweene the infinite God, and the finite Man.

The Schoole-men resemble the Minde or Soule of Man to God, in this respect especially; because that as in the Minde there are three distinct powers, or faculties (to wit) Memorie, Vnderstanding, and Will, and yet all these, being of reall differences, are but one minde: so in God there are three distinct persons, the Father, Sonne, and holy Ghost, and yet but one God. They also make the Image and Similitude diuers; and againe, they distinguish betweene *imaginem Dei*, and *ad imaginem Dei*, and spinne into small threds, with subtile distinctions, many times the plainenesse, and sinceritie of the Scriptures: their wits being like that strong water, that eateth through and dissolueth the purest gold. . . .

But howsoeuer the Schoole-men and others distinguish, or whatsoeuer the Fathers conceiue, sure I am that S^t. *Paul* maketh the same sense of the image, which *Victorinus* doth of the similitude, who saith: *As we haue borne the image of the earthly, so shall we beare the image of the heauenly*; and it cannot bee gathered out of the Scriptures, that the wordes image and similitude were vsed but in one sense, and in this place the better to expresse each other; whatsoeuer *Lombard* hath said to the contrarie. For God knowes, what a multitude of meanings the wit of man imagineth to himselfe in the Scriptures, which neither *Moses*, the *Prophets*, or *Apostles*, euer conceiued. Now as S[t]. *Paul* vseth the word (image) for both: so S[t]. *Iames* vseth the word (similitude) for both in these wordes. *Therewith blesse wee God euen the Father, and therewith curse we Men, which are made after the similitude of God.* . . .

God is a spirituall substance, inuisible, and most simple; God is a iust God: God is mercifull: God is charitie it selfe, and (in a word) goodnesse it selfe, and none else simply good. And thus much it hath pleased God himselfe to teach vs, and to make vs know of himselfe. What then can be the shadow of such a substance, the image of such a nature, or wherein can man be said to resemble his vnexcogitable power and perfectnesse? certainely, not in dominion alone: for the Deuill is said to be the Prince of this world, and the Kingdome of Christ was not thereof, who was the true and perfect image of his Father; neither, because man hath an immortall soule, and therein the faculties of Memorie, Vnderstanding, and Will, for the Deuils are also immortall, and participate those faculties, being called *Dæmones*, because *scientes* of Knowledge, and subtility; neither because we are reasonable creatures, by which we are distinguished from beasts: for who haue rebelled against God? who haue made Gods of the vilest beasts, of Serpents, of Cats, of Owles, yea euen of shamefull parts, of lusts and pleasures, but reasonable men? Yet doe I not condemne the opinion of S[t]. *Chrysostome* and *Ambrose*, as touching dominion, but that, in respect thereof, man was in some sort after the image of God, if we take Dominion, such as it ought to bee, that is, accompanied with iustice and pietie: for God did not only make man a ruler and Gouernour ouer the Fishes of the Sea, the Fowles of Heauen (or of the aire) and ouer the

Beasts of the field; but God gaue vnto man a dominion
ouer men, he appointed Kings to gouerne them, and Iudges,
to iudge them in equitie. Neither doe I exclude reason, as it
is the abilitie of vnderstanding. For I doe not conceiue, that
Irenæus did therefore call man, the image of God, because
hee was *animal rationale* only; but that he vnderstood it
better, with *Sybilla: Imago mea est homo, rectam rationem
habens, Man, that is endued with right reason, is said to
resemble God,* (that is) by right reason to know and confesse
God his Creatour, and the same God to serue, loue, and
obey: and therefore said S^t. *Augustine* (who herein came
nearer the truth) *fecit Deus hominem ad imaginem &
similitudinem suam in mente, God made man, in respect of the
intellect, after his owne image and similitude;* and *Reynerivs;
Homo, quòd habet mentem, factus est ad imaginem Dei, Man
was made after the image of God, in minde,* or *in that he had
a minde.*

§2. *Of the intellectuall minde of man, in which there is much
of the image of God: and that this image is much deformed
by sinne.*

But *Mens* is not taken here for *anima physica,* according to
Aristotle, which is *forma, vel natura hominis, The forme or
nature of man;* but this facultie or gift of God, called *Mens,*
is taken for *prima vis animi, the principall strength of the minde,*
or soule, *cuius actus est perpetua veritatis contemplatio; whose
act,* exercise, or office, *is the perpetuall contemplation of truth;*
and therefore it is also called *intellectus diuinus, intellectus
contemplatiuus, & anima contemplatiua, A diuine vnderstanding, and an intellect or minde contemplatiue. Est autem mens nos-
tra* (saith *Cvsanvs*) *vis comprehendendi, & totum virtuale ex
omnibus comprehendendi virtutibus compositum: Our intellectuall
minde* (saith he) *is a power of comprehending, euen the whole,
that is in this kinde powerfull, compounded of all the powers of
comprehension:* vnto which *Mercurius* attributeth so much (if
his meaning accompanie his wordes) that he esteemeth it to
be the very essence of God (which was also the errour of the
Manichees and others) and no otherwise separate from God

(saith he) then the light from the Sunne: for this *Mens* or vnderstanding (saith Mercurius) *est Deus in hominibus, Is God in men,* or rather (and which I take to be his meaning) is the image of God in man. For as the Sunne is not of the same essence or nature with the diuine light, but a body illightned, and an illumination created; so is this *Mens* or vnderstanding in men, not of the essence of Gods infinite vnderstanding, but a power and facultie of our soules the purest; or the *lumen animæ rationalis,* by the true and eternall light illightned. And this *Mens* others call *animam animæ, The soule of the soule,* or with S^t. *Augustine,* the eye of the soule, or receptacle of Sapience and diuine knowledge, *quæ amorem sapientiæ tanquàm ducem sequitur, Which followeth after the loue of sapience as her guide* (saith *Philo*) between which and reason, between which and the minde, called *anima,* betweene which and that power which the Latines call *animas,* there is this difference. Reason is that facultie by which we iudge and discourse; *Anima,* by which we liue. . . .

Howsoeuer the truth bee determined, wee must conclude, that it is neither in respect of reason alone, by which we discourse, nor in respect of the minde it selfe, by which we liue, nor in respect of our soules simply, by which we are immortall, that we are made after the image of God. But most safely may wee resemble our selues to God *in mente,* and in respect of that pure facultie which is neuer separate from the contemplation and loue of God. Yet this is not all. For S^t. *Bernard* maketh a true difference betweene the nature and faculties of the minde or Soule, and betweene the infusion of qualities, endowments and gifts of grace, wherewith it is adorned and enriched, which, being added to the nature, essence, and faculties, maketh it altogether to be after the image of God, whose words are these: *Non proptereà imago Dei est, quià sui meminit Mens, seque intelligit & diligit* (which was also the opinion of S. *Avgvstine*) *sed quia potest meminisse, intelligere ac diligere eum à quo facta est,* (that is) *The minde* (or *Mens*) *was not therefore the image of God, because it remembreth, vnderstandeth, and loueth it selfe, but because it can remember, understand, and loue God, who created it.* And, that this image may be deformed and made vnprofitable, heare *Basil*: *Homo ad imaginem & similitudinem Dei factus est, peccatum verò imaginis huius pulchritudinem deformauit, & inutilem reddidit, dum animam corruptis concupiscentiæ affectibus immersit, Man was made after the image and similitude of God, but Sinne hath deformed the beautie of this image, and made it vnprofitable by drawing our mindes into corrupt concupiscence.*

It is not therefore (as aforesaid) by reason of Immortalitie, nor in Reason, nor in Dominion, nor in any one of these by it selfe, nor in all these ioyned, by any of which, or by all which we resemble, or may be called the shadow of God, though by reason and vnderstanding, with the other faculties of the Soule, we are made capable of this print; but chiefly, in respect of the habit of Originall righteousnesse, most perfectly infused by God into the minde and Soule of man in his first creation. For it is not by nature, nor by her liberalitie, that wee were printed with the seale of Gods image (though Reason may be said to be of her gift, which ioyned to the Soule is a part of the essentiall constitution of our proper *Species*) but from the bountifull grace of the Lord of all goodnesse, who breathed life into earth, and contriued within the truncke of dust and clay, the inimitable habilitie of his owne iustice, pietie, and righteousnesse.

So long therefore (for that resemblance which Dominion hath) doe those that are powerfull retaine the image of God, as according to his Commandements they exercise the Office or Magistracie to which they are called, and sincerely walke in the waies of God, which in the Scriptures is called *walking with God*; and all other men so long retaine this image, as they feare, loue, and serue God, truly, (that is) for the loue of God alone, and doe not bruise and deface his seale by the waight of manifold and voluntarie offences, and obstinate sinnes. For the vniust minde cannot bee after the image of God, seeing God is iustice it selfe; The bloudthirstie hath it not; for God is charitie, and mercie it selfe: Falshood, cunning practise, and ambition, are properties of Sathan; and therefore cannot dwell in one soule, together with God; and to be short, there is no likelihood betweene pure light and blacke darkenesse, betweene beautie and deformitie, or betweene righteousnesse and reprobation. And though Nature, according to common vnderstanding,

haue made vs capable by the power of reason, and apt
enough to receiue this image of Gods goodnesse, which the
sensuall soules of beasts cannot perceiue; yet were that
aptitude naturall more inclinable to follow and imbrace the
false and durelesse pleasures of this stage-play world, then
to become the shadow of God by walking after him, had not
the exceeding workemanship of Gods wisedome, and the
liberalitie of his mercy, formed eyes to our soules, as to our
bodies, which, piercing through the impuritie of our flesh,
behold the highest heauens, and thence bring knowledge and
Obiect to the minde and Soule, to contemplate the euer-
during glorie, and termelesse ioy, prepared for those, which
retaine the image and similitude of their Creatour, pre-
seruing vndefiled and vnrent the garment of the new man,
which, after the image of God, is created in righteousnesse,
and true holinesse, as saith S^t. *Paul*. Now whereas it is
thought by some of the Fathers, as by S^t. *Augustine* with
whom S. *Ambrose* ioyneth, that, by sinne, the perfection of
the image is lost, and not the image it selfe; both opinions
by this distinction may be well reconciled (to wit) that the
image of God, in man, may be taken two waies; for either
it is considered, according to naturall gifts, and consisteth
therein: namely, to haue a reasonable and vnderstanding
nature, &c. and in this sense, the image of God is no more
lost by sinne, then the very reasonable or vnderstanding
nature, &c. is lost: (for sinne doth not abolish and take
away these naturall gifts) or, the image of God is considered,
according to supernaturall gifts, namely, of diuine grace,
and heauenly glorie, which is indeede the perfection and
accomplishment of the naturall image; and this manner of
similitude and image of God, is wholly blotted out and
destroyed by sinne.

§3. *Of our base and fraile bodies: and that the care thereof
should yeeld to the immortall Soule.*

§4. *Of the Spirit of life, which God breathed into man, in his
Creation.*

§5. *That Man is (as it were) a little world: with a digression touching our mortalitie.*

Man, thus compounded and formed by God, was an abstract or modell, or briefe Storie of the Vniuersall: in whom God concluded the creation, and worke of the world, and whom he made the last and most excellent of his creatures, being internally endued with a diuine vnderstanding, by which he might contemplate and serue his Creatour, after whose image he was formed, and endued with the powers and faculties of reason and other abilities, that thereby also he might gouerne and rule the world, and all other Gods creatures therein. And whereas God created three sorts of liuing natures, (to wit) Angelicall, Rationall, and Brutall; giuing to Angels an intellectuall, and to Beasts a sensuall nature, he vouchsafed vnto man, both the intellectuall of Angels, the sensitiue of Beasts, and the proper rationall belonging vnto man; and therefore (saith *Gregorie Nazianzene:) Homo est vtriusque naturæ vinculum, Man is the bond* and chaine *which tieth together both natures:* and because in the little frame of mans body there is a representation of the Vniuersall, and (by allusion) a kind of participation of all the parts thereof, therefore was man called *Microcosmos,* or the little world. *Deus igitur hominem factum, velut alterum quendam mundum, in breui magnum, atque exiguo totum, in terris statuit, God therefore placed in the earth the man whom he had made, as it were another world, the great and large world in the small and little world:* for out of earth and dust was formed the flesh of man, and therefore heauie and lumpish; the bones of his body we may compare to the hard rockes and stones, and therefore strong and durable: of which *Ouid:*

> *Inde genus durum sumus, experiensque laborum,*
> *Et documenta damus, qua simus origine nati.*

> From thence our kinde hard-hearted is, enduring paine and care,
> Approuing, that our bodies of a stonie nature are.[1]

His bloud, which disperseth it selfe by the branches of veines through all the bodie, may be resembled to those waters, which are carried by brookes and riuers ouer all the

[1] *Metamorphoses,* 1 414–15.

earth; his breath to the aire; his naturall heate to the
inclosed warmth, which the Earth hath in it selfe, which
stirred vp by the heate of the Sunne, assisteth Nature in the
speedier procreation of those varieties, which the Earth
bringeth forth; Our radicall moisture, oile, or Balsamum
(whereon the naturall heat feedeth and is maintained) is
resembled to the fat and fertilitie of the earth; the haires of
mans body, which adornes or ouershadowes it, to the grasse,
which couereth the vpper face and skin of the earth; our
generatiue power, to Nature, which produceth all things;
our determinations, to the light, wandring, and vnstable
clowds, carried euery where with vncertaine winds; our eies,
to the light of the Sunne and Moone, and the beauty of our
youth, to the flowers of the Spring, which, either in a very
short time, or with the Sunnes heat drie vp, & wither away,
or the fierce puffes of wind blow them from the stalks; the
thoughts of our minde, to the motion of Angels; and our
pure vnderstanding (formerly called *Mens,* and that which
alwaies looketh vpwards) to those intellectuall natures,
which are alwayes present with God; and lastly our immortal
soules (while they are righteous) are by God himselfe
beautified with the title of his own image and similitude:
And although, in respect of God, there is no man iust, or
good, or righteous: (for *in Angelis depræhensa est stultitia,*
Behold, he found folly in his Angels, saith *Iob*) yet with such a
kind of difference, as there is between the substance, and
the shadow, there may be found a goodnesse in man: which
God being pleased to accept, hath therefore called man, the
image and similitude of his owne righteousnes. In this also
is the little world of man compared, and made more like the
Vniuersall (man being the measure of all things; *Homo est*
mensura omnium rerum, saith *Aristotle* and *Pythagoras*) that
the foure complexions resemble the foure Elements, and
the seuen Ages of man the seuen Planets: Whereof our
Infancie is compared to the Moone, in which we seeme onely
to liue and growe, as Plants; the second age to *Mercurie,*
wherein we are taught and instructed; our third age to
Venus, the dayes of loue, desire, and vanitie; the fourth to
the *Sunne,* the strong, flourishing, and beautifull age of mans
life; the fifth to *Mars,* in which we seeke honour and

victorie, and in which our thoughts trauaile to ambitious
ends; the sixth age is ascribed to *Iupiter*, in which we begin
to take accompt of our times, iudge of our selues, and grow
to the perfection of our vnderstanding; the last and seuenth
to *Saturne*, wherein our dayes are sad and ouer-cast, and in
which wee finde by deere and lamentable experience, and
by the losse which can neuer be repaired, that of all our
vaine passions, and affections past, the sorrow onely abideth:
Our attendants are sicknesses, and variable infirmities; and
by how much the more we are accompanied with plentie, by
so much the more greedily is our end desired, whome when
Time hath made vnsociable to others, we become a burthen
to our selues: being of no other vse, then to hold the riches
we haue, from our successours. In this time it is when (as
aforesaid) we, for the most part, and neuer before, prepare
for our eternall habitation, which we passe on vnto, with
many sighes, grones, and sad thoughts, and in the end, by
the workemanship of death, finish the sorrowfull businesse
of a wretched life, towards which we always trauaile both
sleeping and waking: neither haue those beloued companions
of honour and riches any power at all, to hold vs any one day,
by the promises of glorious entertainments; but by what
crooked path so euer wee walke, the same leadeth on directly
to the house of death: whose doores lie open at all houres,
and to all persons. For this tide of mans life, after it once
turneth and declineth, euer runneth with a perpetuall ebbe
and falling streame, but neuer floweth againe: our leafe
once fallen, springeth no more, neither doth the Sunne or
the Summer adorne vs againe, with the garments of new
leaues and flowers.

> *Redditur arboribus florens reuirentibus ætas,*
> *Ergò non homini, quod fuit ante, redit.*

To which I giue this sense,

> The Plants and trees made poore and old
> By Winter enuious,
> The Spring-time bounteous
> Couers againe, from shame and cold:
> But neuer Man repair'd againe
> His youth and beautie lost,

> Though art, and care, and cost,
> Doe promise Natures helpe in vaine.[1]

And of which *Catvllvs*, Epigram 53.

> *Soles occidere & redire possunt:*
> *Nobis cùm semel occidit breuis lux,*
> *Nox est perpetua vna dormienda.*

> The Sunne may set and rise:
> But we contrariwise
> Sleepe after our short light
> One euerlasting night.[2]

For if there were any baiting place, or rest, in the course or race of mans life, then, according to the doctrine of the *Academickes*, the same might also perpetually bee maintained; but as there is a continuance of motion in naturall liuing things, and as the sappe and iuyce, wherein the life of Plants is preserued, doth euermore ascend or descend: so is it with the life of man, which is alwaies either encreasing towards ripenesse and perfection, or declining and decreasing towards rottennesse and dissolution.

§6. *Of the free power, which man had in his first creation, to dispose of himselfe.*

These be the miseries which our first Parents brought on all mankinde, vnto whom God in his creation gaue a free and vnconstrained will, and on whom he bestowed the liberall choice of all things, with one only prohibition, to trie his gratitude and obedience. God set before him, a mortall and immortall life, a nature celestiall and terrene, and (indeed) God gaue man to himselfe, to be his owne guide, his owne workeman, and his owne painter, that he might frame or describe vnto himselfe what hee pleased, and make election of his owne forme. *God made man in the beginning* (saith *Siracides*) *and left him in the hands of his own counsaile.* Such was the liberalitie of God, and mans felicitie: whereas beasts, and all other creatures reasonlesse brought with them into the world (saith *Lucilius*) and that euen when they first fell

---

[1] Albinovanus, *Elegia II in obitum Mæcenatis*, 113–14.
[2] *Carmina*, v 4–6.

from the bodies of their Dammes, the nature, which they
could not change; and the supernall spirits or Angels were
from the beginning, or soone after, of that condition, in
which they remaine in perpetuall eternitie. But (as aforesaid)
God gaue vnto man all kinde of seedes and grafts of life,
(to wit) the vegetatiue life of Plants, the sensuall of beastes,
the rationall of man, and the intellectuall of Angels, whereof
which soeuer he tooke pleasure to plant and cultiue, the
same should futurely grow in him, and bring forth fruit,
agreable to his owne choyce and plantation. This freedome
of the first man *Adam*, and our first Father, was ænigmatically
described by *Asclepius Atheniensis* (saith *Mirandula*) in the
person and fable of *Proteus*, who was said, as often as hee
pleased, to change his shape. To the same end were all those
celebrated *Metamorphoses* among the Pythagorians, and
ancient Poets, wherein it was fained, that men were trans-
formed into diuers shapes of beasts, thereby to shew the
change of mens conditions, from reason to brutalitie, from
vertue to vice, from meekenesse to crueltie, and from iustice
to oppression. For by the liuely image of other creatures did
those *Ancients* represent the variable passions, and affections
of mortall men; as by Serpents were signified deceiuers; by
Lions, oppressours, and cruell men; by swine, men giuen
ouer to lust and sensualitie; by wolues, rauening and greedy
men; which also S. *Matthew* resembleth to false Prophets,
*which come to you in sheepes clothing, but inwardly they are
rauening Wolues*, by the images of stones and stockes,
foolish and ignorant men, by Vipers, vngratefull men: of
which Saint *Iohn Baptist*, *O yee generation of vipers, &c.*

§7. *Of Gods ceasing to create any more: and of the cause
thereof, because the Vniuersall created was exceeding good.*

In this worke of man God finished the creation; not that God
laboured as a man, and therefore rested: for God commanded
and it was finished, *Cui voluisse est fecisse*, *with whom, to will
is to make*, saith *Beda*. Neither did God so rest, that hee
left the world made, and the creatures therein to themselues:
for *my father worketh to this day* (saith *Christ*) *and I worke;*

but God rested, (that is) he created no new *species* or kinds of creatures, but (as aforesaid) gaue vnto man a power generatiue, and so to the rest of liuing creatures, and to Plants and flowers their seedes in themselues; and commanded man to multiply and fill the earth, and the earth and Sea to bring forth creatures according to their seuerall kinds: all which being finished, God saw that his workes were good; not that he fore-knew not, and comprehended not the beginning and end before they were; for God made euery Plant of the field before it was in the earth, but he gaue to all things which he had created the name of good, thereby to teach men, that from so good a God there was nothing made, but that which was perfect good, and from whose simple puritie and from so excellent a cause, there could proceede no impure or imperfect effect. For man hauing a free will and liberall choyce, purchased by disobedience his owne death and mortalitie, and for the crueltie of mans heart, was the earth afterward cursed, and all creatures of the first age destroied: but the righteous man *Noah*, and his familie, with those creatures which the Arke contained, reserued by God to replenish the earth.

Ch. III. *Of the place of Paradise*

§1. *That the seate of Paradise is greatly mistaken: and that it is no maruaile that men should erre.*

§2. *A recitall of strange opinions, touching Paradise.*

§3. *That there was a true locall Paradise Eastward, in the Countrie of Eden.*

To the first therefore, that such a place there was vpon the earth, the words of *Moses* make it manifest, where it is written. *And the Lord God planted a garden Eastward in*

Eden, and there he put the man whom he had made. And how-soeuer the vulgar translation, called *Hieromes* translation, hath conuerted this place thus, *Plantauerat Dominus Deus Paradisum voluptatis à principio*; *The Lord God planted a Paradise of pleasure from the beginning*; putting the word (*pleasure*) for *Eden*, and (*from the beginning*) for Eastward: It is manifest, that in this place *Eden* is the proper name of a Region. For what sense hath this translation (saith our *Hopkins*, in his Treatise of *Paradise*) that he planted a garden in pleasure, or that a Riuer went out of pleasure to water the garden? But the seuentie Interpreters call it *Paradisum Edenis*, the *Paradise of Eden*, and so doth the *Chaldæan Paraphrast* truly take it for the proper name of a place, and for a Nowne appellatiue; which Region, in respect of the fertilitie of the soile, of the many beautifull riuers, and goodly woods, and that the trees (as in the *Indies*) doe alwaies keep their leaues, was called *Eden*, which signifieth in the *Hebrew*, pleasantnesse or delicacie, as the *Spaniards* call the Countrie, opposite to the *Isle of Cuba*, *Florida:* and this is the mistaking, which may end the dispute, as touching the double sense of the word, that as *Florida* was a Countrie, so called for the flourishing beautie thereof, so was *Eden* a Region called pleasure, or delicacie, for the pleasure, or delicacie: and as *Florida* signifieth flourishing: so *Eden* signifieth pleasure, and yet both are the proper names of Countries; for *Eden* being the proper name of a Region (called Pleasure in the *Hebrew*) and *Paradise* being the choice seat of all that Region, *Paradise* was truly the Garden of *Eden*, and truly the Garden of pleasure. . . .[1]

§4. *Why it should be needfull to intreate diligently of the place of Paradise.*

§5. *That the floud hath not vtterly defaced the markes of Paradise . . .*

[1] Ralegh's firm insistence on the primacy of the literal meaning – in itself entirely traditional – is the core of the present chapter. The paragraphs here omitted consist largely of the usual invocation of authorities to support the stated thesis.

§6. *That Paradise was not the whole earth, as some haue thought . . .*

§7. *Of their opinion, which make Paradise as high as the Moone . . .*

§8. *Of their opinion that seate Paradise under the Æquinoctiall . . .*

§9. *Of the change of the names of places . . .*

§10. *Of diuers other testimonies of the land of Eden . . .*

§11. *Of the difficultie in the Text, which seemeth to make the foure riuers to rise from one streame.*

§12. *Of the strange fertilitie and happinesse of the Babylonian soile, as it is certaine that Eden was such.*

§13. *Of the Riuer Pison, and the land of Hauilah.*

§14. *Of the Riuer Gehon and the land of Cush . . .*

§15. *A conclusion by way of repetition of some things spoken of before.*

But now to conclude this dispute, it appeareth to me by the testimonies of the Scriptures, that *Paradise* was a place created by God, and a part of this our earth and habitable world, seated in the lower part of the Region of *Eden*, afterward called *Aram fluuiorum*, or *Mesopotamia*, which taketh into it also a portion of *Shinar* and *Armenia*: this Region standing in the most excellent temper of all other, (to wit) 35 degrees from the *Aequinoctiall*, and 55 from the North pole: in which Climate the most excellent wines, fruites, oyle, graine of all sorts are to this day found in abundance. And there is nothing that better proueth the excellencie of this sayd soile and temper, then the abundant growing of the Palme-trees, without the care and labour of man. For wherein soeuer the Earth, Nature, and the Sunne

can most vaunt, that they haue excelled, yet shall this Plant
be the greatest wonder of all their works: this tree alone
giueth vnto man whatsoeuer his life beggeth at Natures
hand. And though it may be sayd, that these trees are
found both in the East and West *Indies*, which Countries
are also blessed with a perpetuall Spring and Summer, yet
lay downe by those pleasures and benefits the fearefull and
dangerous thunders and lightnings, the horrible and
frequent Earthquakes, the dangerous diseases, the multitude
of venimous beasts and wormes, with other inconueniences,
and then there will be found no comparison betweene the
one and the other.

What other excellencies this garden of *Paradise* had,
before God, (for mans ingratitude and crueltie,) cursed the
earth, we cannot iudge; but I may safely thinke, that by how
much *Adam* exceeded all liuing men in perfection, by being
the immediate workemanship of God, by so much did that
chosen and particular garden exceede all parts of the
Vniuersall world, in which God had planted (that is) made
to grow the trees, of Life, of Knowledge; Plants only
proper, and becomming the *Paradise*, and Garden of so
great a Lord. . . .

Ch. IV. *Of the two chiefe Trees in the Garden of Paradise*

§1. *That the tree of Life was a materiall tree: and in what
sense it is to be taken, that man by his eating the forbidden
fruit, is made subiect to death.*

For eating the forbidden fruit of the Tree of Knowledge
was *Adam* driuen out of *Paradise, in exilium vitæ temporalis,
into the banishment of temporall life,* saith *Beda.* That these
trees of Life and Knowledge were materiall trees (though
Figures of the Law and of the Gospell) it is not doubted by

the most religious and learned writers: although the wits of men, which are so volatile, as nothing can fixe them, and so slipperie, as nothing can fasten them, haue in this also deliuered to the world an imaginarie doctrine.

The tree of Life (say the Hebrewes) hath a plurall construction, and is to be vnderstood, *Lignum vitarum*, *The tree of liues*, because the fruit thereof had a propertie, to preserue both the growing, sensitiue, and rationall life of man; and not only (but for *Adams* transgression) had prolonged his owne dayes, but also giuen a durefull continuance to all posteritie; and that, so long, as a bodie compounded of Elements could last.

And although it is hard to thinke, that flesh and bloud could be immortall, but that it must once perish and rot, by the vnchanged law of God imposed on his creatures, Man (notwithstanding) should haue enioyed thereby a long, healthfull, and vngrieued life: after which (according to the opinion of most Diuines) he should haue beene translated, as *Enoch* was. And as before the floud, the daies of men had the long measure of eight hundred or nine hundred yeares; and soone after the floud of two hundred yeares and vpwards euen to fiue hundred: so if *Adam* had not disobeyed Gods first and easie Commandement, the liues of men on earth might haue continued double, treble, or quadruple to any of the longest times of the first age, as many learned men haue conceiued. *Chrysostome*, *Rupertus*, *Tostatus*, and others were of beliefe, that (but for *Adams* fall and transgression) *Adam* and his posteritie had beene immortall. But such is the infinite wisedome of God, as he foresaw that the Earth could not haue contained mankinde; or else, that Millions of soules must haue been vngenerated, and haue had no being, if the first number, wherewith the Earth was replenished, had abode thereon for euer: and therefore that of *Chrysostome* must be vnderstood of immortalitie of bodies, which should haue beene translated and glorified.

But of what kinde or *Species* this tree of Life was, no man hath taken on him to teach: in which respect many haue conceiued, that the same was not materiall, but a meere *Allegorie*, taking their strength out of *Salomon*, where Wisedome is compared to the Tree of Life, and from other places, where also *Christ* is called the Tree of Life, and out of the *Apocalypsis, I will giue to him that ouercommeth, to eate of the Tree of life, which is in the Paradise of God.* But to this place S^t. *Augustines* answere may suffice, (which is) That the one doth not exclude the other, but that, as there was a terrestriall *Paradise,* so there was a celestiall. For although *Agar* and *Sara* were Figures of the *Old,* and *New Testament,* yet to thinke that they were not Women, and the maide and wife of *Abraham,* were meere foolishnesse. And so in this place the sense of the Scripture is manifest. *For God brought out of the earth euery tree faire to sight, and sweet to taste; the tree also of life in the midst of the garden:* which sheweth, that among the trees, which the Earth by Gods commandement produced, the tree of Life was one, and that the fruit thereof was also to be eaten. The report of this Tree was also brought to the ancient Poets: for as from the indigested matter or *Chaos, Hesiodus, Homer, Ouid,* and others steale the inuention of the created world; so from the Garden of *Paradise,* they tooke the Plat-forme of the Orchard of *Alcinous,* and another of the *Hesperides:* and from the tree of Life, their *Nectar* and *Ambrosia;* for *Nectar,* according to *Suidas,* signifieth *making young,* and *Ambrosia, immortalitie;* and therefore said to be the meate and drinke of the Gods.

§2. *Of* Becanvs *his opinion that the Tree of Knowledge was* Ficus Indica.

Now for the Tree of Knowledge of good and euill, some men haue presumed farther, especially *Goropius Becanus,* who giueth himselfe the honour to haue found out that kind of this Tree, which none of the Writers of former times could euer ghesse at, whereat *Goropius* much maruaileth. But as he had an inuentiue braine, so there neuer liued any man, that beleeued better thereof, and of himselfe. Surely howsoeuer his opinion may be valued, yet he vsurpeth the praise due to others, at least if the inuention be at that price at which he setteth it. For *Moses Bar-cephas* fastened on this coniecture aboue six hundred yeares before *Becanus* was borne: and *Bar-cephas* himselfe refereth the inuention to an antiquitie more remote, citing for his Authour *Philoxenus Maburgensis*, and others, whose very wordes *Goropius* vseth, both concerning the Tree, and the reasons wherewith he would induce other men to that beliefe. For *Moses Bar-cephas* in his Treatise of *Paradise* (the first Part and *fol.* 49.) saith, That the Tree of Knowledge was *Ficus Indica, the Indian Fig-tree,* of which the greatest plentie (saith *Becanus*) are found vpon the bankes of *Acesines,* one of the Riuers which falleth into *Indus,* where *Alexander* built his Fleet of Gallies in, or neare the Kingdome of *Porus.*

This Tree[1] beareth a fruit of the bignesse of a great peaze, or (as *Plinie* reporteth) somewhat bigger, and that it is a tree *se semper serens, alwaies planting it selfe;* that it spreadeth it selfe so farre abroade, as that a troupe of horsemen may hide themselues vnder it. *Strabo* saith, that it hath branches bending downewards, and leaues no lesse then a shield. *Aristobulus* affirmeth that fiftie horsemen may shadow themselues vnder one of these trees. *Onesicritus* raiseth this number to foure hundred. This tree (saith *Theophrastus*) exceedeth all other in bignesse, which also *Plinie* and *Onesicritus* confirme: to the truncke of which these Authours giue such a magnitude as I shame to repeate. But it may be, they all speake by an ill-vnderstood report. For this *Indian* Fig-tree is not so rare a Plant, as *Becanus* conceiueth, who because he found it no where else, would needes draw the garden of *Paradise* to the Tree, and set it by the riuer *Acesines.* But many parts of the world haue them, and I my selfe haue seene twentie thousand of them in one Valley, not farre from *Paria* in *America.* They grow in moist grounds, and in this manner. After they are first shot vp some twentie or thirtie foote in length, (some more, some lesse, according to the soile) they spread a very large toppe, hauing no bough nor twigge in the truncke or stemme: for from the vtmost end of the head branches there issueth out a gummie iuyce, which hangeth downeward like a cord or sinnew, and within a few Moneths reacheth the ground; which it no sooner toucheth but it taketh roote, and then being filled both from the toppe boughes, and from his owne

---

[1] The account here may be compared with Milton's version, quoted above, p. 38.

proper roote, this corde maketh it selfe a Tree exceeding
hastily. From the vtmost boughes of these young trees there
fall againe the like cordes, which in one yeare and lesse (in
that world of a perpetuall spring) become also trees of the
bignesse of the nether part of a launce, and as straight, as
art or nature can make anything, casting such a shade, and
making such a kinde of groue, as no other Tree in the world
can doe. Now one of these trees considered with all his
young ones may (indeede) shrowde foure hundred or foure
thousand horsemen, if they please; for they couer whole
vallies of ground where these Trees grow neare the Sea-
banke, as they doe by thousands in the inner part of
Trinidado. The cordes which fall downe ouer the bankes into
the Sea, shooting alway downeward to finde roote vnder
water, are in those Seas of the *Indies*, where Oisters breed,
intangled in their beddes, so as by pulling vp one of these
cordes out of the Sea, I haue seene fiue hundred Oysters
hanging in a heape thereon; whereof the report came, that
Oysters grew on trees in India. But that they beare any such
huge leaues, or any such delicate fruit I could neuer finde,
and yet I haue trauailed a dozen miles together vnder them:
but to returne to *Goropius Becanus*. This tree (saith he) was
good for meate and pleasing to the sight, as the tree of
Knowledge of good and euill is described to be.

Secondly, this tree hauing so huge a truncke (as the
former Authours report, and *Becanus* beleeueth) it was in
this tree that *Adam* and *Eue* hidde themselues from the
presence of God, for no other tree (saith he) could containe
them. But first it is certaine, that this Tree hath no extraordinarie magnitude, as touching the trunke or stemme, for
among ten thousand of them it is hard to finde any one
bigger then the rest, and these are all but of a meane size.
Secondly, the wordes of *Moses* translated *in medio ligni*, are
by all the intepreters vnderstood in the plurall number,
(that is) *in the middest of the trees*. But his third argument (or
rather the argument of *Moses Bar-cephas*, word for word) is,
that when *Adam* and *Eue* found themselues naked, they
made them breeches of Fig-leaues; which proueth (indeede)
that either the tree it selfe was a Fig-tree, or that a Fig-tree
grew neare it: because *Adam* being possest with shame did

not runne vp and downe the garden to seeke out leaues to couer him, but found them in the place it selfe; and these leaues of all other were most commodious by reason of their largenesse, which *Plinie* auoweth in these wordes; *Latitudo foliorum peltæ effigiem Amazoniæ habet, The breadth of the leaues hath the shape of an Amazonian shield:* which also *Theophrast* confirmeth; the forme of which Targets *Virgil* toucheth:

> *Ducit Amazonidum lunatis agmina peltis*
> *Penthesilæa furens.*
>
> The Amazons with Crescent-formed shield
> Penthesilæa leades into the field.[1]

Here *Becanus* desireth to be beleeued, or rather threatneth vs all that reade him, to giue credit to this his borrowed discouerie, vsing this confident (or rather cholericke) speech. *Quis erit tam impudenter obstinatus, si hæc à nobis de ficu hac ex antiquis scriptoribus cum* Mosis *narratione comparet, vt audeat dicere aliam arborem inueniri posse, quæ cum illa magis quadret, Who will be so impudently obstinate, if he compare these thinges which we haue reported of this Fig-tree, and out of ancient Writers deliuered, with the narration of* Moses, *as to dare to auow, that any other tree can be found, which doth more properly answere, or agree therewith.* But for my selfe, because I neither find this tree, sorting in body, in largenesee of leaues, nor in fruit to this report, I rather incline to the opinion of *Philo:* That the Earth neuer brought forth any of these trees neither before nor after; but I leaue euery man to his owne beleefe, for the matter is of no great weight as touching his kinde: only thereby, and by the easie Commandement by God giuen to *Adam*, to forbeare to feede thereon, it pleased God to make triall of his obedience: *Prohibita, non propter aliud, quàm ad commendandum puræ ac simplicis Obedientiæ bonum, Being forbidden, not for any other respect, then thereby to commend the goodnesse of pure and simple Obedience.*

[1] *Aeneid*, 1 490–91.

§3. *Of Becanvs his not vnwittie allegorizing of the Storie of his*
Ficus Indica.

But in this I must doe *Becanus* right, that he hath very
wittily allegorized this tree, allowing his supposition of the
Tree it selfe to be true. The effects whereof, because his
discourses are exceeding ample, I haue gathered in these
few wordes. As this Tree (saith he) so did Man, grow
straight and vpright towards God, vntill such time as hee
had transgressed and broken the Commandement of his
Creatour; and then like vnto the boughes of this tree, he
beganne to bend downeward, and stouped toward the earth,
which all the rest of *Adams* posteritie after him haue done,
rooting themselues therein, and fastning themselues to this
corrupt world. The exceeding vmbragiousnesse of this tree
he compareth to the darke and shadowed life of man,
through which the Sunne of iustice being not able to pierce,
we haue all remained in the shadow of death, till it pleased
Christ to climbe the tree of the Crosse for our enlightning
and redemption. The little fruit which it beareth, and which
is hard to finde among so many large leaues, may be compared (saith he) to the little vertue, and vnperceiued knowledge among so large vanities, which obscure and shadow
it ouer. And as this fruit is exceeding sweet, and delicate to
the taste and palate, so are the delights and pleasures of the
world, most pleasing while they dure. But as all those thinges
which are most mellifluous, are soonest changed into choller
and bitternesse: so are our vanities and pleasures conuerted
into the bitterest sorrowes and repentances. That the
leaues are so exceeding large, the fruit (for such leaues)
exceeding little, in this, by comparison we behold (saith he)
the many cares and great labours of worldly men, their
sollicitude, their outward shewes, and publike ostentation,
their apparent pride and large vanities; and if we seeke for
the fruit, which ought to be their vertuous and pious actions,
we find it of the bignesse of the smallest peaze; glorie, to all
the world apparent; goodnesse, to all the world inuisible.
And furthermore, as the leaues, bodie, and boughes of this
tree, by so much exceede all other Plants, as the greatest
men of power and worldly abilitie surpasse the meanest: so

is the little fruit of such men, and such trees, rather fitting and becomming the vnworthiest shrubbe, and humblest bryar, or the poorest and basest man, then such a flourishing statelinesse, and magnitude. Lastly, whereas *Adam*, after he had disobayed God, and beheld his owne nakednesse and shame, sought for leaues to couer himselfe withall, this may serue to put vs in minde of his and our sinnes, as often as we put on our garments, to couer and adorne our rotten and mortall bodies: to pamper and maintaine which wee vse so many vncharitable and cruell practises in this world.

§4. *Of the name of the tree of Knowledge of good and euill: with some other notes touching the Storie of* Adams *sinne.*

Now, as touching the sense of this tree of Knowledge of good and euill, and what operation the fruit thereof had, and as touching the propertie of the Tree it selfe, *Moses Barcephas* an ancient *Syrian* Doctor (translated by *Masius*) giueth this iudgement: That the fruit of this tree had no such vertue or qualitie, as that by the tasting thereof, there was any such knowledge created in *Adam*, as if he had beene ignorant before; but as *Iunius* also noteth, *Arbor scientiæ boni & mali (id est) experientiæ boni & mali ab euentu, The Tree of Knowledge of good and euill (that is) the experience of good and euill by the euent.* For thus much we may conceiue, that *Adam* being made (according to the Hebrew phrase) by the workemanship of Gods owne hand, in greater perfection then euer any man was produced by generation, being (as it were) the created plant, out of whose seede all men liuing haue growne vp; and hauing receiued immortalitie from the breath or spirit of God, he could not (for these respects) be ignorant, that the disobaying of Gods commandement was the fearfullest euill, and the obseruation of his precepts the happiest good. But as men in perfect health doe (notwithstanding) conceiue, that sicknesse is grieuous, and yet in no such degree of torment, as by the suffering and experience in themselues they afterwards witnesse: so was it with *Adam*, who could not be ignorant of the punishments, due to neglect and disobedience; and yet felt by the proofe thereof in himselfe another terrour then he had forethought, or could imagine. For looking into the glasse of his owne guiltie soule, he beheld therein the horrour of Gods iudgements, so as he then knew, he feelingly knew, and had triall of the late good, which could not be prized, and of the new purchased euill, which could not be exprest. He then saw himselfe naked both in bodie and minde; that is, depriued of Gods grace and former felicitie: and therefore was this tree called the tree of Knowledge, and not because the fruit thereof had any such operation, by any selfe qualitie or effect: for the same phrase is vsed in many places of the Scriptures, and names are giuen to Signes and Sacraments, as to acts performed, and thinges done. In such sort as this tree was called the tree of Knowledge, by cause of the euent. . . .

But *Adam* being both betrayed and maistered by his affections, ambitious of a farther knowledge then he had perceiued in himselfe, and looking but slightly (as all his issues doe) into the miseries and sorrowes incident, and greatly affecting the supposed glorie which he might obtaine by tasting the fruit forbidden, he was transported and blowne forward by the gentle winde of pleasing perswasions vnawares; his progression being strengthened by the subtile arguments of *Sathan*, who laboured to poyson mankinde in the very roote, which he moistned with the liquor of the same ambition, by which himselfe perished for euer.

But what meanes did the Deuill finde out, or what instruments did his owne subtletie present him, as fittest and aptest to worke this mischiefe by? euen the vnquiet vanitie of the woman; so as by *Adams* hearkening to the voice of his wife, contrarie to the expresse commandement of the liuing God, Mankind by that her incantation became the subiect of labour, sorrow, and death: the woman being giuen to man for a comforter and companion, but not for a Counsellour. *But because thou hast obayed the voice of thy wife, &c.* (said God himselfe) *Cursed is the earth for thy sake, in sorrow shalt thou eate of it all thy life.* It is also to be noted, by whom the woman was tempted; euen by the most vgley and unworthy of all beasts, into whom the Deuill entred and perswaded.

Secondly, what was the motiue of her disobedience: euen a desire to know what was most vnfitting her knowledge, an affection which hath euer since remained in all the posteritie of her Sexe. Thirdly, what was it that moued the man to yeeld to her perswasions? euen the same cause which hath moued all men since to the like consent, namely an vnwillingnesse to grieue her and make her sadde, least she should pine and be ouercome with sorrow. But if *Adam* in the state of perfection, and *Salomon* the sonne of *Dauid* Gods chosen seruant, and himselfe a man endued with the greatest wisedome, did both of them disobay their Creatour, by the perswasion and for the loue they bare to a woman, it is not so wonderfull as lamentable, that other men in succeeding ages haue beene allured to so many inconuenient and wicked practises by the perswasions of their wiues, or other beloued Darlings, who couer ouer and shadow many malicious purposes with a counterfait passion of dissimulate sorrow and vnquietnesse.

Ch. V. *Of diuers memorable things betweene the fall of* Adam, *and the floud of* Noah

§1. *Of the cause and the reuenge of* Cains *sinne* . . .

§2. *Of* Cains *dwelling in the Land of* Nod . . .

§3. *Of* Moses *his omitting sundry things concerning* Cains *generation.*

§4. *Of the diuersities in the ages of the Patriarchs* . . .

§5. *Of the long liues of the Patriarchs: and some of late memorie.*

. . . if we seeke for a cause of this long life in nature, then is it reasonable, that the first man, created in highest perfection, should also beget children of equall strength or little differing: for of the first and purest seede there must of necessitie spring vp the fairest and fruitfullest Plants. Secondly, the earth it selfe was then much lesse corrupt, which yeelded her increase, and brought forth fruit and foode for man, without any such mixture of harmefull qualitie, as since that time the curse of God for the crueltie of mans heart brought on it and mankinde: Neither had the waters of the floud infused such an impuritie, as thereby the naturall and powerfull operation of all Plants, Hearbes, and fruits vpon the earth receiued a qualification and harmefull change. And as all things vnder the Sunne haue one time of strength, and another of weakenesse, a youth and beautie, and then age and deformitie: so Time it selfe (vnder the deathfull shade of whose winges all things decay and wither) hath wasted and worne out that liuely vertue of Nature in Man, and Beasts, and Plants; yea the Heauens themselues being of a most pure and cleansed matter shall waxe old as a garment; and then much more the power generatiue in inferiour Creatures, who by the ordinance of God receiue operatiue vertue from the superiour.[1]

But besides the old age of the world, how farre doth our education and simplicitie of liuing differ from that old time? the tender bringing vp of children, first fedde and nourished with the milke of a strange Dugge; an vnnaturall curiositie hauing taught all women (but the begger) to finde out Nurses, which necessitie only ought to commend vnto them: The hastie marriages in tender yeares, wherein, Nature being but yet greene and growing, we rent from her and replant her branches, while her selfe hath not yet any roote sufficient to maintaine her owne toppe; and such halfe-ripe seedes (for the most part) in their growing vp wither in the

[1] Ralegh's espousal of nature's decay is placed within context of the controversy then in progress by Victor Harris, *All Coherence Gone* (Chicago, 1949) esp. pp. 133 f.

budde, and waxe old euen in their infancie. But aboue all things the exceeding luxuriousnesse of this gluttonous age, wherein we presse nature with ouerwaightie burdens, and finding her strength defectiue we take the worke out of her hands, and commit it to the artificiall helpe of strong waters, hot spices, and prouoking sawces; of which *Lucan* hath these elegant Verses.

O prodiga rerum
Luxuries, nunquam paruo contenta paratu:
Et quæsitorum terra pelagoque ciborum
Ambitiosa fames, & lautæ gloria mensæ,
Discite quàm paruo liceat producere vitam:
Et quantum Natura petat.
Non auro myrrhâque bibunt: sed gurgite puro
Vita redit: satis est populis fluuiusque Ceresque.

O wastfull Riot, neuer vvell content
With low-priz'd fare; hunger ambitious
Of cates by land and sea farre fetcht and sent;
Vaine glorie of a table sumptuous,
Learne vvith how little life may be preserued.
In Gold and Myrrhe they neede not to carrouse,
But vvith the brooke the peoples thirst is serued:
Who fedde vvith bread and vvater are not sterued....[1]

§6. *Of the Patriarchs deliuering their knowledge by Tradition* ...

§7. *Of the men of renowne before the floud.*

§8. *That the Giants by* Moses *so called were indeede men of huge bodies* ...

[1] *Pharsalia,* iv 373–8, 380–81.

Ch. VI. *Of idolatrous corruptions, quickly rising, and hardly at length vanishing in the world: and of the Reliques of Truth touching these ancient times, obscurely appearing in fables and old Legends*

§1. *That in old corruptions we may finde some signes of more ancient truth.*

Here before we proceede any further, the occasion offereth it selfe for vs to consider, how the Greekes and other more ancient Nations, by fabulous inuentions, and by breaking into parts the Storie of the Creation, and by deliuering it ouer in a mysticall sense, wrapping it vp mixed with other their owne trumperie, haue sought to obscure the truth thereof; and haue hoped, that after-ages, being thereby brought into many doubts, might receiue those intermixt discourses of God and Nature for the inuentions of Poets and Philosophers, and not as any thing borrowed or stolne out of the bookes of God. But as a skilfull and learned *Chymist* can aswell by separation of visible elements draw helpfull medicines out of poyson, as poyson out of the most healthfull hearbs and plants (all things hauing in themselues both life and death) so, contrarie to the purposes and hopes of the Heathen, may those which seeke after God and Truth finde out euery where, and in all the ancient Poets and Philosophers, the Storie of the first Age, with all the workes and maruailes thereof, amply and liuely exprest.

§2. *That the corruptions themselues were very ancient: as in the familie of* Noah, *and in the old* Ægyptians.

But this defection and falling away from God, which was first found in Angels, and afterwards in Men (the one hauing erred but once, the other euer) as concerning man-kinde it tooke such effect, that thereby (the liberall grace of God being withdrawne) all the posteritie of our first Parents were afterwards borne and bred in a world, suffering a perpetuall Eclipse of spirituall light. Hence it was that it produced plants of such imperfection and harmefull qualitie, as the waters of the generall floud could not so wash out or depure, but that the same defection hath had continuance in the very generation and nature of mankinde. Yea, euen among the few sonnes of *Noah* there were found strong effects of the former poyson. For as the children of *Sem* did inherit the vertues of *Seth*, *Enoch*, and *Noah*; so the sonnes of *Cham* did possesse the vices of the sonnes of *Cain*, and of those wicked Giants of the first Age. Whence the *Chaldæans* beganne soone after the floud to ascribe diuine power and honour to the creature, which was only due to the Creatour. First, they worshipped the Sunne, and then the fire. So the *Ægyptians* and *Phœnicians* did not only learne to leaue the true God, but created twelue seuerall Gods, and diuine powers, whom they worshipped; and vnto whom they built Altars and Temples.

§3. *That in processe of time these lesser errours drew on greater: as appeareth in the grosse superstitions of the* Ægyptians.

But as men once fallen away from vndoubted truth, doe then after wander for euermore in vices vnknowne, and daylie trauaile towards their eternall perdition: so did these grosse and blinde Idolaters euery age after other descend lower and lower, and shrinke and slide downewards from the knowledge of one true and very God; and did not thereby erre in worshipping mortall men only, but they gaue diuine reuerence, and had the same respect to Beasts, Birds, Fishes, Fowles, Winds, Earth, Water, Ayre, Fire, to the Morning,

to the Euening, to Plants, Trees and Rootes, to Passions and
Affections of the minde, to Palenesse, Sicknesse, Sorrowes,
yea to the most vnworthy and basest of all these. Which
barbarous blasphemie *Rhodius Anaxandrides* derideth in this
manner.

> *Bouem colis, ego Deis macto bouem.*
> *Tu maximum Anguillam Deum putas: ego*
> *Obsoniorum credidi suauissimum.*
> *Carnes suillas tu caues, at gaudeo*
> *Hijs maximè: canem colis, quem verbero*
> *Edentem vbi deprehendo fortè obsonium.*

> I sacrifice to God the Beefe, which you adore.
> I broile the Ægyptian Eeles, which you (as God) implore:
> You feare to eate the flesh of Swine, I finde it sweet.
> You worship Dogs, to beate them I thinke meete,
> When they my store deuoure.[1]

And in this manner *Ivvenal*.

> *Porrum aut cæpe nefas violare aut frangere morsu:*
> *O sanctas gentes, quibus hæc nascuntur in hortis*
> *Numina!*

> The Ægyptians thinke it sinne to root vp, or to bite
> Their Leekes or Onyons, which they serue with holy rite:
> O happie Nations, which of their owne sowing
> Haue store of Gods in euery garden growing.[2]

§4. *That from the reliques of ancient records among the
Ægyptians and others, the first Idols and fables were
inuented: and that the first* Ivpiter *was* Cain, Vvlcan,
Tvbalcain, *&c.*

But in so great a confusion of vanities, where among the
Heathens themselues there is no agreement or certaintie, it
were hard to find out from what example the beginnings of
these inuentions were borowed or after what ancient patterne
they erected their building, were it not certaine, that the

---

[1] Quoted from Natalis Comes (Noël Conti), *Mythologiæ sive explicationis
fabvlarvm libri decem*, Bk I, Ch. vii. I consulted a later edition (Passau,
1616) p. 6.
[2] Juvenal, xv 9–11.

Ægyptians had knowledge of the first Age, and of whatsoeuer was done therein, partly from some inscriptions vpon stone or mettall remayning after the floud, and partly from *Mizraim* the sonne of *Cham*, who had learnt the same of *Cham*, and *Cham* of his father *Noah*. For all that the *Ægyptians* write of their ancient Kings and date of times cannot be fained. And though other Nations after them had by imitation their *Iupiters* also, their *Saturnes*, *Vulcans*, and *Mercuries* with the rest which S^t. *Augustine* out of *Varro*; *Eusebius* out of many prophane Historians; *Cicero*, *Diodorus Siculus*, *Arnobius*, and many more haue obserued, to wit, the *Phœnicians*, *Phrygians*, *Cretians*, *Greekes*, and other Nations; yet was *Cain* the sonne of *Adam* (as some very learned men conceiue) called and reputed for the first and ancient *Iupiter*; and *Adam* for the first *Saturne*: for *Iupiter* was said to haue inuented the founding of Citties; and the first Cittie of the world was built by *Cain*, which he called *Enoch*, of whom were the *Henochij* before remembred. And so much may be gathered out of *Plato* in *Protagoras*, which also *Higinus* in his 275. chapter confirmeth. For besides that, many Citties were founded by diuers men, *Tamen primam latissimam à primo et antiquissimo Ioue ædificatam. Yet the first and largest was built by the first and most ancient* Ivpiter, seated in the East parts, or in *India*, according to that of *Moses*: *And Cain dwelt towardes the East side of Eden &c.* where also the *Henochij* were found after the floud. And therefore was *Iupiter* by the *Athenians* called *Polieus*, a Founder of Citties, and *Herceios*, an Incloser or strengthener of Citties; (say *Phornutus* and *Pausanias*) and that to *Iupiter Herceios* there were in very many places Altars and Temples erected. And that there were Citties built before the floud. *Plato* also witnesseth, as may be gathered in this his affirming, that soone after mankind began to increase, they built many Citties; which as his meaning he deliuereth in plaine termes, in his third booke of lawes: for hee saith, that Citties were built an exceeding space of time before the destruction by the great floud.

This first *Iupiter* of the Ethnickes was then the same *Cain*, the sonne of *Adam*, who marrying his owne sister (as also *Iupiter* is said to haue done) inhabited the East, where

Stephanus [in] *de vrbibus* placeth the Cittie *Henochia*. And besides this Cittie of *Henoch*, *Philo Iudæus* conceiueth that *Cain* built sixe others, as *Maich*, *Iared*, *Tehe*, *Iesca*, *Selet* and *Gebat*: but where *Philo* had this I know not. Now as *Cain* was the first *Iupiter*, and from whome also the Ethnickes had the inuention of sacrifice: so were *Iubal*, *Tubal* and *Tubalcain* (inuentors of pastorage, smiths-craft, and musick) the same, which were called by the ancient prophane writers *Mercurius*, *Vulcan* and *Apollo*; and as there is a likelihood of name betweene *Tubalcain* and *Vulcan*: so doth *Augustine* expound the name of *Noema* or *Naamath*, the sister of *Tubalcain*, to signifie *Venusta*, or beautifull *Voluptas*, or pleasure; as the wife of *Vulcan* is said to be *Venus*, the Lady of pleasure and beautie. And as *Adam* was the ancient and first *Saturne*, *Cain* the eldest *Iupiter*, *Eua Rhea*, and *Noema* or *Naamath* the first *Venus*: so did the fable of the diuiding of the world betweene the three brethren the sonnes of *Saturne* arise, from the true story of the diuiding of the earth betweene the three brethren the sonnes of *Noah*: so also was the fiction of those golden apples kept by a dragon taken from the Serpent, which tempted *Euah*: so was *Paradyse* it selfe transported out of *Asia* into *Africa*, and made the garden of the *Hesperides*: the prophecies, that *Christ* should breake the Serpents head, and conquer the power of Hell, occasioned the fables of *Hercules* killing the Serpent of *Hesperides*, and descending into Hell, and captiuating *Cerberus*: so out of the taking vp of *Henoch* by God who borrowed the conuersion of their *Heroes* (the Inuentors of Religion and such artes as the life of man had profit by) into starres and heauenly signes, and (withall) that leauing of the world, and ascension of *Astræa*; of which *Ouid*,

Vltima cælestûm terras Astræa reliquit

Astræa last of heauenly wights the earth did leaue....[1]

§5. *Of the three chiefest* Ivpiters . . .

[1] *Metamorphoses*, I I50.

§6. *Of* Cham, *and other wicked ones, whereof some gat, some affected the name of Gods.*

§7. *That the wiser of the ancient Heathen had farre better opinions of God.*

But that euer *Pythagoras,* or *Plato,* or *Orpheus,* with many other ancient and excellently learned, belieued in any of these fooleries, it cannot be suspected, though some of them (ouer busily) haue mixed their owne inuentions with the Scriptures: for, in punishment for their fictions, did *Pythagoras* hang both *Homer* and *Hesiodus* in Hell, where hee fained that they were perpetually stung and pinched with Serpents. Yet it cannot be doubted, but that *Homer* had read ouer all the bookes of *Moses,* as by places stolne thence, almost word for word, may appeare; of which *Iustine Martyr* remembreth many in that Treatise conuerted by *Mirandula.* As for *Plato,* though he dissembled in some things, for feare of the inquisition of the *Areopagites,* yet St *Augustine* hath already answered for him (as before remembred) *Et mirificè ijs delectatus est, quæ de vno Deo tradit a fuerant, And he was greatly delighted in the doctrine of one God,* saith *Iustine Martyr.* Now howsoeuer *Lactantius* pleased to reprehend *Plato,* because (saith he) *Plato* sought knowledge from the *Ægyptians,* and the *Chaldæans,* neglecting the *Iewes,* and the bookes of *Moses: Eusebius, Cyrillus,* and *Origen,* finde reason to beleeue the contrarie, thinking that from thence he tooke the grounds of all by him written of God, or sauouring of Diuinitie: and the same opinion had S^t. *Ambrose* of *Pythagoras. . . .*[1]

And this is certaine, that if we looke into the wisedome of all ages, wee shall finde that there neuer was man of solid vnderstanding or excellent iudgement: neuer any man whose minde the art of education hath not bended; whose eyes a foolish superstition hath not afterward blinded; whose apprehensions are sober, and by a pensiue inspection aduised; but that he hath found by an vnresistable necessitie, one true

[1] In a long disquisition here omitted, Ralegh argues the monotheistic inclinations of both Egyptians and Greeks through a series of quotations from a variety of sources.

God, and euerlasting being, all for euer causing, and all for euer sustaining; which no man among the Heathen hath with more reuerence acknowledged, or more learnedly exprest, then that *Ægyptian Hermes*, howsoeuer it failed afterward in his posteritie: all being at length by deuilish pollicie of the *Ægyptian* Priests purposely obscured; who inuented new Gods, and those innumerable, best sorting (as the Deuill perswaded them) with vulgar capacities, and fittest to keepe in awe and order their common people.

§8. *That Heathenisme and Iudaisme, after many wounds were at length about the same time vnder* Ivlian *miraculously confounded.*

But all these are againe vanished: for the inuentions of mortall men are no lesse mortall then themselues. The Fire, which the *Chaldæans* worshipped for a God, is crept into euery mans chimney, which the lacke of fewell starueth, water quencheth, and want of aire suffocateth: *Iupiter* is no more vexed with *Iunoes* ielousies; Death hath perswaded him to chastitie, and her to patience; and that Time which hath deuoured it selfe, hath also eaten vp both the bodies and images of him and his: yea, their stately Temples of stone and durefull Marble. The houses and sumptuous buildings erected to *Baal*, can no where bee found vpon the earth; nor any monument of that glorious Temple consecrated to *Diana*. There are none now in *Phœnicia*, that lament the death of *Adonis*; nor any in *Lybia, Creta, Thessalia*, or elsewhere, that can aske counsaile or helpe from *Iupiter*. The great God *Pan* hath broken his Pipes, *Apolloes* Priests are become speechlesse; and the Trade of riddles in Oracles, with the Deuils telling mens fortunes therein, is taken vp by counterfait *Ægyptians*, and cousening *Astrologers*.

But it was long ere the Deuill gaue way to these his ouer-throwes and dishonours: for after the Temple of *Apollo* at *Delphos* (one of his chiefe Mansions) was many times robbed, burnt, and destroyed; yet by his diligence the same was often enriched, repaired, and reedified againe, till by the hand of God himselfe it receiued the last and vtter subuersion. For it was first robbed of all the Idols and ornaments therein by the *Eubæan Pyrates:* Secondly, by the *Phlegians* vtterly sackt: Thirdly, by *Pyrrhus* the Sonne of *Achilles:* Fourthly, by the Armie of *Xerxes:* Fiftly, by the Captaines of the *Phocenses:* Sixtly, by *Nero*, who carried thence fiue hundred brazen images: all which were new made, and therein againe set vp at the common charge. But whatsoeuer was gathered betweene the time of *Nero* and *Constantine*, the Christian Armie made spoile of, defacing as much as the time permitted them; notwithstanding all this it was againe gloriously rebuilt, and so remained till such time as *Iulian* the *Apostata* sent thither to know the successe of his *Parthian* enterprise, at which time it was vtterly burnt and consumed with fire from Heauen; and the image of *Apollo* himselfe, and all the rest of the Idols therein molten downe and lost in the earth. . . .

§9. *Of the last refuges of the Deuill to maintaine his Kingdome.*

Now the Deuill, because he cannot play vpon the open stage of this world (as in those dayes) and being still as industrious as euer, findes it more for his aduantage to creepe into the mindes of men; and inhabiting in the Temples of their hearts, workes them to a more effectuall adoration of himselfe then euer. For whereas hee first taught them to sacrifice to Monsters, to dead stones cut into faces of beasts, birds, and other mixt Natures; hee now sets before them the high and shining Idoll of glorie, the all-commanding Image of bright Gold. Hee tels them that Truth is the Goddesse of dangers and oppressions: that chastitie is the enemie of nature; and lastly, that as all vertue (in generall) is without taste: so pleasure satisfieth and delighteth euery sense: for true wisedome (saith he) is exercised in nothing else, then in the obtaining of power to oppresse, and of riches to maintaine plentifully our worldly delights. And if this *Arch-politician* finde in his Pupils any remorse, any feare or feeling of Gods future iudgement, hee perswades them that God hath so great neede of mens soules, that he will accept them at any time, and vpon any conditions: interrupting by his vigilant endeuours all offer of timefull returne towards God, by laying those great blockes of rugged pouertie, and despised contempt in the narrow passage leading to his diuine presence. But as the minde of man hath two ports, the one alwaies frequented by the entrance of manifold vanities; the other desolate and ouergrowne with grasse, by which enter our charitable thoughts and diuine contemplations: so hath that of death a double and twofold opening: worldly miserie passing by the one, worldly prosperitie by the other: at the entrance of the one we finde our sufferings and patience, to attend vs: (all which haue gone before vs to prepare our ioyes) at the other our cruelties, couetousnesse, licentiousnesse, iniustice, and oppressions (the Harbingers of most fearefull and terrible sorrow) staying for vs. And as the Deuill our most industrious enemie was euer most diligent: so is he now more laborious then euer: the long day of mankinde drawing fast towards an euening, and the worlds Tragedie and time neare at an end.

Ch. VII. *Of* Noahs *Floud*

§1. *Of Gods fore-warning: and some humane testimonies . . .*

§2. *Of the floud in the time of* Ogyges: *and that this was not* Noahs *floud.*

§3. *Of* Devcalions *floud: and that this was not* Noahs *Floud . . .*

§4. *Of some other records testifying the universall floud . . .*

§5. *That the floud of* Noah *was supernaturall . . .*

§6. *That there was no neede of any new creation of matter to make the universall floud . . .*

§7. *Of some remainder of the memorie of* Noah *among the* Heathen.

§8. *Of sundrie particulars touching the Arke* . . .

§9. *That the Arke was of sufficient capacitie.*

§10. *That the Arke rested vpon part of the hill Taurus (or* Caucasus*)* . . .

Ch. VIII. *Of the first planting of Nations after the floud; and of the Sonnes of* Noah, Sem, Ham, *and* Iaphet, *by whom the earth was repeopled*

§1. *Whether* Shem *and* Ham *were elder than* Iaphet.

§2. *Of diuers things* . . . *touching the first planting of the world* . . .

§3. *Of the Iles of the Gentiles in* Iaphets *portion* . . .

§4. *Of* Gog *and* Magog, Tvbal *and* Mesech . . .

§5. *Against the* . . . *fiction, That the Italian* Ianus *was* Noah.

§6. *That* Gomer *also and his Sonne* Togorma . . . *were first seated about Asia the lesse* . . .

§7. *Of* Iavan *the fourth sonne of* Iapheth . . .

§8. *Of* Ascanez *and* Riphath, *the two elder Sonnes of* Gomer.

§9. *Of foure Sonnes of* Iavan . . .

§10. *That the seate of* Chvsh *the eldest sonne of* Ham *was in Arabia* . . .

§11. *Of the Plantation and Antiquities of Ægypt.*

§12. *Of the eleuen sonnes of* Canaan, *the fourth sonne of* Ham.

§13. *Of the sonnes of* Chvsh (*excepting* Nimrod) *of whom hereafter.*

§14. *Of the issue of* Mizraim . . .

§15. *Of the issue of* Sem.

Ch. IX. *Of the beginning and establishing of Gouernement*

§1. *Of the proceeding from the first Gouernement vnder the eldest of families to Regall, and from Regall absolute to Regall tempered with Lawes.*

It followeth now to entreate how the world beganne to receiue Rule and Gouernement, which (while it had scarcitie of people) vnder-went no other Dominion then Paternitie and Eldership. For the Fathers of Nations were then as Kings, and the eldest of families as Princes . . .

But as men and vice beganne abundantly to increase: so obedience, (the fruit of naturall reuerence, which but from excellent seede seldome ripeneth) being exceedingly ouer-shadowed with pride, and ill examples vtterly withered and fell away. And the soft weapons of paternall perswasions (after mankinde beganne to neglect and forget the originall and first giuer of life) became in all ouer-weake, either to resist the first inclination of euill, or after (when it became habituall) to constraine it. So that now, when the hearts of men were only guided and steered by their owne fancies, and tost too and fro on the tempestuous Seas of the world, while wisedome was seuered from power, and strength from charitie: Necessitie (which bindeth euery nature but the immortall) made both the Wise and Foolish vnderstand at once, that the estate of reasonable men would become farre more miserable then that of beasts, and that a generall floud of confusion would a second time ouerflow them, did they not by a generall obedience to order and dominion preuent it. For the Mightie, who trusted in their owne strengths, found others againe (by interchange of times) more mightie then themselues: the feeble fell vnder the forcible; and the equall from equall receiued equall harmes. In so much that licentious disorder (which seemed to promise a libertie vpon the first acquaintance) proued vpon a better triall, no lesse perilous then an vnindurable bondage.

These Arguments by Necessitie propounded, and by Reason maintained and confirmed, perswaded all Nations which the Heauens couer, to subiect themselues to a Master, and to Magistracie in some degree. Vnder which Gouernement, as the change (which brought with it lesse euill, then the former mischiefes) was generally pleasing: so time (making all men wise that obserue it) found some imperfection and corrosiue in this cure. And therefore the same Necessitie which inuented, and the same Reason which approued soueraigne power, bethought themselues of certaine equall rules, in which Dominion (in the beginning boundlesse) might also discerne her owne limits. For before the inuention of Lawes, priuate affections in supreme Rulers made their owne fancies both their Treasurers and Hangmen: measuring by this yard, and waighing in this ballance both good and euill. . . .

And though (speaking humanely) the beginning of Empire may bee ascribed to reason and necessitie; yet it was God himselfe that first kindled this light in the minds of men, whereby they saw that they could not liue and bee preserued without a Ruler and Conductor: God himselfe by his eternall prouidence hauing ordayned Kings; and the law of Nature leaders, and Rulers ouer others. For the verie Bees haue their Prince; the Deere their Leaders; and Cranes (by order imposed) watch for their owne safetie. *The most High beareth rule ouer the Kingdomes of men; and appointeth ouer it whomsoeuer he pleaseth.* By me (saith *Wisedome,* spoken by the Son of God) *Kings raine; by me Princes rule,* and *it is God* (saith *Daniel*) *that setteth vp Kings, and taketh away Kings:* and that this power is giuen from God, *Christ* himselfe witnesseth, speaking to *Pilate. Thou couldest haue no power at all against mee, except it were giuen thee from aboue.*

It was therefore by a threefold iustice that the world hath beene gouerned from the beginning, (to wit) by a iustice naturall: by which the Parents and Elders of families gouerned their children, and nephewes, and families, in which gouernement the obedience was called naturall pietie; againe, by a iustice diuine, drawne from the lawes and ordinances of God: and the obedience hereunto was called conscience; and lastly by a iustice ciuill, begotten by both the former: and the obedience to this we call dutie. That by these three those of the eldest times were commanded: and that the rule in generall was paternall, it is most euident: for *Adam* being Lord ouer his owne children, instructed them in the seruice of God his Creatour; as wee reade, *Cain* and *Abel* brought Oblations before God, as they had beene taught by their Parent, the Father of mankinde.

§2. *Of the three commendable sorts of Gouernement with their opposites: and of the degrees of humane societie.*

. . . The first, the most ancient, most generall, and most approued, was the Gouernement of one, ruling by iust lawes, called *Monarchie:* to which *Tyrannie* is opposed, being also a sole and absolute rule, exercised according to the will of the Commander, without respect or obseruation of the lawes of God, or Men. For a lawfull Prince or Magistrate (saith *Aristotle*) is the keeper of right and equitie: and of this condition ought euery Magistrate to be, according to the rule of Gods word. *Iudges and Officers shalt thou make thee in thy Citties: And these shall iudge the people with righteous iudgement.*

The second Gouernement is of diuers principall persons established by order, and ruling by lawes, called *Aristocracie*, or *Optimatum potestas*; to which *Oligarchia* (or the particular faction and vsurpation of a few great ones) is opposed: as the *Decemviri*, or *Triumviri*, and the like.

The third is a State popular, (or Gouernement of the people) called *Democratia*, to which is opposed *Ochlocratia*, or the turbulent vniust ruling of the confused multitude, seditiously swaying the state, contrarie to their owne lawes and ordinances. These three kinds of Gouernement are briefly exprest by *Tholosanus*; *Vnius, paucorum, & multorum, Of one, of few, of many.*

Now as touching the beginning and order of pollicie since the second increase of mankinde, the same grew in this sort: First of all, euery Father, or eldest of the familie, gaue lawes to his owne issues, and to the people from him and them increased. These as they were multiplyed into many housholds (man by nature louing societie) ioyned their Cottages together in one common field or Village, which the Latines call *Vicus*; of the *Greeke οἶκος*, which signifieth a house, or of the word (*Via*) because it hath diuers waies and paths leading to it. And as the first house grew into a Village, so the Village into that which is called *Pagus*, (being a societie of diuers Villages) so called of the *Greeke πηγή*, which signifieth a fountaine: because many people (hauing their habitations not farre asunder) dranke of one spring or streame of water. To this word the English Hundreds, or (as some thinke) Shires answereth not vnfitly.

But as men and impietie beganne to gather strength, and as emulation and pride betweene the races of the one and the other daylie increased: so both to defend themselues from outrage, and to preserue such goods as they had gathered, they beganne to ioyne and set together diuers of their Villages, inuironing them first with banks and ditches, and afterwards with wals. . . .

Lastly, as many Fathers erected many Cottages for their many children: and as (for the reason before remembred)

many housholds ioyned themselues together, and made
Villages; many Villages made Citties: so when these Citties
and Cittizens ioyned together, and established lawes by
consent, associating themselues vnder one Gouernour and
gouernment, they so ioyned were called a Commonwealth:
the same being sometimes gouerned by Kings; sometimes
by Magistrates; sometimes by the people themselues.

§3. *Of the good Gouernement of the first Kings.*

Now this first Age after the floud, and after such time as the
people were increased, and the families became strong, and
dispersed into seuerall parts of the world, was by ancient
Historians called Golden: Ambition and Couetousnesse
being as then but greene, and newly growne vp, the seedes
and effects whereof were as yet but potentiall, and in the
blowth and budde. For while the Law of Nature was the
rule of mans life, they then sought for no larger Territorie
then themselues could compasse and manure: they erected
no other magnificent buildings, then sufficient to defend
them from cold and tempest: they cared for no other delicacie
of fare, or curiositie of dyet, then to maintayne life: nor for
any other apparell then to couer them from the cold, the
Raine and the Sunne.

　　And sure if we vnderstand by that Age (which was called
Golden) the ancient simplicity of our forefathers, this name
may then truly bee cast vpon those elder times: but if it be
taken otherwise, then, whether the same may be attributed
more to any one time then to another, (I meane to one
limited time and none else) it may bee doubted. For good
and golden Kings make good and golden Ages: and all
times haue brought forth of both sorts. And as the infancie
of Empirie, (when Princes played their prizes, and did then
only woo men to obedience) might bee called the golden
Age: so may the beginning of all Princes times bee truly
called golden, for be it that men affect honour it is then best
purchased; or if honour affect men, it is then that good
deseruings haue commonly the least impediments: and if
euer Liberalitie ouerflow her bankes and bounds, the same

is then best warranted both by pollicie and example. But
Age and Time doe not only harden and shrinke the openest
and most *Iouiall* hearts, but the experience which it bringeth
with it layeth Princes torne estates before their eyes, and
(withall) perswadeth them to compassionate themselues.
And although there bee no Kings vnder the Sunne whose
meanes are answerable vnto other mens desires; yet such as
value all things by their owne respects, doe no sooner finde
their appetites vnanswered, but they complaine of alteration,
and account the times iniurious and yron. And as this
falleth out in the raigne of euery King, so doth it in the life
of euery man, if his dayes bee many: for our younger yeares
are our golden Age; which being eaten vp by time, we praise
those seasons which our youth accompanied: and (indeede)
the grieuous alterations in our selues, and the paines and
diseases which neuer part from vs but at the graue, make the
times seeme so differing and displeasing: especially the
qualitie of mans nature being also such, as it adoreth and
extolleth the passages of the former, and condemneth the
present state how iust soeuer. *Fit humanæ malignitatis vitio,
vt semper vetera in laude, præsentiæ in fastidio sint, It comes
to passe* (saith *Tacitus*) *by the vice of our malignitie, that we
alwaies extoll the time past, and hold the present fastidious:*
For it is one of the errours of wayward age. *Quod sint
laudatores temporis acti, That they are praisers of forepassed
times,* forgetting this aduise of *Salomon. Say not then why is it
that the former dayes were better then these? for thou doest not
inquire wisely of this thing:* to which purpose *Seneca. Maiores
nostri questi sunt, & nos querimur, posteri querentur, euersos
esse mores, regnare nequitiam, in deterius res hominum, &
in omne nefas labi, Our Ancesters haue complained, we doe
complaine, our children will complaine, that good manners are
gone, that wickednesse doth raigne, and all thinges grow worse
and worse, and fall into all euill.* These are the vsuall discourses of Age and misfortune. But hereof what can we adde
to this of *Arnobius. Noua res quandoque vetus fiet, & vetus
temporibus quibus cœpit noua fuit & repentina, Whatsoeuer is
new, in time shall be made old: and the ancientest thinges when
they tooke beginning were also new and sodaine.* Wherefore not
to stand in much admiration of these first times, which the

discontentments of present times haue made golden, this wee may set downe for certaine, That as it was the vertue of the first Kings, which (after God) gaue them Crownes: so the loue of their people thereby purchased, held the same Crownes on their heads. And as God gaue the obedience of subiects to Princes: so (relatiuely) he gaue the care and iustice of Kings to the Subiects; hauing respect, not only to the Kings themselues, but euen to the meanest of his Creatures. *Nunquàm particulari bono seruit omne bonum, The infinite goodnesse of God doth not attend any one only:* for he that made the small and the great, careth for all alike: and it is the care which Kings haue of all theirs, which makes them beloued of all theirs; and by a generall loue it is, that Princes hold a generall obedience: For *Potestas humana radicatur in voluntatibus hominum, All humane power is rooted in the will or dispositions of men.*

§4. *Of the beginning of Nobilitie: and of the vaine vaunt thereof without vertue.*

. . . Nobilitie, or difference from the Vulgar, was not in the beginning giuen to the succession of bloud, but to succession of vertue, as hereafter may bee proued. Though at length it was sufficient for those whose Parents were aduanced, to be knowne for the Sonnes of such Fathers: and so there needed then no endeauour of well-doing at all, or any contention for them to excell, vpon whom glorie or worldly Nobilitie necessarily descended. Yet hereof had Nobilitie denomination in the beginning, That such as excelled others in vertue were so called. *Hinc dictus Nobilis, quasi virtute præ alijs notabilis.* But after such time as the deserued Honour of the Father was giuen in reward to his posteritie, S^t. *Hierome* iudged of the succession in this manner. *Nihil aliud video in Nobilitate appetendum, nisi quod Nobiles quadam necessitate constringantur, ne ab antiquorum probitate degenerent, I see no other thing to be affected in Nobilitie, then that Noblemen are by a kinde of necessitie bound not to degenerate from the vertue of their Ancesters.* For if Nobilitie be *virtus & antiquæ diuitiæ, Vertue and ancient riches,* then to exceede in all those thinges which are *extra hominem*, as riches, power, glorie, and the like, doe no otherwise define Nobilitie, then the word (*animal*) alone doth define a reasonable man. Or if honour (according to *L. Viues*) be a witnesse of vertue and well-doing: and Nobilitie (after *Plutarch*) the continuance of vertue in a race or linage: then are those in whom vertue is extinguished, but like vnto painted and printed papers, which ignorant men worship in steade of *Christ*, our Ladie, and other Saints: men, in whom there remaine but the dregges and vices of ancient vertue: Flowers, and hearbes, which by change of soile and want of manuring are turned to weedes. For what is found praise-worthy in those waters, which had their beginning out of pure fountaines, if in all the rest of their course they runne foule, filthie, and defiled? *Ex terra fertili producitur aliquando cicuta venenosa, & ex terra sterili pretiosum aurum, Out of fruitfull ground ariseth sometimes poysoning henbane: and out of barren soile pretious gold.* For as all thinges consist of matter and forme, so doth *Charron* (in his Chapter of Nobilitie) call the race and linage but the matter of Nobilitie: the forme (which giues life and perfect being) he maketh to be vertue, and qualitie, profitable to the Commonweale. For hee is truly and entirely Noble, who maketh a singular profession of publike vertue, seruing his Prince and Countrie, and being descended of Parents and Ancesters that haue done the like. And although that Nobilitie, which the same Authour calleth personall, (the same which our selues acquire by our vertue and well deseruings) cannot bee ballanced with that which is both naturall by descent, and also personall; yet if vertue bee wanting to the naturall, then is the personall and acquired Nobilitie by many degrees to be preferred: For (saith this *Charron*) this Honour (to wit) by descent, may light vpon such a one, as in his owne nature is a true Villaine. There is also a third Nobilitie which he calleth Nobilitie in Parchment, bought with siluer or fauour: and these be indeede but Honours of affection, which Kinges with the change of their fancies wish they knew well how to wipe off againe. But surely, if we had as much sense of our degenerating in worthinesse, as we haue of vanitie in deriuing our selues of such and such Parents, wee should rather know such

Nobilitie (without vertue) to be shame and dishonour, then Noblenesse, and glorie to vaunt thereof. *What calamitie is wanting* (saith *Bernard*) *to him that is borne in sinne, of a potshare body and barren minde?* for (according to the same Father,) *Dele fucum fugacis honoris huius, & male coronatæ nitorem gloriæ, &c. Wipe away the painting of this fleeting honour, and the glittering of the ill-crowned glorie, that then thou maiest consider thy selfe nakedly: for thou camest naked out of thy Mothers wombe. Camest thou thence with thy Myter, or glissening with Iewels, or garnished with silkes, or adorned with feathers, or stuffed with gold? If thou scatter and blow away all these by thy consideration as certaine morning cloudes, which doe or will soone passe ouer, thou shalt meete with a naked, and poore, and wretched, and miserable man, and blushing, because he is naked, and weeping because he is borne, and repining because he is borne to labour, and not to honour.*

For as touching the matter of all men, there is no difference betweene it and dust: which if *thou doest not beleeue* (saith S. *Chrysostome*) *looke into the Sepulchers and Monuments of thy Ancesters, and they shall easily perswade thee by their owne example, that thou art dust and dirt: so that if man seeme more Noble and beautifull then dust, this proceedeth not from the diuersitie of his nature, but from the cunning of his Creatour.*

> For true Nobilitie standeth in the Trade
> Of vertuous life; not in the fleshly line :
> For bloud is brute, but Gentrie is diuine.

And howsoeuer the custome of the world haue made it good, that Honours be cast by birth vpon vnworthy issues: yet *Salomon* (as wise as any King) reprehendeth the same in his fellow-Princes. *There is an euill* (saith he) *that I haue seene vnder the Sunne, as an errour that proceedeth from the face of him that ruleth. Follie is set in great excellencie.*

Ch. X. *Of* Nimrod, Belvs, *and* Ninvs: *and of memorable thinges about those times*

§1. *That* Nimrod *was the first after the floud that raigned like soueraigne Lord* . . .

§2. *That* Nimrod, Belvs, *and* Ninvs *were three distinct persons.*

§3. *That* Nimrod, *not* Assur, *built* Niniue . . .

§4. *Of the acts of* Nimrod *and* Belvs, *as farre as now they are knowne.*

§5. *That wee are not to meruaile how so many Kingdomes could bee erected about these times* . . .

§6. *Of the name of* Belvs . . .

§7. *Of the worshipping of Images begunne from* Belvs *in Babel.*

§8. *Of the Warres of* Ninvs: *and lastly of his warre against* Zoroaster.

Ch. XI. *Of* Zoroaster, *supposed to haue beene the chiefe Authour of Magick Arts; and of the diuers kinds of Magicke*

§1. *That* Zoroaster *was not* Cham, *nor the first inuentor of Astrologie, or of Magicke: and that there were diuers great Magitians of this name.*

§2. *Of the name of Magia: and that it was anciently farre diuers from coniuring, and Witchcraft.*[1]

Now for *Magicke* it selfe; which Art (saith *Mirandula*) *pauci intelligunt, multi reprehendunt,* Few *vnderstand,* and many *reprehend: Et sicut canes ignotos semper allatrant,* As dogges barke at those they know not: so they condemne and hate the things they vnderstand not: I thinke it not amisse (leauing *Ninus* for a while) to speake somewhat thereof. . . .

Magus is a *Persian* word primitiuely; whereby is exprest such a one as is altogether conuersant in things diuine. And (as *Plato* affirmeth) the art of *Magicke* is the art of worshipping God. To which effect *Apollonius* in his Epistles expounding the word μάγος saith, that the *Persians* called their Gods μάγους: whence he addeth that *Magus* is either ὁ κατὰ φύσιν Θεὸς or θεραπευτὴς Θεῶν (that is) that *Magus* is a name sometime of him that is a God by nature; sometimes of him that is in the seruice of God: in which latter sense it is taken *Matt. c.2. v.1.* And this is the first and highest kinde: which *Piccolominie* calleth diuine *Magicke:* and these did the Latines newly intitle *sapientes* or *wisemen: For the feare and worship of God is the beginning of knowledge.* These *Wisemen* the *Greekes* call *Philosophers:* the *Indians Brachmans:* which name they somewhat nearely retaine to this day, calling their Priests *Bramines*; among the *Ægyptians* they were termed Priests; with the *Hebrewes* they were called *Cabalistes, Prophets, Scribes,* and *Pharisees:* amongst the *Babylonians* they were differenced by the name of *Chaldæans:* and among the *Persians Magicians.* . . .

A second kinde of *Magicke* was that part of *Astrologie,* which had respect to sowing and planting, and all kinds of agriculture and husbandrie: which was a knowledge of the

---

[1] In another section not made available here (1 xi 6), Ralegh expounds the 'diuers kindes of vnlawfull Magick', including necromancy, theurgy, and especially witchcraft. But the distinctions attempted in these two sections are fundamental to his interpretation of 'magic'.

motions and influences of the Starres into those lower
elements. . . .

The third kinde of *Magicke* containeth the whole Philosophie of nature; not the brablings of the *Aristotelians*, but
that which bringeth to light the inmost vertues, and draweth
them out of natures hidden bosome to humane vse, *Virtutes in
centro centri latentes, Vertues hidden in the center of the center*,
according to the *Chymists*. . . .

In all these three kindes which other men diuide into
foure, it seemeth that *Zoroaster* was exceedingly learned:
especially in the first and highest. For in his *Oracles* hee
confesseth God to bee the Creatour of the Vniuersal: he
beleeueth of the *Trinitie*, which he could not inuestigate by
any naturall knowledge: hee speaketh of Angels, and of
Paradise: approueth the immortalitie of the soule: teacheth
Truth, Faith, Hope, and Loue, discoursing of the Abstinence
and Charitie of the *Magi:* which *Oracles* of his, *Psellus*,
Ficinus, Patritius, and others haue gathered and translated.

Of this *Zoroaster, Eusebius* in the *Theologie* of the *Phœnicians* vsing *Zoroasters* owne wordes. *Hæc ad verbum scribit:*
(saith *Evsebivs*) *Deus primus incorruptibilium, sempiternus,
ingenitus, expers partium, sibi ipsi simillimus, bonorum omnium
auriga, munera non expectans, optimus, prudentissimus,
pater iuris, sine doctrina iustitiam per doctus, natura perfectus,
sapiens, sacræ naturæ vnicus inuentor, &c.* Thus writeth
Zoroaster, word for word. God the first incorruptible, euerlasting, vnbegotten, without parts, most like himselfe, the guide of
all good, expecting no reward, the best, the wisest, the father of
right, hauing learn'd iustice without teaching, perfect wise by
nature, the only inuentour thereof. . . .

§3. *That the good knowledge in the ancient Magicke is not to
be condemned: though the Deuill here as in other kinds hath
sought to obtrude euill things vnder the name and colour of
good things.*

Seeing therefore it is confessed by all of vnderstanding, that
a *Magician* (according to the *Persian* word) is no other then
diuinorum cultor & interpres, A studious obseruer and expounder

of diuine things: and the art it selfe (I meane the Art of naturall *Magicke*) no other, *quàm naturalis Philosophiæ absoluta consummatio, Then the absolute perfection of naturall Philosophie:* Certainly then it proceedeth from common ignorance, and no way sorteth with wise and learned men *promiscuè*, and without difference and distinction, to confound lawfull and praise-worthy knowledge with that impious, and (to vse S. *Paules* wordes) *with those beggerly rudiments*, which the Deuill hath shuffled in, and by them bewitcheth and befooleth gracelesse men. For if we condemne naturall *Magicke*, or the wisedome of nature, because the Deuill (who knoweth more then any man) doth also teach Witches and Poysoners the harmefull parts of hearbs, drugges, minerals, and excrements: then may wee by the same rule condemne the Physition, and the Art of healing. For the Deuill also in the Oracles of *Amphiaraus*, *Amphilochus*, *Trophonius*, and the like, taught men in dreames what hearbs and drugges were proper for such and such diseases. Now no man of iudgement is ignorant, that the Deuill from the beginning hath sought to thrust himselfe into the same imployment among the ministers and seruants of God, changing himselfe for that purpose into an Angell of light. He hath led men to Idolatrie as a doctrine of religion; he hath thrust in his Prophets among those of the true God; he hath corrupted the Art of *Astrologie*, by giuing a diuine power to the Starres teaching men to esteeme them as Gods, and not as instruments. And (as *Bunting* obserueth) it is true, that iudiciall *Astrologie* is corrupted with many superstitions: but the abuse of the thing takes not away the Art; considering that heauenly bodies (as euen generall experience sheweth) haue and exercise their operation vpon the inferiour. For the Sunne, and the Starre of *Mars* doe drie; the Moone doth moisten, and gouerne the Tides of the Sea. Againe, the Planets, as they haue seuerall and proper names, so haue they seuerall and proper vertues: the Starres doe also differ in beautie and in magnitude; and to all the Starres hath God giuen also their proper names, which (had they not influences and vertues different) needed not: *He counteth the number of the Starres, and calleth them by their names.* But into the good and profitable knowledge of the celestiall influences, the Deuil ceaseth not to shuffle in his superstitions: and so to the knowledge of the secret vertues of nature hath he fastened his doctrine of *Characters*, numbers, and incantations; and taught men to beleeue in the strength of wordes and letters: (which without faith in God are but inke or common breath) thereby either to equall his owne with the all-powerfull word of God, or to diminish the glorie of Gods creating word, by whom are all thinges. . . .

§4. *That* Daniels *misliking* Nabvchodonosors *condemning of the Magicians doth not iustifie all their practises.*

§5. *The abuse of things which may be found in all kinds, is not to condemne the right vse of them.*

§6. *Of the diuers kindes of vnlawfull Magick.*

§7. *Of diuers waies by which the Deuill seemeth to worke his wonders.*

§8. *That none was euer raised from the dead by the power of the Deuill* . . .

Ch. XII. *Of the memorable buildings of* Ninvs, *and of his wife* Semiramis: *and of other of her actes*

§1. *Of the magnificent building of Niniue by* Ninvs: *and of Babylon by* Semiramis.

But to come backe to *Ninus* the amplifier and finisher of *Niniue:* whether he performed it before or after the ouer-throw of *Zoroaster*, it is vncertaine. As for the Citty it selfe,

it is agreed by all prophane writers, and confirmed by the
Scriptures, that it exceeded all other in circuit, and answerable magnificence. For it had in compasse 440. *stadia,* or
furlongs; the walles whereof were an hundred foot vpright,
and had such a bredth as three charriots might passe on the
rampire in front: these walles were garnished with 1500.
towers which gaue exceeding beautie to the rest, and a
strength no lesse admirable for the nature of those times.

But this Cittie (built in the Plaines of *Assyria,* and on the
bankes of *Tigris,* and in the Region of *Eden,*) was founded
long before *Ninus* time; and (as ancient Historians report,
and more lately *Nauclerus*) had the name of *Campsor,* at such
time as *Ninus* amplified the same, and gaue it a wall, and
called it after his owne name.

For these workes of *Babylon* and *Niniue* begun by
Nimrod in *Chaldæa,* and in *Assyria, Ninus* and *Semiramis*
made perfect. *Ninus* finished *Niniue, Semiramis Babylon*:
wherein shee fought to exceed her husband by farre. Indeed
in the first Age when Princes were moderate, they neither
thought how to inuade others, nor feared to be inuaded:
labouring to build Townes and Villages for the vse of themselues and their people without either Walles or Towers;
and how they might discharge the earth of woods, briars,
bushments, and waters, to make it the more habitable and
fertile. But *Semiramis* liuing in that age, when Ambition
was in strong youth: and purposing to follow the conquest
which her husband had vndertaken, gaue that beauty and
strength to *Babylon* which it had.

§2. *Of the end of* Ninvs: *and beginning of* Semiramis *reigne.*

This she did after the death of her husband *Ninus*: who after
he had maistred *Bactria,* and subiected vnto his Empire all
those Regions betweene it and the *Mediterran Sea* and
Hellespont (*Asia* the lesse excepted) and finished the worke
of *Niniue,* he left the world in the yeare thereof 2019. after
he had raigned 52. yeares. *Plutarch* reporteth that *Semiramis*
desired her husband *Ninus,* that he would graunt vnto her the
absolute souereigne power for one day. *Diod. Siculus* out of

Athenæus, and others, speakes of fiue daies. In which time (moued either with desire of rule, or licentious liberty, or with the memory of her husband *Menon*, who perished for her) she caused *Ninus* her husband to be slaine. But this seemeth rather a scandall cast on her by the *Greekes*, then that it had any truth.

Howsoeuer *Ninus* came to his ende, *Semiramis* tooke on her after his death the sole rule of the *Assyrian* empire: of which, *Ninus* was said to be the first *Monarch* because he changed his seat from *Babylonia* in *Chaldæa* to *Niniue* in *Assyria*. *Iustine* reports that *Semiramis* (the better to inuest herselfe, and in her beginning without murmure or offense to take on her so great a charge) presented herselfe to the people in the person of her sonne *Ninias* or *Zameis*, who bare her externall forme and proportion without any sensible difference.

This report I take also to be fained, for which many arguments might bee made. But as she ruled long, so she performed all those memorable actes which are written of her by the name of *Semiramis*, and subscribed that letter which she sent to the King of *India* (her last challenge and vndertaken conquest) by her owne name. And were it true that her sonne *Ninias* had such a stature at his Fathers death, as that *Semiramis* (who was very personable) could be taken for him; yet it is very vnlikely that she could haue held the Empire from him 42. yeares after by any such subtilety: (for so long shee reigned after the death of her Husband:) but it may bee true that *Ninias* or *Zameis* (being wholly giuen to his pleasures as it is written of him) was well pleased with his Mothers prosperous gouernment and vndertakings.

§3. *Of* Semiramis *parentage, and education, and* Metamorphosis *of her Mother.*

Some writers (of which *Plutarch* is one) make this famous woman to haue beene of base parentage, calling her after the name of her Countrey, a *Syrian*. *Berosus* cals her after the name of her Citty wherein she was borne, *Semiramis Ascalonitis*; of *Ascalon*, the ancient Citty and *Metropolis* of the *Philistims*. Others report her to be the daughter of *Derceta*, a *Curtizan* of *Ascalon* exceeding beautifull. Others say that this *Derceta* or *Dercetis* the mother of *Semiramis* was sometimes a Recluse, and had profest a holy and a religious life, to whom there was a Temple dedicated seated on the banke of a Lake adioyning to *Ascalon*; and afterward falling in loue with a goodly yong man she was by him made with child, which (for feare of extreme punishment) she conuaied away, and caused the same to be hidden among the high reedes which grew on the bankes of the Lake: in which (while the child was left to the mercy of wild beasts) the same was fed by certaine birds, which vsed to feed vpon or neere those waters. But I take this tale to be like that of *Lupa* the harlot that fostered *Romulus*. For some one or other adioyning to this Lake had the charge and fosteridge of this child, who being perchance but some base and obscure creature, the mother might thereby hope the better to couer her dishonour and breach of vow; notwithstanding which she was cast from the top of her Temple into the Lake adioining, and (as the Poets haue fained) changed by *Venus* into a fish, all but her face, which still held the same beauty and humane shape. It is thought that from this *Derceta* the inuention of that Idoll of the *Philistims* (called *Dagon*) was taken: for it is true, that *Dagon* had a mans face, and a fishes body: into whose Temple when the *Arke* of God was brought, the Idoll fell twice to the ground: and at the second fall there remained only the Trunck of *Dagon*, the head being broken of: For so S^t. *Hierome* hath conuerted that place. *Vatablus*, *Pagninus*, and *Iunius* write it by *Dagon* onely, which signifieth a fish, and so it only appeared: the head thereof by the second fall being sundred from the body.

For my selfe I rather thinke, that this *Dagon* of the *Philistims* was an Idoll representing *Triton*, one of those imaginary Sea-gods vnder *Neptune*. For this Citty being maritimate (as all those of the *Philistims* were, and so were the best of *Phœnicia*) vsed all their deuotions to *Neptune*, and the rest of the pettie Gods which attended him.

§4. *Of her expedition into India, and death after discomfiture:
with a note of the improbabilitie of her vices.*

But for her Pedigree I leaue it to the *Assyrian Heralds:* and
for her vitious life I ascribe the report thereof to the enuious
and lying *Grecians.* For delicacie and ease do more often
accompanie licentiousnesse in men and women, then labour
and hazzard do. And if the one halfe bee true which is
reported of this Lady, then there neuer liued any Prince or
Princesse more worthy of fame then *Semiramis* was, both for
the workes she did at *Babylon* and elsewhere, and for the
warres she made with glorious successe: all but her last
enterprise of *India*; from whence both *Strabo* and *Arianus*
report that she neuer returned: and that of all her most
powerfull Army there suruiued but only twenty persons: the
rest being either drowned in the riuer of *Indus,* dead of the
famine, or slaine by the sword of *Staurobates.* But as the
multitude which went out are more then reason hath
numbred: so were those that returned lesse then could
haue escaped of such an Army, as consisted of foure millions
and vpwards. For these numbers which she leuied by her
Lieutenant *Dercetæus* (saith *Suidas*) did consist of Foot-men
three millions; of Horsemen one million; of Charriots
armed with hookes on each side one hundred thousand; of
those which fought vpon Camels as many; of Camels for
burden two hundred thousand; of raw Hides for all vses
three hundred thousand; of Galleies with brazen heads three
thousand, by which she might transport ouer *Indus* at once
three hundred thousand souldiers: which Gallies were
furnished with *Syrians, Phœnicians, Cilicians,* and men of
Cyprus. These incredible and impossible numbers, which
no one place of the earth was able to nourish (had euery
man and beast but fed vpon grasse) are taken from the
authority of *Ctesias* whom *Diodorus* followeth. But as the
one may be taxed with many friuolous reports: so *Diodorus*
himselfe hath nothing of certainty, but from *Xerxes* expedition into *Greece* and afterwards: whose Armie (though the
same was farre inferior to that of *Semiramis*) yet had it
weight enough to ouerlode the beliefe of any reasonable
man. For all Authors consent, that *Xerxes* transported into

Greece an Army of 1700000. and gathered together (therein to passe the *Hellespont*) three thousand Gallies, as *Herodotus* out of the seuerall Prouinces whence those Galleies were taken hath collected the number.

But of what multitude soeuer the Armie of *Semiramis* consisted: the same being broken and ouerthrown by *Staurobates* vpon the banks of *Indus, canticum cantauit extremum: she sang her last song*; and (as Antiquity hath fained) was changed by the Gods into a Doue, (the bird of *Venus*) whence it came that the *Babylonians* gaue a Doue in their ensignes.

§5. *Of the Temple of* Belvs *built by* Semiramis: *and of the Pyramides of Ægypt.*

Among all her other memorable and more then magnificent workes (besides the wall of the Citty of *Babylon*) was the Temple of *Bel*, erected in the middle of this Citty, inuironed with a wall carried foure-square of great heighth and beauty, hauing on each square certaine brazen gates curiously engrauen. In the *Core* of the square she raised a Tower of a furlong high, which is halfe a quarter of a mile; and vpon it againe (taking a *Basis* of a lesse circuit) she set a second Tower; and so eight in all, one aboue an other: vpon the top whereof the *Chaldæans* Priests made the obseruation of the starres, because this Tower ouer-topped the ordinary cloudes.

By beholding the ruines of this Tower haue many Trauailers beene deceiued; who suppose that they haue seene a part of *Nimrods* Tower, when it was but the Foundation of this Temple of *Bel*: (except this of *Bel* were founded on that of *Nimrod*.) There were burnt in this Temple one hundred thousand talents of frankincense euery yeare (saith *Herodotus*). This Temple did *Nabuchodonosor* adorne with the spoiles of *Hierusalem*, & of the temple of *Salomon*: all which vessels & ornaments *Cyrus* redeliuered. This Temple *Zerxes* euened with the soile; which *Alexander* is said to haue repaired by the perswasions of the *Chaldæans*. I deny not that it might haue been in his desire so to do; but he enioyed but a few yeares after *Babylon* taken, and therefore could not performe any such worke. The *Ægyptians* (saith *Proclus*) inhabiting a low and leauell ground, and giuen to the same superstition of the stars that the *Chaldæans* were, erected in imitation, and for the same seruice and vse, the *Pyramides* by *Memphis*, which were *conspicuæ vndique nauigantibus*, saith *Plinie*.[1] Of these *Pyramides Bellonius* a carefull obseruer of rarities (who being in *Ægypt* mounted by steps to the top of the highest) maketh this report. *Le meilleur archer qui seroit a sa sommite, et tirant vne fleche en l'air, a peine pouroit l'enuoyer hors de sa base qu'elle ne se tombast sur les degrez. The best Archer standing on the top of one of these Pyramides, and shooting an arrow from thence into the aier as farre as he can, with great difficulty shall be able so to force the same, but that it will fall vpon some of the degrees or steppes.*

[1] In *Historia naturalis*, XXXVI 12: 'conspicuous to travellers approaching from any direction'.

THE FIRST PART
OF THE HISTORIE
OF THE WORLD:

Intreating of the times from the birth of Abraham to the destruction of the Temple of Salomon.

THE SECOND BOOKE.

Ch. I. *Of the time of the birth of Abraham: and of the vse of this question, for the ordering of the Storie of the Assyrian Empire*

§1. *Of some of the successours of* Semiramis: *with a briefe transition to the question, about the time of the birth of* Abraham.

After the death of *Semiramis*, *Ninias* or *Zameis* succeeded her in the Empire, on whom *Berosus Annianus* bestowes the conquest of *Bactria*, and the ouerthrow of *Zoroaster*; contrary to *Diodorus*, *Iustine*, *Orosius*, and all other approued writers. For *Ninias* being esteemed no man of warre at all, but altogether feminine, and subiected to ease and delicacie, there is no probability in that opinion.[1] Now because there was nothing performed by this *Ninias* of any moment, other then that out of iealousie he euery yeare changed his Prouinciall Gouernors, and built Colledges for the *Chaldæan* Priests, his Astronomers: nor by *Arius* his successor, whom *Suidas* calleth *Thuras*; but that he reduced againe the *Bactrians* and *Caspians*, reuolted as it seemeth in *Ninias* his time: nor of *Aralius*, the successor of *Arius*; but that he added sumptuosity, inuented iewels of gold and stone, and some engins for the warre: I will for this present passe them ouer, and a while follow *Abraham*. . . .

Ch. II. *Of the Kings of Ægypt from the first peopling of it after the Floud, to the time of the deliuerie of the Israelites from thence*

[1] On the possibility that Ninias represents James I, see above, p. 19.

Ch. III. *Of the delivery of Israel out of Ægypt*

§1. *Of the time of* Moses *birth* . . .

§2. *Of diuers Cities and places in Ægypt, mentioned in this Storie* . . .

§3. *Of the crueltie against the Israelites yong children in Ægypt* . . .

§4. *Of* Moses *his flying out of Ægypt* . . .

§5. *Of* Pharaohs *pursuit of the Israelites* . . .

§6. *Of the Solarie and Lunarie yeares: and how they are reconciled: with the forme of the Hebrew yeare, and their manner of intercalation.*

§7. *Of the passage of* Israel *from Succoth towards the Red Sea* . . .

§8. *Of their passage ouer the Red Sea: and of the Red Sea it selfe.*

§9. *That the passage through the Red Sea was miraculous, and not at a low Ebbe.*

The *Ægyptians*, and of them the *Memphites*, and other Heathen Writers, who in hatred of the *Hebrewes* haue obiected that *Moses* past ouer the red Sea at a low ebbe, vpon a great spring-tide, and that *Pharao* conducted more by furie then discretion, pursued him so far, as before he could recouer the coast of *Ægypt*, he was ouertaken by the floud and therein perished, did not well consider the nature of this place with other circumstances. For not to borrow strength from that part of the Scriptures, which makes it plaine, that the waters were diuided, and that God wrought this miracle by an Easterly winde, and by the hand and rod of *Moses* (which authoritie to men that beleeue not therein perswadeth nothing) I say that by the same naturall reason vnto which they fasten themselues, it is made manifest, that had there beene no other working power from aboue or assistance giuen from God himselfe to *Moses*, and the children of *Israel* than ordinarie and casuall, then could not *Pharao* and all his armie haue perished in that pursuite.

For wheresoeuer there is any ebbing of the Sea in any gulfe, or indraught, there doe the waters fall away from the land: and runne downeward towards the *Ocean:* leauing all that part towards the land as farre as the Sea can ebbe, or fall off, to bee drie land. Now *Moses* entring the Sea at *Migdoll* vnder *Balzephon* (if hee had taken the aduantage and opportunitie of the tyde) must haue left all that end of the Red Sea towards *Sues*, on his left hand drie and vn- couered. For if a passage were made by falling away of the water, ten or twelue mile farther into the Sea then *Sues*; much more was it made at *Sues*, and betweene it and where *Moses* past: who entred the same so farre below it, and towards the body of the same Sea. It followeth then, that if all that part of the Sleeue or Strait, had beene by the ebbe of a spring-tide discouered, when *Pharao* found the floud in- creasing, he needed not to haue returned by the same way toward *Ægypt* side, but might haue gone on in his returne before the tide, on his right hand: and so taken ground againe at the end of that sea, at *Sues* it selfe, or elsewhere. But the Scriptures doe truly witnesse the contrarie, that is, That the sea did not fall away from the land, as naturally it doth; but that *Moses* past on betweene two seas: and that the waters were diuided. Otherwise, *Pharao* by any returne of waters could not haue perished, as he did: and therefore the effects of that great Armies destruction, proue the cause to haue beene a power aboue nature, and the miraculous worke of God himselfe. Againe, those words of the Scriptures, that *God caused the Sea to runne backe by a strong east-winde*, doe rather proue the miracle, than that thereby was caused an ebbe more then ordinarie: for that sea doth not lie East and

West, but, in effect, North and South. And it must haue
been a West and North-west winde, that must haue driuen
those waters away through their proper channels, and to the
South-east into the Sea. But the East-winde blew athwart
the sea, and cut it asunder: so as one part fell backe towards
the South, and maine body thereof: the other part remained
towards *Sues*, and the North. Which being vnknowne to
Pharao; while he was checkt by that sea, which vsed in all
times before to ebbe away: the floud prest him and ouer-
whelmed him. Thirdly, seeing *Iosephus* auoweth, that *Moses*
was not only of excellent iudgement generally, but also so
great a Captaine, as he ouerthrew the *Æthiopians* in many
battels, being imploied by *Pharao*, and wan diuers Cities
seeming impregnable: it were barbarous to condemne him
of this grossenesse, and distraction: that rather then he
would haue endured the hardnesse of a mountainous passage
at hand, (had not God commanded him to take that way,
and foretold him of the honour which hee would there winne
vpon *Pharao*) he would haue trusted to the aduantage of an
ebbing water. For hee knew not the contrarie, but that
Pharao might haue found him, and prest him, as well when
it flowed as when it ebbed, as it seemeth he did. For the
people, beholding *Pharaos* approch, cried out against
Moses, and despaired altogether of their safetie: and when
Moses praied vnto God for helpe, he was answered by God:
*Wherefore criest thou vnto me: speake vnto the children of Israel
that they goe forward, and lift thou vp thy rod, and stretch out
thy hand vpon the Sea, and diuide it:* which proues that there
was not at the time of *Pharaos* approch any ebbe at all; but
that God did disperse and cut through the weight of waters,
by a strong East-winde, whereby the sands discouered
themselues betweene the sea on the left hand toward *Sues*,
from whence the waters moued not, and the sea which was
towards the South on the right hand, *so that the waters were
a wall vnto them on the right hand, and on the left hand*, that
is, the waters so defended them on both sides, as the
Ægyptians could only follow them in the same path; not
that the waters stood vpright as walls doe, as some of the
Schoolemen haue fancied. For had *Pharaoh* and the *Ægyptians*
perceiued any such buildings in the sea, they would soone

haue quitted the chace and pursuit of *Israel*. Furthermore,
there is no man of iudgement, that can thinke, that *Pharaoh*
and the *Ægyptians*, who then excelled all Nations in the
obseruations of heauenly motions, could be ignorant of the
fluxes, and refluxes of the sea, in his owne Countrie, on his
owne coast, and in his owne most traded and frequented
Ports and Hauens, and wherein, his people hauing had so
many hundreds of yeares experience of the tides, he could
not be caught, as he was, through ignorance, nor by any
foreknowne or naturall accident, but by Gods powerfull
hand only; which then falleth most heauily on all men, when
looking through no other spectacle but their owne prosperitie, they least discerne it comming, and least feare it.
Lastly, if the Armie of the *Ægyptians* had beene ouertaken
by the ordinarie returne of the floud, before they could
recouer their owne coast; their bodies drowned would haue
beene carried with the floud which runneth vp to *Sues*, and
to the end of that sea, and not haue beene cast ashore on that
coast of *Arabia* where *Moses* landed, to wit, vpon the sea-
banke ouer against *Baalzephon*, on *Arabia* side: where it was
that the *Israelites* saw their dead bodies; and not at the end
of the *Red Sea*, to which place the ordinarie floud would haue
carried them: Which floud doth not any where crosse the
Channell, and runne athwart it, as it must haue done from
Ægypt side to *Arabia*, to haue cast the *Ægyptians* bodies
there; but it keepes the naturall course towards the end of
that sea: and to which their carcases should haue beene
carried, if the worke had not beene supernaturall and
miraculous. *Apollonius* in the liues of the *Fathers* affirmeth,
that those of the *Ægyptians* which staied in the Countrie,
and did not follow *Pharaoh* in the pursuit of *Israel*, did euer
after honour those Beasts, Birds, Plants, or other Creatures,
about which they were busied at the time of *Pharaohs*
destruction: as he that was then labouring in his garden
made a God of that Plant or Roote, about which he was
occupied: and so of the rest. But how those multitudes of
Gods were erected among them, a more probable reason shall
be giuen elsewhere. *Orosius* in his first Booke and tenth
Chapter against the *Pagans* tells vs, that in his time, who
liued some 400. yeares after *Christ*, the prints of *Pharaohs*

Chariot wheeles were to be seene at a low water on the *Ægyptian* sands: and though they were sometime defaced by winde and weather, yet soone after they appeared againe. But hereof I leaue euery man to his owne beleefe.

Ch. IV. *Of the iournying of the Israelites from the Red Sea, to the place where the Law was giuen them: with a discourse of Lawes*

§1. *A transition, by way of recapitulation of some things touching Chronologie: with a continuance of the storie . . .*

§2. *Of the Amalekites, Madianites, and Kenites . . .*

§3. *Of the time when the Law was giuen: with diuers commendations of the inuention of Lawes.*

§4. *Of the name and meaning of the words, Law, and Right.*

The word *Lex*, or *Law*, is not alwaies taken alike, but is diuersly, and in an indifferent sense vsed. For if we consider it at large, it may be vnderstood for any rule prescribing a necessarie meane, order, and methode, for the attaining of an end. And so the rules of *Grammer*, or other Arts, are called Lawes. Or it is taken for any priuate ordinance of Superiours to Inferiours: for the commandements of Tyrants, which they cause to be obserued by force, for their decrees doe also vsurpe that title, according to the generall acceptation of the word *Law:* of which *Esay, Woe vnto them that decree wicked decrees, and write grieuous things.* Likewise, the word is vsed for the tumultuarie resolutions of the people. For such constitutions doth *Aristotle* also call lawes, though euill and vnsufficient. *Mala lex est, quæ tumultuariè posita est*; *It is an ill law that is made tumultuously.* So as all ordinances, good or euill, are called by the name of lawes.

The word *Law* is also taken for the morall habit of our minde, which doth (as it were) command our thoughts, words, and actions: framing and fashioning them according to it selfe, as to their patterne and platforme. And thus the law of the flesh which the Diuines call *legem fomitis*, is to be understood. For euery law is a kinde of patterne of that which is done according vnto it: in which sense as else-where, this morall habit or disposition of the heart is called the frame or *figmentum* of the heart: so in S^t. *Paul* to the *Romanes* it is called a *Law. But I see another law in my members, rebelling against the law of my minde, and leading me captiue vnto the law of sinne.* Againe, the nature and inclinations of all creatures are sometime called *lawes*, so farre as they agree with the reason of the law eternall; as the law of a *Lyon*, to bee fierce or valiant.

Also priuate contracts among Merchants and other Tradesmen, doe often put on the name of lawes. But law commonly and properly is taken, for a right rule, prescribing a necessarie meane, for the good of a Common-wealth, or Ciuill communitie. The rest, to wit, the commandements of Tyrants, &c. which haue not the common good for their end, but being *leges iniquæ*, are by *Thomas* called *violentiæ magis quàm leges*; *rather compulsions then lawes:* And what-soeuer is not iust, Saint *Augustine* doth not allow for lawes, howsoeuer established: for he calls them *iniqua hominum constituta, quæ nec iura dicenda, nec putanda sunt*; *The vniust constitutions of men which are neither to be termed nor thought lawes.* For saith *Aristotle, Legalia iusta sunt factiua, & conseruatiua fœlicitatis*; *Iust lawes are the workers and pre-seruers of happinesse:* because by them we are directed *ad vitam quietam, to a quiet life,* according to *Cicero.* Yea, *to life euerlasting,* according to the Scriptures. For the end of the law, saith *Plato,* is God and his worship. *Finis legis Deus & cultus eius. Lex,* or the Law is so called by the *Latines à legendo,* or *à ligando, of reading* or *binding: Leges quia lectæ*

& ad populum latæ, saith *Varro*; For after Lawes were written and published, all men might reade them, and behold in them whereto they were bound. The other *Etymologie, à ligando*, is no lesse agreeable with the nature of a Law: whence in the Scripture it is called also a yoke, and a band: as *confregerunt iugum, diruperunt vincula:* they haue broken the yoke, they haue broken the bands. And in the second *Psalme, dirumpamus vincula corum, & projiciamus à nobis funes ipsorum*; *Let vs breake their bands in sunder, and cast away their cordes from vs.*

The *Couenant* it is called, because of the conditionall promises of God: and because of Gods peoples voluntarie submission of themselues vnto it: for which word the *Septuagint*, and the *Epistle* to the *Hebrewes*, vse the word διαθήκη, *a Testament or last will:* which name it hath, because it is not otherwise effectuall for our saluation, but in respect of the death of the Testator, for without the death of the Testator, the Testament is of no force: *as Hebr.* 9.17. it is said, *Testamentum in mortuis ratum est.*

The *Hebrewes* call the law *Thorah* of teaching, because euery man is thereby taught his dutie, both to God and Men. The *Greekes* call it *Nomos* of distributing, because it distributeth to euery man his owne due; the power of the law is the power of God: Iustice being an attribute proper vnto God himselfe. *Imperium legis imperium Dei est*; *The raigne of the law, is the raigne of God.*

Law in generall is thus defined by the *Philosophers*: *Lex est vitæ regula, præcipiens quæ sunt sequenda, & quæ fugienda*; *Law is the rule of life, commanding what to follow and what to shunne*, or *Lex est omnium diuinarum & humanarum rerum Regina*; *Law is the Queene* or *Princesse of things both humane and diuine.* But this description is grounded vpon the opinion of ineuitable fate. Law is the very wisedome of Nature: the reason and vnderstanding of the prudent: and the rule of right and wrong. For as a right line is called *Index sui & curui*, the demonstrance of it selfe, and of the crooked: so is the law, the Iudge and measure of right and wrong.

M^r. *Hooker* calls the Law a directiue rule to goodnesse of operation: and though law as touching the substance and essence, consist in vnderstanding: *Concludit tamen actum voluntatis*; *Yet it comprehends the act of our will.* The word *Ius* is also diuersly taken, as sometime for the matter of the law and for common right: sometime for the law it selfe: as *Ius Ciuile*, or *Ius gentium*. *Isidore* distinguisheth the two generall words *Ius* and *Fas*: whereof *Ius*, saith he, hath reference to men, *Fas* to God. *Fas lex diuina, Ius lex humana.* To goe ouer an other mans field, is permitted by Gods law, not by mans: and therefore in a thing out of controuersie, *Virgil* vsed both those words: as *Fas & iura sinunt*: God and Men permit.

The word *Ius* or Right, is deriued or taken from the old substantiue Nowne *iussus*, a bidding or commandement: or perhaps from the *Greeke* Ζεὺς, which is the name of *Iupiter*: or of the *Latine* genitiue case *Iouis*: because as the Scripture speaks, *the iudgement is Gods*. For as it is certaine that *iusiurandum* came of *Iouis-iurandum* (for so we finde it written in *Nonius* out of the ancient, in which sense the Scripture calls it *iuramentum Iehouæ*) so also we may say, that *Ius* came of *Iouis, quia Iouis est*: because as God is the Author, and Patterne, and Maintainer of right, so also in his *Vicegerents* the *Magistrates*, he is the pronouncer and exequutor of right. Of this *Ius* the iust are denominated, *iustus à iure*, and *iustitia à iusto*; *The right giues name to the righteous*: and *iustice takes her name from the iust.*

§5. *Of the definition of Lawes, and of the law eternall.*

But because lawes are manifold, and that euery kinde hath a proper and peculiar definition, it agreeth with order, first to diuide and distinguish them. I meane those sorts of lawes, from whence all other particulars are drawne: leauing the indiuiduals of humane lawes to their infinite and horrible confusion.

The law eternall is thus defined by *Thomas*. *Lex æterna est æternus diuinæ sapientiæ conceptus, secundum quod ordinatur ad gubernationem rerum ab ipso præcognitarum*; *The eternall law is the eternall conceipt of Gods wisedome, as it is referred to the gouernement of things foreknowne by himselfe.* Or *Lex æterna est summa atque æterna ratio diuinæ sapientiæ: quatenus*

Lawes are of 3. kindes.

- *Eternall, or vncreated.*
- *Naturall, Nationall, or Internall.*
- *Law imposed or of addition, commonly called positiue.*
  - *Lawes positiue or imposed explicating, and perfecting the Law of Nature, are double.*
    - *Diuine which hath two parts.*
    - *Humane which is also twofold.*

res omnes ad destinatos fines ita dirigit, vt illis iuxta condition-em ipsarum modum aliquem necessitatis adferat; It is the high and eternall reason of diuine sapience: as it directeth all things in such sort to their proper ends, imposing a kinde of necessitie according to their seuerall natures, or conditions. Now the difference lieth in this: That as the same diuine vnderstand-ing directeth all these to their proper ends; so it is called prouidence: but as it imposeth a necessitie according to the natures of all things which it directeth, so it is called a law.

Of this eternall law *Cicero* tooke knowledge, when in his booke of Lawes, hee wrote in this manner. *Erat ratio perfecta, rerum natura, & ad rectè faciendum impellens & à delicto auocans: quæ non tum incipit lex esse cum scripta est: sed tum cum orta est. Orta autem simul est cum mente diuina: quamobrem lex vera atque princeps, apta ad iubendum & ad vetandum ratio est recta summi Iouis;* That perfect reason and nature of things incouraging or impelling to rightfull actions, and calling vs backe from euill, did not (saith he) then beginne to be a law when it was written: but when it had being. Being and beginning it had together with diuine vnderstanding, and therefore a true law

{ Written. { The written is also double. { The law of Moses. { The Gospell.

{ Vnwritten. { As the doctrine and religion of the Patriarks before the written law of Moses, which some call Cabala.

{ Written. { Which Cicero in his second booke of inuention cal-*leth* Ius legiti-mum, *diuided* into the { Ecclesiasticall, and Secular.

{ Vnwritten. { As the Lawes of custome and *vse.*

and a fit Princesse to command and forbid is the right reason of the most high God. This eternall law, (if we consider it in God, or as God,) is alwaies one and the same; the nature of God being most simple: but as it is referred to diuers obiects, so the reason of man finds it diuers and manifold. It also seemeth one law in respect of things necessarie, as the motions of the heauens, stabilitie of the earth, &c. but it appeareth otherwise to things contingent: another law to men: another to other creatures, hauing life, and to all those that be inanimate.

By this eternall law all things are directed, as by the counsaile and prouidence of God: from this law all lawes are deriued, as from the rule vniuersall: and thereto referred, as the operation of the second to the first.

The eternall, and the diuine Law, differ only in consideration; the eternall directing more largely, aswell euery creature, to their proper and naturall ends, as it doth man to his supernaturall: but the diuine law to a supernaturall end only: the Naturall law is thence deriued, but an effect of the eternall: as it were a streame from this fountaine.

The Lawe humane or temporall is also thence drawne: in that it hath the forme of right reason: from which if it differ, it is then *impositio iniqua, a wicked imposition:* and only borroweth the name of a law.

To this eternall law all things are subiected: aswell *Angels* and *Men*, as all other creatures, or things created; whether necessarie or contingent, naturall, or morall, and humane. For the law eternall runneth through all the vniuersall, and therefore it is the law also of things which are simple, naturall, and inanimate.

Hence it is, that all things created are commanded to praise God their Creatour and Directour: as *Praise him all yee his Angels: praise yee him Sunne and Moone, all bright Starres: heauens of heauens, for he hath established them for euer and euer. Hee hath made an ordinance which shall not passe: Praise yee the Lord from the earth yee Dragons and all depths: Fire, and haile, snow, and vapours, stormie winds, which exequute his Word: mountaines, and hils: fruitfull trees and all Cedars: Beasts, and all Cattell, &c.* Now as the reasonable Creatures are by this eternall law bound, by the glorie and felicitie proposed vnto them (beatitude being both the attractiue, and the end) so all other naturall things and creatures, haue in themselues, and in their owne natures, an obedience formall to it: without any proper intention, knowne cause, or end proposed. For beasts are led by sense, and naturall instinct: things without life by their created forme, or formall appetites, as that which is heauie to fall downeward: things light to mount vpward, &c. and fire to heate whatsoeuer is apposed. This kinde of working the *Aristotelians* ascribe to common nature: others to fate; a difference vsed in termes only; it being no other then Gods generall prouidence: for as it is truly said of God, that he is *omnia super omnia:* so are all things which appeare in themselues, thence deriued: there-vnder subiected: thence-from by his eternall law and prouidence directed, euen from the greatest to the least of his creatures, in heauen and in earth.

The *Schoolemen* are very curious and ample in the consideration of these lawes: and in discourse of the profit, and of the matter, and obiect of the eternall law. But as the profit is manifest in the good of all creatures, who haue thence-from, either reason, sense, vegetation, or appetition, to conduct them: so is the obiect and matter of the law, the whole creature. For according to S^t. *Avgvstine. Lex æterna est, qua iustum est vt omnia sint ordinatissima*; *The law eternall is that, whereby it is iust, that all things should be disposed in the best and goodliest order.*

Lastly, it is disputed, whether the eternall law be immutable, yea or no? But the resolution is, that it changeth not; for which S^t. *Augustine* vseth a sufficient argument in his first Booke of *Free-will* the sixth Chapter. For the law of *Moses* which had a time prefixed, was eternally by God ordained to last vntill the time of the *Pædagogia* of Gods people, or introduction to *Christ* should be expired: which time of expiration some thinke our Sauiour noted to be come, when on the Crosse hee said, *Consummatum est.* But I rather thinke these words of our Sauiour to haue no other signification, then that now the prophecie of their giuing him Vineger to drinke was fulfilled. For so S. *Iohn* expounds it, when he saith *v.* 28. *That Christ seeing all* (other) *things to be fulfilled, Vt consummaretur Scriptura, That the Scripture* in this also *might be fulfilled,* said *I thirst:* though I denie not, but at the same time also the date of the Law was expired, to wit, of the law cerimoniall, and of so much of the iudiciall, as appertained peculiarly to the *Iewes,* and agreeth not with the law of the new *Testament* and Gospell of *Christ.* For the immutable law of God, though prescribing things mutable, is not therefore changed in it selfe: but the things prescribed change according to this eternall ordinance; of which the *Wisedome* of *Salomon. And being one shee can doe all things, and remaining in her selfe reneweth all.*

§6. *Of the Law of Nature.*

Of the law of Nature as it is taken in generall, I finde no definition among the *Schoolemen:* only as it is considered in man, it is called *the impression of diuine light, and a participation of the eternall law in the reasonable creature. Lex naturalis est impressio diuini luminis in nobis, & participatio legis æternæ in rationali creatura. Vlpian* defines the *naturall law to be the same which nature hath taught all liuing creatures*; *Ius naturale est quod Natura omnia animalia docuit:* and he afterward addeth, *Ius istud non humani generis proprium, sed omnium animalium quæ terra marique nascuntur, auium quoque commune est*; *The law of nature is not proper to man alone, but the same is common to all liuing creatures: aswell to birds, as to those which the Land and Sea produceth.* But this definition is not generall, but of the naturall law in things of life.

The law of nature in generall, I take to be that disposition, instinct, and formall qualitie, which God in his eternall prouidence hath giuen and imprinted in the nature of euery creature, animate, and inanimate. And as it is *diuinum lumen* in men, inlightning our formall reason: so is it more then sense in beasts: and more then vegetation in plants. For it is not sense alone in beasts, which teacheth them at first sight, and without experience or instruction, to flie from the enemies of their liues: seeing that Bulls and Horses appeare vnto the sense more fearefull and terrible, then the least kinde of Dogs: and yet the Hare and Deere feedeth by the one, and flieth from the other, yea though by them neuer seene before, and that as soone as they fall from their Dammes. Neither is it sense which hath taught other Beasts to prouide for Winter, Birds to build their nests, high or low, according to the tempestuous or quiet seasons: or the Birds of *India* to make their nests on the smallest twigs which hang ouer Riuers, and not on any other part of the tree, or elsewhere: to saue their egges and yong ones from the Monkies, and other beasts, whose weight such a twig will not beare: and which would feare to fall into the water. The instances in this kinde are exceeding many which may bee giuen. Neither is it out of the vegetable or growing nature of plants, that some trees, as the female of the *Palmitto*, will not beare any fruit except the male grow in sight. But this they doe by that law which the infinite and vnsearchable wisdome of God, had in all eternitie prouided for them, and for euery nature created. In man this law is double: corrupt, and incorrupt; corrupt where the reason of man hath made it selfe subiect, and a Vassall to passions, and affections brutall: and where time and custome hath bred in men a new nature, which also, as is aforesaid, is a kinde of Law. For it was not by the law of Nature incorrupt, which S[t]. *Augustine* calleth the law of reason, but by a nature blinded and corrupted, that the *Germans* did anciently allow of theft: and that other Nations were by law constrained to become Idolaters; that by the lawes of *Lycurgus* it was permitted to men to vse one an others wife, and to the women to choose them others besides their husbands, to beget them with child: which law in those parts hath lasted long, and is not forgotten to this day.

The *Scythians*, and the people of both *Indies*, hold it lawfull to burie with them the best beloued wiues: as also they haue many other customes remembred by *G. Valentia*, against nature and right reason.

And I know not from what authoritie it is that these lawes some men auow to be naturall: except it be of this corrupt nature, as (among others) to pay guile with guile: to become faithlesse among the faithlesse: to prouide for our selues by another mans destruction: that iniurie is not done to him that is willing: to destroy those whom we feare: and the like. For taking the definition of naturall lawes, either out of S[t]. *Augustine* or *Aquinas*, (the one calling it *the impression of diuine light*; the other, *the dictate* or sentence *of practique reason*) the same can teach vs, or incline vs to no other thing, then to the exercise of Iustice and vprightnesse: and not to offer or performe any thing toward others, saue that which wee would bee content should be offered or performed toward our selues. For such is the law of nature to the minde, as the eie is to the bodie; and that which according to *Dauid* sheweth vs good, that is, the obseruation of those things which leade vs thereby to our last end; which is eternall life: though of themselues not sufficient without faith and grace.

Now, that which is truly and properly the law of Nature, where the corruption is not taken for the law, is, as aforesaid, the impression of Gods diuine light in men, and a participation of the law increated and eternall. For without any law written the right reason and vnderstanding, which God hath giuen vs, are abilities within our selues, sufficient to giue vs knowledge of the good and euill, which by our gratitude to God, and distribution of right to men, or by the contrarie, wee prepare and purchase for our selues. *For when the Gentiles* (saith S. *Pavl*) *which haue not the Law, doe by nature those things contained in the law: they hauing not the law, are a law vnto themselues.* Now, to loue God by whom wee are, and to doe the same right to all men, which we desire should be done vnto vs, is an effect of the purest reason: in whose highest Turrets, the quiet of conscience hath made her resting place, and habitation. *In arce altissima rationis quies habitat;* Therefore, the *Gentiles* (saith S. *Pavl*) *which shew the effects of the law written in their hearts, haue their consciences for witnesses of those effects: and the reprobate their thoughts to accuse them.*

And it is most true, that whosoeuer is not a law vnto him-selfe (while he hopeth to abuse the world by the aduantage of hypocrisie) worketh nothing else, but the betraying of his owne soule, by craftie vnrighteousnesse, purchasing eternall perdition. For it helpeth vs not to hide our corrupt hearts from the worlds eie, seeing from him, who is an infinite eie, we cannot hide them: some Garlands wee may gather in this May-game of the world, *Sed flos ille, dum loquimur, arescit; Those flowers wither while we discourse of their colours, or are in gathering them.* That we should therefore inhabite and dwell within our selues, and become fearefull witnesses of our secretest euils, did that reuerend *Philosopher Pythagoras* teach in this golden precept. *Nil turpe committas, neque coram alijs, neque tecum, maxime omnium verere teipsum; Commit nothing foule or dishonest,* saith he, *neither to be knowne to others, nor to thine owne heart: but aboue all men reuerence thine owne conscience.* And this may bee a precept of nature and right reason: by which law, men, and all creatures, and bodies, are inclined to those operations, which are answerable to their owne forme; as fire to giue heate. Now, as the reasonable minde is the forme of man, so is he aptly moued to those things which his proper forme presenteth vnto him: to wit, to that which right reason offereth; and the acts of right reason, are the acts of vertue: and in the breach of the rules of this reason, is man least excusable: as being a reasonable creature. For all else, both sensitiue, growing, and inanimate, obay the law which God imposed on them at their first creation.

The Earth performeth her office, according to the Law of God in nature: for it bringeth forth the budde of the hearbe which seedeth seede, &c. and the Beast, which liueth thereon. He gaue a Law to the Seas, and commanded them to keepe their bounds: which they obay. He made a decree for the raine, and a way for the lightning of the thunders. He caused the Sunne to moue, and to giue light, and to serue for signes and for seasons. Were these as rebellious as man, for whose sake they were created, or did they once breake the law of their natures and formes, the whole world would then perish, and all returne to the first *Chaos*, darkenesse, and confusion.

By this naturall Law, or Law of humane reason, did *Caine* perceiue his owne wickednesse, and offence, in the murther of *Abel:* for he not only feared the displeasure of God, but the reuenge of Men: it being written in his reason, that whatsoeuer he performed towards others, the same by others might bee done vnto him againe. And that this iudgement of well and euill doing, was put into our natures by God, and his eternall law, before the law written: *Moses* in the person of God witnesseth, *Gen.* the fourth. *If thou doe well shalt thou not be accepted? and if thou doe not well, sinne lyeth at thy dore.*

The *Schoolemen* are large also in this question of the naturall Law: the same being opened amply by *Reinerius, Antoninus,* and *Valentia.* But it is not my purpose to write a volume of this subiect.

But this law which *Thomas Aquinas* calleth *an act of reason taken properly,* and not a habite, as it is an euident naturall iudgement of practique reason: they diuide into indemonstrable, or needing no demonstration (as that good is to be followed, and euill eschewed) and demonstrable, which is euidently proued, out of higher and more vniuersall propositions. Againe, as it answereth the naturall appetite, prescribing things to be desired as good, or to be auoided as euill (as of the first to desire to liue, and to satisfie hunger, &c. and of the second, to eschew paines, sorrow, and death) in this consideration they diuide it, according to the diuers kinds of appetites that are in vs. For in euery man there are three sorts of appetites, which answere the three degrees of

naturall Law. The first is, to bee that which we are; in which
is comprehended the desire, both to liue, and to preserue our
being and life, also the desire of issue, with care to prouide
for them: for the Father after his death liues in his children;
and therefore the desire of life comprehends the desire of
children. And to these appetites are referred the first indemonstrable lawes of nature, for the most part. For it
needes no proofe, that all creatures should desire to be, to
liue, and to be defended, and to liue in their issue, when they
cannot in themselues. And as man is a being, *Ens* or *Res*:
so hee doth desire good, and shunne euill. For it is common
to all things, to desire things agreable to their owne natures,
which is, to desire their owne good. And so is Good defined
by *Aristotle*, to be that which all desire. Which definition
Basil vpon the 44. *Psalme* approueth: *Recte quidem Bonum
definierunt, Quod omnia expetunt*; *Rightly haue some men
defined Good, or Goodnesse, to be that which all things desire.*

The second kinde of appetite is of those things which
appertaine to us, as wee haue sense. Whence, by the law of
Nature, wee desire the delight of euery sense; but with such
moderation, as may neither glut vs with satietie, nor hurt
vs with excesse. For as Sense it selfe is for the preseruation
of life and being: so is it meete, euen by the law of nature,
that the sensitiue appetite should not carrie vs to the
destruction, either of our life or being. And although (seeing
both these kinds of appetites are in beasts) wee may well
say, that Nature hath giuen diuers lawes vnto them: In
which sense the *Ciuilians* define *Naturall right*, or *Ius
naturale*, to bee the same which Nature hath taught all
liuing creatures; Yet the *Schoolemen* admit not, that the
instincts of beasts can be properly called a Law, but only a
Ius, or *Right*, which is the matter, and aime of euery Law.
For so they distinguish it, where *Vlpian* affirmeth, that *Ius
naturale* is that, which Nature hath taught all liuing creatures.
In this place (saith *Valentia*) *Ius* is not to be taken for a Law,
but for the matter of the Law. And yet where *Vlpian* also
distinguisheth the right belonging to liuing creatures in
generall, from the right belonging to men; calling the one
Ius naturæ, the other *Ius gentium:* the Diuines vnderstand the
law of nature more largely, that is, for all euident dictates,

precepts, or biddings of diuine reason: both in beasts and men; and restraine the law of Nations to a kinde of humane right.

The third appetite is of those things which appertaine properly to man, as he is a liuing creature reasonable: as well with relation to God, and to our Neighbour, as for our selues: and the lawes of this appetite are the Commandements of our religion.

Now although there are many other branches and diuisions of this law of nature answering the diuision of matter, which it prescribeth, and as manifold, as the morall actions are which it commandeth or forbiddeth: yet is the law of nature but one law, according to *Aquinas*: first, because it hath one fountaine or roote in the naturall or motiue facultie, which is but one, stirring vp to good, and declining the contrarie: secondly, because all is contained in that generall naturall precept, That good is to be followed, and ill auoided: and thirdly, because all the parts are reduced to one and the same last end.

That this law of nature bindeth all creatures, it is manifest: and chiefly man; because he is indued with reason; in whom as reason groweth, so this band of obseruing the law of nature increaseth, *Post quam ratio ad perfectum venit, tunc fit quod scriptum est, Adueniente mandato peccatum reuixit*; *When reason grew to perfection, then it came to passe, which was written by* S. *Pavl, When the Commandement came, sinne reuiued.* Neither is it a small warrant for this law of nature, when those which breake the same, are said by S. *Pavl, To be deliuered ouer into a reprobate sense* (or minde) *to doe those things which are not conuenient:* and againe, *that their consciences beare witnesse, and their thoughts accuse them.* For, though this law of nature stretch not to euery particular: as to command fasting and the like: yet, it commandeth in generall all good, and whatsoeuer is agreeable to right reason. And therefore, said *Damascene*; *homines facti sunt mali, declinando in id quod contra naturam est*; *Men* (saith he) *are made euill, by declining vnto that which is contrarie to nature:* and S. *Avgvstine, Omne vitium naturæ nocet, ac per hoc contra naturam est*; *Euery vice doth wrong to nature, and is therefore contrarie vnto it.*

Neither yet are the rules of this law of nature so streight, but that they suffer exceptions in some particulars. For whereas by this law all men are borne Lords of the earth, yet it well alloweth inequalitie of portions, according to vnequall merit: by taking from the euill, and giuing to the good: and by permitting and commanding that all men shall enioy the fruits of their labours to themselues: according to the rules of justice and equitie.

And though the law of nature command, that all things bee restored which are left in trust, yet in some causes this her law shee suffereth to be broken: as to denie a madde man his weapons, and the like, which he left in keeping while hee was sober. But the vniuersall principles can no more bee changed, than the decrees of God are alterable: who according to St. *Pavl, abideth faithfull, and cannot denie himselfe*.

§7. *Of the written Law of God.*

After the eternall, and naturall, the law *Positiue* or imposed is the next in order, which law, being nothing but an addition, or rather explication of the former, hath two kinds: Diuine, and Humane. Againe, the diuine positiue law is double; the old and new: The old was giuen vnto *Moses* in Mount *Sinai* or *Horeb*, at such time as the world had stood 2513. whole yeeres: and in the 67. day of this yeere when as *Ascatades* or *Ascades* gouerned the *Assyrians, Marathus* the *Sycionians, Triopus* the *Argiues, Cecrops Attica,* and *Acherres Ægypt:* to wit, after the promise to *Abraham* 430. yeeres. And this, it seemes, was the first written law which the world receiued. For the very word *Nomos,* signifying a law, was not then, nor long after inuented by the *Græcians:* no not in *Homers* time: who liued after the fall of *Troy* 80. yeeres at least: and *Troy* it selfe was cast downe 335. yeeres, after *Moses* led *Israel* out of *Ægypt.* This law, it pleased God to ingraue in stone, that it might remaine a lasting booke of his exprest will in the Church; and that the Priests and people might haue, whereof to meditate, till the comming of *Christ:* and that so these children of *Israel,* though bred among an Idolatrous people in *Ægypt*, might be without excuse: the slight defences of ignorance being taken from them.

The reason knowne to vs why this law was not written before, is, that when the people were few, and their liues long, the *Elders* of families might easily without any written law instruct their owne children: and yet as they increased, so doubtlesse they had besides the law of Nature, many precepts from God, before the law written. But now at length, forasmuch as the law of nature did not define all kinds of good, and euill; nor condemne euery sinne in particular: nor sufficiently terrifie the consciences of offenders: nor so expound diuine worship, as for those after-ages was required, who gaue euery day lesse authoritie than other to the naturall law; In these respects it was necessarie, that the law should be written, and set before the eies of all men: which before, they might, but would not reade, in their owne consciences. The *Schoolemen*, and the Fathers before them, inlarge the causes and necessitie, why the law was written, whereof these are the chiefest.

The first, for restraining of sinne, directly grounded vpon this place of *David, The law of the Lord is vndefiled, conuerting soules: The testimonies of the Lord are faithfull, giuing wisedome to children*. For the humane law, saith S[t]. *Augustine*, meeteth not with all offences, either by way of prohibition or punishment; seeing thereby it might take away something seeming necessarie, and hinder common profit: but the diuine law written, forbiddeth euery euill, and therefore by *Dauid* it is called vndefiled.

Secondly, it serueth for the direction of our minds. For the lawes of men, can only take knowledge of outward actions, but not of internall motions, or of our disposition and will: and yet it is required, that we be no lesse cleane in the one, than in the other. And therefore were the words *conuerting our soules*, added by *Dauid*: wherein are all our outward acts first generated, according to the *Cabalists*. *Actiones hominum nullæ essent, nisi prius in mente dicerentur; The actions of men* (say they) *would be none at all, were they not first conceiued in the minde*.

Thirdly, it leadeth vs to the knowledge of truth, by which reason of diuersitie of opinion, and difference of peculiar

lawes among sundrie Nations, wee cannot bee assured of;
but the law of God bindeth all men, and is without errour:
and therefore also said *David, That the testimonie of the law
of God is faithfull: giuing wisedome to children.*

§8. *Of the vnwritten law of God, giuen to the Patriarks by
Tradition.*

§9. *Of the Morall, Iudiciall, and Ceremoniall Law . . .*

§§10–12. *A proposall of nine other points . . .*

§13. *Of the seuerall Commandements of the* Decalogue . . .

§14. *If there were not any Religion nor Iudgement to come, yet
the* Decalogue *were most necessarie to be obserued.*

§15. *Of humane Law, written and vnwritten.*

§16. *That only the Prince is exempt from humane lawes, and in
what sort.*

Ch. V. *The Storie of the Israelites from the receiuing of the Law, to the death of* Moses[1]

§10. *Obseruations out of the Storie of* Moses, *how God disposeth both the smallest occasions, and the greatest resist-
ances, to the effecting of his purpose.*

---

[1] The single section from Chapter v, which follows, is directly related to the
single one from Chapter xix (below, p. 210). The titles of the intervening
chapters are given to remind us of Ralegh's constant efforts to interlock the
histories of Israel and other nations.

Now let vs a little, for instruction, looke backe to the occasions of sundrie of the great euents, which haue beene mentioned in this Storie of the life of *Moses*, for (excepting Gods miracles, his promise, and fore-choise of this people) hee wrought in all things else by the *medium* of mens affections, and naturall appetites. And so we shall find that the feare which *Pharao* had of the increase of the *Hebrewes*, multiplied by God to exceeding great numbers, was the next naturall cause of the sorrowes and losse, which befell himselfe, and the *Ægyptian* Nation: which numbers when he sought by cruell and vngodly pollicies to cut off and lessen, as when he commanded all the male-children of the *Hebrewes* to be slaine, God (whose prouidence cannot bee resisted, nor his purposes preuented by all the foolish and saluage craft of mortall men) moued compassion in the heart of *Pharao's* owne Daughter, to preserue that child, which afterward became the most wise, and of all men the most gentle and milde, the most excellently learned in all Diuine and Humane knowledge, to be the Conductor and deliuerer of his oppressed Brethren, and the ouerthrow of *Pharao*, and all the flower of his Nation; euen then, when he sought by the strength of his men of Warre, of his Horse, and Chariots, to tread them vnder and burie them in the dust. The griefe which *Moses* conceiued of the iniuries, and of the violence offered to one of the *Hebrewes* in his owne presence, moued him to take reuenge of the *Ægyptian* that offered it: the ingratitude of one of his owne Nation, by threatning him to discouer the slaughter of the *Ægyptian*, moued him to flie into *Midian*: the contention betweene the sheep-heards of that place, and *Iethro's* Daughters, made him knowne to their Father: who not only entertained him, but married him to one of those Sisters: and in that solitarie life of keeping of his Father in lawes sheepe, farre from the presse of the world, contenting himselfe (though bred as a Kings Sonne) with the lot of a poore Heards-man, God found him out in that Desart, wherein he first suffered him to liue many yeares, the better to know the waies and passages through which he purposed that hee should conduct his people, toward the Land promised: and therein appearing vnto him, he made him know his Will and diuine Pleasure for his returne into *Ægypt*. The like may be said of all things else, which *Moses* afterward by Gods direction performed in the Storie of *Israel* before remembred. There is not therefore the smallest accident, which may seeme vnto men as falling out by chance, and of no consequence: but that the same is caused by God to effect somewhat else by: yea, and oftentimes to effect things of the greatest worldly importance, either presently, or in many yeares after, when the occasions are either not considered, or forgotten.

Ch. VI. *Of the Nations with whom the Israelites had dealing after their comming out of Ægypt . . .*

Ch. VII. *Of the Tribes of Israel . . .*

Ch. VIII. *Of the Kingdom of Phœnicia*

Ch. IX. *Of the Tribe of Ephraim . . .*

Ch. X. *Of the memorable places of* Dan, Simeon, Ivda, Rvben, Gad . . .

Ch. XI. *The Historie of the Syrians* . . .

Ch. XII. *Of the Tribe of* Beniamin, *and of Hierusalem*

Ch. XIII. *Of the memorable thinges that happened in the world, from the death of* Iosva *to the Warre of Troy: which was about the time of* Iephtha

§1. *Of the* inter-regnum *after* Iosva's *death: and of* Othoniel.

§2. *Of the memorable thinges of this Age in other Nations* . . .

§3. *Of* Ehvds *time, and of* Proserpina, Orithya, Terevs, Tantalvs . . .

§4. *Of* Debora *and her Contemporaries.*

§5. *Of* Gideon, *and of* Dædalvs, Sphinx, Minos . . .

§6. *Of the expedition of the Argonauts.*[1]

About the eleuenth yeere of *Gideon*, was that famous
expedition of the *Argonauts:* of which many fabulous discourses haue beene written, the summe of which is this.

Pelias the sonne of *Neptune*, brother by the mothers side
to *Æson*, who was *Iasons* father, reigning in *Iolcus* a towne
of *Thessalie*, was warned by the *Oracle of Apollo* to take heede
of him that ware but one shoe. This *Pelias* afterward
sacrificing to *Neptune*, inuited *Iason* to him, who comming
hastily, lost one shoe in passing ouer a brooke: whereupon
Pelias demaunded of him what course he would take
(supposing he were able) against one of whom an *Oracle*
should aduise him to take heede: to which question when
Iason had briefly answered, that he would send him to
Colchos, to fetch the golden fleece, *Pelias* immediatly commaunded him to vndertake that seruice. Therefore *Iason*
prepared for the voyage, hauing a shippe built by *Argus*,
the sonne of *Phryxus*, by the Counsell of *Pallas:* wherein
hee procured all the brauest men of *Greece* to saile with him:
as *Typhis* the Master of the shippe, *Orpheus* the famous Poet,
Castor and *Pollux* the sonnes of *Tyndarus*, *Telamon* and
Peleus, sonnes of *Æacus*, and fathers of *Aiax* and *Achilles*,
Hercules, *Theseus*, *Zetes* and *Calais* the two winged sonnes of
Boreas, *Amphiaraus* the great Southsayer, *Meleager* of *Calidon*
that slew the great wilde boare: *Ascalaphus* and *Ialmenus* or
Almenus the sonnes of *Mars*, who were afterwards at the last
warre of *Troy*, *Laertes* the father of *Vlysses*, *Atalanta* a warlike
virgine, *Idas* and *Lynceus* the sonnes of *Aphareus*, who afterwards in fight with *Castor* and *Pollux* slew *Castor*, and
wounded *Pollux*, but were slaine themselues: *Lynceus* by
Pollux, *Idas* by *Iupiter* with lightning.

These and many other went with *Iason* in the ship *Argo:*
in whose prowe was a table of the beech of *Dodona*, which
could speake. They arriued first at *Lemnos*; the women of

---

[1] Not the least significant aspect of this section is its allegorical interpretation of the legends recited. It stands in marked contrast to Ralegh's insistence
on the primacy of the literal meaning in the Bible (above, p. 132).

which *Iland*, hauing slaine all the males, purposing to lead an *Amazonian* life, were neuerthelesse contented to take their pleasure of the *Argonauts*. Hence they came to the Country about *Cyzicus*: where dwelt a people called *Doliones*: ouer whom then reigned one *Cyzicus*: who entertained them friendly: but it so fell out, that loosing thence by night they were driuen by contrary winds back into his port, neither knowing that it was the same Hauen, nor being knowne by the *Doliones*, to be the same men: but rather taken for some of their bordering enemies: by which meanes they fell to blowes, insomuch that the *Argonautes* slew the most part of the *Doliones* together with their King *Cyzicus*: which when by daylight they perceiued, with many teares they solemnized his funerall. Then departed they againe and arriued shortly in *Mysia*, where they left *Hercules* and *Polyphemus* the sonne of *Elates*, who went to seeke *Hylas* the darling of *Hercules*, that was rauished by the *Nymphes*.

Poliphemus built a towne in *Mysia*, called *Cios*, wherein he reigned. *Hercules* returned to *Argos*. From *Mysia* the *Argonautes* sailed into *Bythinia*, which then was peopled by the *Bebryces*, the auncient inhabitants of the Country, ouer whom *Amycus* the sonne of *Neptune* was then King. He beeing a strong man, compelled all strangers to fight with him, at whorlebattes, in which kinde of fight hee had slaine many, and was now himselfe slaine by *Pollux*. The *Bebryces* in reuenge of his death flew all vpon *Pollux*, but his companions rescued him, with great slaughter of the people. They sailed from hence to *Salmydessus*, a towne in *Thrace* (somwhat out of their way) wherein *Phineus* a Soothsayer dwelt, who was blinde and vexed with the *Harpyes*. The *Harpyes* were said to be a kinde of birds, which had the faces of women and foule long clawes, very filthy creatures, which when the table was furnished for *Phineus*, came flying in, and deuouring or carrying away the greater part of the victuals, did so defile the rest, that they could not be endured. When therefore the *Argonautes* craued his aduise, and direction for their voyage: you shall doe well (quoth he) first of all to deliuer me from the *Harpyes*, and then afterwards to aske my Counsaile. Whereupon they caused the table to be couered, and meat set on; which was no sooner set downe, then that presently in came the *Harpyes*, and played their accustomed prancks: when *Zetes* and *Calais* the winged young men saw this, they drew their swords, and pursued them through the ayre; some say that both the *Harpyes* and the young men died of wearinesse in the flight, and pursuit. But *Apollonius* saith that the *Harpyes* did couenant with the youthes, to doe no more harme to *Phineus*, and were thereupon dismissed. For this good turne *Phineus* gaue them informations of the way, and aduertised them withal of the daungerous rockes, called *Symplegades*, which by force of windes running together, did shut vp the passage: wherefore he willed them to put a pigeon before them into the passage: and if that passed safe, then to aduenture after her: if not, then by no meanes to hazard themselues in vaine. They did so, and perceiuing that the pigeon had only lost a piece of her taile, they obserued the next opening of the rockes and then rowing with all their might, passed through safe, onely the end of the poope was bruised.

From thence forward, (as the tale goeth) the *Symplegades* haue stood still: for the Gods, say they, had decreed that after the passage of a shippe, they should be fixed. Thence the *Argonautes* came to the *Mariandyni*, a people inhabiting about the mouth of the riuer *Parthenius*, where *Lycus* the King entertained them courteously. Here *Idmon* a Southsayer of their company was slaine by a wild boare; also heere *Typhis* died: and *Ancæus* vndertooke to steare the shippe. So they passed by the riuer *Thermodon*, and mount *Caucasus*, and came to the riuer *Phasis*, which runnes through the land of *Colchos*. When they were entred the hauen, *Iason* went to *Æetes* the King of *Colchos*, and told him the Commaundement of *Pelias*, and cause of his comming, desiring him to deliuer the golden Flece, which *Æetes*, as the Fable goeth, promised to doe, if he alone would yoake together two brazen hooft bulles, and plowing the ground with them, sowe dragons teeth, which *Minerua* had giuen to him, being part of those which *Cadmus* did sowe at *Thebes*. These bulles were great and fierce, and breathed out fier: *Vulcan* had giuen them to *Æetes*.

Whilest *Iason* was in a great perplexitie about this taske, *Medæa* the daughter of *Æetes*, fell into a most vehement loue of him, so farre foorth, that being excellent in *Magique*, she came priuily to him, promising her helpe, if he would assure her of his marriage. To this *Iason* agreed, and confirmed his promise by oath. Then gaue she to him a medicine wherewith she bad him to annoint both his bodie and his armour, which would preserue him from their violence: further she told him, that armed men would arise out from the ground, from the teeth which hee should sowe, and set vpon him. To remedie which inconuenience, shee bad him throw stones amongst them as soone as they came vp thicke, whereupon they would fall together to blowes, in such wise that he might easily slay them. *Iason* followed her counsaile; whereto when the euent had answered, hee againe demaunded the Fleece. But *Æetes* was so farre from approuing such his desire, that hee deuised how to destroy the *Argonautes*, and burne their shippe, which *Medæa* perceiuing, went to *Iason*, and brought him by night to the Fleece, which hung vppon an oake in the groue of *Mars*, where they say it was kept by a Dragon, that neuer slept. This Dragon was by the *Magique* of *Medæa* cast into a sleepe: so taking away the golden Fleece, she went with *Iason* into the shippe *Argo*; hauing with her, her brother *Absyrtus*.

Æetes vnderstanding the practises of *Medæa*, prouided to pursue the ship, whom when *Medæa* perceiued to be at hand, she slew her brother, & cutting him in pieces she scattered his limbes in diuerse places, of which *Æetes* finding some, was faine to seeke out the rest, and suffer his daughter to passe: the parts of his sonne hee buried in a place which thereupon he called *Tomi*; the *Greeke* word signifieth *Diuision*. Afterwards he sent many of his subiectes to seeke the shippe *Argo*, threatning that if they brought not back *Medæa* they should suffer in her stead. In the meane while the *Argonauts* were driuen about the Seas, and were come to the Riuer *Eridanus*, which is *Po* in *Italie*.

Iupiter offended with the slaughter of *Absyrtus*, vexed them with a great tempest, and carried them they knew not whither; when they came to the *Ilands Absyrtides*, there the shippe *Argo* (that there might want no incredible thing in this Fable) spake to them, and said that the anger of *Iupiter* should not cease, till they came to *Ausonia*, and were

clensed by *Circe*, from the murther of *Absyrtus*. Now they
thereupon sayling betwene the coastes of *Lybia*, and *Gallia*,
and passing through the sea of *Sardinia* and along the coast
of *Hetruria*, came to the Ile of *Æea*, wherein *Circe* dwelt,
who cleansed them. Thence they sayled by the coast of the
Syrens, who sang to allure them into danger: but *Orpheus*
on the other side sang so well that he stayed them. Only
Butes swamme out vnto them, whom *Venus* rauished, and
carried to *Lylibæum* in *Sicilie* to dwell.

Hauing past the *Syrens*, they came betweene *Scylla* and
Charybdis, and the stragling rockes which seemed to cast
out great store of flames and smoke. But *Thetis* and the
Nereides, conueyed them safe through at the appointment of
Iuno. So they coasted *Sicilie* where the beeues of the Sunne
were, and touched at *Corcyra* the Iland of the *Phæaces*,
where King *Alcinous* reigned. Meane while the men of
Colchos that had beene sent by *Æetes* in quest of the shippe
Argo, hearing no newes of it, and fearing his anger if they
fulfilled not his will, betooke themselues to new habitations:
some of them dwelt in the mountaines of *Corcyra*, others in
the Ilands *Absyrtides*, and some comming to the *Phæaces*,
there found the shippe *Argo*, and demanded *Medæa* of
Alcinous: whereto *Alcinous* made answere, that if shee were
not *Iasons* wife they should haue her, but if shee were
alreadie married he would not take her from her husband.
Arete the wife of *Alcinous* hearing this, married them:
wherefore they of *Colchos* not daring to returne home,
stayed with the *Phæaces*, so the *Argonautes* departed thence,
and after a while came to *Crete*. In this Iland *Minos* reigned,
who had a man of brasse giuen to him (as some of the
Fablers say) by *Vulcan*. This man had one veine in his bodie
reaching from the necke to the heele, the end whereof was
closed vp with a brazen naile, his name was *Talus*: his
custome was to runne thrice a day about the Iland for the
defence of it. When hee saw the shippe *Argo* passe by, he
threw stones at it, but *Medæa* with her *Magique* destroyed
him. Some say that she slew him by potions, which made
him madde; others that promising to make him immortall,
she drew out the naile that stopt his veine, by which meanes
all his blood ranne out, and he died; others there are that

say he was slaine by *Pæan*, who wounded him with an arrow in the heele. From hence the *Argonautes* sailed to *Ægina* where they were faine to fight for fresh water. And lastly from *Ægina* they sailed by *Eubæa* and *Locris* home to *Iolcos*, where they arriued, hauing spent foure whole moneths in the expedition.

Some there are that by this iourney of *Iason*, vnderstand the mysterie of the Philosophers Stone, called the golden Fleece, to which also other superfine *Chymists*, draw the twelue labours of *Hercules*. *Suidas* thinkes that by the golden Fleece, was ment a booke of Parcement, which is of sheepe-skinne, and therefore called golden, because it was taught therein how other mettals might be transmuted. Others would signifie by *Iason* wisdome, and moderation, which ouercommeth all perils: but that which is most probable is the opinion of *Dercilus*, that the Storie of such a passage was true, and that *Iason* with the rest went indeed to robbe *Colchos*, to which they might arriue by boate. For not farre from *Caucasus* there are certaine steepe falling torrents which wash downe many graines of gold, as in many other parts of the world, and the people there inhabiting vse to set many fleeces of wooll in those descents of waters, in which the graines of gold remaine, and the water passeth through, which *Strabo* witnesseth to be true. The many rockes, straites, sands, and Currents, in the passage betweene *Greece* and the bottome of *Pontus*, are Poetically conuerted into those fierie bulles, the armed men rising out of the ground, the Dragon cast asleepe, and the like. The man of brasse, the *Syrens*, *Scylla* and *Charybdis*, were other hazards and aduentures which they fell into in the *Mediterran* sea, disguised, as the rest, by *Orpheus*, vnder poeticall morrals: all which *Homer* afterward vsed (the man of brasse excepted) in the description of *Vlysses* his trauailes on the same Inland-seas.

Ch. XIV. *Of the Warre of Troy*

SWR H

Ch. XV. *Of* Sampson, Eli, *and* Samvel

Ch. XVI. *Of Savl*

Ch. XVII. *Of David*

Ch. XVIII. *Of Salomon*

Ch. XIX. *Of* Salomons *Successors vntil the end of* Iehosaphat

§3. *Of the great battaile betweene* Ieroboam *and* Abia, *with a Corolarie of the examples of Gods iudgements.*

Abijah the Sonne of *Rehoboam*, inherited his Fathers Kingdome, and his vices. He raised an Armie of foure hundred thousand, with which he inuaded *Ieroboam*, who encountred him with a double number of eight hundred thousand; both Armies ioyned neare to the Mount *Ephraim*, where *Ieroboam* was vtterly ouerthrowne, and the strength of *Israel* broken; for there fell of that side fiue hundred thousand, the greatest ouerthrow that euer was giuen or receiued of those Nations. *Abijah* being now master of the field, recoured *Bethel*, *Ieshanah*, and *Ephron*, soone after which discomfiture, *Ieroboam* died: who raigned in all 22. yeares. *Abijah*, the better to strengthen himselfe, entred into league with

Hesion, the third of the *Adads* of *Syria;* as may be gathered out of the 2. of *Chron.* He raigned but three yeares and then died: the particulars of his acts were written by *Iddo* the Prophet, as some part of his Fathers were.

Here wee see how it plased God to punish the sinnes of *Salomon* in his Sonne *Rehoboam:* first, by an Idolator and a Traitor: and then by the successor of that *Ægyptian*, whose daughter *Salomon* had maried, thereby the better to assure his estate, which while he serued God, was by God assured against all and the greatest neighbouring Kings, and when hee forsooke him, it was torne a-sunder by his meanest Vassalls; Not that the Father wanted strength to defend him from the *Ægyptian Sesac*. For the sonne *Abijah* was able to leuie foure hundred thousand men, and with the same number he ouerthrew eight hundred thousand *Israelites*, and slew of them fiue hundred thousand, God giuing spirit, courage, and inuention, when and where it pleaseth him. And as in those times the causes were exprest, why it pleased God to punish both Kings and their People: the same being both before, and at the instant deliuered by Prophets; so the same iust God who liueth and gouerneth all thinges for euer, doeth in these our times giue victorie, courage, and discourage, raise, and throw downe Kinges, Estates, Cities, and Nations, for the same offences which were committed of old, and are committed in the present: for which reason in these and other the afflictions of *Israel*, alwaies the causes are set downe, that they might bee as precedents to succeeding ages. They were punished with famine in *Dauids* time for three yeeres, *For Saul and his bloudie house, &c.* And *Dauid* towards his latter end suffred all sorts of afflictions, and sorrowes in effect, for *Vriah*. *Salomon* had tenne tribes of twelue torne from his sonne for his idolatrie. *Rehoboam* was spoiled of his riches and honour by *Sesac* of *Ægypt*, because the people of *Iuda* made images, high places, and groues &c. And because they suffered *Sodomites* in the land. *Ieroboam* was punished in himselfe & his posteritie for the golden *Calues* that he erected. *Ioram* had all his sonnes slaine by the *Philistims*, and his very bowels torne out of his bodie by an excoriating flix, for murthering his brethren. *Ahab* and *Iezabel* were slaine, the bloud of the one, the bodie of the other eaten with dogs: for the false accusing and killing of *Naboth*. So also hath God punished the same and the like sinnes in all after-times, and in these our daies by the same famine, plagues, warre, losse, vexation, death, sicknesse, and calamities, howsoeuer the wise men of the world raise these effectes no higher than to second causes, and such other accidents, which, as being next their eyes and eares, seeme to them to worke euery alteration that happeneth.

Ch. XX. *Of* Iehoram *the sonne of* Iehosaphat, *and* Ahazia

Ch. XXI. *Of* Athalia

§6. *A digression, wherein is maintained the libertie of vsing coniecture in Histories.*

Thvs much concerning the person of *Ioas*, from whom, as from a new roote, the tree of *Dauid* was propagated into many branches. In handling of which matter, the more I consider the nature of this Historie, and the diuersitie beweene it and others, the lesse, me thinkes, I neede to suspect mine owne presumption, as deseruing blame, for curiositie in matter of doubt, or boldnesse in libertie of coniecture. For all Histories doe giue vs information of humaine counsailes and euents, as farre forth as the knowledge and faith of the writers can affoord; but of Gods will, by which all things are ordered, they speake onely at randome, and many times falsly. This we often finde in prophane writers, who ascribe the ill successe of great vndertakings to the neglect of some impious rites, whereof indeed God abhorred the performance as vehemētly, as they thought him to be highly offended with the omission. Hereat we

may the lesse wonder, if we consider the answere made by
the *Iewes* in *Ægypt* vnto *Ieremie* the Prophet reprehending
their idolatrie. For, howsoeuer the written Law of *God* was
knowne vnto the people, and his punishmens laid vpon
them for contempt thereof were very terrible, and euen then
but newly executed; yet were they so obstinatly bent vnto
their owne wils, that they would not by any meanes be
drawne to acknowledge the true cause of their affliction. But
they told the Prophet roundly, that they would worship the
Queene of Heauen, as they and their fathers, their Kings and
their Princes had vsed to do; *For then* (said they) *had we
plentie of victuals, and were well, and felt no euill:* adding that
all manner of miseries were befallen them, since they left
off the seruice of that *Queene of Heauen*. So blinde is the
wisdome of man, in looking into the counsaile of God, which
to finde out there is no better nor other guide than his
owne written wil, not peruerted by vaine additions.

But this Historie of the Kings of *Israel* and *Iuda* hath
herein a singular prerogatiue aboue all that haue beene
written by the most sufficient of meerly humane authours:
it setteth downe expresly the true, and first causes of all that
happened; not imputing the death of *Ahab* to his ouer-
forwardnesse in battaile; the ruine of his familie, to the
securitie of *Ieroboam* in *Izreel;* nor the victories of *Hazael*,
to the great commotions raised in *Israel*, by the comming
in of *Iehu;* but referring all vnto the will of God, I meane, to
his reuealed will: from which that his hidden purposes doe
not varie, this storie, by many great examples, giues most
notable proofe. True it is that the concurrence of second
causes with their effects, is in these bookes nothing largely
described; nor perhaps exactly in any of those Histories
that are in these points most copious. For it was well noted
by that worthie Gentleman Sir *Philip Sidnie*, that Historians
doe borrow of Poets, not onely much of their ornament, but
somewhat of their substance. Informations are often false,
records not alwaies true, and notorious actions commonly
insufficient to discouer the passions, which did set them
first on foote. Wherefore they are faine (I speake of the best,
and in that which is allowed: for to take out of *Liuie* euery
one circumstance of *Claudius* his iourney against *Asdrubal* in

Italie, fitting all to another businesse, or any practise of that kinde, is neither Historicall nor Poeticall) to search into the particular humours of Princes, and of those which haue gouerned their affections, or the instruments by which they wrought, from whence they doe collect the most likely motiues, or impediments of euery businesse; and so figuring, as neere to the life as they can imagine, the matter in hand, they iudiciously consider the defects in counsaile, or obliquitie in proceeding.

Yet all this, for the most part, is not enough to giue assurance, howsoeuer it may giue satisfaction. For the heart of man is vnsearchable: and Princes, howsoeuer their intents be seldome hidden from some of those many eyes which prie both into them, and into such as liue about them; yet sometimes either by their owne close temper, or by some subtill miste, they conceale the trueth from all reports. Yea, many times the affections themselues lie dead, and buried in obliuion, when the preparations which they begate, are conuerted to another vse. The industrie of an Historian, hauing so many things to wearie it, may well be excused, when finding apparent cause enough of things done, it forbeareth to make further search; though it often fall out, where sundry occasions worke to the same end, that one small matter in a weake minde is more effectuall, than many that seeme farre greater. So comes it many times to passe, that great fires, which consume whole houses or Townes, begin with a few strawes, that are wasted or not seene; when the flame is discouered, hauing fastned vpon some wood-pile, that catcheth all about it. Questionlesse it is that the warre commenced by *Darius*, and pursued by *Xerxes* against the *Greekes*, proceeded from desire of the *Persians* to enlarge their Empire: howsoeuer the enterprize of the *Athenians* vpon *Sardes*, was noised abroad as the ground of that quarrell: yet *Herodotus* telleth vs, that the wanton desire of *Queene Atossa*, to haue the *Grecian* dames her bondwomen, did first moue *Darius* to prepare for this warre, before he had receiued any iniurie; and when he did not yet so much desire to get more, as to enioy what was alreadie gotten.

I will not here stand to argue whether *Herodotus* be more iustly reprehended by some, or defended by others, for

alleadging the vaine appetite, and secret speech of the
Queene in bed with her husband, as the cause of those great
euils following; this I may boldlie affirme, (hauing I think, in
euery estate some sufficient witnesses) that matter of much
consequence, founded in all seeming vpon substantiall
reasons, haue issued indeed from such pettie trifles, as no
Historian would either thinke vpon, or could well search out.

Therefore it was a good answere that *Sixtus Quintus* the
Pope made to a certaine Frier, comming to visite him in his
Popedome, as hauing long before in his meaner estate, beene
his familiar friend. This poore Frier, being emboldened by
the Pope to vse his old libertie of speech, aduentured to tell
him, that he verie much wondred how it was possible for his
holinesse, whom he rather tooke for a direct honest man,
than any cunning polititian, to attaine vnto the Papacie; in
compassing of which, all the subtiltie (said he) of the most
craftie braines, finde worke enough: and therfore the more
I thinke vpon the arte of the conclaue, and your vnaptnesse
thereto, the more I needs must wonder. Pope *Sixtus* to
satisfie the plaine dealing Friar, dealt with him againe as
plainly, saying, Hadst thou liued abroad as I haue done, and
seene by what folly this world is gouerned, thou wouldest
wonder at nothing.

Surely, if this be referred vnto those exorbitant engines,
by which the course of affaires is mooued; the Pope said
true. For the wisest of men are not without their vanities,
which requiring and finding mutuall toleration; worke more
closely, and earnestly, than right reason either needes or can.
But if we lift vp our thoughts to that supreame gouernour,
of whose Empire all that is true, which by the Poet was said
of *Iupiter*.

> *Quiterram inertem, qui mare temperat*
> *Ventosum, & vrbes, regnaque tristia*
> *Diuosque, mortalesque turmas,*
> *Imperio regit vnus æquo.*

> Who rules the duller earth, the wind-swolne streames,
> The ciuill Cities, and th'infernall realmes,
> Who th'host of heauen and the mortall band,
> Alone doth gouerne by his iust commaund.[1]

[1] Horace, *Carmina*, III iv 45–8.

Then shall we finde the quite contrarie. In him there is no vncertaintie nor change; he foreseeth all things, and all things disposeth to his owne honour; Hee neither deceiueth nor can be deceiued, but continuing one and the same for euer, doth constantly gouerne all creatures by that law, which hee hath prescribed and will neuer alter. The vanities of men beguile their vaine contriuers, and the prosperitie of the wicked, is the way leading to their destruction: yea, this broad and headlong passage to hell, is not so delightfull as it seemeth at the first entrance, but hath growing in it, besides the poisons which infect the soule, many cruell thornes deepely wounding the bodie, all which, if any few escape, they haue onely this miserable aduantage of others, that their descent was the more swift and expedite. But the seruice of God is the path guiding vs to perfect happinesse, and hath in it a true, though not compleat felicitie, yeelding such abundance of ioy to the conscience, as doth easilie counteruaile all afflictions whatsoeuer: though indeed those brambles that sometimes teare the skinne of such as walke in this blessed way, doe commonly laie hold vpon them at such time as they sit downe to take their ease, and make them with themselues at their iournies end, in presence of their Lord whom they faithfully serue, in whose *presence is the fulnesse of ioy, and at whose right hand are pleasures for euermore.*

Wherfore it being the end and scope of al Historie, to teach by example of times past, such wisdome as may guide our desires and actions, wee should not meruaile though the *Chronicles of the Kings of Iuda and Israel,* being written by men inspired with the spirit of God, instruct vs cheifly, in that which is most requisite for vs to know, as the meanes to attaine vnto true felicitie, both here, and hereafter, propounding examples which illustrate this infallible rule, *The feare of the Lord is the beginning of Wisdome.* Had the expedition of *Xerxes* (as it was foretold by *Daniel*) beene written by some Prophet after the captiuitie: wee may well beleeue that the counsaile of God therein, and the execution of his righteous will, should haue occupied either the whole, or the principall roome in that narration. Yet had not the purpose of *Darius,* the desire of his wife, and the businesse at *Sardes*, with other occurrents, beene the lesse true, though they might haue beene omitted, as the lesse materiall: but these things it had beene lawfull for any man to gather out of prophane Histories, or out of circumstances otherwise appearing, wherein he should not haue done iniurie to the sacred writings, as long as hee had forborne to derogate from the first causes, by ascribing to the second more than was due.

Such, or litle different, is the businesse that I haue now in hand: wherin I cannot beleeue that any man of iudgement will taxe mee as either fabulous or presumptuous. For he doth not faine, that rehearseth probabilities as bare coniectures; neither doth he depraue the text, that seeketh to illustrate and make good in humane reason, those things, which authoritie alone, without further circumstance, ought to haue confirmed in euery mans beliefe. And this may suffice in defence of the libertie, which I haue vsed in coniectures, and may hereafter vse when occasion shall require, as neither vnlawfull, nor misbeseeming an Historian.

Ch. XXII. *Of* Ioas *and* Amasia . . . ; *where somewhat of the building of Carthage*

Ch. XXIII. *Of* Vzzia

Ch. XXIV. *Of the Antiquities of Italie, and foundation of Rome in the time of* Ahas

SWR H 2

Ch. XXV. *Of* Ezekia, *and his Contemporaries*

Ch. XXVI. *Of the Kings that raigned in Ægypt* . . .

Ch. XXVII. *Of* Manasse(s) *and his Contemporaries*

Ch. XXVIII. *Of the times from the death of* Manasses *to the destruction of* Ierusalem

THE FIRST PART OF THE HISTORIE OF THE WORLD:

Intreating of the times from the destruction of Ierusalem to the time of Philip of Macedon.

THE THIRD BOOKE.

Ch. I. *Of the time passing betweene the destruction of Ierusalem, and the fall of the Assyrian Empire*

§1. *Of the connexion of sacred and prophane Historie.*

The course of Time, which in prophane Histories might rather bee discerned through the greatest part of his way, hitherto passed in some out-worne foot-steps, than in any beaten path, hauing once in *Greece* by the *Olympiads,* and in the Easterne Countries by the accompt from *Nabonassar,* left surer marks, and more appliable to actions concurrent, than were the warre of *Troy,* or any other token of former date; begins at length in the ruine of *Hierusalem* to discouer the connexion of antiquitie fore-spent, with the storie of succeeding ages. Manifest it is, that the originall and progresse of thinges could ill bee sought in those that were ignorant of the first creation: as likewise that the affaires of Kingdomes and Empire afterwards growne vp are not to be found among those, that haue now no state nor policie remaining of their owne. Hauing therefore pursued the storie of the world vnto that age, from whence the memorie of succeeding accidents is with little interruption or fabulous discourse deriued vnto vs, I hold it now conuenient briefly to shew, by what meanes and circumstances the historie of the *Hebrewes,* which of all other is the most ancient, may bee conioyned with the following times, wherein that Image of sundrie mettalls, discouered by God vnto *Nabuchadnezzar,* did raigne ouer the earth, when *Israel* was either none, or an vnregarded Nation. . . .

Ch. II. *Of the originall and first greatnesse of the Persians*

Ch. III. *Of* Cyrvs

Ch. IV. *The estate of things from the death of* Cyrvs *to the Raigne of* Darivs

Ch. V. *Of* Darivs *the Sonne of* Hyspaspes

Ch. VI. *Of* Xerxes[1]

§1. *The preparation of* Xerxes *against Greece.*

§2. Xerxes *Armie entertained by* Pythius: *his cutting off Mount Athos from the Continent* . . .

§3. *Of the fights at Thermopylæ and Artemisium.*

§4. *The attempt of* Xerxes *vpon* Apollo's *temple: and his taking of Athens.*

[1] Xerxes' invasion of Greece may appear to be a unit independent of the rest of the *History*; but the final section (pp. 231 f.) places the account within Ralegh's comprehensive design. Cf. above, p. 32.

When *Xerxes* had passed the straites of *Thermopylæ* he wasted the Country of the *Phocians* and the regions adioining: as for the inhabitants they chose rather to flie, and reserue themselues to a day of battaile, than to aduenture their liues into his hands, vpon hope of sauing their wealth by making proffer vnto him of their seruice. Part of his armie he sent to spoile the Temple of *Delphi*; which was exceeding rich by meanes of many offerings that had there been made by diuers Kings and great personages; Of all which riches it was thought that *Xerxes* had a better Inuentorie than of the goods left in his owne Palace. To make relation of a great astonishment that fell vpon the companies which ariued at the Temple to haue sacked it, and of two Rockes that breaking from the mount *Parnassus* ouerwhelmed many of the *Barbarians*, it were peraduenture somewhat superstitious. Yet *Herodotus*, who liued not long after, saith, That the broken Rocks remained euen to his memorie in the Temple of *Minerua*, whither they rowled in their fall. And surely this attempt of *Xerxes* was impious; for seeing he beleeued that *Apollo* was a God, he should not haue dared to entertaine a couetous desire of inriching himselfe by committing sacriledge vpon his Temple. Wherefore it may possibly be true, that licence to chastise his impietie, in such manner as is reported, was granted vnto the Deuill, by that Holie one, who saith, *Will a man spoile his Gods?* and elsewhere; *Hath any nation changed their Gods, which yet are no Gods? Go to the Iles of Kittim, and behold, and send to Kedar and take diligent heed, and see whether there be any such things.* Now this impietie of *Xerxes* was the more inexcusable, for that the *Persians* alleadged the burning of *Cybeles* Temple by the *Athenians*, when they set fire on the Citie of *Sardis* in *Asia*, to be the ground and cause of the wast which they made in burnings of Cities and Temples in *Greece*. Whereas indeed, in the enterprise against *Delphos*, this Vizzor of holie and zealous reuenge falling off, discouered the face of couetousnesse so much the more ouglie, by how much the more themselues had professed a detestation of the offence which the *Athenians* had committed in that kind by meere mischance.

The remainder of that which *Xerxes* did may be expressed

briefly thus. *He came to Athens, which finding forsaken he tooke, & burnt the Cittadel and temple which was therein.* The Cittadell indeed was defended a while by some of more courage than wisedome, who literally interpreting *Apollo's* Oracle; *that Athens should bee safe in woodden walls,* had fortified that place with boords and *Palissadoes:* too weake to hold out long, though by their desperate valour so well maintained at the first assault, that they might haue yeelded it vpon tolerable conditions, had they not vainely relied vpon the prophecie: whereof (being somewhat obscure) it was wisely done of *Themistocles,* to make discretion the interpreter, applying rather the wordes to the present neede, than fashioning the businesse to wordes.

§5. *How* Themistocles *the Athenian drew the Greekes to fight at Salamis.*

The *Athenians* had, before the comming of *Xerxes,* remoued their wiues and children into *Trœzene, Ægina,* and *Salamis,* not so highly prizing their houses, and lands, as their freedome, and the common libertie of *Greece.* Neuerthelesse this great zeale, which the *Athenians* did shew for the generall good of their Countrie, was ill requited by the other *Greekes,* who with much labour were hardly intreated to stay for them at *Salamis,* whilest they remoued the wiues and children out of their Citie. But when the Citie of *Athens* was taken, it was presently resolued vpon, that they should forsake the Ile of *Salamis,* and with-draw the fleet to *Isthmus:* which neck of land they did purpose to fortifie against the *Persians,* and so to defend *Peloponnesus* by Land, and Sea, leauing the rest of *Greece,* as indefensible, to the furie of the enemie. So should the Ilands of *Salamis* and *Ægina* haue beene abandoned, and the Families of the *Athenians* (which were there bestowed as in places of securitie) haue beene giuen ouer into mercilesse bondage. Against this resolution *Themistocles,* Admirall of the *Athenian* fleet, very strongly made opposition; but in vaine. For the *Peloponnesians* were so possessed with feare of loosing their owne, which they would not hazard, that no perswasions could obtaine of them, to regard the estate of their distressed friends, and Allies. Many remonstrances *Themistocles* made vnto them, to allure them to abide the enemie at *Salamis*; As first in priuate vnto *Eurybiades* the *Lacedæmonian*, Admirall of the whole fleet; That the selfe same feare which made them forsake those coasts of *Greece*, vpon which they then anchored, would afterward (if it found no check at the first) cause them also to disseuer the fleet, and euery one of the Confederates to with-draw himselfe to the defence of his owne Citie and estate; Then to the Councell of Warre which *Eurybiades* vpon this motion did call together (forbearing to obiect what want of courage might worke in them hereafter) he shewed that the fight at *Isthmus* would be in an open Sea, whereas it was more expedient for them, hauing the fewer ships, to determine the matter in the straights; and that, besides the safeguard of *Ægina*, *Megara*, and *Salamis*, they should by abiding, where they then were, sufficiently defend *Isthmus*, which the *Barbarians* should not so much as once looke vpon, if the *Greekes* obtained victorie by Sea: which they could not so well hope for else-where, as in that present place which gaue them so good aduantage. All this would not serue to retaine the *Peloponnesians*, of whom one, vnworthy of memorie, vpbraided *Themistocles* with the losse of *Athens*, blaming *Eurybiades* for suffering one to speake in the Councell, that had no Countrie of his owne to inhabite. A base and shamefull obiection it was, to lay as a reproch that losse, which being voluntarily sustained for the common good, was in true estimation by so much the more honourable, by how much it was the greater. But this indignitie did exasperate *Themistocles*, and put into his mouth a reply so sharpe, as auailed more than all his former perswasions. Hee told them all plainely, That the *Athenians* wanted not a fairer Citie, than any Nation of *Greece* could boast of; hauing well-neare two hundred good ships of Warre, the better part of the *Græcian* fleet, with which it was easie for them to transport their Families and substance into any part of the world, and settle themselues in a more secure habitation, leauing those to shift as well as they might, who in their extremitie had refused to stand by them. Herewithall he mentioned a Towne in *Italie* belonging of old to the State of *Athens*, of which Towne he said an Oracle had foretold, That the *Athenians* in processe of time should build it a-new, and there (quoth hee) will we plant our selues, leauing vnto you a sorrowfull remembrance of my words, and of your owne vnthankfulnesse. The *Peloponnesians* hearing thus much, beganne to enter into better consideration of the *Athenians*, whose affaires depended not, as they well perceiued, vpon so weake termes, that they should be driuen to crouch to others; but rather were such, as might inforce the rest to yeeld to them, and condescend euen to the vttermost of their owne demands.

For the *Athenians*, when they first embraced that Heroicall resolution of leauing their grounds and houses to fire and ruine, if necessitie should inforce them so farre, for the preseruation of their libertie; did imploy the most of their priuate wealth, and all the common treasure, in building a great Nauie. By these meanes they hoped (which accordingly fell out) that no such calamitie should befall them by land, as might not well be counterpoised by great aduantages at Sea: Knowing well, that a strong fleet would either procure victorie at home, or a secure passage to any other Countrie. The other States of *Greece* held it sufficient, if building a few new ships they did somewhat amend their Nauie. Whereby it came to passe, that, had they beene vanquished, they could not haue expected any other fortune than either present death, or perpetuall slauerie; neither could they hope to be victorious without the assistance of the *Athenians*, whose forces by Sea did equall all theirs together; the whole consisting of no more than three hundred and fourescore bottomes. Wherefore these *Peloponnesians* beginning to suspect their owne condition, which would haue stood vpon desperate points, if the fleet of *Athens* had forsaken them; were soone perswaded, by the greater feare of such a bad euent, to forget the lesser, which they had conceiued of the *Persians:* and laying a-side their insolent brauerie, they yeelded to that most profitable counsaile of abiding at *Salamis*.

§6. *How the Persians consulted about giuing battaile: and how*
Themistocles *by policie held the Greekes to their resolution;*
with the victorie at Salamis thereupon ensuing.

In the meane season the *Persians* had entred into consultation, whether it were conuenient to offer battaile to the
Greekes, or no. The rest of the Captaines giuing such aduise
as they thought would best please the King their Master,
had soone agreed vpon the fight: but *Artemisia* Queene of
Halicarnassus, who followed *Xerxes* to this warre in person,
was of contrarie opinion. Her counsaile was, that the King
himselfe directly should march toward *Peloponnesus*, whereby
it would come to passe that the *Greeke* Nauie, (vnable otherwise to continue long at *Salamis* for want of prouision) should
presently be disseuered, and euery one seeking to preserue
his owne Citie and goods, they should, being diuided, proue
vnable to resist him, who had wonne so farre vpon them
when they held together. And as the profit will bee great in
forbearing to giue battaile; so on the other side the danger
will bee more (said shee) which wee shall vnder-goe, than
any neede requireth vs to aduenture vpon; and the losse, in
case it fall vpon vs, greater than the profit of the victorie
which we desire. For if we compell the enemies to flie, it
is no more than they would haue done, wee sitting still:
but if they, as better Sea-men than ours, put vs to the worst,
the iourney to *Peloponnesus* is vtterly dasht, and many that
now declare for vs, will soone reuolt vnto the *Greekes*.
Mardonius, whom *Xerxes* had sent for that purpose to the
fleet, related vnto his Master the common consent of the
other Captaines, and withall this disagreeing opinion of
Artemisia. The King well pleased with her aduise, yet
resolued vpon following the more generall, but farre-worse
counsaile of the rest; which would questionlesse haue beene
the same which *Artemisia* gaue, had not feare and flatterie
made all the Captaines vtter that as out of their owne
iudgement, which they thought most conformable to their
Princes determination. So it was indeede that *Xerxes* had
entertained a vaine perswasion of much good, that his owne
presence vpon the shore to behold the conflict, would worke
among the Souldiers. Therefore he incamped vpon the

Sea-side, pitching his owne Tent on the mount *Ægaleus* which is opposite vnto the Ile of *Salamis*, whence at ease hee might safely view all which might happen in that action, hauing Scribes about him to write downe the acts and behauiour of euery Captaine. The neare approch of the *Barbarians*, together with the newes of that timorous diligence, which their Countrimen shewed in fortifying the *Isthmus*, and of a *Persian* Armie marching a-pace thither, did now againe so terrifie and amaze the *Peloponnesians*, that no intreatie, nor contestation would suffice to hold them together. For they thought it meere madnesse to fight for a Countrie alreadie lost, when they rather should endeauour to saue that which remained vnconquered; propounding chiefly to themselues what miserie would befall them, if loosing the victorie, they should be driuen into *Salamis*, there to bee shut vp, and besieged round in a poore desolate Iland.

Hereupon they resolued forth-with to set saile for *Isthmus*: which had presently beene done, if the wisedome of *Themistocles* had not preuented it. For he perceiuing what a violent feare had stopt vp their cares against all good counsaile, did practise another course, and forth-with labour to preuent the execution of this vnwholsome decree; not suffering the very houre of performance to find him busie in wrangling altercation. As soone as the Councell brake vp, hee dispatched secretly a trustie Gentleman to the *Persian* Captaines, informing them truly of the intended flight, and exhorting them to send part of their Nauie about the Iland, which incompassing the *Greekes* might preuent their escape: giuing them withall a false hope of his assistance. The *Persians* no sooner heard than beleeued these good newes, well knowing that the victorie was their owne assured, if the *Athenian* fleet ioyned with them; which they might easily hope, considering what abilitie their Master had to recompence for so doing, both the Captaines with rich rewards, and the People with restitution of their Citie, and Territories. By these meanes it fell out, that when the *Greekes* very early in the morning were about to waigh Anchor, they found themselues inclosed round with *Persians*, who had laboured hard all night, sending many of their ships about the Ile of *Salamis*, to charge the enemie in reare, and landing many of their men in the Isle of *Psyttalea*, which lieth ouer against *Salamis*, to saue such of their owne, and kill such of the *Græcian* partie, as by any misfortune should be cast vpon the shore. Thus did meere necessitie enforce the *Græcians* to vndertake the battaile in the Straights of *Salamis*, where they obtained a memorable victorie, stemming the formost of their enemies, and chasing the rest, who falling foule one vpon another, could neither conueniently fight nor flie. I doe not finde any particular occurrences in this great battaile to be much remarkeable. Sure it is that the Scribes of *Xerxes* had a wearisome taske of writing downe many disasters that befell the *Persian* fleet, which ill acquited it selfe that day, doing no one peece of seruice worthie the presence of their King, or the registring of his Notaries. As for the *Greekes*, they might well seeme to haue wrought out that victorie with equall courage, were it not that the principall honour of that day was ascribed to those of *Ægina*, and to the *Athenians*, of whom it is recorded, That when the *Barbarians* did flie towards *Phalerus*, where the Land-Armie of *Xerxes* lay, the ships of *Ægina* hauing possessed the straights did sinke or take them, whilest the *Athenians* did valiantly giue charge vpon those that kept the Sea, and made any countenance of resisting.

§7. *Of thinges following after the battaile of Salamis: and of the flight of* Xerxes.

After this victorie, the *Greekes* intending, by way of scrutinie, to determine which of the Captaines had best merited of them, in all this great seruice; euery Captaine, being ambitious of that honour, did in the place write downe his owne name, but in the second place, as best deseruing next vnto himselfe, almost euery Suffrage did concurre vpon *Themistocles*. Thus priuate affection yeelded vnto vertue, as soone as her owne turne was serued. The *Persian* King, as not amazed with this calamitie, beganne to make new preparation for continuance of warre; but in such fashion, that they which were best acquainted with his temper, might easily discerne his faint heart, through his painted lookes. Especially *Mardonius*, Author of the warre, began to

cast a warie eie vpon his Master, fearing least his counsaile
should bee rewarded according to the euent. Wherefore
purposing rather to aduenture his life in pursuit of the
victorie, than to cast it away by vnder-going his Princes
indignation; he aduised the King to leaue vnto him three
hundred thousand men, with which forces he promised
to reduce all *Greece* vnder the subiection of the *Persian*
Scepter. Herewithall he forgot not to sooth *Xerxes* with
many faire wordes; telling him, that the cowardise of those
Ægyptians, *Phœnicians*, and *Cilicians*, with others of the like
mettall, nothing better than slaues, who had so ill behaued
themselues in the late Sea-seruice, did not concerne his
honour, who had alwaies beene victorious, and had alreadie
subdued the better part of *Greece*, yea taken *Athens* it selfe,
against which the Warre was principally intended. These
wordes found very good acceptance in the Kings eare, who
presently betooke himselfe to his iourney homewards, making
the more hast, for that he vnderstood, how the *Greekes* had
a purpose to saile to *Hellespont*, and there to breake downe
his bridge, and intercept his passage. True it was that the
Greekes had no such intent, but rather wished his hastie
departure, knowing that he would leaue his Armie not so
strong, as it should haue beene, had he in person remained
with it. And for this cause did *Eurybiades* giue counsaile that
by no meanes they should attempt the breaking of that
bridge, least necessitie should inforce the *Persians* to take
courage, and rather to fight like men, than die like beasts.
Wherefore *Themistocles* did, vnder pretence of friendship,
send a false aduertisement to this timorous Prince, aduising
him to conuay himselfe into *Asia* with all speede, before his
bridge were dissolued: which counsaile *Xerxes* tooke very
kindly, and hastily followed, as before is shewed. Whether
it were so that he found the bridge whole, and thereby
repassed into *Asia*; or whether it were torne in sunder by
tempests, and he thereby driuen to imbarke himselfe in
some obscure vessell, it is not greatly materiall; though the
Greekes did most willingly imbrace the later of these reports.
Howsoeuer it were, this flight of his did well ease the
Countrie; that was thereby disburdened of that huge throng
of people, which, as Locusts, had before ouer-whelmed it.

§8. *The negotiations betweene* Mardoniv̄s *and the Athenians* ...

§9. *The great battaile of Plataea.*

§10. *The battaile of Mycale* ...

§11. *Of the barbarous qualitie of* Xerxes: *with a transition from the Persian affaires, to matters of Greece, which from this time grew more worthie of regard.*

Xerxes lay at *Sardis,* not farre from the place of this battaile; but little minde had hee to reuenge either this or other his great losses, being wholly giuen ouer to the loue of his Brothers Wife: with whom when hee could not preuaile by intreatie, nor would obtaine his desire by force, because hee respected much his Brother her husband, he thought it best to make a match betweene his owne Sonne *Darius,* and the Daughter of this Woman; hoping by that meanes to finde occasion of such familiaritie, as might worke out his desire. But whether it were so, that the chastitie of the Mother did still reject him, or the beautie of her Daughter allure him; hee soone after fell in loue with his owne Sonnes wife, being a vitious Prince, and as ill able to gouerne himselfe in peace, as to guide his Armie in Warre. This yong Ladie hauing once desired the King to giue her the Garment which hee then wore, being wrought by his owne Wife; caused the Queene thereby to perceiue her husbands conuersation with her, which shee imputed not so much to the beautie of her Daughter-in-law, as to the cunning of the Mother, against whom thereupon shee conceiued extreme hatred. Therefore at a Royall feast, wherein the custome was that the King should grant euery request, shee craued that the Wife of *Masistes,* her husbands Brother, the yong Ladies Mother, might bee giuen into her disposition. The barbarous King, who might either haue reformed the abuse of such a custome, or haue deluded the importunate crueltie of his Wife, by threatning her selfe with the like, to whatsoeuer shee should inflict vpon the innocent Ladie, granted the request; and sending for his brother perswaded him to put away the Wife which hee had, and take one of his Daughters in her stead. Hereby it seemes, that hee vnderstood how vilainously that poore Ladie should bee intreated, whom hee knew to bee vertuous, and whom himselfe had loued. *Masistes* refused to put her away; alleaging his owne loue, her deseruing, and their common Children, one of which was married to the Kings Sonne, as reasons important to moue him to keepe her. But in most wicked manner *Xerxes* reuiled him; saying, That hee now should neither keepe the Wife which hee had, nor haue his Daughter whome hee had promised vnto him. *Masistes* was much grieued with these wordes, but much more, when returning home, hee found his Wife most butcherly mangled by the Queene *Amestris*, who had caused her Nose, Lips, Eares, and Tongue to bee cut off, and her Breasts in like manner, which were cast vnto Dogs. *Masistes* enraged with this vilanie, tooke his way with his children, and some Friends, towards *Bactria*, of which Prouince hee was Gouernour, intending to rebell and auenge himselfe. But *Xerxes* vnderstanding his purpose, caused an Armie to bee leauied which cut him off by the way, putting him and all his Companie to the sword. Such was the tyrannicall condition of the *Persian* Gouernement; and such are generally the effects of Luxurie, when it is ioyned with absolute power.

Yet of *Xerxes* it is noted, that he was a Prince of much vertue. And therefore *Alexander* the Great, finding an Image of his ouer-throwne, and lying vpon the ground, said, That hee doubted, whether, in regard of his vertue, hee should againe erect it, or, for the mischiefe done by him to *Greece*, should let it lie. But surely whatsoeuer his other good qualities were, he was foolish, and was a coward, and consequently mercilesse. . . .

Ch. VII. *Of things that passed in Greece from the end of the Persian Warre to the beginning of the Peloponnesian*

Ch. **VIII**. *Of the Peloponnesian Warre*

Ch. **IX**. *Of matters concurring with the Peloponnesian Warre*

Ch. **X**. *Of the expedition of* Cyrvs *the younger*

Ch. **XI**. *Of the affaires of Greece, whilest they were managed by the Lacedæmonians*

Ch. **XII**. *Of the flourishing estate of Thebes, from the battaile of Leuctra to the battaile of Mantinæa*

§1. *How Thebes and Athens ioyned together against Sparta.* . . . *The battaile of Leuctra, and beginning of the Theban greatnesse.*

§2. ... Epaminondas *inuadeth and wasteth the Territorie of Lacedæmon.*

§3. ... *the Thebans ... againe inuade and spoile Peloponnesus* ...

§4. *The great growth of the Theban Estate* ...

§5. *How all Greece was diuided, betweene the Athenians and Lacedæmonians, on the one side, and Thebans on the other* ...

§6. *A terrible inuasion of Peloponnesus by* Epaminondas.

Certaine it is, that the condition of things did at that time require a verie firme consent, and vniforme care of the common safetie. For beside the great forces raised out of the other parts of *Greece*, the *Argiues*, and *Messenians*, prepared with all their strength to joyne with *Epaminondas*; who hauing lien a while at *Nemea*, to intercept the *Athenians*, receiued there intelligence, that the Armie comming from *Athens* would passe by Sea, whereupon he dislodged, and came to *Tegea*, which Citie, and the most of all *Arcadia* besides, forth-with declared themselues his. The common opinion was, that the first attempt of the *Thebans*, would be vpon such of the *Arcadians* as had reuolted; which caused the *Lacedæmonian* Captaines to fortifie *Mantinæa* with all diligence, and to send for *Agesilaus* to *Sparta*, that he bringing with him all that small force of able men, which remained in the Towne, they might be strong enough to abide *Epaminondas* there. But *Epaminondas* held so good espiall vpon his Enemies, that had not an vnknowne fellow brought hastie aduertisement of his purpose to *Agesilaus*, who was then well onward in the way to *Mantinæa*, the Citie of *Sparta* had sodainely beene taken. For thither with all speede and secrecie did the *Thebans* march, who had surely carried the Citie, notwithstanding anie defence that could haue beene made by that handfull of men remaining within it; but that *Agesilaus* in all flying hast got into it with his Companies, whom the Armie of his Confederates followed thither to the rescue as fast as it was able. The arriuall of the

Lacedæmonians and their friends, as it cut off all hope from
Epaminondas of taking *Sparta*, so it presented him with a
faire aduantage vpon *Mantinæa*. It was the time of Haruest,
which made it very likely that the *Mantinæans*, finding the
warre to be carried from their walls into an other quarter,
would vse the commoditie of that vacation, by fetching in
their corne, and turning out their cattaile into their fields,
whilest no enemie was neare that might empeach them.
Wherefore hee turned away from *Sparta* to *Mantinæa*,
sending his horse-men before him, to seize vpon all that
might be found without the Citie. The *Mantinæans*
(according to the expectation of *Epaminondas*) were scattered
abroade in the Countrie; farre more intent vpon their
haruest-businesse, than vpon the warre, whereof they were
secure, as thinking themselues out of distance. By which
presumption it fell out, that great numbers of them, and all
their Cattaile, being vnable to recouer the Towne, were in a
desperate case; and the Towne it selfe in no great likelihood
of holding out, when the enemie should haue taken all their
prouision of victuals with so many of the people, as had not
ouer-dearely beene redeemed, by that Cities returning to
societie with *Thebes*. But at the same time, the *Athenians*
comming to the succour of their Confederates, whom they
thought to haue found at *Mantinæa*, were very earnestly
entreated by the Citizens to rescue their goods, and people,
from the danger whereinto they were fallen, if it were
possible by any couragious aduenture to deliuer those who
otherwise were giuen as lost. The *Thebans* were knowne at
that time to bee the best Souldiers of all the *Greekes*, and the
commendation of good horsemanship had alwaies beene
giuen to the *Thessalians*, as excelling in that qualitie all other
Nations; yet the regard of honour so wrought vpon the
Athenians, that for the reputation of their Citie, which had
entred into this warre, vpon no necessitie of her owne, but
only in desire of relieuing her distressed friends, they issued
forth of *Mantinæa*, not abiding so long as to refresh themselues, or their horses with meat, and giuing a lustie charge
vpon the enemie, who as brauely receiued them, after a long
and hot fight they remained masters of the field, giuing by
this victorie a safe and easie retrait to all that were without

the walls. The whole power of the *Bœotians* arriued in the place soone after this battaile, whom the *Lacedæmonians* and their Assistants were not farre behinde.

§7. *The great battaile of Mantinæa. The honourable death of* Epaminondas, *with his commendation.*

Epaminondas, considering that his Commission was almost now expired, and that his attempts of surprising *Sparta* and *Mantinæa* hauing failed, the impression of terrour which his name had wrought in the *Peloponnesians*, would soone vanish, vnlesse by some notable act he should abate their courage in their first grouth, and leaue some memorable character of his expedition; resolued to giue them battaile, whereby he reasonably hoped both to settle the doubtfull affections of his owne Associates, and to leaue the *Spartans* as weake in spirit and abilitie, as he found them, if not wholly to bring them into subjection. Hauing therefore warned his men to prepare for that battaile, wherein victorie should be rewarded with Lordship of all *Greece*; and finding the alacritie of his Souldiers to be such, as promised the accomplishment of his owne desire; he made shew of declining the enemie, and intrenching himselfe in a place of more aduantage, that so by taking from them all expectation of fighting that day, he might allay the heate of their valour, and afterward strike their senses with amazement, when hee should come vpon them vnexpected. This opinion deceiued him not. For with verie much tumult, as in so great and sodaine a danger, the enemie ranne to Armes, necessitie enforcing their resolution, and the consequence of that daies seruice vrging them to doe as well as they might. The *Theban* Armie consisted of thirtie thousand foot, and three thousand horse; the *Lacedæmonians* and their friends were short of this number, both in horse and in foot, by a third part. The *Mantinæans* (because the warre was in their Countrie) stood in the right wing, and with them the *Lacedæmonians*: the *Athenians* had the left wing, the *Achæans*, *Eleans*, and others of lesse account, filled the bodie of the Armie. The *Thebans* stood in the left wing of their owne battaile, opposite to the *Lacedæmonians*, hauing by them the *Arcadians*; the *Eubœans*, *Locrians*, *Sicyonians*, *Messenians*, and *Thessalians* with others, compounding the maine battaile; the *Argiues* held the right wing; the horse-men on each part were placed in the flancks, only a troupe of the *Eleans* were in reare. Before the footmen could joyne, the encounter of the horse on both sides was very rough, wherein finally the *Thebans* preuailed, notwithstanding the valiant resistance of the *Athenians:* who not yeelding to the enemie either in courage or skill, were ouer-laied with numbers, and so beaten vpon by *Thessalian* slings, that they were driuen to forsake the place, and leaue their infanterie naked. But this retrait was the lesse disgracefull, because they kept themselues together, and did not fall backe vpon their owne foot-men; but finding the *Theban* horse to haue giuen them ouer, and withall discouering some Companies of foot, which had beene sent about by *Epaminondas*, to charge their battaile in the reare, they brake vpon them, routed them, and hewed them all in peeces. In the meane season the battaile of the *Athenians* had not only to doe with the *Argiues*, but was hardly pressed by the *Theban* Horse-men, in such wise that it beganne to open, and was readie to turne back, when the *Elean* squadron of Horse came vp to the reliefe of it, and restored all on that part. With farre greater violence did the *Lacedæmonians* and *Thebans* meete, these contending for Dominion, the other for the maintenance of their ancient honour, so that equall courage and equall losse on both sides made the hope and appearance of victorie to either equally doubtfull: vnlesse perhaps the *Lacedæmonians* being very firme abiders, might seeme the more likely to preuaile, as hauing borne the first brunt, and furie of the on-set, which was not hitherto remitted; and being framed by Discipline, as it were by Nature, to excell in patience, whereof the *Thebans*, by practise of a few yeares, cannot bee thought to haue gotten a habite so sure and generall. But *Epaminondas* perceiuing the obstinate stiffenesse of the Enemies to bee such, as neither the badde successe of their owne horse, nor all the force of the *Bœotian* Armie, could abate so farre, as to make them giue one foote of ground; taking a choise Companie of the most able men, whom he cast into the forme of a Wedge, or Diamond, by the aduantage of that figure against a squadron, and by his owne exceeding vertue, accompanied with the great strength and resolution of them which followed him, did open their rancks, and cleaue the whole battaile in despight of all resistance. Thus was the honour of that day wonne by the *Thebans*, who may justly bee said to haue carried the victorie, seeing that they remained Masters of the ground whereon the battaile was fought, hauing driuen the Enemie to lodge farther off. For that which was alleaged by the *Athenians*, as a token that the victorie was partly theirs, the slaughter of those Mercenaries vpon whom they lighted by chance in their owne flight, finding them behinde their Armie, and the retayning of their dead bodies; it was a Ceremonie regardable only among the *Greekes*, and serued meerely for ostentation, shewing that by the fight they had obtayned somewhat, which the Enemie could not get from them otherwise than by request. But the *Thebans* arriued at the generall immediate end of battaile; none daring to abide them in the field: whereof a manifest confession is expressed from them, who forsake the place which they had chosen or accepted, as indifferent for triall of their abilitie and prowesse. This was the last worke of the incomparable vertue of *Epaminondas*, who being in the head of that Warlike troupe of men, which broke the *Lacedæmonian* esquadron, and forced it to giue back in disaray, was furiously charged on the sodaine, by a desperate Companie of the *Spartans*, who all at once threw their Darts at him alone; whereby receiuing many wounds, hee neuerthelesse with a singular courage maintayned the fight, vsing against the Enemies many of their Darts, which hee drew out of his owne bodie; till at length by a *Spartan*, called *Anticrates*, hee receiued so violent a stroke with a Dart, that the wood of it brake, leauing the yron and a peece of the tronchion in his breast. Hereupon hee sunke downe, and was soone conueighed out of the fight by his friends; hauing by his fall somewhat animated the *Spartans* (who faine would haue got his bodie) but much more inflamed with reuengefull indignation, the *Thebans*, who raging at this heauie mischance did with great slaughter compell their disordered enemies to leaue the field; though long they followed not the chase, being wearied more with the sadnesse of this disaster, than with all the trauaile of the day. *Epaminondas* being brought into his Tent, was told by the Phisitians, That when the head of the Dart should bee drawne out of his bodie, hee must needes die. Hearing this, hee called for his shield, which to haue lost was held a great dishonour: It was brought vnto him. Hee bad them tell him which part had the victorie; answere was made, that the *Bœotians* had wonne the field. Then said hee, it is faire time for mee to die, and withall sent for *Iolidas*, and *Diophantes*, two principall men of Warre, that were both slaine; which being told him, He aduised the *Thebans* to make Peace, whilest with aduantage they might, for that they had none left that was able to discharge the office of a Generall. Herewithall he willed that the head of the weapon should be drawne out of his bodie; comforting his friends that lamented his death, and want of issue, by telling them that the victories of *Leuctra* and *Mantinæa* were two faire Daughters, in whom his memorie should liue.

So died *Epaminondas*, the worthiest man that euer was bred in that Nation of *Greece*, and hardly to bee matched in any Age or Countrie: for hee equalled all others in the seuerall vertues, which in each of them were singular. His Iustice, and Sinceritie, his Temperance, Wisedome, and high Magnanimitie, were no way inferiour to his Militarie vertue; in euery part whereof hee so excelled, That hee could not properly bee called a Warie, a Valiant, a Politique, a Bountifull, or an Industrious, and a Prouident Captaine; all these Titles, and many other, being due vnto him, which with his notable Discipline, and good Conduct, made a perfect composition of an Heroique Generall. Neither was his priuate Conuersation vnanswerable to those high parts, which gaue him praise abroad. For hee was Graue, and yet very Affable and Curteous; resolute in publique businesse, but in his owne particular easie, and of much mildnesse; a louer of his People, bearing with mens infirmities, wittie and pleasant in speech, farre from insolence, Master of his owne affections, and furnished with all qualities that might winne and keepe loue. To these Graces were added great abilitie of bodie, much Eloquence, and very deepe

knowledge in all parts of Philosophie and Learning, wherewith his minde being enlightened, rested not in the sweetnesse of Contemplation, but brake forth into such effects
as gaue vnto *Thebes*, which had euer-more beene an vnder-
ling, a dreadfull reputation among all people adjoyning, and
the highest command in *Greece*.

§8. *Of the peace concluded in Greece after the battaile of
Mantinæa. . . .*

THE FIRST PART
OF THE HISTORIE
OF THE WORLD:

Intreating of the times from
the raigne of Philip of
Macedon, to the establishing
of that Kingdome, in the race
of Antigonvs.

THE FOVRTH BOOKE.

Ch. I. *Of* Philip, *the Father of* Alexander *the Great, King of* Macedon

Ch. II. *Of* Alexander *the Great*

§1. *A briefe rehearsall of* Alexanders *doings, before hee inuaded* Asia.

Alexander, afterward called the Great, succeeded vnto *Philip* his Father; being a Prince no lesse valiant by Nature, than by Education, well instructed, and inriched in all sorts of Learning and good Arts. He began his raigne ouer the *Macedonians* foure hundred and seuenteene years after *Rome* built, and after his owne birth twentie yeares. The strange dreames of *Philip* his Father, and that one of the Gods, in the shape of a Snake, begat him on *Olympias* his Mother, I omit as foolish tales; but that the Temple of *Diana* (a worke the most magnificent of the World) was burnt vpon the day of his birth, and that so strange an accident was accompanied with the newes of three seuerall victories obtained by the *Macedonians*, it was very remarkeable, and might with the reason of those times be interpreted for ominous, and fore-shewing the great thinges by *Alexander* afterward performed. Vpon the change of the King, the Neighbour-Nations, whom *Philip* had opprest, beganne to consult about the recouerie of their former libertie, and to aduenture it by force of Armes. *Alexanders* yong-yeares gaue them hope of preuailing, and his suspected seueritie increased courage in those, who could better resolue to die, than to liue slauishly. But *Alexander* gaue no time to those swelling humours, which might speedily haue endangered the health of his estate. For after reuenge taken vpon the Conspirators against his Father, whom he slew vpon his Tombe; and the cele-bration of his Funeralls, hee first fastened vnto him his owne

Nation, by freeing them from all exactions, and bodily slauerie, other than their seruice in his warres; and vsed such Kingly austeritie towards those that contemned his yong yeares, and such clemencie to the rest that perswaded themselues of the crueltie of his disposition, as all affections being pacified at home, He made a present journey into *Peloponnesus*, and so well exercised his spirits among them, as by the Counsell of the States of *Greece*, he was according to the great desire of his heart, elected Captaine-Generall against the *Persians*, vpon which warre *Philip* his Father had not only resolued, (who had obtained the same title of Generall Commander) but had transported vnder the leading of *Parmenio*, and *Attalus*, a part of his Armie, to recouer some places on *Asia*-side, for the safe descent of the rest.

This enterprise against the *Persian* occupied all *Alexanders* affections; those faire markes of riches, Honour, and large Dominion, hee now shot at both sleeping and waking: all other thoughts and imaginations were either grieuous or hatefull. But a contrarie winde ariseth; for hee receiueth aduertisement that the *Athenians*, *Thebans*, and *Lacedæmonians*, had vnited themselues against him, and, by assistance from the *Persian*, hoped for the recouerie of their former freedome. Hereto they were perswaded by *Demosthenes*, himselfe being thereto perswaded by the gold of *Persia*; the deuise he vsed was more subtile than profitable, for he caused it to be bruted that *Alexander* was slaine in a battaile against the *Triballes*, and brought into the assembly a Companion whom hee had corrupted to affirme, That himselfe was present and wounded in the battaile. There is indeede a certaine Doctrine of Policie (as Policie is now a-daies defined by falshood and knauerie) that deuised rumours and lies, if they serue the turne, but for a day or two, are greatly auaileable. It is true that common people are sometime mockt by them, as Souldiers are by false alarums in the Warres; but in all that I haue obserued, I haue found the successe as ridiculous as the inuention. For as those that finde themselues at one time abused by such like brutes, doe at other times neglect their duties, when they are vpon true reports, and in occasions perilous, summoned to assemble;

so doe all men in generall condemne the Venters of such trumperie, and for them feare vpon necessarie occasions to entertaine the truth it selfe. This labour vnlooked for, and losse of time, was not only very grieuous to *Alexander*, but by turning his sword from the ignoble and effeminate *Persians*, against which he had directed it, towards the manly and famous *Græcians*, of whose assistance he thought himselfe assured, his present vndertaking was greatly disordered. But he that cannot indure to striue against the winde, shall hardly attaine the Port which hee purposeth to recouer: and it no lesse becommeth the worthiest men to oppose misfortunes, than it doth the weakest children to bewaile them.

He therefore made such expedition towards these Reuolters, as that himselfe, with the Armie that followed him, brought them the first newes of his preparation. Hereupon all stagger, and the *Athenians*, as they were the first that moued, so were they the first that fainted, seeking by their Embassadours to pacifie the King, and to be receiued againe into his grace. *Alexander* was not long in resoluing; for the *Persians* perswaded him to pardon the *Græcians*. Wise men are not easily drawne from great purposes by such occasions as may easily be taken off, neither hath any King euer brought to effect any great affaire, who hath intangled himselfe in many enterprises at once, not tending to one and the same certaine end.

And hauing now quieted his borderers towards the South, he resolued to assure those Nations which lay on the Northside of *Macedon*, to wit, the *Thracians*, *Triballes*, *Peones*, *Getes*, *Agrians*, and other saluage people, which had greatly vexed with incursions, not only other of his Predecessours, but euen *Philip* his Father: with all which after diuers ouerthrowes giuen them, hee made peace, or else brought them into subjection. Notwithstanding this good successe he could not yet find the way out of *Europe*. There is nothing more naturall to man than libertie; the *Greekes* had enjoyed it ouer-long, and lost it too late to forget it; they therefore shake off the yoke once againe. The *Thebans*, who had in their Citadell a Garrison of a thousand *Macedons*, attempt to force it; *Alexander* hasteth to their succour, and presents himselfe with thirtie thousand foot, all old Souldiers, and three thousand horse, before the Citie, and gaue the Inhabitants some daies to resolue, being euen heart-sicke with the desire of passing into *Asia*. So vnwilling, indeede, he was to draw bloud of the *Græcians*, by whom hee hoped to serue himselfe elsewhere, that hee offered the *Thebans* remission, if they would only deliuer into his hands *Phœnix* and *Prothytes*, the stirrers vp of the Rebellion. But they, opposing the mounting fortune of *Alexander*, (which bare all resistance before it, like the breaking-in of the Ocean-Sea) in steed of such an answere, as men besieged and abandoned should haue made, demanded *Philotas* and *Antipater* to bee deliuered vnto them; as if *Thebes* alone, then laied in the ballance of Fortune with the Kingdome of *Macedon*, and many other Prouinces, could either haue euened the scale or swaied it. Therefore in the end they perished in their obstinacie. For while the *Thebans* oppose the Armie assailant, they are charged at the back by the *Macedonian* Garrison, their Citie taken and razed to the ground, sixe thousand slaine, and thirtie thousand sold for slaues, at the price of four hundred and fortie talents. This the King did to the terrour of the other *Græcian* Cities.

Many Arguments were vsed by *Cleadas* one of the prisoners, to perswade *Alexander* to forbeare the destruction of *Thebes*. He praied the King to beleeue that they were rather misse-led by giuing hastie credit to false reports, than any way malicious; for being perswaded of *Alexanders* death, they rebelled but against his Successour. Hee also besought the King to remember, that his father *Philip* had his education in that Citie, yea that his Ancestor *Hercules* was borne therein: but all perswasions were fruitlesse; the times wherein offences are committed, doe greatly aggrauate them. Yet for the honour he bare to learning, he pardoned all of the race of *Pindarus* the Poet, and spared, and set at libertie *Timoclea*, the sister of *Theagenes*, who died in defence of the libertie of *Greece* against his Father *Philip*. This Noble-woman being taken by a *Thracian*, and by him rauished, hee threatned to take her life vnlesse shee would confesse her treasure, shee led the *Thracian* to a Well, and told him that shee had therein cast it, and when the *Thracian* stooped to looke into the Well, shee suddainly thrust him into the mouth thereof, and stoned him to death.

Now because the *Athenians* had receiued into their Citie so many of the *Thebans*, as had escaped and fled vnto them for succour, *Alexander* would not grant them peace, but vpon condition to deliuer into his hands both their Orators which perswaded this second reuolt, and their Captaines; yet in the end it being a torment vnto him to retard the enterprise of *Persia*, he was content that the Orators should remaine, and accepted of the banishment of the Captaines, wherein he was exceeding ill aduised, had not his fortune, or rather the prouidence of God, made all the resistance against him vnprofitable: for these good Leaders of the *Græcians* betooke themselues to the seruice of the *Persian*, whom after a few daies he inuadeth.

§2. *How* Alexander *passing into Asia, fought with the Persians vpon the Riuer of Granicus.*

When all was now quieted at home, *Alexander*, committing to the trust of *Antipater* both *Greece* and *Macedon*, in the first of the Spring did passe the *Hellespont*, and being readie to disimbarke, hee threw a Dart towards the *Asian* shore, as a token of defiance, commanding his Souldiers not to make any wast in their owne Territorie, or to burne, or deface those buildings which themselues were presently, and in the future to possesse. He landed his Armie, consisting of two and thirtie thousand foot, and fiue thousand horse, all old Souldiers, neare vnto *Troy*, where he offered a solemne sacrifice vpon *Achilles* Tombe, his maternall Ancestor.

But before he left his owne coast, he put to death, without any offence giuen him, all his Mother-in-lawes Kinsmen, whom *Philip* his Father had greatly aduanced, not sparing such of his owne as he suspected. Hee also tooke with him, many of his tributarie Princes, of whose fidelitie he doubted; thinking by vnjust crueltie to assure all things, both in the present and future. Yet the end of all fell out contrarie to the policie which his Ambition had commended vnto him, though agreeing verie well with the justice of God; for all that he had planted, was soone after withered, and rooted vp; those, whom he most trusted, were the most traiterous; his mother, friends, and children, fell by such another mercilesse sword as his owne, and all manner of confusion followed his dead bodie to the graue, and left him there.

When the knowledge of *Alexanders* landing on *Asia*-side was brought to *Darius*, he so much scorned the Armie of *Macedon*, and had so contemptible an opinion of *Alexander* himselfe, as hauing stiled him his seruant on a letter which hee wrote vnto him, reprehending his disloialtie and audacitie (for *Darius* intitled himselfe King of Kings, and the Kinsmand of the Gods) hee gaue order withall to his Lieutenants of the lesser *Asia*, that they should take *Alexander* a-liue, whip him with rods, and then conuey him to his presence: that they should sinke his ships, and send the *Macedons* taken prisoners beyond the Red-Sea, belike into *Æthiopia*, or some other vnhealthfull part of *Affrica*.

In this sort did this glorious King, confident in the glittering, but heartlesse, multitude which he commanded, dispose of the alreadie-vanquished *Macedonians*; But the ill destinies of men beare them to the ground, by what strong confidence soeuer armed: The great numbers which he gathered together, and brought in one heape into the field, gaue rather an exceeding aduantage to his enemies, than any discouragement at all. For besides that they were men vtterly vnacquainted with dangers, men who by the name and countenance of their King were wont to preuaile against those of lesse courage than themselues, men that tooke more care how to embroder with gold and siluer their vpper garments, as if they attended the inuasion but of the Sunne-beames, than they did to arme themselues with yron and steele against the sharpe-pikes, swords, and darts of the hardie *Macedonians*; I say besides all these, euen the opinion they had of their owne numbers, of which euery one in particular hoped that it would not fall to his turne to fight, filled euery of them with the care of their owne safetie, without any intent at all to hazard any thing but their owne breath, and that of their horses, in running away. The *Macedonians* as they came to fight, and thereby to inrich themselues with the gold and jewells of *Persia*, both which they needed, so the *Persians* who expected nothing in that Warre but blowes and wounds, which they needed not, obaied the King, who had power to constraine them in assembling themselues for his seruice; but their owne feares and cowardice, which in time of danger had most power ouer them, they only then obaied, when their rebellion against so seruile a passion did justly and violently require it. For saith *Vegetivs: Quemadmodum bene exercitatus miles prælium cupit, ita formidat indoctus; nam sciendum est in pugnâ vsum amplius prodesse quàm vires; As the well-practised Souldier desires to come to battaile, so the raw one feares it: for we must vnderstand, that in fight it more auailes to haue beene accustomed vnto the like, than only to haue rude strength.* What manner of men the *Persians* were, *Alexander* discouered in the first encounter, before which time it is said, by those that writ his Storie, That it was hard to judge, whether his daring to vndertake the Conquest of an Empire so well peopled, with a handfull of men, or the successe he had, were more to be wondred at. For at the Riuer of *Granick*, which seuereth the Territorie of *Troy* from *Propontis*, the *Persians* sought to stop his passage, taking the higher ground and banck of the riuer to defend, which *Alexander* was forced (as it were) to clime vp vnto, and scale from the Leuell of the water; Great resistance (saith *Curtius*) was made by the *Persians*, yet in the end *Alexander* preuailed. But it seemes to mee, that the victorie then gotten was exceeding easie, and that the twentie thousand *Persian* footmen, said to be slaine, were rather kil'd in the back, in running away, than hurt in the bosomes by resisting. For had those twentie thousand foot, and two hundred and fiftie horse-men, or, after *Plutarch*, two thousand and fiue hundred horse-men, died with their faces towards the *Macedonians*, *Alexander* could not haue bought their liues at so small a rate, as with the losse of foure and thirtie of all sorts of his owne. And if it were also true, that *Plutarch* doth report, how *Alexander* encountred two of the *Persian* Commanders, *Spithridates* and *Rhœsaces*; and that the *Persian* horse-men fought with great furie, though in the end scattered; and lastly how those *Grœcians* in *Darius* his pay holding themselues in one bodie vpon a peece of ground of

aduantage, did (after mercie was refused them) fight it out
to the last; how doth it then resemble truth, that such
resistance hauing beene made, yet of *Alexanders* Armie there
fell but twelue Foote-men, and two and twentie Horse-men.

§3. *A digression concerning the defence of hard passages. Of
things following the battaile of Granick.*

The winning of this passage did greatly encourage the
Macedonians, and brought such terrour vpon all those of the
lesser *Asia*, as hee obtained all the Kingdomes thereof
without a blow, some one or two Townes excepted. For in
all inuasions, where the Nations inuaded haue once beene
beaten vpon a great aduantage of the place, as in defence of
Riuers, Streights, and Mountaines, they will soone haue
perswaded themselues, that such an enemie, vpon equall
termes and euen ground, can hardly be resisted. It was
therefore *Machiauels* counsell, that he which resolueth to
defend a passage, should with his ablest force oppose the
Assailant. And to say truth, few Regions of any great
circuit are so well fenced, that Armies, of such force as may
be thought sufficient to conquer them, can be debarred all
entrance, by the naturall difficultie of the waies. One passage
or other is commonly left vnguarded: if all be defended,
then must the forces of the Countrie be distracted, and yet
lightly, some one place will be found that is defended very
weakely. How often haue the *Alpes* giuen way to Armies,
breaking into *Italie?* Yea, where shall we finde that euer they
kept out an inuadour? Yet are they such, as (to speake
briefly) afflict with all difficulties those that trauaile ouer
them; but they giue no securitie to those that lie behinde
them: for they are of too large extent. The Townes of
Lumbardie perswaded themselues that they might enjoy
their quiet, when the Warlike Nation of the *Switzers* had
vndertaken to hinder *Francis* the *French* King from descending into the Duchie of *Milan:* but whilest these Patrons of
Milan, whom their owne dwelling in those Mountaines
had made fittest of all other for such a seruice, were busied
in custodie of the *Alpes*; *Francis* appeared in *Lumbardie*, to

so much the greater terrour of the Inhabitants, by how much the lesse they had expected his arriuall. What shall we say of those Mountaines, which locke vp whole Regions in such sort, as they leaue but one Gate open? The Streights, or (as they were called) the Gates of *Taurus* in *Cilicia*, and those of *Thermopylæ*, haue seldome beene attempted, perhaps because they were thought impregnable: but how seldome (if euer) haue they been attempted in vaine? *Xerxes*, and long after him, the *Romans*, forced the entrance of *Thermopylæ*; *Cyrus* the yonger, and after him *Alexander*, found the Gates of *Cilicia* wide open; how strongly soeuer they had beene locked and barred, yet were those countries open enough to a fleet that should enter on the back-side. The defence of Riuers how hard a thing it is, wee finde examples in all histories that beare good witnesse. The deepest haue many Foords; the swiftest and broadest may bee passed by Boates, in case it be found a matter of difficultie to make a Bridge. He that hath men enough to defend all the length of his owne banke, hath also enough to beate his enemie; and may therefore doe better to let him come ouer, to his losse, than by striuing in vaine to hinder the passage, as a matter tending to his owne disaduantage, fill the heads of his Souldiers with an opinion, that they are in ill case, hauing their meanes of safeguard taken from them, by the skill or valour of such as are too good for them. Certainely if a Riuer were sufficient defence against an Armie, the Isle of *Mona*, now called *Anglesey*, which is diuided from North-Wales by an arme of the Sea; had beene safe enough against the *Romans*, inuading it vnder conduct of *Iulius Agricola*. But he wanting, and not meaning to spend the time in making vessells to transport his forces, did assay the foords. Whereby hee so amazed the enemies attending for ships and such like prouision by Sea, that surely beleeuing nothing could bee hard or inuincible to men, which came so minded to Warre, they humbly intreated for peace, and yeelded the Iland. Yet the *Britaines* were men stout enough; the *Persians* verie dastards.

It was therefore wisely done of *Alexander*, to passe the Riuer of *Granick* in face of the enemie; not marching higher to seeke an easier way, nor labouring to conuey his men ouer it by some safer meanes. For hauing beaten them vpon their owne ground, hee did thereby cut off no lesse of their reputation, than of their strength, leauing no hope of succour to the partakers and followers of such vnable Protectors.

Soone after this victorie he recouered *Sardis*, *Ephesus*, the Cities of the *Trallians* and *Magnesia*, which were rendred vnto him. The Inhabitants of which, with the people of the Countrie, he receiued with great grace, suffering them to be gouerned by their owne lawes. For hee obserued it well; *Nouum Imperium inchoantibus vtilis elementiæ fama*; *It is commodious vnto such as lay the foundations of a new Soueraignetie to haue the fame of being mercifull.* Hee then by *Parmenio* wanne *Miletus*, and by force mastred *Halicarnassus*, which, because it resisted obstinately, hee razed to the ground. From thence hee entred into *Caria*, where *Ada* the Queene, who had beene cast out of all that shee held (except the Citie of *Alinda*) by *Darius* his Lieutenants, presented her selfe vnto him, and adopted him her sonne and successor; which *Alexander* accepted in so gracious part as hee left the whole Kingdome to her disposing. Hee then entred into *Lycia*, and *Pamphilia*, and obtained all the Sea-coasts, and subjecting vnto him *Pisidia*, he directed himselfe towards *Darius* (who was said to be aduanced towards him with a maruailous Armie) by the way of *Phrygia:* For all the Prouince of *Asia* the lesse, bordering vpon the Sea, his first victorie laied vnder his feet.

While he gaue order for the gouernement and setling of *Lycia*, and *Pamphilia*, he sent *Cleander* to raise some new Companies in *Peloponnesus*; and marching towards the North he entred *Celenas*, seated on the Riuer *Mæander*, which was abandoned vnto him, the Castle only holding out, which also after fortie daies was giuen vp: for so long time he gaue them to attend succour from *Darius*. From *Celenas* he past on through *Phrygia* towards the *Euxine* Sea, till he came to a Citie called *Gordium*, the Regall-seate, in former times, of King *Midas*. In this Citie it was that he found the *Gordian*-knot, which when hee knew not how to vndoe, hee cut it a-sunder with his sword. For there was an ancient prophecie did promise to him that could vntie it, the Lordship of all *Asia*; whereupon *Alexander*, not respecting the manner how, so it were done, assumed to himselfe the fulfilling of the prophesie, by hewing it in peeces.

But before he turned from this part of *Asia* the lesse towards the East, hee tooke care to cleare the Sea-coast on his backe, and to thrust the *Persians* out of the Ilands of *Lesbos, Scio,* and *Coos,* the charge whereof he cõmitted vnto two of his Captaines, giuing them such order as he thought to be most conuenient for that seruice; and deliuering vnto them fiftie talents to defray the charge; and withall out of his first spoile gotten, he sent threescore talents more to *Antipater* his Lieutenant in *Greece,* and *Macedon.* From *Celenas* he remoued to *Ancira,* now called *Anguori,* standing on the same Riuer of *Sangarius,* which runneth through *Gordium:* there hee mustred his Armie, and then entred *Paphlagonia,* whose people submitted themselues vnto him, and obtained freedome of tribute: where hee left *Catus* Gouernour with one Regiment of *Macedonians* lately arriued.

Here he vnderstood of the death of *Memnon, Darius* Lieutenant, which heartned him greatly to passe on towards him, for of this only Captaine hee had more respect than of all the multitude by *Darius* assembled, and of all the Commanders hee had besides. For so much hath the spirit of some one man excelled, as it hath vndertaken and effected the alteration of the greatest States and Common-weales, the erection of Monarchies, the conquest of Kingdomes and Empires guided handfuls of men against multitudes of equall bodily strength, contriued victories beyond all hope and discourse of reason, conuerted the fearefull passions of his owne followers into magnanimitie, and the valour of his enemies into cowardize; such spirits haue beene stirred vp in sundrie Ages of the world, and in diuers parts thereof, to erect and cast downe againe, to establish and to destroy, and to bring all things, Persons and States; to the same certaine ends, which the infinite spirit of the *Vniuersall,* piercing, mouing, and gouerning all thinges hath ordained. Certainely the things that this King did were maruailous, and would hardly haue beene vndertaken by any man else: and though his Father had determined to haue inuaded the lesser *Asia* it is like enough that he would haue contented himselfe with some part thereof, and not haue discouered

the Riuer of *Indus*, as this man did. The swift course of
victorie, wherewith he ranne ouer so large a portion of the
World, in so short a space, may justly be imputed vnto this,
That he was neuer encountred by an equall spirit, concurring
with equall power against him. Hereby it came to passe
that his actions being limited by no greater opposition,
than Desert places, and the meere length of tedious journies
could make, were like the *Colossus* of *Rhodes*, not so much to
bee admired for the workemanship, though therein also
praise-worthie, as for the huge bulke. For certainly the
things performed by *Xenophon*, discouer as braue a spirit
as *Alexanders*, and working no lesse exquisitely, though the
effects were lesse materiall, as were also the forces and power
of command, by which it wrought. But he that would finde
the exact patterne of a noble Commander, must looke vpon
such as *Epaminondas*, that encountring worthie Captains,
and those better followed than themselues, haue by their
singular vertue ouer-topped their valiant enemies, and still
preuailed ouer those, that would not haue yeelded one foot
to any other. Such as these are doe seldome liue to obtaine
great Empires. For it is a worke of more labour and longer
time, to master the equall forces of one hardie and well-
ordered State, than to tread downe and vtterly subdue a
multitude of seruile Nations, compounding the bodie of a
grosse vnweldie Empire. Wherefore these *Paruo Potentes*,
men that with little haue done much vpon enemies of like
abilitie, are to be regarded as choise examples of worth;
but great Conquerors, to bee rather admired for the substance of their actions, than the exquisite menaging: exact-
nesse and greatnesse concurring so seldome, that I can finde
no instance of both in one, saue only that braue *Roman Cæsar*.

Hauing thus farre digressed, it is now time that wee
returne vnto our Easterne Conqueror; who is trauailing
hastily towards *Cilicia*, with a desire to recouer the Streights
thereof before *Darius* should arriue there. But first making
a dispatch into *Greece*, he sent to those Cities, in which he
reposed most trust, some of the *Persian* Targets which he
had recouered in his first battaile; vpon which, by certaine
inscriptions, he made them partakers of his victorie. Herein
hee well aduised himselfe; for he that doth not aswell impart

of the honour which he gaineth in the Warres, as hee doth
of the spoiles, shall neuer bee long followed by those of the
better sort. For men which are either well borne or well
bred, and haue more of wealth than of reputation, doe as
often satisfie themselues with the purchase of glorie; as the
weake in fortune, and strong in courage, doe with the gaine
of gold and siluer.

The Gouernour of *Cilicia* hearing of *Alexander* comming
on, left some Companies to keepe the Streights, which were
indeede very defencible; and withall, as *Curtius* noteth, hee
beganne ouer-late to prise and put in execution the Counsell
of *Memnon:* who in the beginning of the Warres aduised
him to wast all the prouisions for Men and Horse, that
could not bee lodged in strong places, and alwaies to giue
ground to the Inuader, till hee found some such notable
aduantage as might assuredly promise him the obtaining of
victorie. For the furie of an inuading Armie is best broken,
by delaies, change of diet, and want, eating sometimes too
little, and sometimes too much, sometimes reposing themselues in beds, and more oftner on the cold ground. These
and the like suddaine alterations bring many diseases vpon
all Nations out of their owne Countries. Therefore if *Darius*
had kept the *Macedonians* but a while from meat and sleepe,
and refusing to giue or take battaile, had wearied them with
his light horse, as the *Parthians* afterward did the *Romans*;
hee might perchance haue saued his owne life, and his
estate: For it was one of the greatest incouragements giuen
by *Alexander* to the *Macedonians*, in the third and last
fatall battaile, that they were to fight with all the strength
of *Persia* at once.

Xerxes when he inuaded *Greece* and fought abroade, in
being beaten, lost only his men; but *Darius* being inuaded
by the *Greekes*, and fighting at home, by being beaten, lost
his Kingdome; *Pericles*, though the *Lacedæmonians* burnt
all in *Attica* to the Gates of *Athens*, yet could not bee drawne
to hazard a battaile: for the inuaded ought euermore to fight
vpon the aduantage of time and place. Because we reade
Histories to informe our vnderstanding by the examples
therein found, we will giue some instances of those that haue
perished by aduenturing in their owne Countries, to charge

an inuading Armie. The *Romans*, by fighting with *Hanibal*,
were brought to the brinke of their destruction.

Pompey was well aduised for a while, when hee gaue
Cæsar ground, but when by the importunitie of his Captaines
he aduentured to fight at *Pharsalia*, he lost the battaile, lost
the freedome of *Rome*, and his owne life.

Ferdinand, in the Conquest of *Naples*, would needs fight
a battaile with the *French* to his confusion, though it was
told him by a man of sound judgement, that those Counsels
which promise suretie in all things, are honourable enough.

The Constable of *France* made frustrate the mightie preparation of *Charles* the First, when he inuaded *Prouence*,
by wasting the Countrie, and forbearing to fight; so did
the Duke of *Alua* wearie the *French* in *Naples*, and dissolue
the boisterous Armie of the Prince of *Orenge* in the low-
Countries.

The *Leigers*, contrarie to the aduise of their Generall,
would needes fight a battaile with the *Bourgonians*, inuading
their Countrie, and could not be perswaded to linger the
time, and stay their aduantage; but they lost eight and
twentie thousand vpon the place. *Philip* of *Valois* set upon
King *Edward* at *Cressie*, and King *Iohn* (when the *English*
were well neare tired out, and would in short time by an
orderly pursuit haue beene wasted to nothing) constrained
the black Prince with great furie, neare *Poitiers*, to joyne
battaile with him: But all men know what lamentable
successe these two *French* Kings found. *Charles* the Fift of
France made an other kinde of *Tabian* Warfare; and though
the *English* burnt and wasted many places, yet this King
held his resolution to forbeare blowes, and followed his
aduise which told him, That the *English* could neuer get his
inheritance by smoake; and it is reported by *Bellarus* and
Herrault, that King *Edward* was wont to say of this *Charles*,
that hee wanne from him the Duchie of *Guien* without euer
putting on his Armour.

But where God hath a purpose to destroy, wise men grow
short liued, and the charge of things is committed vnto such
as either cannot see what is for their good, or know not how
to put in execution any sound aduise. The course which
Memnon had propounded, must in all appearance of reason

haue brought the *Macedonian* to a great perplexitie, and
made him stand still a while at the Streights of *Cilicia*,
doubting whether it were more shamefull to returne; or
dangerous to proceede. For had *Cappadocia* and *Paphlagonia*
beene wasted whilest *Alexander* was farre off; and the
Streights of *Cilicia* beene defended by *Arsenes*, Gouernor of
that Prouince, with the best of his forces: hunger would not
haue suffered the enemie, to stay the triall of all meanes that
might be thought vpon, of forcing that passage; or if the
place could not haue beene maintained, yet might *Cilicia*
at better leisure haue beene so throughly spoiled, that the
heart of his Armie should haue beene broken; by seeking
out miseries with painefull trauaile.

But *Arsenes* leauing a small number to defend the
Streights, tooke the best of his Armie with him, to wast,
and spoile the Countrie; or rather, as may seeme, to find
himselfe some worke, by pretence of which hee might
honestly runne further away from *Alexander*. Hee should
rather haue aduentured his person in custodie of the
Streights, whereby hee might perhaps haue saued the
Prouince; and in the meane time, all that was in the fields,
would haue beene conueighed into strong Townes. So
should his Armie, if it were driuen from the place of
aduantage, haue found good entertainement within walled
Cities, and himselfe with his horse-men haue had the lesse
worke in destroying that little which was left abroad.
Handling the matter as he did, he gaue the *Cilicians* cause
to wish for *Alexanders* comming, and as great cause to the
Keepers of the passage not to hinder it. For cowards are
wise in apprehending all formes of danger. These Guardians
of the Streights, hearing that *Arsenes* made all hast to joyne
himselfe with *Darius*, burning downe all as he went, like
one despairing of the defence, beganne to grow circumspect,
and to thinke that surely their Generall, who gaue as lost
the Countrie behind their backs, had exposed themselues
vnto certaine death, as men that were good for nothing else,
but to dull the *Macedonian* swords. Wherefore, not affecting
to die for their Prince and Countrie (which honour they
saw that *Arsenes* himselfe could well forbeare) they speedily
followed the foote-steps of their Generall, gleaning after his

Haruest. Thus *Alexander* without labour got both the entrance of *Cilicia*, abandoned by the cowardise of his Enemies, and the whole Prouince that had beene alienated from the *Persian* side by their indiscretion.

§4. *Of the vnwarlike Armie leauied by* Darivs *against* Alexander. *The vnaduised courses which* Darivs *tooke in this expedition. Hee is vanquished at Issus; where his Mother, Wife, and Children are made prisoners. Of some thinges following the battaile of Issus.*

In the meane season *Darius* approched; who (as *Curtius* reports) had compounded an Armie of more than two hundred and ninetie thousand Souldiers, out of diuers Nations; *Iustine* musters them at three hundred thousand Foot, and a hundred thousand Horse; *Plutarch* at sixe hundred thousand.

The manner of his comming on, as *Curtius* describes it, was rather like a masker than a man of Warre, and like one that tooke more care to set out his glorie and riches, than to prouide for his owne safetie, perswading himselfe, as it seemed, to beat *Alexander* with pompe and sumptuous Pageants. For, before the Armie there was carried the holy fire which the *Persians* worshipped, attended by their *Priests*, and after them three hundred and threescore and fiue yong-men, answering the number of the daies of the yeare, couered with Scarlet; then the Chariot of *Iupiter* drawne with white Horses, with their Riders cloathed in the same colour, with rods of gold in their hands; And after it, the Horse of the *Sunne*: Next after these followed ten sumptuous Chariots, inlaied and garnisht with siluer and gold, and then the Vantguard of their horse, compounded of twelue seuerall Nations, which the better to auoide confusion, did hardly vnderstand each others language, and these marshalled in the head of the rest, being beaten, might serue very fitly to disorder all that followed them; in the taile of these Horses the Regiment of foote marched, with the *Persians* called immortall, because if any died the number was presently supplied: and these were armed with chaines of gold, and their coates with the same mettall imbrodered, whereof the sleeues were garnished with pearle, baites, either to catch the hungrie *Macedonians* withall, or to perswade them that it were great inciuilitie to cut and to deface such glorious garments. But it was well said. . . . *Let no man thinke that he exceedeth those in valour, whom hee exceedeth in gay garments, for it is by men armed with fortitude of minde, and not by the apparell they put on, that enemies are beaten.* And it was perchance from the *Roman Papyrius* that this aduice was borrowed, who when he fought against the *Samnites* in that fatall battaile, wherein they all sware either to preuaile or die, thirtie thousand of them hauing apparelled themselues in white garments, with high crests and great plumes of feathers, bad the *Roman* Souldiers to lay aside all feare: *Non enim cristas vulnera facere, & per picta atque aurata scuta transire Romanum pilum*; *For these plumed crests would wound no bodie, and the Roman pile would bore holes in painted and gilded shields.*

To second this Court-like companie, fifteene thousand were appointed more rich and glittering than the former, but apparelled like Women (belike to breede the more terrour) and these were honoured with the Title of the Kings Kinsmen. Then came *Darius* himselfe, the Gentleman of his Guarde-robe, riding before his Chariot, which was supported with the Gods of his Nation, cast and cut in pure gold; these the *Macedonians* did not serue, but they serued their turnes of these, by changing their massie-bodies into thinne portable and currant coine. The head of this Chariot was set with pretious stones, with two little golden Idols, couered with an open-winged-Eagle of the same metall: The hinder part being raised high wheron *Darius* sate, had a couering of inestimable value. This Chariot of the King was followed with ten thousand Horse-men, their Lances plated with sluer, and their heads guilt; which they meant not to imbrew in the *Macedonian* bloud, for feare of marring their beautie. He had for the proper Guard of his person two hundred of the bloud Royall, bloud too Royall and pretious to be spilt by any valorous aduenture, (I am of opinion that two hundred sturdie fellowes, like the *Switzers*, would haue done him more seruice) and these were backt with thirtie

thousand foot-men, after whome againe were led foure
hundred spare horses for the King, which if hee had meant
to haue vsed he would haue marshalled somewhat nearer
him.

Now followed the Reareward, the same being led by
Sisygambis the Kings Mother, and by his Wife, drawne in
glorious Chariots, followed by a great traine of Ladies their
attendants on horse-back, with fifteene Wagons of the Kings
children, and the wiues of the Nobilitie, waited on by two
hundred and fiftie Concubines, and a world of Nurses, and
Eunuchs, most sumptuously apparelled, By which it should
seeme that *Darius* thought that the *Macedonians* had beene
Comedians or *Tumblers*; for this troupe was farre fitter to
behold those sports than to bee present at battailes. Betweene these & a companie of slight-armed slaues, with a
world of Vallets, was the Kings treasure, charged on six
hundred Mules, and three hundred Camels, brought, as it
proued, to pay the *Macedonians*. In this sort came this
Maygame-King into the field, incombred with a most vnnecessarie traine of Strumpets, attended with troupes of
diuers Nations, speaking diuers languages, and for their
numbers impossible to be marshalled, and for the most part
so effeminate, and so rich in gold and in garments, as the
same could not but haue incouraged the nakeddest Nation
of the world against them. We finde it in daily experience
that all discourse of magnanimitie, of Nationall Vertue, of
Religion, of Libertie, and whatsoeuer else hath beene wont
to moue and incourage vertuous men, hath no force at all
with the common-Souldier in comparison of spoile and
riches, The rich ships are boorded vpon all disaduantages,
the rich Townes are furiously assaulted, and the plentifull
Countries willingly inuaded. Our *English* Nation haue
attempted many places in the *Indies*, and runne vpon the
Spaniards head-long, in hope of their Royalls of plate, and
Pistolets, which had they beene put to it vpon the like
disaduantages in *Ireland*, or in any poore Countrie, they
would haue turned their Peeces and Pikes against their
Commanders, contesting that they had beene brought without reason to the Butcherie and slaughter. It is true that the
warre is made willingly, and for the most part with good

successe, that is ordained against the richest Nations; for as the needie are alwaies aduenturous, so plentie is wont to shunne perill, and men that haue well to liue, doe rather studie how to liue well, I meane wealthily, than care to die (as they call it) honourably. *Car où il ny' a rien a gaigner, que des coups volontiers il ny' va pas*; *No man makes hast to the market, where there is nothing to be bought but blowes.*

Now if *Alexander* had beheld this preparation before his consultation with his Southsaiers, hee would haue satisfied himselfe by the out-sides of the *Persians*, and neuer haue looked into the intrailes of Beasts for successe. For leauing the description of this second battaile (which is indeede no-where well described, neither for the confusion and hastie running away of the *Asians* could it be) we haue enough by the slaughter that was made of them, and by the few that fell of the *Macedonians*, to informe vs what manner of resistance was made. For if it be true that threescore thousand *Persian* foot-men were slaine in this Battaile, with ten thousand of their horsemen, Or (as *Curtius* saith) an hundred thousand footmen, with the same number of horse-men, and besides this slaughter, fortie thousand taken prisoners, while of *Alexanders* Armie there miscarried but two hundred and fourescore of all sorts, of which numbers *Arianus* and other Historians cut off almost the one halfe: I doe verily beleeue that this small number rather died with the ouer-trauaile and paines-taking in killing their enemies, than by any strokes receiued from them. And surely if the *Persian* Nation (at this time degenerate and the basest of the World) had had any sauour remaining of the ancient valour of their forefathers; they would neuer haue sold so good cheape, and at so vile a price, the Mother, the Wife, the Daughters, and other the Kings children; had their owne honor beene valued by them at nothing, and the Kings safetie and his estate at lesse. *Darius* by this time found it true that *Charidemus* a banished *Grædian* of *Athens* had told him, when hee made a view of his Armie about *Babylon*, to wit, That the multitude which hee had assembled of diuers Nations, richly attired, but poorely armed, would bee found more terrible to the Inhabitants of the countrie, whom in passing by they would deuour, than to the *Macedonians*, whom they meant to assaile; who being all old and obedient Souldiers, imbattailed in grosse squadrons, which they call their *Phallanx*, well couered with Armour for defence, and furnished with weapons for offence of great aduantage, would make so little accompt of his delicate *Persians*, louing their ease and their palat, being withall ill armed and worse disciplined, as except it would please him to entertaine (hauing so great aboundance of treasure to doe it withall) a sufficient number of the same *Græcians*, and so to encounter the *Macedonians* with men of equall courage, hee would repent him ouer-late, as taught by the miserable successe like to follow.

But this discourse was so vnpleasing to *Darius* (who had beene accustomed to nothing so much as to his owne praises, and to nothing so little as to heare truth;) as he commanded that this poore *Græcian* should bee presently slaine: who while hee was a sundring in the Tormentors hand, vsed this speech to the King, That *Alexander*, against whom hee had giuen this good counsell, should assuredly reuenge his death, and lay deserued punishment vpon *Darius* for despising his aduise.

It was the saying of a Wise man. *Desperata eius Principis salus est, cuius aures ita formatæ sunt, vt aspera quæ vtilia, nec quicquam nisi iucundum accipiat*; That Princes safetie is in a desperate case, whose eares iudge all that is profitable to bee too sharpe, and will entertaine nothing that is vnpleasant.

For *libertie in counsell is the life and essence of counsell*; *Libertas consilij est eius vita, & essentia, qua erepta consilium euanescit.*

Darius did likewise value at nothing the Aduise giuen him by the *Græcian* Souldiers that serued him, who intreated him not to fight in the Streights: but had they beene Counsellers and directors in that Warre, as they were vnderlings and commanded by others, they had with the helpe of a good troupe of horse-men beene able to haue opposed the furie of *Alexander*, without any assistance of the *Persian* foot-men. For when *Darius* was ouerthrowne with all his cowardly and confused rabble, those *Græcians*, vnder their Captaine *Amyntas*, held firme, and marched away in order in despight of the vanquishers. Old Souldiers are not easily dismaied: we reade in Histories ancient and moderne, what braue retraits haue beene made by them, though the rest of the Armie in which they haue serued, hath beene broken.

At the battaile of *Rauenne* where the Imperialls were beaten by the *French*, a squadron of *Spaniards*, old Souldiers, came off vnbroken and vndismaied; whom when *Gaston de Foix*, Duke of *Nemures*, and Nephew to *Lewis* the twelfth, charged, as holding the victorie not intire by their escape, hee was ouer-turned and slaine in the place. For it is truely said of those men, who, by being acquainted with dangers feare them not, That, *Neglecto periculo imminentis mali opus ipsum quantumuis difficile aggrediuntur*; *They goe about the businesse it selfe, how hard soeuer it be, not standing to consider of the danger, which the mischiefe hanging ouer their heads may bring:* and as truely of those that know the warres but by heare-say. *Quod valentes sunt & preualentes ante pericula, in ipsis tamen periculis discedunt*; *They haue abilitie enough, and to spare, till dangers appeare; but when perill indeede comes they get them gone.*

These *Græcians* also that made the retract, aduised *Darius* to retire his Armie into the plaine of *Mesopotamia*, to the end that *Alexander* being entred into those large fields and great Champions, he might haue inuironed the *Macedonians* on all sides with his multitude; and withall they counselled him to diuide that his huge Armie into parts, not committing the whole to one stroke of Fortune, whereby he might haue fought many battailes, and haue brought no greater numbers at once then might haue beene well marshalled and con-ducted. But this counsell was so contrarie to the cowardly affections of the *Persians*, as they perswaded *Darius* to inuirone the *Græcians* which gaue the aduise, and to cut them in peeces as Traitors. The infinite wisedome of God doth not worke alwaies by one and the same way, but very often in the alteration of Kingdomes and Estates, by taking vnderstanding from the Gouernours, so as they can neither giue nor discerne of Counsels. For *Darius* that would needes fight with *Alexander* vpon a straightned peece of ground, neare vnto the Citie of *Issus*, where he could bring no more hands to fight than *Alexander* could, (who by the aduise of

Parmenio staied there, as in a place of best aduantage) was vtterly ouerthrowne, his Treasure lost, his Wife, Mother, and Children (whom the *Grœcians* his followers had perswaded him to leaue in *Babylon*, or elsewhere) taken prisoners, and all their traine of Ladies spoiled of their rich Garments, Iewels, and Honour. It is true, that both the Queene, with her Daughters, who had the good hap to be brought to *Alexanders* presence, were entertained with all respect due vnto their birth, their Honours preserued, and their Iewels and rich Garments restored vnto them; and though *Darius* Wife was a most beautifull Ladie, and his Daughters of excellent forme, Yet *Alexander* mastred his affections towards them all: only it is reported out of *Aristobulus* the Historian, That he imbraced the Wife of the valiant *Memnon*, her Husband lately dead, who was taken flying from *Damascus* by *Parmenio*, at which time the Daughters of *Ochus*, who raigned before *Darius*, and the Wiues and Children of all the Nobilitie of *Persia* in effect, fell into captiuitie; At which time also *Darius* Treasure (not lost at *Issus*) was seized, amounting to sixe thousand and two hundred talents of coine, and of *Bullion* fiue hundred talents, with a world of riches besides.

Darius himselfe leauing his brother dead, with diuers other of his chiefe Captaines (casting the Crowne from his head) hardly escaped.

After this ouerthrow giuen vnto *Darius*, all *Phœnicia* (the Citie of *Tyre* excepted) was yeelded to *Alexander*, of which *Parmenio* was made Gouernour.

Aradus, *Zidon*, and *Biblos*, Maritimate Cities of great importance, of which one *Strato* was King (but hated of the people) acknowledged *Alexander*. Good fortune followed him so fast that it troade on his heeles, for *Antigonus*, *Alexanders* Lieutenant in *Asia* the lesse, ouerthrew the *Cappadocians*, *Paphlagonians*, and others lately reuolted; *Aristodemus*, *Darius* Admirall, had his Fleet partly taken, and in part drowned by the *Macedonians* newly leauied; the *Lacedæmonians* that warred against *Antipater* were beaten; foure thousand of those *Greekes* which made the retrait at the last battaile, forsaking both the partie of *Darius* and of *Alexander*, and led by *Amyntas* into *Ægypt*, to hold it for themselues, were buried there; for the time was not yet come to diuide Kingdomes.

Alexander, to honour *Ephestion*, whom hee loued most, gaue him power to dispose of the Kingdome of *Zidon*. A man of a most poore estate, that laboured to sustaine his life, being of the Royall bloud, was commended by the people vnto him, who changed his Spade into a Scepter, so as he was beheld both a Beggar and a King in one and the same houre.

It was a good desire of this new King, when speaking to *Alexander*, he wisht that hee could beare his prosperitie with the same moderation, and quietnesse of heart, that he had done his aduersitie; but ill done of *Alexander*, in that he would not performe in himselfe that which hee commended in an other mans desire: for it was a signe that he did but accompanie, and could not gouerne, his felicitie.

While he made some stay in those parts, he receiued a letter from *Darius*, importing the ransome of his Wife, his Mother, and his Children, with some other conditions of peace, but such as rather became a Conqueror, than one that had now been twice shamefully beaten, not vouchsafing, in his direction, to stile *Alexander* King. It is true, that the *Romans*, after that they had receiued an ouerthrow by *Pyrrhus*, returned him a more scornefull answere vpon the offer of peace, than they did before the triall of his force. But as their fortunes were then in the Spring, so that of *Darius* had alreadie cast leafe, the one a resolued well armed and disciplined Nation, the other cowardly and effeminate. *Alexander* disdained the offers of *Darius*, and sent him word that he not only directed his letter to a King, but to the King of *Darius* himselfe.

§5. *How* Alexander *besieged and wanne the Citie of Tyre.*

Alexander comming neare to the Citie of *Tyre*, receiued from them the present of a golden Crowne, with great store of victualls, and other presents, which hee tooke very thankefully, returning them answere, That he desired to offer a sacrifice to *Hercules*, the Protector of their Citie, from whom hee was descended. But the *Tyrians* like not his companie within their Walles, but tell him that the Temple of *Hercules* was seated in the old Citie adjoyning, now abandoned and desolate: To bee short, *Alexander* resolued to enter it by force, and though it were a place in all mens opinion impregnable, because the Iland whereon it was built, was eight hundred furlongs from the Maine; yet with the labour of many hands, hauing great store of stone from the old *Tyre*, and timber sufficient from *Lybanus*, hee filled the passage of the Sea betweene the Iland and the Maine, which being more than once carried away by the strength of the Sea vpon a storme of winde, sometime by the *Tyrians* fired, and sometime torne a-sunder, yet with the helpe of his Nauie which arriued (during the siege) from *Cyprus*, he ouercame all difficulties and preuailed, after he had spent seuen Moneths in that attempt. The *Tyrians* in the beginning of the siege had barbarously drowned the messengers sent by *Alexander*, perswading them to render the Citie, in respect whereof, and of the great losse of time and men, he put eight thousand to the sword, and caused two thousand of those, that escaped the first furie, to bee hanged on Crosses on the Sea-shore, and reserued for slaues (saith *Diodore*) thirteene thousand; *Arrianus* reckons them at thirtie thousand. Many more had died had not the *Zidonians*, that serued *Alexander*, conueied great numbers away by shipping vnto their owne Citie.

Happie it was for *Apollo* that the Towne was taken, for one of the *Tyrians* hauing dreamt, that this God meant to forsake the Citie, they bound him fast with a golden chaine to the Idoll of *Hercules*; but *Alexander* like a gratious Prince loosened him againe.

It is true, that it was a notable enterprise and a difficult, but great things are made greater. For *Nabuchodonosor* had taken it before, and filled vp the channell, that lay betweene the Iland and the Maine.

The gouernement of this Territorie he gaue to *Philotas*, the Sonne of *Parmenio*; *Cilicia*, he committed to *Socrates*, and *Andromachus* Lieutenant vnder *Parmenio*; *Ephestion* had the charge of the Fleet, and was directed to finde *Alexander* at *Gaza* towards *Ægypt*.

§6. *How* Darivs *offered conditions of peace to* Alexander.
Alexander *winnes Gaza*; *and deales graciously with the*
Iewes.

In the meane while *Darius* sends againe to *Alexander*, sets
before him all the difficulties of passing on towards the
East; and laieth the losse of the last battaile to the straight-
nesse of the place: he hoped to terrifie him, by threatning to
incompasse him in the plaine Countries, he bids him consider, how impossible it was to passe the Riuers of *Euphrates*,
Tigris, *Araxes*, and the rest, with all such other fearefull
thinges: for, hee that was now filled with nothing but feare,
had arguments enough of that nature to present vnto another.
All the Kingdomes betweene the Riuer of *Alys*, and the
Hellespont, he offered him in Dower with his beloued
daughter. But *Alexander* answered, That he offered him
nothing but his owne, and that which victorie and his owne
vertue had possest him of; That he was to giue conditions,
and not to receiue any; and that he hauing passed the Sea it
selfe, disdained to thinke of resistance in transporting himselfe ouer Riuers. It is said that *Parmenio*, who was now old
and full of honour and riches, told the King, that were he
Alexander hee would accept of *Darius* his offers, to which
Alexander answered, That so would he if he were *Parmenio*.

But he goes on towards *Ægypt*, and comming before *Gaza*,
Betis a faithfull seruant to *Darius*, shuts the Gate against
him, and defends the Towne with an obstinate resolution,
at the siege whereof *Alexander* receiued a wound in the
shoulder, which was dangerous, and a blow on his legge
with a stone; Hee found better men in this place than he
did at the former battailes, for he left so many of his
Macedonians buried in the sands of *Gaza*, that he was forst
to send for a new supply into *Greece*. Here it was that
Alexander first beganne to change condition, and to exercise
crueltie. For after that he had entred *Gaza* by assault, and
taken *Betis*, (whom *Iosephus* calleth *Babemeses*) that was
weakened with many wounds, and who neuer gaue ground
to the Assailants; he bored holes through his feete, and
caused him to bee drawne about the streets, whilest he was
as yet aliue; who being as valiant a man as himselfe,

disdained to aske him either life or remission of his torments. And what had hee to countenance this his tyrannie, but the imitation of his ancestor *Achilles*, who did the like to *Hector?* It is true, that crueltie hath alwaies somewhat to couer her deformitie.

From *Gaza* (saith *Iosephus*) he led his Armie towards *Ierusalem*, a Citie, for the antiquitie and great fame thereof, well knowne vnto him while he lay before *Tyre*; He had sent for some supply thither, which *Iaddus* the high Priest, being subject and sworne to *Darius*, had refused him. The *Iewes* therefore fearing his reuenge, and vnable to resist, committed the care of their estates and safetie to *Iaddus*, who, being taught by God, issued out of the Citie couered with his Pontificall-Robes, to wit, an vpper garment of purple, embrodered with gold, with his Miter, and the plate of gold wherein the name of God was written, the Priests & Leuites in their rich ornaments, and the people in white garments, in a maner so vnusuall, stately, and graue, as *Alexander* greatly admired it. *Iosephus* reports it, that he fell to the ground before the high Priest, as reuerencing the name of God, and that *Parmenio* reprehended him for it; Howsoeuer it was, I am of opinion, That he became so confident in his enterprise, and so assured of the successe after the prophecie of *Daniel* had been read vnto him, wherein he saw himselfe, and the conquest of *Persia* so directly pointed at, as nothing thence-forth could discourage him or feare him. He confessed to *Parmenio* (saith *Iosephus*) That in *Dio* a Citie of *Macedon*, when his mind laboured the conquest of *Asia*, hee saw in his sleepe such a person as *Iaddus*, and so apparailed, professing one and the same God, by whom he was incouraged to pursue the purpose hee had in hand with assurance of victorie. This apparition, formerly apprehended only by the light of his phantasie, he now beheld with his bodily eies; wherewith he was so exceedingly pleased and imboldened, as contrarie to the practice of the *Phœnicians*, (who hoped to haue sackt and destroied *Ierusalem*) he gaue the *Iewes* all, and more than they desired, both of libertie and immunitie, with permission to liue vnder their owne lawes, and to exercise and enjoy their owne Religion.

§7. Alexander *winnes Ægypt: and makes a iournie to the Temple of* Hammon.

From *Ierusalem Alexander* turned againe towards *Ægypt*, and entred it, where *Darius* his Lieutenant, *Astaces*, receiued him and deliuered into his hand the Citie of *Memphis*, with eight hundred talents of treasure, and all other the Kings riches. By this wee see that the Kings of *Persia*, who had more of affection than of judgement, gaue to the valiantest man hee had but the command of one Citie, and to the veriest coward the gouernement of all *Ægypt*. When he had set thinges in order in *Ægypt*, he beganne to trauaile after *God-head*, towards *Iupiter Hammon*, so foolish had pro-speritie made him, He was to passe ouer the dangerous and drie sands, where, when the water which he brought on his Camels-back was spent, hee could not but haue perished, had not a maruailous shower of raine fallen vpon him, when his Armie was in extreme despaire. All men that know *Ægypt*, and haue written thereof, affirme, That it neuer raines there; but the purposes of the Almightie God are secret, and he bringeth to passe what it pleaseth him; for it is also said, That when he had lost his way in those vast desarts, that a flight of Crowes flew before the Armie; who making faster wing when they were followed, and fluttering slowly when the Armie was cast back, guided them ouer those pathlesse sands to *Iupiters* Temple.

Arrianus from the report of *Ptolomie*, the sonne of *Lagus*, saies, That hee was led by two Dragons, both which reports may be a-like true; But many of these wonders and thinges prodigious, are fained by those that haue written the Storie of *Alexander*, as that an Eagle lay houering directly ouer his head at the battaile of *Issus;* That a Swallow flew about his head when hee slept, and could not be feared from him, till it had wakened him, at *Halicarnasseus*, fore-shewing the treason of *Æropus*, practised by *Darius* to haue slaine him; That from the yron barres of which the *Tyrians* made their defensiue ingines, when *Alexander* besieged them, there fell drops of bloud; and that the like drops were found in a loafe of bread, broken by a *Macedonian* Souldier, at the same time; That a Turfe of earth fell on his shoulder, when he lay before *Gaza*, out of which there flew a Bird into the aire. The *Spaniards* in the conquest of the West *Indies* haue many such pretie tales; telling how they haue been assisted in battaile, by the presence of our *Ladie*, and by *Angels* riding on white horses, with the like *Romish* miracles, which I thinke themselues doe hardly beleeue. The strangest things that I haue read of in this kind being certainely true was, That the night before the battaile at *Nouarre*, all the Dogges which followed the *French* Armie, ranne from them to the *Switzers*, leaping and fawning vpon them, as if they had beene bred and fed by them all their liues, and in the morning following, *Triuulzi* and *Tremouille*, Generals for *Lewis* the twelfth, were by these *Imperiall Switzers* vtterly broken and put to ruine.

The place of this Idoll of *Iupiter Hammon* is ill described by *Curtius*, for he bounds it by the *Arabian Troglodites* on the south, between whom and the territorie of *Hammon*, the Region *Thebais*, or the superiour *Ægypt*, with the Mountaines of *Lybia*, and the Riuer of *Nilus*, are interiacent, and on the North he ioynes it to a Nation, called *Nassamones*, who bordering the Sea-shore, liue (saith hee) vpon the spoiles of shipwrack, whereas the Temple or Groue of this Idoll hath no Sea neare it by two hundred miles and more, being found on the South part of *Lybia;* these *Nassamones* being due West from it, in the South part of *Marmarica*.

When *Alexander* came neare the place, he sent some of his Parasites before him to practise the Priests attending the Oracle, That their answere might bee giuen in all thinges, agreeable to his madde ambition, who affected the title of *Iupiters* sonne. And so hee was saluted *Sonne of Iupiter* by the Deuils Prophet, whether prepared before to flatter him, or rather (as some thinke) defectiue in the *Greeke* tongue; For whereas he meant to say *Opaidion*, he said *Opaidios*, that is; *O sonne of Iupiter*, in stead of, *O deare sonne:* for which Grãmaticall error he was richly rewarded, and a rumor presently spread, that the great *Iupiter* had acknowledged *Alexander* for his owne.

He had heard that *Perseus* and *Hercules* had formerly consulted with this Oracle, The one, when he was imploied against *Gorgon*, The other, against *Anteus* and *Busiris;* and seeing these men had deriued themselues from the Gods, why might not hee? By this it seemes, that he hoped to make his followers and the world fooles, though indeede he made himselfe one, by thinking to couer from the Worlds knowledge his vanities and vices; and the better to confirme his followers in the beliefe of his *Deitie*, hee had practized the Priests to giue answere to such as consulted with the Oracle, that it should be pleasing to *Iupiter* to honour *Alexander* as his Sonne.

Who this *Ammon* was, and how represented, either by a bosse carried in a Boate, or by a *Ramme*, or a *Rammes*-head; I see that many wise-men haue troubled themselues to finde out; but, as *Arrianus* speakes of *Dionysius*, or *Liber Pater* (who liued saith S^t. *Augustine* in *Moses* time), *Ea quæ de dijs veteres fabulis suis conscripsere non sunt nimium curiosè peruestiganda; We must not ouer-curiously search into the fables, which the Ancients haue written of their Gods.*

But this is certaine and notable, that after the Gospell beganne to be preached in the World, the Deuill in this and in all other Idols became speechlesse. For that this *Hammon* was neglected in the time of *Tiberius Cæsar*, and in the time of *Traian* altogether forgotten, *Strabo* and *Plutarch* witnesse.

There is found neare his Temple a Fountaine called *Fons solis* (though *Ptolomie* in his third *African* Table sets it farther off) that at mid-night is as hot as boiling water, and at Noone as cold as any yce, to which I cannot but giue credit, because I haue heard of some other Wells of like nature, and because it is reported by Saint *Augustine*, by *Diodore*, *Herodotus*, *Plinie*, *Mela*, *Solinus*, *Arianus*, *Curtius*, and others, and indeede our Bathes in *England* are much warmer in the night, than in the day.

§8. *How* Alexander *marching against* Darivs, *was opposed very vnskilfully by the Enemie.*

From the Temple of *Hammon* he returned to *Memphis*, where among many other learned men he heard the Philosopher *Psammones*, who, belike vnderstanding that he affected the title of *Iupiters* Sonne, told him that God was the

Father-King of all men in generall; and refining the pride of this haughtie King, brought him to say, That God was the Father of all mortall men, but that hee acknowledged none for his children saue good men.

He gaue the charge of the seuerall Prouinces of *Ægypt* to seuerall Gouernours, following the rule of his Master *Aristotle*, That *a great Dominion should not bee continued in the hands of any one:* whom therein the *Roman* Emperours also followed, not daring to commit the gouernement of *Ægypt* to any of their *Senators*, but to men of meaner ranck and degree. He then gaue order for the founding of *Alexandria* vpon the Wester-most branch of *Nilus*. And hauing now setled (as he could) the estate of *Ægypt*, with the Kingdomes of the lesser *Asia*, *Phœnicia*, and *Syria*, (which being but the pawnes of *Darius* his ill fortune, one happie victorie would readily haue redeemed;) he led his Armie towards *Euphrates*, which passage though the same was committed to *Mazeus* to defend, yet was it abandoned, and *Alexander* without resistance past it. From thence he marched towards *Tigris*, a Riuer for the swiftnesse thereof called by the *Persians* The Arrow. Here, as *Curtius*, and Reason it selfe tells vs, might *Darius* easily haue repelled the inuading *Macedonian:* for the violent course of the streame was such, as it draue before it many waightie stones, and those that moued not but lay in the bottome, were so round and well polished by continuall rolling, that no man was able to fight on so slipperie a footing; nor the *Macedonian* foot-men to wade the Riuer, otherwise than by joyning their handes and enterlacing their Armes together, making one waightie and entire bodie to resist the swift passage and furious race of the streame. Besides this notable helpe, the Channell was so deepe towards the Easterne shore, where *Darius* should haue made head, as the foot-men were inforst to lift their Bowes and Arrowes and Darts ouer their heads, to keepe them from being moistned, and made vnseruiceable by the Waters. But it was truely and vnderstandingly said of *Homer*.

> *Talis est hominum terrestrium mens,*
> *Qualis quotidie ducit pater virorumque Deorumque.*

The mindes of men are euer so affected,
As by Gods will they daily are directed.

And it cannot be denied, that as all Estates of the World by the surfeit of misgouernement haue beene subject to many grieuous, and sometimes mortall diseases, So had the Empire of *Persia* at this time brought it selfe into a burning and consuming Feuer, and thereby become frantick and without vnderstanding, foreshewing manifestly the dissolution and death thereof.

But *Alexander* hath now recouered the Easterne shores of *Tigris*, without any other difficultie, than that of the nature of the place; where *Mazeus* (who had charge to defend the passage both of *Euphrates* and it) presented himselfe to the *Macedonians*, followed with certaine companies of Horsemen, as if with vneuen forces hee durst haue charged them on euen ground, when as with a multitude farre exceeding them hee forsooke the aduantage which no valour of his enemies could easily haue ouer-come. But it is commonly seene, that fearefull and cowardly men doe euer follow those waies, and counsells, whereof the opportunitie is alreadie lost.

It is true that he set all prouisions a fire wherewith the *Macedonians* might serue themselues ouer *Tigris*, thinking thereby greatly to haue distressed them; but the execution of good counsell is fruitlesse when vnseasonable. For now was *Alexander* so well furnished with carriages, as nothing was wanting to the competencie of the Armie which he conducted. Those thinges also which he sought to wast, *Alexander* being now in sight, were by his Horse-men saued and recouered. This, *Mazeus* might haue done some daies before at good leisure; or at this time with so great a strength of horse-men, as the *Macedonians* durst not haue pursued them, leauing the strength of their foote out of sight, and farre behinde.

§9. *The new prouisions of* Darivs. *Accidents foregoing the battaile of Arbela.*

Darivs, vpon *Alexanders* first returne out of *Ægypt*, had assembled all the forces, which those Regions next him could furnish, and now also were the *Arians, Scythians, Indians,*

SWR K

and other Nations arriued; Nations (saith *Curtius*) that rather serued to make vp the names of men, than to make resistance. *Arianus* hath numbred them with their Leaders; and finds of foot-men of all sorts ten hundred thousand, and of horse foure hundred thousand, besides armed Chariots, and some few Elephants. *Curtius* who musters the Armie of *Darius* at two hundred thousand foote, and neare fiftie thousand horse, comes (I thinke) nearer to the true number; and yet seeing he had more confidence in the multitude than in the valour of his Vassalls, it is like enough that hee had gathered together of all sorts some three or foure hundred thousand, with which hee hoped in those faire plaines of *Assyria* to haue ouer-borne the few numbers of the inuading Armie. But it is a Rule in the Philosophie of the Warre, *In omni prælio non tam multitudo, & virtus indocta, quam ars & exercitium solent præstare victoriam; In euerie battaile skill and practise doe more towards the victorie, than multitude and rude audacitie.*

While *Alexander* gaue rest to his Armie after their passage ouer *Tigris*, there happened an Eclipse of the Moone, of which the *Macedonians*, not knowing the cause and reason, were greatly affrighted. All that were ignorant, (as the multitude alwaies are) tooke it for a certaine presage of their ouerthrow and destruction, in so much as they began not only to murmur, but to speake it boldly, That for the ambition of one man, a man that disdained *Philip* for his Father, and would needes bee called the Sonne of *Iupiter*, they should all perish; For hee not only inforst them to make warre against Worlds of enemies, but against Riuers, Mountaines, and the Heauens themselues.

Hereupon *Alexander* being readie to march forward made a *halt*, and to quiet the mindes of the multitude, he called before him the *Ægyptian Astrologers*, which followed him thence, that by them the Souldiers might bee assured that this defection of the Moone was a certaine presage of good successe; for that it was naturall they neuer imparted to the common people, but reserued the knowledge to themselues, so as a sorrie Almanack-maker had beene no small foole in those daies.

Of this kinde of superstitious obseruation *Cæsar* made

good vse, when he fought against *Ariouistus* and the *Germans*: for they being perswaded by the casting of lots, that if they fought before the change of the Moone, they should certainely loose the battaile, *Cæsar* forst them to abide it, though they durst not giue it, wherein hauing their mindes alreadie beaten by their owne superstition, and being resolutely charged by the *Romans*, the whole Armie in effect perished.

These *Ægyptians* gaue no other reason than this, That the *Græcians* were vnder the aspect of the *Sunne*, the *Persians* of the *Moone*; and therefore the Moone failing and being darkened, the state of *Persia* was now in danger of falling, and their glorie of being obscured. This judgement of the *Ægyptian* Priests being noised through all the Armie, all were satisfied, and their courage redoubled. It is a principle in the Warre, which, though deuised since, was well obserued then. *Exercitum terrore plenum Dux ad pugnam non ducat; Let not a Captaine leade his Armie to the fight, when it is possessed with matter of terrour.*

It is truely obserued by *Curtius*, that the people are led by nothing so much as by superstition; yea, we finde it in all Stories, and often in our owne, that by such inuentions, deuised tales, dreames, and prophesies, the people of this Land haue beene carried head-long into many dangerous tumults and insurrections, and still to their owne losse and ruine.

As *Alexander* drew neare the *Persian* Armie, certaine letters were surprized written by *Darius* to the *Græcians*, perswading them for great summes of money, either to kill or betray *Alexander*. But these by the aduice of *Parmenio* he suppressed.

At this time also *Darius* his faire Wife, opprest with sorrow, and wearied with trauell, died. Which accident *Alexander* seemed no lesse to bewaile than *Darius*, who vpon the first brute suspected that some dishonourable violence had beene offered her, but being satisfied by an *Eunuch* of his owne that attended her, of *Alexanders* Kingly respect towards her, from the day of her being taken, he desired the immortall Gods, That if they had decreed to make a new Master of the *Persian Empire*, then it would please them to conferre it on so just and continent an enemie as *Alexander*, to whom he once againe before the last triall by battaile offered these conditions of peace.

That with his Daughter in marriage he would deliuer vp and resigne all *Asia* the lesse, and with *Ægypt*, all those Kingdomes betweene the *Phœnician* Sea, and the Riuer of *Euphrates;* That he would pay him for the ransome of his Mother, and his other Daughter thirtie thousand talents, and that for the performance thereof, hee would leaue his Sonne *Occhus* in hostage: To this they sought to perswade *Alexander* by such arguments as they had. *Alexander* causing the Embassadours to be remoued, aduised with his Counsell, but heard no man speake but *Parmenio*, the very right hand of his good fortune; who perswaded him to accept of these faire conditions. Hee told him, that the Empire betweene *Euphrates* and *Hellespont* was a faire addition to *Macedon;* that the retayning of the *Persian* prisoners was a great cumber, and the treasure offered for them of farre better vse than their persons, with diuers other arguments; all which *Alexander* rejected. And yet it is probable that if he had followed his aduise, and bonded his ambition within those limits, he might haue liued as famous for vertue as for fortune, and left himselfe a Successor of able age to haue enjoyed his estate, which afterward, indeed, he much inlarged, rather to the greatning of others than himselfe: who to assure themselues of what they had vsurped vpon his issues, left not one of them to draw breath in the world within a few yeares after. The truth is, That *Alexander* in going so farre into the East, left behinde him the reputation which he brought out of *Macedon;* the reputation of a just and prudent Prince, a Prince temperate, aduised and gratefull: and being taught new lessons by aboundance of prosperitie, became a louer of wine, of his owne flatterie, and of extreame crueltie. Yea, as *Seneca* hath obserued, the taint of one vnjust slaughter, amongst many, defaced and withered the flourishing beautie of all his great acts and glorious victories obtained. But the *Persian* Embassadors stay his answere, which was to this effect, That whatsoeuer he had bestowed on the Wife and Children of *Darius*, proceeded from his owne naturall clemencie and magnanimitie, without all respect to their Master; that thankes to an enemie was improper; that he made no warres against aduersitie, but against those that resisted him, Not against Women and Children, but against armed enemies: and although by the reiterated practice of *Darius*, to corrupt his Souldiers, and by great summes of money to perswade his friends to attempt vpon his person, he had reason to doubt that the peace offered was rather pretended than meant, yet hee could not (were it otherwise and faithfull) resolue in hast to accept the same, seeing *Darius* had made the Warre against him, not as a King with Royall and ouert-force, but as a Traitor by secret and base practice; That for the Territorie offered him, it was alreadie his owne, and if *Darius* could beate him back againe ouer *Euphrates*, which hee had alreadie past, hee would then beleeue that he offered him somewhat in his owne power: Otherwise he propounded to himselfe for the reward of the Warre, which hee had made, all those Kingdomes as yet in *Darius* possession, wherein, whether he were abused by his owne hopes or no, the battaile which hee meant to fight in the day following should determine. For conclusion, hee told them, that hee came into *Asia* to giue, and not to receiue; That the Heauens could not hold two Sunnes: and therefore if *Darius* could bee content to acknowledge *Alexander* for his Superiour, hee might perchance bee perswaded to giue him conditions fit for a second Person, and his Inferiour.

§ 10. *The battaile of Arbela: and that it could not bee so strongly fought as report hath made it.*

With this answer the Embassadors returne; *Darius* prepares to fight, and sends *Mazeus* to defend a passage, which he neuer yet dared so much as to hazard. *Alexander* consults with his Captaines, *Parmenio* perswades him to force *Darius* his Camp by night; so that the multitude of enemies might not moue terrour in the *Macedonians*, being but few. *Alexander* disdaines to steale the victorie, and resolues to bring with him the day-light, to witnesse his valour. But it was the successe that made good *Alexanders* resolution, though the

counsell giuen by *Parmenio* was more sound: For it is a
ground in Warre, *Si pauci necessario cum multitudine pugnare
cogantur, consilium est noctis tempus belli fortunam tentare.* Notwithstanding vpon the view of the multitude at hand, he
staggers & intrenches himselfe vpon a ground of aduantage,
which the *Persian* had abandoned: And whereas *Darius* for
feare of surprise had stood with his Armie in armour all the
day, and forborne sleepe all the night; *Alexander* gaue his
men rest and store of foode, for reason had taught him this
Rule in the Warre, *In pugna Milites validius resistunt, si cibo
potuque refecti fuerint, nam fames intrinsecus magis pugnat,
quam ferrum exterius; Souldiers doe the better stand to it in
fight; if they haue their bellies full of meate and drinke; for
hunger within, fights more eagrely than steele without.*

The numbers which *Alexander* had, saith *Arianus*, were
fortie thousand foote, and seuen thousand horse; these belike
were of the *Europæan* Armie; for hee had besides both
Syrians, Indians, Ægyptians, and *Arabians,* that followed him
out of those Regions. He vsed but a short speech to his
Souldiers to incourage them; and I thinke that he needed
little Rhetorick; for by the two former battailes vpon the
Riuer of *Granick* and in *Cilicia,* the *Macedonians* were best
taught with what men they were to encounter. And it is a
true saying, *Victoria Victoriam parat, animumque victoribus
auget, & aduersarijs aufert; One victorie begets an other, and
puts courage into those that haue alreadie had the better, taking
spirit away from such as haue beene beaten.*

Arrianus and *Curtius* make large descriptions of this
battaile, fought at *Gaugamela;* They tell vs of many charges
and re-charges; That the victorie inclined sometime to the
Persians, sometime to the *Macedonians;* That *Parmenio* was
in danger of being ouerthrowne, who led the left wing; That
Alexanders Reare-guard was broken and his carriages lost;
That for the fierce and valorous encounters on both sides,
Fortune her selfe was long vnresolued on whom to bestow the
Garland: And lastly, That *Alexander* in person wrought
wonders, being charged in his retrait. But, in conclusion,
Curtius deliuers vs in accompt but three hundred dead
Macedonians, in all this terrible daies-worke; saying, That
Ephestion, Perdiccas, and others of name, were wounded.

Arrianus findes not a third part of this number slaine; of the *Persians* there fell fortie thousand (saith *Curtius*,) thirtie thousand according to *Arrianus:* Ninetie thousand, if we beleeue *Diodor*. But what can we judge of this great encounter, other than that, as in the two former battailes, the *Persians* vpon the first charge ranne away, and that the *Macedonians* pursued? For if of these foure or fiue hundred thousand *Asians* brought into the field by *Darius*, euery man had but cast a Dart, or a Stone, the *Macedonians* could not haue bought the Empire of the East at so easie a rate, as sixe or seuen hundred men in three notorious battailes. Certainely, if *Darius* had fought with *Alexander* vpon the bankes of *Euphrates*, and had armed but fiftie or threescore thousand of this great multitude, only with Spades (for the most of all he had were fit for no other weapon) it had beene impossible for *Alexander* to haue past that Riuer so easily, much lesse the Riuer of *Tigris*. But as a man whose Empire God in his prouidence had *determined*, Hee abandoned all places of aduantage, and suffered *Alexander* to enter so far into the bowells of his Kingdome, as all hope and possibilitie of escape by retrait being taken from the *Macedonians*, they had presented vnto them the choise, either of death or victorie; to which election *Darius* could no way constraine his owne, seeing they had many large Regions to runne into from those that inuaded them.

§11. *Of thinges following the battaile of Arbela. The yeelding of Babylon and Susa.*

Darivs after the rout of his Armie recouered *Arbela* the same night, better followed in his flight, than in the fight. He propounded vnto them that ranne after him his purpose of making a retrait into *Media*, perswading them that the *Macedonians*, greedie of spoile and riches, would rather attempt *Babylon, Susa*, and other Cities, filled with treasure, than pursue the vanquished. This miserable resolution his Nobilitie rather obeied than approued.

Alexander soone after *Darius* his departure arriues at *Arbela*, which with a great masse of treasure, and Princely ornaments, was rendred vnto him: for the feare which conducted *Darius* tooke nothing with it but shame and dishonour. Hee that had beene twice beaten, should rather haue sent his treasure into *Media*, than brought it to *Arbela*, so neare the place where he abid the comming of his enemies; if he had beene victorious he might haue brought it after him at leisure, but being ouer-come, hee knew it vnpossible to driue Mules and Cammels laden with gold from the pursuing Enemie, seeing himselfe, at the ouerthrow hee had in *Cilicia*, cast the Crowne from his head to runne away with the more speede. But errours are then best discerned when most incurable. *Et præterita magis reprehendi possunt quam corrigi; It is easier to reprehend than amend what is past.*

From *Arbela Alexander* tooke his way towards *Babylon*, where *Mazeus* in whom *Darius* had most confidence rendred himselfe, his children and the Citie. Also the Captaine of the Castle, who was keeper of the treasure, strewed the streetes with flowers, burnt franckinsence vpon Altars of siluer as *Alexander* passed by, and deliuered vnto him whatsoeuer was committed to his trust. The *Magi* (the *Chaldean* Astrologers) followed this Captain in great solemnitie to entertaine their new King: after these came the *Babylonian* horsemen, infinite riche in attire, but exceeding poore in warlike furniture. Betweene these (though not greatly to be feared) and him-selfe, *Alexander* caused his *Macedonian* foote-men to march. When hee entred the Castle hee admired the glorie thereof, and the aboundance of treasure therein found amounting to fiftie thousand talents of siluer vncoyned. The Citie it selfe I haue elsewhere described[1] with the Walles, the Towers, the Gates and the Circuite, with the wonderfull place of pleasure about two miles in Circuite, surrounded with a Wall of fourescore foote high, and on the toppe thereof (being vnder-borne with Pillars) a Groue of beautifull and fruitfull trees, which it is said that one of the Kings of *Babylon* caused to be built, that the Queene and other Princesses might walke priuately therein. In this Citie, rich in all things but most of all in Voluptuous pleasures, the King rested himselfe and the whole Armie foure and thirtie daies, consuming that

[1] In III III 5 – a more expansive version of the account provided here.

time in banqueting and in all sorts of effeminate exercise, which so much softened the mindes of the *Macedonians*, not acquainted till now with the like delicacies, as the seuere discipline of warre which taught them the sufferances of hunger and thirst, of painefull trauaile, and hard lodging, began rather to be forgotten, than neglected.

Heere it was that those bands of a thousand Souldiers were erected, & Commanders appointed ouer them, who thereupon were stiled *Chiliarchi*. This new order *Alexander* brought in, was to honor those Captaines which were found by certain selected Iudges to haue deserued best in the late warre. For before this time the *Macedonian* companies consisted but of fiue hundred. Certainely the drawing downe of the foote-bands in this latter age hath beene the cause (saith the *Marshal Monluct*) that the title and charge of a Captaine hath beene bestowed on euery *Picque Bœuf* or Spurn-Cow, for when the Captaines of foote had a thousand Souldiers vnder one Ensigne, and after that fiue hundred, as in the time of *Francis* the first, the title was honorable and the Kings were lesse charged, and farre better serued. King *Henrie* the eighth of *England* neuer gaue the commandement of any of his good shippes, but to men of knowne valour, and of great estate, nay sometime he made two Gentlemen of qualitie commanders in one ship: but all orders and degrees are fallen from the reputation they had.

While *Alexander* was yet in *Babylon*, there came to him a great supply out of *Europe*, for *Antipater* sent him sixe thousand foote and fiue hundred horse, out of *Macedon*, of *Thracians* three thousand foote and the like number of horse, and out of *Greece* foure thousand foote and foure hundred horse, by which his Armie was greatly strengthned: for those that were infected with the pleasures of *Babylon* could hardly be brought againe, *De quitter la plume pur dermir sur la dure; To change from soft beds to hard boards.*

He left the Castle and Citie of *Babylon* with the Territories about it in charge vnto three of his owne Captaines, deliuering withall into their handes to supply al wants a thousand talents: but to grace *Mazeus* who rendred the citie vnto him, he gaue him the title of his Lieutenant ouer all, and tooke with him *Bagislines* that gaue vp the Castle, and hauing distributed to euery Souldier a part of the Treasure, he left *Babylon* and entred into the Prouince *Satrapene:* from thence he went on towards *Susa* in *Persia*, the same which *Ptolomie, Herodotus,* and *Elianus* call *Memnonia*, sytuate on the riuer *Euleus*, a Citie sometime gouerned by *Daniel* the prophet. *Abulites* also, gouernour of this famous Citie, gaue it vp to the Conquerer with fiftie thousand talents of siluer in bullion, and twelue *Elephants* for the warre, with all other the treasures of *Darius*. In this sort did those Vassalls of fortune, louers of the Kings prosperitie, not of his person (for so all ambitious men are) purchase their owne peace and safetie with the Kings treasures.

While *Alexander* spoiled *Arbela*, *Mazeus* might haue furnisht his owne King from *Babylon*, and while he staid foure and thirtie daies at *Babylon*, *Abulites* might haue holpen him from *Susa:* and while he feasted there, *Tiridates* from *Persepolis* might haue relieued him: for the great masse of treasure was laied vp in that Citie. But who hath sought out and friended fearefull aduersitie? It is certaine, that benefits binde not the ambitious, but the honest: for those that are but greedie of themselues, doe in all changes of fortune only studie the conseruation of their owne greatnesse.

And therefore was *Alexander* well aduised, that whatsoeuer titles he gaue to the *Persians*, yet he left all places of importance in trust with his owne Captaines, to wit, *Babylon, Susa,* and *Persepolis*, with other Cities and Prouinces by him conquered; for if *Darius* (as yet liuing) had beaten the *Macedonians* but in one battell, all the Nobilitie of *Persia* would haue returned to their naturall Lord. Those that are Traitors to their owne Kings are neuer to bee vsed alone in great enterprises by those Princes that entertaine them, nor euer to be trusted with the defences of any frontier-Towne, or Fortresse of waight, by the rendring whereof they may redeeme their libertie and estates lost.

Hereof the *French* had experience, when *Don Petro de Nauarra*, being banished out of *Spaine*, was trusted with *Fontarabe*, in the yeare 1523.

It is said, that *Charles* the fifth hauing promised *Charles*

of *Bourbon* the gouernement of *Marseilles*, if he could haue
forst it, and whereof he made sure accompt, told some of his
nearest Counsellers, that hee meant nothing lesse than the
performance of that promise, because hee should thereby
haue left the Duke (reuolted from his Master) very well
wherewithall to haue recouered his fauour.

The gouernement of *Susa*, with the Castle and Treasure,
Alexander cōmitted to his owne *Macedonians*, making
Abulites who rendred it vnto him his Lieutenant, as he had
done *Mazeus* and others, in giuing them Titles, but neither
trust nor power; for he left three thousand old Souldiers in
Garrison to assure the place; and *Darius* his Mother and her
children to repose themselues.

§12. *How* Alexander *came to Persepolis, and burnt it.*

From *Susa Alexander* leadeth his Armie toward *Persepolis*,
and when he sought to passe those Mountaines which sunder
Susiana and *Persia*, hee was soundly beaten by *Ariobarzanes*,
who defended against him those Straights, called *Pylæ
Persidis*, or *Susœidæ;* and after the losse of many Companies
of his *Macedonians*, he was forst to saue himselfe by retrait,
causing his foote to march close together, and to couer themselues with their Targets from the stones tumbled on them
from the Mountaine-top. Yet in the end he found out an
other path, which a *Lycian*, liuing in that Countrie, discouered vnto him, and came thereby suddenly in view of
Ariobarzanes, who being inforst to fight vpon euen ground,
was by *Alexander* broken, whereupon hee fled to *Persepolis*,
but (after that they of *Persepolis* had refused to receiue him)
hee returned and gaue a second charge vpon the *Macedonians*,
wherein he was slaine. In like manner did King *Francis* the
first, in the yeare 1515. finde a way ouer the *Alpes*, the
Switzers vndertaking to defend all the passages, who, if
their footmanship had not saued them vpon the Kings
descent on the other side, they had beene ill paied for their
hard lodging on those Hils.

Foure thousand *Greekes*, saith *Curtius*, (*Iustine* numbers
them but at eight hundred) hauing beene taken prisoners

by the *Persians*, presented themselues to *Alexander* now in sight of *Persepolis*. These had the barbarous *Persians* so maimed and defaced, by cutting off their Hands, Noses, Eares, and other Members, as they could no way haue beene knowne to their Countrie-men, but by their voices; to each of these *Alexander* gaue three hundred Crownes, with new garments, and such Lands as they liked to liue vpon.

Tiridates, one of *Darius* his false-hearted *Grandes*, hearing of *Alexanders* approch, made him know that *Persepolis* was readie to receiue him, and praied him to double his pace, because there was a determination in the people to spoile the Kings treasure. This Citie was abandoned by many of her Inhabitants vpon *Alexanders* arriuall, and they that staied followed the worst counsell, for all was left to the libertie of the Souldiers, to spoile and kill at their pleasure. There was no place in the world at that time, which, if it had beene laied in ballance with *Persepolis*, would haue waighed it downe. *Babylon*, indeede, and *Susa*, were very rich; but in *Persepolis* lay the bulke and maine store of the *Persians*. For after the spoile that had beene made of money, curious plate, bullion, Images of gold and siluer, and other jewells; there remained to *Alexander* himselfe one hundred and twentie thousand talents. He left the same number of three thousand *Macedonians* in *Persepolis*, which he had done in *Susa*, and gaue the same formall honour to the Traitor *Tiridates*, that he had done to *Abulites*; but he that had the trust of the place was *Nicarides*, a creature of his owne. The bodie of his Armie hee left here for thirtie daies, of which the Commanders were *Parmenio* and *Craterus*, and with a thousand horse and certaine troupes of chosen foote, he would needes view in the Winter-time those parts of *Persia*, which the Snow had couered, a fruitlesse and foolish enterprise, but as *Seneca* saies: *Non ille ire vult, sed non potest stare*; *He hath not a will to goe, but he is vnable to stand still.* It is said and spoken in his praise, That when his Souldiers cried out against him, because they could not indure the extreame frost, and make way, but with extreme difficultie, through the snow, that *Alexander* forsooke his horse, and led them the way. But what can bee more ridiculous than to bring other men into extreamitie, thereby to shew how well himselfe can indure it? His walking on foote did no otherwise take off their wearinesse that followed him, than his sometime forbearing to drinke did quench their thirst, that could lesse indure it. For mine owne little judgement I shall rather commend that Captaine, that makes carefull prouision for those that follow him, and that seekes wisely to preuent extreme necessitie, than those witlesse arrogant fooles, that make the vaunt of hauing indured equally with the common-Souldier, as if that were a matter of great glorie and importance.

We finde in all the Warres that *Cæsar* made, or the best of the *Roman* Commanders, that the prouision of victualls was their first care. For it was a true saying of *Coligni*, Admirall of *France*; *That who so will shape that beast* (meaning Warre) *must beginne with his bellie.*

But *Alexander* is now returned to *Persepolis*, where those Historians, that were most amorous of his vertues, complaine, that the opinion of his valour, of his liberalitie, of his clemencie, towards the vanquished, and all other his Kingly conditions, were drowned in drinke; That he smothered in carrowsing cups all the reputation of his actions past, and that by descending, as it were, from the reuerend Throne of the greatest King, into the companie and familiaritie of base Harlots, he beganne to be despised both of his owne and all other Nations. For being perswaded, when he was inflamed with wine, by the infamous Strumpet *Thais*, he caused the most sumptuous and goodly Castle and Citie of *Persepolis*, to bee consumed with fire, notwithstanding all the arguments of *Parmenio* to the contrarie, who told him that it was a dishonour to destroy those thinges by the parswasions of others, which by his proper vertue and force he had obtained; and that it would be a most strong perswasion to the *Asians*, to thinke hardly of him, and thereby aliene their hearts: For they might well beleeue that hee which demolished the goodliest Ornaments they had, meant nothing lesse than (after such vastation) to hold their possession. *Fere vinolentiam crudelitas sequitur*; *Crueltie doth commonly follow drunkennesse:* For so it fell out soone after, and often, in *Alexander*.

§13. *The Treason of* Bessvs *against* Darivs. Darivs *his death*.

About this time he receiued a new supply of Souldiers out of *Cilicia*, and goes on to finde *Darius* in *Media*. *Darius* had there compounded his fourth and last Armie, which hee meant to haue increased in *Bactria*, had he not heard of *Alexanders* comming on, with whom (trusting to such companies as hee had, which was numbred at thirtie or fortie thousand) he determined once againe to trie his fortune. Hee therefore calls together his Captains and Commanders, and propounds vnto them his resolution, who being desperate of good successe vsed silence for a while. *Artabazus*, one of his eldest men of Warre, who had sometime liued with *Philip* of *Macedon*, brake the yce, and protesting that hee could neuer be beaten by any aduersitie of the Kings, from the faith which he had euer ought him, with firme confidence, that all the rest were of the same disposition (whereof they likewise assured *Darius* by the like protestation) he approued the Kings resolution. Two only, and those the greatest, to wit, *Naburzanes*, and *Bessus*, whereof the latter was Gouernour of *Bactria*, had conspired against their Master, and therefore aduised the King to lay a new foundation for the Warre, and to pursue it by some such person for the present, against whom neither the Gods nor Fortune had in all things declared themselues to bee an enemie: this preamble *Naburzanes* vsed, and in conclusion aduised the election of his fellow Traitor *Bessus*, with promise that, the warres ended, the Empire should againe be restored to *Darius*. The King swollen with disdaine prest towards *Naburzanes* to haue slaine him, but *Bessus* and the *Bactrians* whom he commanded, being more in number than the rest, with-held him. In the meane while *Naburzanes* with-drew himselfe, and *Bessus* followed him making their quarter a-part from the rest of the Armie. *Artabazus*, the Kings faithfull seruant, perswaded him to be aduised, and serue the time, seeing *Alexander* was at hand, and that hee would at least make shew of forgetting the offence made, which the King being of a gentle disposition willingly yeelded vnto. *Bessus* makes his submission and attends the King, who remoues his Armie. *Patron*, who commanded a Regiment of foure thou-

sand *Greekes* which had in all the former battailes serued
Darius with great fidelitie, and alwaies made the retrait
in spight of the *Macedonians*, offered himselfe to guard his
person, protesting against the treason of *Bessus*, but it was
not in his destinie to follow their aduice, who from the
beginning of the Warre gaue him faithfull counsell, but hee
inclined still to *Bessus*, who told him, that the *Greekes* with
Patron their Captaine were corrupted by *Alexander*, and
practised the diuision of his faithfull seruants. *Bessus* had
drawne vnto him thirtie thousand of the Armie, promising
them all those thinges by which the louers of the world and
themselues, are wont to be allured, to wit, riches, safetie,
and honour.

Now the day following *Darius* plainely discouered the
purposes of *Bessus*, and being ouer-come with passion, as
thinking himselfe vnable to make head against these
vngratefull and vnnaturall Traitors, he praied *Artabazus* his
faithfull seruant to depart from him, and to prouide for
himselfe. In like sort he discharged the rest of his attendants,
all saue a few of his *Eunuchs*; for his guards had voluntarily
abandoned him, His *Persians* being most base cowards,
durst not vndertake his defence against the *Bactrians*, notwithstanding that they had foure thousand *Greekes* to joyne
with him, who had beene able to haue beaten both Nations.
But it is true, that him, which forsakes himselfe, no man
followes. It had beene farre more manlike and King-like,
to haue died in the head of those foure thousand *Greekes*,
which offered him the disposition of their liues, (to which
Artabazus perswaded him) than to haue lien bewailing himselfe on the ground, and suffering himselfe to bee bound like
a slaue by those ambitious Monsters that laied hand on him,
whom neither the consideration of his former great estate,
nor the honors he had giuen them, nor the trust reposed in
them, nor the world of benefits bestowed on them, could
moue to pittie: no, nor his present aduersitie, which aboue
all thinges should haue moued them, could pierce their
viperous and vngratefull hearts. Vaine it was indeed to hope
it, for infidelitie hath no compassion.

Now *Darius*, thus forsaken, was bound and laied in a
Cart, couered with hides of beasts, to the end that by any

other ornament he might not bee discouered; and to adde despight and derision to his aduersitie, they fastened him with chaines of gold, and so drew him on among their ordinarie carriages and Carts. For *Bessus* and *Nabarzanes* perswaded themselues to redeeme their liues and the Prouinces they held either by deliuering him a prisoner to *Alexander*, or if that hope failed, to make themselues Kings by his slaughter, and then to defend themselues by force of Armes. But they failed in both. For it was against the nature of God, who is most just, to pardon so strange villanie, yea though against a Prince purely Heathenish, and an Idolater.

Alexander hauing knowledge that *Darius* was retired towards *Bactria*, and durst not abide his comming, hasted after him with a violent speed, and because he would not force his foot-men beyond their powers, hee mounted on horse backe certaine selected Companies of them, and best armed, and with six thousand other Horse, rather ranne than marched after *Darius*. Such as hated the treason of *Bessus*, and secretly forsooke him, gaue knowledge to *Alexander* of all that had happened, informing him of the way that *Bessus* tooke, and how neare hee was at hand: for many men of worth daily ranne from him. Hereupon *Alexander* againe doubled his pace, and his Vant-guard being discouered by *Bessus* his reare, *Bessus* brought a horse to the Cart, where *Darius* lay bound, perswading him to mount thereon, and to saue himselfe. But the vnfortunate King refusing to follow those that had betraied him, they cast Darts at him, wounded him to death, and wounded the beasts that drew him, and slew two poore seruants that attended his person. This done, they all fled that could, leauing the rest to the mercie of the *Macedonian* Swords.

Polystratus a *Macedonian*, being by pursute of the vanquished prest with thirst, as he was refreshing himselfe with some water that he had discouered, espying a Cart with a Teame of wounded beasts breathing for life, and not able to moue, searched the same, and therein found *Darius* bathing in his owne bloud. And by a *Persian* captiue which followed this *Polystratus*, he vnderstood that it was *Darius*, and was informed of this barbarous Tragedie. *Darius* also seemed greatly comforted (if dying men ignorant of the liuing God

can bee comforted) that hee cast not out his last sorrowes
vnheard, but that by this *Macedonian, Alexander* might know
and take vengeance on those Traitors, which had dealt no
lesse vnworthily than cruelly with him, recommending their
reuenge to *Alexander* by this Messenger, which hee besought
him to pursue, not because *Darius* had desired it, but for his
owne honor, and for the safetie of all that did, or should
after weare Crownes. Hee also, hauing nothing else to
present, rendred thankes to *Alexander* for the Kingly grace
vsed towards his Wife, Mother, and Children, desiring the
immortall Gods to submit vnto him the Empire of the whole
world. As hee was thus speaking, impatient death pressing
out his few remaining spirits, he desired water, which
Polystratus presented him, after which he liued but to tell
him, that of all the best thinges that the world had, which
were lately in his power, he had nothing remaining but his
last breath, where-with to desire the Gods to reward his
compassion.

§14. *How* Alexander *pursued* Bessvs, *and tooke into his grace*
     Darivs *his Captaines.*

It was now hoped by the *Macedonians,* that their trauells
were neare an end, euery man preparing for his returne.
Hereof when *Alexander* had knowledge, hee was greatly
grieued; for the bounded earth sufficed not his boundlesse
ambition. Many arguments hee therefore vsed to draw on
his Armie farther into the East, but that which had most
strength was, that *Bessus,* a most cruell Traitor to his
Master *Darius,* hauing at his deuotion the *Hyrcanians,* and
Bactrians, would in short time (if the *Macedonians* should
returne) make himselfe Lord of the *Persian* Empire, and
enjoy the fruits of all their former trauailes. In conclusion,
hee wanne their consents to goe on: which done, leauing
Craterus with certaine Regiments of foot, and *Amyntas* with
six thousand Horse in *Parthenia,* hee enters not without
some opposition into *Hyrcania;* for the *Mardons,* and other
barbarous Nations, defended certaine passages for a while.
Hee passeth the Riuer of *Zioberis,* which taking beginning

in *Parthia* dissolues it selfe in the *Caspian* Sea: it runneth
vnder the ledge of Mountaines, which bound *Parthia* and
Hyrcania, where hiding it selfe vnderground for three hundred furlongs, it then riseth againe and followeth its former
course. In *Zadracarta* or *Zeudracarta*, the same Citie which
Ptolomie writes *Hyrcania*, the *Metropolis* of that Region,
hee rested fifteene daies, banquetting, and feasting therein.

  Phataphernes, one of *Darius* his greatest Cōmanders, with
other of his best followers, submit themselues to *Alexander*,
and were restored to their places and gouernements. But of
all other he graced *Artabazus* most highly for his approued
& constant faith to his Master *Darius*. *Artabazus* brought
with him ten thousand and fiue hundred *Greekes*, the remainder of all those that had serued *Darius*; He treats with
Alexander for their pardon, before they were yet arriued,
but in the end they render themselues simply without
promise or composition: he pardons all but the *Lacedæmonians*, whom he imprisoned, their Leader hauing slaine himselfe. Hee was also wrought, (though to his great dishonour) to receiue *Nabarzanes* that had joyned with *Bessus*
to murder *Darius*.

§15. *Of* Thalestris *Queene of the Amazons; where, by way of
digression it is shewed, that such Amazons haue beene,
and are.*

Here it is said, that *Thalestris* or *Minothea*, a Queene of the
Amazones, came to visite him, and her sute was, (which shee
easily obtayned) That shee might accompanie him till shee
were made with child by him: which done (refusing to
follow him into *India*) shee returned into her owne Countrie.

  Plutarch citeth many Historians, reporting this meeting
of *Thalestris* with *Alexander*, and some contradicting it. But,
indeede, the letters of *Alexander* himselfe to *Antipater*, re-
counting all that befell him in those parts, and yet omitting
to make mention of this *Amazonian* businesse, may justly
breede suspition of the whole matter as forged. Much more
justly may we suspect it as a vaine tale, because an Historian
of the same time reading one of his bookes to *Lysimachus*

(then King of *Thrace*) who had followed *Alexander* in all his
voiage; was laught at by the King for inserting such newes
of the *Amazons*, as *Lysimachus* himselfe had neuer heard of.
One that accompanied *Alexander* tooke vpon him to write
his acts; which to amplifie, He told how the King had fought
single with an Elephant, and slaine it. The King hearing
such stuffe, caught the booke, and threw it into the Riuer of
Indus; saying, that it were well done to throw the writer
after it, who by inserting such fables disparaged the truth
of his great exploits. Yet as wee beleeue and know that
there are Elephants, though it were false that *Alexander*
fought with one; so may we giue credit vnto writers, making
mention of such *Amazons*, whether it were true or false that
they met with *Alexander*; as *Plutarch* leaues the matter
vndetermined. Therefore I will here take leaue to make
digression, as well to shew the opinions of the ancient
Historians, Cosmographers, and others, as also of some
moderne discouerers touching these warlike Women,
because not only *Strabo*, but many others of these our times
make doubt, whether, or no, there were any such kinde of
people. *Iulius Solinus* seates them in the North parts of
Asia the lesse. *Pom. Mela* finds two Regions filled with
them; the one, on the Riuer *Thermodoon*; the other, neare
the *Caspian* Sea; *Quas* (saith hee) *Sauromatidas appellant*;
Which the people call Sauromatidas. The former of these two
had the *Cimerians* for their Neighbours; *Certum est* (saith
Vadianus, who hath Commented vpon *Mela*) *illos proximos
Amazonibus fuisse*; *It is certaine that the Cimerians were the
next Nations to the Amazones.* *Ptolomie* sets them farther into
the Land North-wards, neare the Mountaines *Hippaci*, not
farre from the Pillars of *Alexander*. And that they had
Dominion in *Asia* it selfe toward *India*, *Solinus* and *Plinie*
tells vs; Where they gouerned a people called the *Pandeans*,
or *Padeans*, so called after *Pandea* the Daughter of *Hercules*,
from whom all the rest deriue themselues. *Claudian* affirmes,
That they commanded many Nations: For he speakes
(largely perhaps as a Poet) thus.

> *Medis leuibusque Sabæis*
> *Imperat hic fexus: Reginarumque sub armis,*
> *Barbariæ pars magna iacet.*

Ouer the Medes, and light Sabæans, raignes
This female sexe: and vnder armes of Queene[s],
Great part of the Barbarian Land remaines.[1]

Diodorus Siculus hath heard of them in *Lybia*, who were more ancient (saith hee) than those which kept the bankes of *Thermodoon*, a Riuer falling into the *Euxine* Sea neare *Heraclium*.

Herodotus doth also make report of these *Amazons*, whom hee tells vs that the *Scythians* call *Æorpatas*, which is as much as *Viricidas*, or Men-killers. And that they made incursion into *Asia* lesse, sackt *Ephesus*, and burnt the Temple of *Diana*, *Manethon* and *Auentinus* report, which they performed fortie yeares after *Troy* was taken. At the siege of *Troy* it selfe wee read of *Penthesilea*, That shee came to the succour of *Priamus*.

Am. Marcellinus giues the cause of their inhabiting vpon the riuer of *Thermodoon*, speaking confidently of the Warres they made with diuers Nations, and of their ouerthrow.

Plutarch in the life of *Theseus*, out of *Philochorus*, *Hellanicus*, and other ancient Historians, reports the taking of *Antiopa* Queene of the *Amazons* by *Hercules*, and by him giuen to *Theseus*, though some affirme, That *Theseus* himselfe got her by stealth when shee came to visit him aboord his ship. But in substance there is little difference; all confessing, That such *Amazons* there were. The same Author in the life of *Pompey* speakes of certaine companies of the *Amazons*, that came to aide the *Albanians* against the *Romans*, by whom, after the battaile, many Targets and Buskins of theirs were taken vp: and he saith farther, That these women entertaine the *Gelæ* and *Lelages* once a yeare, Nations inhabiting betweene them and the *Albanians*.

But to omit the many Authors, making mention of *Amazons* that were in the old times, *Fran. Lopez* who hath written the nauigation of *Orellana*, which he made down the Riuer of *Amazons* from *Peru*, in the yeare 1542. (vpon which Riuer, for the diuers turnings, he is said to haue sailed sixe thousand miles) reports from the relation of the said *Orellana*, to the Councell of the *Indies*, That hee both

[1] Claudian, *In Eutropium,* 1 321-3.

saw those women and fought with them, where they sought
to impeach his passage towards the East-Sea.

It is also reported by *Vlricus Schmidel*, that in the yeare
1542. where he sailed vp the Riuers of *Paragna* and *Parabol*,
that he came to a King of that Countrie, called *Scherues*,
inhabiting vnder the *Tropick* of *Capricorne*, who gaue his
Captaine *Ernando Rieffere*, a Crowne of siluer, which hee
had gotten in fight from a Queene of the *Amazons* in those
parts.

Ed. Lopes, in his description of the Kingdome of *Congo*,
makes relation of such *Amazons*, telling vs, That (agreeable
to the reports of elder times) they burne off their right breast,
and liue a-part from men, saue at one time of the yeare,
when they feast and accompanie them for one moneth.
These (saith he) possesse a part of the Kingdome of *Mono-
motapa* in *Africa*, nineteene degrees to the Southward of the
line: and that these women are the strongest guards of this
Emperour, all the East *Indian Portugals* know.

I haue produced these authorities, in part, to iustifie
mine owne relation of these *Amazons*, because that which
was deliuered mee for truth by an ancient *Casique*[1] of *Guiana*,
how vpon the Riuer of *Papamena* (since the *Spanish* dis-
coueries called *Amazons*) that these women still liue and
gouerne, was held for a vaine and vnprobable report.

§16. *How* Alexander *fell into the Persians Luxurie: and how
hee further pursued* Bessvs.

Now as *Alexander* had begunne to change his conditions
after the taking of *Persepolis*: so at this time his prosperitie
had so much ouer-wrought his vertue, as he accompted
clemencie to bee but basenesse, and the temperance which
he had vsed all his life-time, but a poore and dejected humor,
rather becomming the instructers of his youth, than the
condition and state of so mightie a King, as the world could
not equall. For he perswaded himselfe that he now represented the greatnesse of the Gods; hee was pleased that those

---

[1] Native chief or 'prince'.

that came before him, should fall to the ground and adore him; hee ware the Robes, and garments of the *Persians*, and commanded that his Nobilitie should doe the like; hee entertained in his Court, and Campe, the same shamelesse rabble of Curtisans, and *Sodomiticall Eunuchs*, that *Darius* had done, and imitated in all thinges the proude, voluptuous, and detested manners of the *Persians*, whom he had vanquished. So licentious is felicitie, as notwithstanding that he was fully perswaded, that the Gods, whom he serued (detesting the vices of the inuaded) assisted him in all attempts against them, he himselfe contrarie to the religion he profest (which how Idolatrous soeuer it were, could not bee but fearefull vnto him by neglecting it) became by imitation, and not by ignorance or education, a more foule and fearefull Monster than *Darius*, from whose tyrannie he vaunted to haue deliuered so many Nations. Yea those that were dearest and nearest vnto him, began to be ashamed of him, entertaining each other with this, and the like scornefull discourse, That *Alexander* of *Macedon* was become one of *Darius* his licentious Courtiers; That by his example the *Macedonians* were in the end of so many trauailes more impouerished in their vertues, than inriched by their victories; and that it was hard to judge whether the Conquerors, or the conquered were the baser slaues. Neither were these opinions so reserued, but that the noise of them came to his eares. He therefore with great gifts sought to pacifie the better sort, and those of whose judgements he was most jealous; and making it knowne to the Armie that *Bessus* had assumed the title of a King, and called himselfe *Artaxerxes*, and that hee had compounded a great Armie of the *Bactrians*, and other Nations, hee had arguments enough to perswade them to goe on, to the end that all alreadie gotten, might not with themselues (so farre ingaged) be cast away. And because they were pestered with the spoiles of so many Cities, as the whole Armie seemed but the guard of their carriages, (not much vnlike the warfare of the *French*) hauing commanded euery mans fardells to be brought into the market-place, he together with his owne, caused all to bee consumed with fire. Certainely, this could not but haue proued most dangerous vnto him, seeing the common-

Souldiers had more interest in these thinges, which they had bought with their painefull trauailes, and with their bloud; than in the Kings ambition; had not (as *Seneca* often obserued) his happie temeritie ouer-come all thinges. As he was in his way, newes came to him that *Satribarzanes,* whom he had established in his former gouernement ouer the *Arrians,* was reuolted, whereupon leauing the way of *Bactria,* he sought him out, but the Rebelle hearing of his comming fled to *Bessus* with two thousand Horse. Hee then went on towards *Bessus,* and by setting a great pile of wood on fire with the aduantage of a strong winde, wonne a passage ouer a high and vnaccessable Rock, which was defended against him with thirteene thousand foote. For the extremitie of the flame and smoke forced them from the place, otherwise inuincible. I saw in the third ciuill Warre of *France* certaine caues in *Languedoc,* which had but one entrance, and that very narrow, cut out in the mid-way of high Rocks, which we knew not how to enter by any ladder or engine, till at last by certaine bundells of straw let downe by an yron chaine, and a waightie stone in the middest, those that defended it were so smothered, as they rendred themselues with their plate, monie, and other goods therein hidden. There were also, some three yeares before my arriuall in *Guiana,* three hundred *Spaniards* well mounted, smothered to death, together with their Horses, by the Countrie people, who did set the long drie-grasse on fire to the eastward of them, (the winde in those parts being alwaies East) so as notwithstanding their flying from the smoke, there was not any one that escaped. Sr *Iohn Borrowes* also, with a hundred *English,* was in great danger of being lost at *Margarita,* in the *West-Indies,* by hauing the grasse fired behinde him, but the smoke being timefully discouered, hee recouered the Sea-shore with the losse of sixteene of his men. I remember these thinges, but to giue caution to those that shall in times to come inuade any part of those Countries, that they alwaies, before they passe into the Land, burne downe the grasse and sedge to the East of them; they may otherwise, without any other enemie than a handfull of straw set on fire, die the death of honnie-Bees, burnt out of the Hiue.

§17. *A conspiracie against* Alexander. *The death of* Philotas *and* Parmenio.

Alexander was after he parted hence no where resisted, till he came into *Asia*, to the East of *Bactria*, where the chiefe Citie of that Prouince, called *Artacoana*, was a while defended against him, by the reuolt of *Sartibarzanes*, but in the end hee receiued the Inhabitants to mercie. At this place his Armie was re-enforced with a new supply of fiue thousand and fiue hundred foote, and neare fiue hundred Horse, out of *Greece*, *Thessalie*, and other places. His journie out of *Persia* into these parts is very confusedly described. For hauing (as all his Historians tell vs) a determination to finde *Bessus* in *Bactria*, he leaues it at the very entrance, and takes the way of *Hyrcania*; from thence hee wanders Northward towards the obscure *Mardi*, vpon the *Caspian*-Sea, and thence ouer the Mountaines *Coronus* into *Aria*, and *Drangiana*.

At this time it was that the treason of *Dimnus* brake out, of which *Philotas* the sonne of *Parmenio* was accused, as accessarie, if not principall. This *Dimnus*, hauing (I know not vpon what ground) conspired with some others against the life of *Alexander*, went about to draw *Nicomachus*, a yong-man whom he loued, into the same treason. The youth, although he was first bound by oath to secrecie, when he heard so foule a matter vttered, beganne to protest against it so vehemently, that his friend was like to haue slaine him for securitie of his owne life. So constrained by feare, hee made shew as if hee had beene wonne by perswasion, and by seeming at length to like well of the businesse, hee was told more at large what they were, that had vndertaken it. There were nine or ten of them, all men of ranke; whose names *Dimnus* (to countenance the enterprise) reckoned vp to *Nicomachus*. *Nicomachus* had no sooner freed himselfe from the companie of this Traitor *Dimnus*, than he acquainted his owne brother *Ceballinus* with the whole Historie: whereupon it was agreed betweene them, that *Ceballinus* (who might with least suspition) should goe to the Court and vtter all. *Ceballinus*, meeting with *Philotas*, told him the whole businesse; desiring him to acquaint the King therewith: which hee promised to doe, but did not. Two daies passed, and

Philotas neuer brake with the King about the matter; but still excused himselfe to *Ceballinus* by the Kings want of leisure. This his coldnesse bred suspition, and caused *Ceballinus* to addresse himselfe to another, one *Metron*, keeper of the Kings Armorie, who forth-with brought him to *Alexanders* presence. *Alexander*, finding by examination what had passed betweene *Ceballinus* and *Philotas*, did fully perswade himselfe that this concealement of the treason argued his hand to haue beene in the businesse. Therefore when *Dimnus* was brought before him, he asked the Traitor no other question than this: *Wherein haue I so offended thee, that thou shouldest thinke* Philotas *more worthie to be King than I? Dimnus* perceiuing, when he was apprehended, how the matter went, had so wounded himselfe that hee liued no longer than to giue his last groane in the Kings presence. Then was *Philotas* called, and charged with the suspition which his silence might justly breede. His answere was, That when the practise was reuealed vnto him by *Nicomachus*, he judging it to be but friuolous, did forbeare to acquaint *Alexander* therewithall, vntill he might haue better information. This errour of his, (if it were only an errour) although *Alexander*, for the notorious seruices of his Father *Parmenio*, of his brother *Nicanor* lately dead, and of *Philotas* himselfe, had freely pardoned and giuen him his hand for assurance; yet by the instigation of *Craterus*, hee againe swallowed his Princely promise, and made his enemies his Iudges: *Curtius* giues a note of *Craterus* in this businesse; How hee perswaded himselfe, that he could neuer finde a better occasion to oppresse his priuate enemie, than by pretending pietie and dutie towards the King. Hereof a Poet of our owne hath giuen a note as much better as it is more generall in his *Philotas*.

> See how these great men cloathe their priuate hate,
> In these faire colours of the publike good,
> And to effect their ends, pretend the State,
> As if the State by their affection stood,
> And arm'd with power and Princes jealousies,
> Will put the least conceit of discontent
> Into the greatest ranke of treacheries,
> That no one action shall seeme innocent;

Yea valour, honour, bountie, shall be made
As accessaries vnto ends vnjust:
And euen the seruice of the State must lade
The needfull'st vndertaking with distrust,
So that base vilenesse, idle Luxurie,
Seeme safer farre, than to doe worthily, &c.[1]

Now although it were so that the King, following the aduise of *Craterus*, had resolued the next day to put *Philotas* to torment, yet in the very euening of the same night in which he was apprehended, he called him to a banquet, and discoursed as familiarly with him as at any other time. But when in the dead of the night *Philotas* was taken in his lodging, and that they which hated him beganne to binde him; he cried out vpon the King in these wordes: *O* Alexander, *the malice of mine Enemies hath surmounted thy mercie, and their hatred is farre more constant than the word of a King.* Many circumstances were vrged against him by *Alexander* himselfe; (for the Kings of *Macedon* did in person examine the accusations of treason) and this was not the least (not the least offence, indeede, against the Kings humour, who desired to be glorified as a God) That when *Alexander* wrote vnto him concerning the title giuen him by *Iupiter Hammon*; He answered, That he could not but rejoyce that he was admitted into that sacred Fellowship of the Gods, and yet hee could not but withall grieue for those that should liue vnder such a one as would exceede the nature of man. This was (saith *Alexander*) a firme perswasion vnto me, that his heart was changed, and that hee held my glorie in despight. See what a strange Monster flatterie is, that can perswade Kings to kill those that doe not praise and allow those thinges in them, which are of all other most to be abhorred. *Philotas* was brought before the multitude to heare the Kings Oration against him: he was brought forth in vilde garments, and bound like a Theefe; where hee heard himselfe, and his absent Father the greatest Captaine of the World, accused, his two other Brothers *Hector* and *Nicanor* hauing beene lost in the present Warre. Hee was

[1] Samuel Daniel, *The Tragedie of Philotas* (1607), sig. B1o [Act III, Chorus, 1–14]. This is Ralegh's most extensive quotation from any contemporary poet.

so greatly opprest with griefe as for a while he could vtter nothing but teares, and sorrow had so wasted his spirits as hee sunke vnder those that led him. In the end the King asked him in what language he would make his defence; he answered, In the same wherein it had pleased the King to accuse him, which hee did to the end that the *Persians*, as well as the *Macedonians*, might vnderstand him. But hereof the King made his aduantage, perswading the assembly that hee disdained the language of his owne Countrie, and so with-drawing himselfe, left him to his mercilesse enemies.

This proceeding of the Kings, *Philotas* greatly lamented, seeing the King who had so sharply inuaied against him, would not vouchsafe to heare his excuse. For, not his enemies only were imboldened thereby against him, but all the rest hauing discouered the Kings disposition and resolution, contended among themselues which of them should exceede in hatred towards him; Among many other arguments which he vsed in his owne defence, this was not the weakest, That when *Nicomachus* desired to know of *Dimnus* what men of marke and power were his partners in the conspiracie (as seeming vnwilling to aduenture himselfe with meane and base Companions) *Dimnus* named vnto him *Demetrius* of the Kings Chamber, *Nicanor*, *Amyntas*, and some others, but spake not a word of *Philotas*, who by being commander of the Horse, would greatly haue valued the partie, and haue incouraged *Nicomachus*. Indeede, as *Philotas* said well for himselfe, it is likely that *Dimnus*, thereby the better to haue heartned *Nicomachus*, would haue named him, though hee had neuer dealt with him in any such practise. And for more certaine proofe that he knew nothing of their intents, that practised against the King, there was not any one of the Conspirators, being many, inforst by torments or otherwise, that could accuse him, and it is true, that aduersitie being seldome able to beare her owne burden, is for the most part found so malicious, as shee rather desires to draw others (not alwaies deseruing it) into the same danger than to spare any that it can accuse. Yet at the last, howsoeuer it were, to auoide the extremitie of resistelesse and vnnaturall torments, deuised by his profest enemies *Craterus*, *Cenus*, *Ephestion*, and others, *Philotas* accused his owne selfe;

being perswaded that they would haue slaine him forthwith. But he failed euen in that miserable hope, and suffering all that could be laied on flesh and bloud, he was forst to deliuer, not what he knew, but whatsoeuer best pleased their eares, that were farre more mercilesse than death it selfe.

Of this kinde of judiciall proceeding S^t. *Augustine* greatly complaineth as a matter to bee bewailed, saith hee, with Fountaines of teares. . . . *What shall we say to it, when one is put to torture in his owne case; and tormented whilest yet it is in question whether he be guiltie; and being innocent suffers assured punishment for a fault of which there is no certaintie, not because he is knowne to haue committed the offence, but because others doe not know that he hath not committed it.*

It had beene enough for *Alexanders* safetie if *Philotas* had been put to death without torment, the rest would not much haue grieued thereat, because he was greatly suspected. But *Hemolaus*, who afterward conspired against him, made the Kings crueltie and delight in bloud the greatest motiue of his owne ill intent. Therefore, *Seneca* speaking of *Alexander*, saith thus: . . . *Crueltie is not a humane vice; it is vnworthie of so mild a spirit. It is euen a beastly rage to delight in bloud and wounds, and casting away the nature of man to become a sauage Monster.*

For the conclusion of this Tragedie, *Curtius* makes a doubt, whether the confession that *Philotas* made were to giue end to the torments which hee could not any longer indure, or that the same was true indeede; For (saith he) in this case, they that speake truely, or they that denie falsly, come to one and the same end. Now while the Kings hands were yet wet in bloud, he commanded that *Lyncestes*, sonne-in-Law to *Antipater*, who had beene three yeares in prison, should bee slaine: The same dispatch had all those that *Nicomachus* had accused: others there were that were suspected, because they had followed *Philotas*, but when they had answered for themselues that they knew no way so direct to winne the Kings fauour, as by louing those whom the King fauoured; they were dismist. But *Parmenio* was yet liuing; *Parmenio*, who had serued with great fidelitie as well *Philip* of *Macedon* the Kings Father, as himselfe; *Parmenio* that first opened the way into *Asia*; That had deprest *Attalus* the Kings enemie; that had alwaies, and in all hazards, the leading of the Kings Vant-guard, that was no lesse prudent in counsell, than fortunate in all attempts; A man beloued of the men of Warre, and, to say the truth, hee that had made the purchase for the King of the Empire of the East, and of all the glorie and fame he had: That he might not therefore reuenge the death of his Sonne, though not vpon the King, (for it was vnlikely that he would haue dishonoured his fidelitie in his eldest age, hauing now liued threescore and ten yeares) yet vpon those that by the witch-craft of flatterie had possest themselues of his affection; it was resolued that he should be dispatcht. *Polydamas* was imploied in this businesse, a man whom of all other *Parmenio* trusted most, and loued best, who (to be short) finding him in *Media*, and hauing *Cleander* and other Murderers with him, slew him walking in his Garden, while he was reading the Kings letters. *Hic exitus* Parmenionis *fuit, militiæ domique clari viri; Multa sine Rege prosperè, Rex sine illo nihil magnæ rei gesserat; This was the end of* Parmenio (saith *Cvrtivs*) *who had performed many notable thinges without the King, but the King, without him, did neuer effect any thing worthie of praise.*

§18. *How* Alexander *subdued the Bactrians, Sogdians, and other people. How* Bessvs *was deliuered into his hands. How he fought with the Scythians.*

When these things had end, *Alexander* went on with his Armie, and brought vnder his obedience the *Araspians* or *Euergitans;* he made *Amenides* (sometime *Darius* his Secre-tarie) their Gouernour; then he subdued the *Arachosians*, and left *Menon* to commaund ouer them. Heere the Armie, sometimes led by *Parmenio*, findes him, consisting of twelue thousand *Macedons* and *Greekes*, with whom he past through some colde regions with difficultie enough. At length hee came to the foote of the Mountaine *Taurus* towards the East, where he built a Citie which he honoured with his owne name, and peopled with seuen thousand of his olde *Macedons*, worne with age and with trauailes of the warre.

The *Arians,* who since he left them were reuolted, hee subdued againe by the industrie and valour of *Caranus* and
Erigius; And now he resolues to finde out the new King
Bessus in *Bactria. Bessus,* hearing of his comming, prepares
to passe ouer the great Riuer of *Oxus* which diuides *Bactria*
from *Sogdiana; Artabazus* is made Gouernour of *Bactria*
abandoned by *Bessus;* The *Macedonian* Armie suffereth for
want of Water, insomuch as when they came to the Riuer
of *Oxus,* there died more of them by drinking inordinately
then *Alexander* had lost in any one battaile against the
Persians. And it may well be; For (as *Clytus* did after obiect
vnto him) he fought against women, not against men, and
not against their persons but their shadowes. He found on
the bankes of this great Riuer no manner of Timber or other
materialls to make either boates, bridges, or raffe, but was
forst to sow together the Hides that couered his carriages,
and stuffe them with straw, and on them in sixe daies to
passe ouer his Armie; which *Bessus* might easily haue
distrest, if he had dared but to beholde the *Macedonian*
Armie afarre-off. He had formerly complained against
Darius for neglecting to defend the bankes of *Tigris,* and
other passages, and yet now, when this traiterous slaue had
styled himselfe a King, hee durst not perfourme any thing
worthie of a slaue. And therefore those that were neerest
vnto him, and whom he most trusted, to wit *Spitamines,*
Dataphernes, Catanes, and others the Commaunders of his
Armie, moued both by the care of their owne safetie, and
by the memorie of *Bessus* his Treason and crueltie against
Darius, bound him in the like manner that he had done his
Master, but with this difference, that he had the chaine
closed about his neck like a mastife Dogge, and so was
dragged along to be presented to his enemie.

In the meane while *Alexander* was arriued at a certaine
Towne inhabited with *Greekes* of *Miletum,* brought thither
by *Xerxes,* when long before hee returned out of *Greece,*
whose issues had well-neere forgotten their Countrie-
language. These most cruelly (after they had receiued him
with great ioy) he put to the sworde, and destroyed their
Citie. At this place he receiued *Bessus,* and, hauing rewarded
Spitamenes with the rest that deliuered him, he gaue the

Traitor into the hands of *Oxatres*, *Darius* his brother, to be tormented.

But while he now thought himselfe secure, some twentie thousand Mountainers assalted his Camp; in repelling whom he receiued a shot in the leg, the arrow-head sticking in the flesh, so as he was carried in a Horse-Lytter, sometime by the horsemen, sometime by the foote.

Soone after he came vnto *Maracanda*, which *Petrus Perondinus* takes to be *Samarchand*, the regall Citie of the great *Tamerlaine*. It had in compasse threescore and ten furlongs (*Curtius* saith). Heere hee receiued the Embassadors of the *Scythians* (called *Auians*) who offered to serue him.

The *Bactrians* are shortly againe with the *Sogdians* stirred to Rebellion by the same *Spitamenes* and *Catanes* who had lately deliuered into his hands the Traitor *Bessus*. Many Cities were resoluedly defended against him, all which, after victorie, hee defaced and rased, killing all therein. At one of these hee receiued a blow on the neck which strucke him to the ground, and much disabled him for many daies after. In the meane while *Spitamenes* had recouered *Maracanda*, against whom he imployed *Menedemus* with three thousand foote and eight hundred horse.

In the heate of these tumults *Alexander* marched on (if we may beleeue *Curtius* and others) till he came to the Riuer of *Tanais*; vpon whose banke he built another *Alexandria* threescore furlongs in compasse, which he beautified with houses within seuenteen daies after the walls built. The building of this Citie is said to haue bin occasion of a war betweene him and the *Scythians*; the *Scythian* King perswading himselfe, that this new Towne was fortified of purpose to keepe him vnder. I doe not well vnderstand, why the *Scythians*, offering warre in such terrible manner that *Alexander* was iudged by his owne Souldiers to counterfeit sicknesse for verie feare, should neuerthelesse make suit for peace: neither finde I the reason why *Alexander* (not intending the conquest of those Northerne deserts, but only the defense of his owne banke) should refuse to let them alone, with whom he could not meddle further than they should agree to suffer him. Yet hereof is made a great matter; and a victorie described; in pursuit of which the

Macedons ranne beyond the boundes and monuments of *Bacchus* his expedition.

The truth is, That *Curtius* and *Trogus* haue greatly mistaken this Riuer which they call *Tanais*. For it was the Riuer of *Iaxartes*, that runnes betweene *Sogdiana* and *Scythia*, which *Alexander* past ouer, while *Menedemus* was imploied in the recouery of *Samarchand:* But *Tanais* which diuides *Asia* from *Europe* is neere two thousand miles distant from any part of *Bactria* or *Sogdiana*, and the way desert and vnknowne. So that *Alexander* had (besides *Iaxartes*) the great Riuer of *Volga* and manie others to swimme ouer, ere hee could recouer *Tanais*; which (from the place where he was) he could hardly haue discouered with the Armie that followed him, if he had imploied all the time that he liued in *Asia* in that trauaile.

Wherefore it is enough to beleeue, that the *Asiatique Scythians*, making some offer to disturbe the erection of this new Citie, which was like to giue some hindrance to their excursions, were driuen away by the *Macedonians;* and being naked of defensiue Armes, easily chased some tenne or twelue miles; which is the substance of *Curtius* his report. As for the limits of *Bacchus* his iournie; like enough it is that *Bacchus* (if in his life time he were as sober a man, as after his death he was held a drunken God) went not verie farre into that wast Countrie, where hee could finde nothing but trees and stones, nor other busines than to set vp a monument.

Threescore of the *Macedons* are said to haue beene slaine, and one thousand one hundred hurt in this fight, which might easily be, in passing a great Riuer, defended against them by good Archers. Of *Scythian* horses one thousand eight hundred were brought into the Campe, and many prisoners. It is forbidden by some Historians, and indeed it is hardly possible, to set downe the numbers of such as perish in battell: yet *Cæsar* commonly did it. And where the diligence of the victors hath beene so inquisitiue into the greatnesse of their owne successe, that writers haue beene able to deliuer such particulars by credible reporte, I hold it not vnlawfull to set downe what we finde; especially when it serues to giue light to the businesse in hand. The small number which the *Macedonians* lost; the omission of the number which they slew (a thing not vsuall in *Curtius*, who forbeares nothing that may set out the greatnesse of *Alexander*) and the little bootie that was gotten; doe make it probable, that this warre was no better than the repulsion of a few rouing *Tartars* (the like being yearely performed by the *Moscouite*, without any boast) and therefore better omitted by some Historians, than so highly extolled as a great exploit by others.

While *Alexander* was assuring himselfe of those *Scythians* bordering vpon *Iaxartes*, he receiued the ill newes that *Menedemus* was slaine by *Spitamenes*, the Armie (by him led) broken, and the greatest numbers slaine, to wit, two thousand foote, and three hundred horse. He therefore, to appease the rebellion and to take reuenge of *Spitamenes*, makes all the hast he can; but *Spitamenes* flies into *Bactria*. *Alexander* kills, burnes, and laies wast all before him; not sparing the innocent children, and so departs, leauing a new Gouernour in that Prouince.

To repaire this losse he receiued a great supply of nineteene thousand Souldiers out of *Greece*, *Lycia*, and *Syria*; with all which, and the old Armie, hee returnes towards the South, and passeth the Riuer of *Oxus*; on the South-side whereof hee built sixe Townes neare each other for mutuall succour. But hee finds a new start-vp-Rebell, called *Arimazes* (a *Sogdian*) followed with thirtie thousand Souldiers that defended against him a strong peece of ground on the top of a high Hill; whom when *Alexander* had sought in vaine to winne by faire words, hee made choise of three hundred yong-men, and promised ten talents to the first, nine to the second, and so in proportion to the rest, that could finde a way to creepe vp to the top thereof. This they performed with the losse of some two and thirtie of their men, and then made a signe to *Alexander*, that they had performed his commandement. Hereupon he sent one *Cophes* to perswade *Arimazes* to yeeld the place; who, being shewed by *Cophes* that the Armie of *Macedon* was alreadie mounted vp, yeelded simply to *Alexanders* mercie, and was (with all his kindred) scourged and crucified to death; which punishment they well deserued for neglecting to keepe good watch in so

SWR L

dangerous a time. For the place, as seemes by the description, might easily haue beene defended against all the Armies of the World. But, what strength cannot doe; Mans wit, being the most forcible engine, hath often effected; Of which I will giue you an example in a place of our owne.

The Iland of *Sarke*, joyning to *Garnsey* and of that gouernement, was in Queene *Maries* time surprised by the *French*, and could neuer haue beene recouered againe by strong hand, hauing cattle and corne enough vpon the place to feede so many men as will serue to defend it, and being euery way so inaccessible that it might bee held against the Great *Turke*. Yet by the industrie of a Gentleman of the Netherlands, it was in this sort regained. Hee anchored in the roade with one ship of small burden, and, pretending the death of his Marchant, besought the *French*, being some thirtie in number, that they might burie their Marchant in hallowed ground, and in the Chappell of that Isle; offering a present to the *French* of such commodities as they had aboord; whereto (with condition that they should not come a-shore with any weapon, no not so much as with a knife) the *French*-men yeelded. Then did the *Flemings* put a Coffin into their boat, not filled with a dead carkasse, but with Swords, Targets, and Harquebusses; The *French* receiued them at their landing; and searching euery of them so narrowly as they could not hide a pen-knife, gaue them leaue to draw their Coffin vp the Rocks with great difficultie; some part of the *French* tooke the *Flemish* boat and rowed aboord their ship, to fetch the commodities promised, and what-else they pleased, but being entred they were taken and bound. The *Flemings* on the Land, when they had carried their Coffin into the Chappell, shut the dore to them, and taking their weapons out of the Coffin set vppon the *French;* they runne to the Cliffe and crie to their companie aboord the *Fleming* to come to their succour, but finding the boat charged with *Flemings* yeelded themselues and the place. Thus a Foxe-taile doth sometimes helpe well to peece out the Lions-skinne, that else would be too short.

§19. *How* Alexander *slew his owne friends.*

After these *Sogdian* and *Scythian* Warres, wee reade of
Alexanders killing of a Lion, and other friuolous matter, and
that he committed the gouernement of *Maracanda,* and the
Countrie about it, to *Clytus,* and how he slew him soone
after, for valuing the vertue of *Philip* the father before that
of *Alexander* the sonne, or rather because hee objected to
the King the death of *Parmenio,* and derided the Oracle of
Hammon: for therein he toucht him to the quick, the same
being deliuered in publike and at a drunken banquet.
Clytus, indeede, had deserued as much at the Kings hands,
as any man liuing had done, and had in particular saued his
life, which the King well remembred when he came to himselfe, and when it was too late. Yet to say the truth, *Clytus*
his insolencie was intolerable. As he in his cups forgat whom
hee offended, so the King in his (for neither of them were
themselues) forgat whom he went about to slay, for the
griefe whereof he tare his owne face and sorrowed so
inordinately, as, but for the perswasions of *Calisthenes,* it is
thought he would haue slaine himselfe.

Wine begat furie, furie matter of repentance: but præceding mischiefs are not amended by succeeding bewailings. . . .
*Drunkennesse both kindles and laies open euery vice; it remoues
out of the way that shame which giues impediment vnto bad
attempts; where wine gets the mastrie, all the ill that before lay
hidden breakes out: drunkennesse indeede rather discouers vices,
than makes them.*

Soone after this, *Spitamenes,* who slew *Bessus,* and had
lately reuolted from *Alexander,* was murdered by his Wife,
and his head presented to *Alexander. Spitamenes* being taken
away, the *Dahans* also seized vpon his fellow-conspirator
Dataphernes, and deliuered him vp. So *Alexander* being now
freed from all these pettie-rebels, disposed of the Prouinces
which he past ouer, and went on with his Armie into
Gabaza, where it suffered so much Hunger, Cold, Lightning,
Thunder, and Storme, as he lost in one Tempest a thousand
of his traine. From hence hee inuaded the *Sacans,* and
destroied their Countrie. Then came he into the Territorie
of *Cohortanes* who submitted himselfe vnto him, feasted him

greatly, and presented him with thirtie beautifull Virgins, among whom *Roxane*, afterward his Wife, was one: which although all the *Macedonians* disdained, yet none of them durst vse any freedome of speech after *Clytus* his death. From hence hee directed his course towards *India*, hauing so increased his numbers, as they amounted to an hundred and twentie thousand armed men.

In the meane while hee would needes bee honoured as a God: whereto that hee might allure the *Macedonians*, hee imploied two pernitious Parasites, *Hagis* and *Cleo*; whom *Calisthenes* opposed: For, among many other honest arguments vsed to the assembly, he told *Cleo*, That he thought that *Alexander* would disdaine the gift of God-head from his Vassalls; That the opinion of Sanctitie, though it did sometime follow the death of those who in their life-time had done the greatest thinges, yet it neuer accompanied any one as yet liuing in the World. He further told him, That neither *Hercules* nor *Bacchus* were Deified at a banquet, and vpon drinke, (for this matter was propounded by *Cleo* at a carowsing feast) but that, for the more than manly acts by them performed while they liued, they were in future and succeeding Ages numbred among the Gods. *Alexander* stood behinde a partition and heard all that was spoken, waiting but an opportunitie to bee reuenged on *Calisthenes*, who being a man of free speech, honest, learned, and a louer of the Kings honour, was yet soone after tormented to death, not for that hee had betraied the King to others, but because hee neuer would condescend to betray the King to himselfe, as all his detestable flatterers did. For in a conspiracie against the King made by one *Hermolaus* and others (which they confest) he caused *Callisthenes* without confession, accusation, or triall, to be torne a-sunder vpon the rack: This deede, vnworthie of a King, *Seneca* thus censureth. . . . *This is the eternall crime of* Alexander, *which no vertue nor felicitie of his in Warre shall euer be able to redeeme. For as often as any man shall say,* He slew many thousand Persians; *it shall be replied,* He did so, and he slew Callisthenes: *When it shall be said,* He slew Darivs, *it shall be replied, and* Callisthenes; *When it shall be said, he wanne all as farre as to the very Ocean, thereon also he aduentured with vnusuall Nauies; and extended his*

Empire from a corner of Thrace, to the vtmost bounds of the Orient, It shall be said with all; But he killed Callisthenes. *Let him haue out-gone all the ancient examples of Captaines and Kings; none of all his acts makes so much to his glorie, as* Callisthenes *to his reproach.*

§20. *Of* Alexanders *iournie into India. The battaile betweene him and* Porvs.

With the Armie before remembred, of one hundred and twentie thousand foot and horse, *Alexander* did enter the borders of *India,* where such of the Princes, as submitted themselues vnto him, he entertayned louingly, the rest hee constrained; killing Man, Woman, and Child, where they resisted. Hee then came before *Nisa* built by *Bacchus,* which after a few daies was rendred vnto him. From thence he remoued to a Hill at hand, which on the top had goodly Gardens filled with delicate fruits and Vines, dedicated to *Bacchus,* to whom hee made feasts for ten daies together. Now when hee had drunke his fill, hee went on towards *Dedala,* and thence to *Acadera,* Countries spoiled and abandoned by the Inhabitants, by reason whereof, victualls failing, he diuides his Armie: *Ptolomie* led one part, *Cenon* an other, and himselfe the rest. They take many Townes, whereof that of greatest fame was *Mazage,* which had in it three hundred thousand men; but after some resistance, it was yeelded vnto him by *Cleophe* the Queene, to whom againe he restored it; at the siege of this Citie he receiued a wound in the legge. After this, *Nora* was taken by *Polysperchon,* and a Rock of great strength by himselfe: he wanne also a passage vpon one *Eryx,* who was slaine by his companie, and his head presented to *Alexander.* This is the summe of *Alexanders* doings in those parts, before such time as hee arriued at the Riuer of *Indus.* Comming to *Indus* hee found there *Ephestion,* who (being sent before) had prepared boates for the transportation of his Armie, and ere *Alexanders* arriuall, had perswaded *Omphis* King of that part of the Countrie to submit himselfe to this great Conquerour. Therefore, soone vpon *Alexanders* comming, *Omphis* presented himselfe with all the strength of his Countrie, and sixe and fiftie Elephants, vnto him; offering him his seruice and assistance. Hee made *Alexander* know that hee was an Enemie to the next two great Kings of that part of *India*, named *Abiasares* and *Porus*; wherewith *Alexander* was not a little pleased, hoping by this disvnion to make his owne victorie by farre the more easie. Hee presented *Alexander* with a Crowne of gold, so did he the rest of his Commanders, and withall fourescore talents of siluer coine, which *Alexander* not only refused, but to shew that he was couetous of glorie, not of gold, he gaue *Omphis* a thousand talents of his owne treasure, besides other *Persian* rarities. *Abiasares*, hauing heard that *Alexander* had receiued his enemie *Omphis* into his protection, resolued to make his owne peace also: For, knowing that his owne strength did but equall that of *Omphis*, and that there was no other difference betweene them, than that which the chance of Warre gaue, hee thought it an ill match when *Alexander*, who had alreadie beaten vnder foote all the greatest Princes of *Asia*, should make himselfe a Partie and Head of the quarrell. So had *Alexander* none now to stand in his way but *Porus*, to whom he sent a commandement, that he should attend him at the border of his Kingdome, there to doe him homage. But from *Porus* hee receiued this manly answere; That hee would satisfie him in his first demand, which was to attend him on his borders, and that well accompanied; but for any other acknowledgement hee was resolued to take counsell of his Sword. To be short, *Alexander* resolues to passe ouer the Riuer *Hydaspes*, and to find *Porus* at his owne home. *Porus* attends him on the farther banke with thirtie thousand foot, fourescore and ten Elephants, and three hundred armed Chariots, and a great troupe of Horse. If *Darius* had done the like on *Tigris*, *Alexander* had surely staid somewhat longer ere he had seene *India*. The Riuer was foure furlong broade, which makes halfe a mile, and withall deepe and swift. It had in it many Ilands, among which there was one well shadowed with wood, and of good capacitie. *Alexander* sent *Ptolomie* vp the Riuer with a great part of the Armie, shrowding the rest from the view of *Porus:* who by this deuice being drawne from his first incamping, sets himself

downe opposite to *Ptolomie*, supposing that the whole Armie
of *Macedon* meant to force their passage there. In the meane
while *Alexander* recouers the farther shore without resistance.
He orders his troups and aduanceth towards *Porus*, who at
first rather beleeues that *Abiasares* his Confederate (but now
the Confederate of fortune) had beene come ouer *Hydaspes*
to his aide, than that *Alexander* had past it. But he finds it
otherwise, and sends his Brother *Hagis* with foure thousand
horse, and a hundred armed waggons to entertaine him.
Each waggon had in it foure to fight, and two to guide it;
but they were at this time of litle vse: for there had fallen
so much raine, and thereby the fields were so moistned, as
the horses could hardly trot. The *Scythians* and *Dahans* had
the Vantguard, who so galled these *Indians* as they brake
their reines, & other furniture, ouerturning the wagons &
those in them. *Perdiccas* also gaue vpon the *Indian* horse-
men, and the one & the other were forst to recoile. *Porus*
moues forward with grosse of his Armie, that those of his
Vantguard scattered might recouer his Reare: *Alexander*
being followed with *Ephestion*, *Ptolomie*, and *Perdiccas*, tooke
on him to charge the *Indian* horse-men on the left wing,
commanding *Cenus* or *Cenon* to inuade the right; *Antigonus*
and *Leonatus*, hee directed to breake vpon *Porus* his battaile
of foote, strengthened with Elephants, *Porus* himselfe being
carried vpon one of them of the greatest stature. By these
beasts the *Macedonian* foot were most offended; but the
Archers and Darters being well guarded with the long and
strong Pikes of the *Macedons*, so galled them, as being
inraged, they turned head and ranne ouer the foote that
followed them: In the end, and after a long and doubtfull
fight, by the aduantage of weapon, and by the courage and
skilfulnesse of the *Macedonian* Captaines, the victorie fell to
Alexander, who also farre exceeded *Porus* in number: for
besides the *Macedonians* and other Easterne and Northern
Nations, *Porus* was assailed by his owne Confederate and
Countrie people. Yet for his owne person he neuer gaue
ground otherwise than with his sword towards his enemies,
till being weakened with many wounds, and abandoned by
his Armie, he became a prisoner to the Conqueror, from
whom againe he receiued his estate with a great enlargement.

§21. *How* Alexander *finished his expedition, and returned out of India.*

I forbeare to trouble my selfe and others with a friuolous discourse of Serpents, Apes, and Peacocks, which the *Macedonians* found in these their trauailes: or of those pettie Wars which *Alexander* made betweene the ouerthrow of *Porus*, and his sailing downe the Riuer of *Indus*. The descriptions of places about the head and branches thereof are better knowne vnto vs in this Age, by meanes of our late Nauigations into those parts, than they were in any former times. The magnificence and riches of those Kings we could in no sort be perswaded to beleeue, till our owne experience had taught vs, that there were many stranger thinges in the World, than are to bee seene betweene *London* and *Stanes*.

Our great traueller *Mandeuile* who died in the yeare 1372. and had seene so much of the World, and of the East *India*, wee accompted the greatest fabler of the World; yet had he an other reputation among other Nations, as well able to judge as we. Witnesse the Monument made of him in the Conuent of the Friers *Guillimins* in *Liege*, where the religious of that place keepe some thinges of his, *Comme pour honorable memoire de son Excellence; For an honorable memorie of his Excellencie*, saith *Guichardine*.

The Countries towards the Springs of *Indus*, and where those many Riuers of *Hydaspes*, *Zaradris*, *Acesines*, and the rest, fall into the maine streame, are now possest by the great *Mogor*, the ninth from *Tamberlane*, who commands all that tract betweene *Persia* and *Indus* towards the West, as also a great extent of Countrie towards *Ganges*. In the mouth of *Indus*, the *Ascension*, a ship of *London*, suffered shipwrack in the yeare 1609. and some of the companie trauailed ouer Land till they came to *Agra*, the same great Citie (as I take it) which our later Cosmographers call *Nagra*, being named of old *Dionysopolis*.

Phylostratus in the life of *Apollonius Tyanæus*, speaking of the expedition of *Bacchus* and *Hercules* into the East *India*, tells vs that those two great Captaines (whom *Alexander* sought by all meanes to out-fame) when they indeuored to subject vnto them the *Oxydracæ*, a people inhabiting be-

tweene the Riuers of *Hyphasis* and *Ganges*, they were beaten
from the assault of their Cities with thunder and lightnings.
This may well be vnderstood by the great Ordinance that
those people had then in vse. For it is now certainely knowne,
that the great Kings of the vttermost East, haue had the
vse of the Cannon, many hundreds of yeares since, and
euen since their first ciuilitie and greatnesse, which was long
before *Alexanders* time. But *Alexander* pierst not so farre into
the East. It sufficed, that hauing alreadie ouer-wearied his
Armie hee discouered the rest of *India* by fame. The *Indian*
Kings whom he had subdued, informed him, that a Prince
called *Aggramenes*, who commanded many Nations beyond
the Riuer of *Ganges*, was the powerfullest King of all those
Regions: and that he was able to bring into the field two
hundred thousand Foot, three thousand Elephants, twentie
thousand Horse, and two thousand armed Chariots. With
this report, though *Alexander* were more inflamed than euer
to proceede in this discouerie and conquest, yet all the art he
had could not perswade the Souldiers to wander ouer those
great desarts beyond *Indus* and *Ganges*, more terrible vnto
them than the greatest Armie that the East could gather.
Yet at the last contented they were, after many perswasiue
Orations, to follow him towards the South, to discouer such
part of the Ocean Sea, as was nearer at hand, whereunto the
Riuer of *Indus* was their infallible guide. *Alexander* seeing
that it would bee no otherwise, deuised a prettie trick,
where-with hee hoped to beguile posteritie, and make himselfe seeme greater than he was. He enlarged his Campe,
made greater trenches, greater cabbines for the Souldiers,
greater Horse-stalls, and higher mangers than his Horses
could feede in. He caused all furniture of Men and Horses
to bee made larger than would serue for vse; and scattered
these Armours and Bridles about his Campe, to be kept as
reliques, and wondered at by the sauages. Proportionable
to these he raised vp twelue great Altars to be the monument
of his journies end. This was a readie way to encrease the
fame of his bignesse; to his greatnesse it could adde nothing
saue a suspition that it was lesse than is thought, seeing he
stroue so earnestly to make it thought more than it was.

This done, he returned againe to the banke of *Acesines*,

and there determined to set vp his fleet where *Acesines* and *Hydaspis* incounter, where to testifie by a surer monument, how farre he had past towards the East, built by those Riuers two Cities: the one hee called *Nicæa*, and the other *Bucephalon*, after the name of his beloued Horse *Bucephalus*. Here againe hee receiued a fourth supply of sixe thousand *Thracian* Horse-men, seuen thousand Foot, and from his Lieutenant at *Babylon* fiue and twentie thousand Armours, garnished with siluer and gold which hee distributed among his Souldiers. About these Riuers he wanne many Townes, and committed great slaughter on those that resisted; It is then written of him, that assaulting a Citie of the *Oxidracans*, he lept from the top of the wall into it, and fought, I know not how long, against all the Inhabitants; tales like those of *Beuis* of *Southampton*, friuolous and incredible. Finally, hee past downe the Riuer with his fleet, at which time also the newes came vnto him of a rebellion in *Bactria*, and then of the arriuall of an hundred Embassadours from a King of *India*, who submitted himselfe vnto him. He feasted these Embassadours vpon a hundred beds of gold, with all the sumptuositie that could be deuised, who soone after their dispatch returned againe with a present of three hundred Horse, one hundred and thirtie Wagons, and to each foure Horses, a thousand Targets, with many other things rare and rich.

Their entertainements ended, he sailes towards the South, passeth through many obscure Nations, which did all yeeld vnto him either quietly or compelled by force: among these he builded another *Alexandria*. Of many places which he tooke in this passage, *Samus* was one, the Inhabitans whereof fought against him with poisoned Swords, with one of which *Ptolomie* (afterward King of *Ægypt*) was wounded and cured by an hearbe which *Alexander* dreamt that he had seene in the mouth of a Serpent.

When he came neare the out-let of *Indus* (being ignorant of the tides of the Sea) his Gallies as they were on a suddaine shuffled one vpon an other by the Floud, so on the Ebbe they were left on the drie ground, and on the sandie bankes of the Riuer, wherewith the *Macedonians* were much amazed, but after hee had a few daies obserued well the course of the

Sea, he past out of the riuers mouth some few miles, and after Sacrifices offered to *Neptune* returned: and the better to informe himselfe, hee sent *Nearchus* and *Onesicritus*, to discouer the coast towards the mouth of *Euphrates*. *Arrianus* in the beginning of his sixt Booke hath written this passage downe the Riuer of *Indus* at length, with the manner of the Vessells, in which hee transported his Armie, the Commanders that were vsed therein, and other the maruailous prouisions made.

Neare the out-lets of this Riuer hee spent some part of the Winter, and in eighteene daies march from thence recouered *Gedrosia*, in which passage his Armie suffered such miserie for want of foode, that of a hundred and twentie thousand foot, and twelue thousand horse, which hee carried into *India*, not the fourth part returned aliue.

§22. *Of* Alexanders *Riot, Crueltie, and death.*

From *Gedrosia Alexander* led his Armie into *Carmania*, and so drawing neare to *Persia*, hee gaue himselfe wholly to feasting and drinking, imitating the triumphs of *Bacchus*. And though this Swinish vice bee hatefull enough in it selfe, yet it alwaies inflamed this King to Crueltie. *For* (saith *Curtius*) *the Hang-man followed the feast, for* Aspastes *one of his Prouinciall Gouernours he commanded to be slaine, so as neither did the excesse of voluptuousnesse qualifie his crueltie, nor his crueltie hinder in ought his voluptuousnesse.*

While he refreshed his Armie in these parts, a new supply of fiue thousand foote and a thousand horse, was brought him by *Cleander*, and his fellowes, that had been imploied in the killing of *Parmenio*. Against these Murderers great complaint was made, by the Deputies of the Prouinces in which they had commanded; and their offences were so outragious, as *Alexander* was perswaded, that, had they not altogether despaired of his returne out of *India*, they durst not haue committed them. All men were glad of the occasion, remembring the vertue of him whom they had slaughtered. The end was, That *Cleander* and the other chiefe, with six hundred Souldiers by them imploied, were deliuered ouer to the Hang-man: euery one rejoycing that the Ire of the King was at last executed on the ministers of his Ire.

Nearchus and *Onesicritus* were now returned from the coast, and made report of an Iland rich in gold, and of other strange thinges; whereupon they were commanded to make some farther discouerie: which done, that they should enter the mouth of *Euphrates*, and finde the King at *Babylon*.

As he drew neare to *Babylon* he visited the Sepulchre of *Cyrus* in *Pasargada*, now called *Chelquera:* where he was presented with many rich gifts by *Orsines*, one of the Princes of *Persia*, of the race of *Cyrus*. But because *Bagoas*, an *Eunuch* in especiall fauour with the King, was neglected, he not only practised certaine loose fellowes to witnesse against *Orsines*, that he had robbed *Cyrus* Tomb, for which he was condemned to die; but hee assisted the Hang-man with his owne handes in tormenting him. At which time also *Alexander* caused *Phradates* to be slaine, suspecting his greatnesse. *Cæperat* (saith *Cvrtivs*) *esse præceps ad repræsentanda supplicia, item ad deteriora credenda*; *He beganne headlongly to shed bloud, and to beleeue false reports*. It is true, that he tooke a way to make all men wearie of his gouernement, seeing crueltie is more fearefull than all the aduentures that can be made against it.

At this time it is said that *Calanus* the Philosopher burnt himselfe, when hee had liued threescore and thirteene yeares. Whether herein he followed the custome of his Countrie, being an *Indian*, Or sought to preuent the griefe and incommoditie of elder age, it is vncertaine: but in this the Historians agree, that fore-seeing and fore-shewing *Alexanders* death, he promised to meete him shortly after at *Babylon*.

From *Pasargada* hee came to *Susa*, where hee married *Statira*, *Darius* his eldest Daughter, giuing her yonger sister to his beloued *Ephestion*, and fourescore other *Persian* Ladies to his Captaines. There were six thousand guests inuited to the feast, to each of which he gaue a cup of gold. Here there came vnto him three thousand yong souldiers out of his conquered Prouinces, whereat the *Macedonians* greatly murmured. *Harpalus*, his Treasurer in *Babylon* hauing lauishly consumed the monies in his keeping, got him going with fiue thousand talents, and sixe thousand hired Souldiers, but he was rejected in *Greece*, and there slaine. *Alexander* greatly rejoyced at the fidelitie of the *Greekes*, whom *Harpalus* with these forces and treasures could not stirre: yet hee sent commandement that they should againe receiue their banished men, whereunto (fearefull of his indignation) all submitted themselues, (except the *Athenians*) though they resolued that it was a manifest preparation towards their bondage. After this there followed a maruailous discontentment in his Armie, because he had resolued to send into *Macedon* all those old Souldiers which could no longer indure the trauell of Warre, and to keepe the rest in *Asia*. He vsed many Orations to satisfie them, but it was in vaine during the tempest of their furie. But afterward, as Whales are drawne to the Land with a twine threed, when they haue tumbled a while, so are the vnconsiderate multitude easily conducted when their first passions are evaporate. With such as were licenced to depart, he sent *Craterus*, to whom he gaue the Lieutenantship of *Macedon*, *Thessalie*, and *Thrace*, which *Antipater* had held from his first departure out of *Europe*, who had beaten the rebellious *Greekes* in his absence, discharged the trust committed vnto him with great fidelitie, and sent him so many strong supplies into *Asia* from time to time. Certainely, if *Alexander* had not taken counsell of his cups, hee would haue cast some better colour on this alteration, and giuen *Antipater* a stronger reason for his remoue, than to haue imploied him in the conduction of a new supply to be brought him to *Babylon*, the warre being now at an end. For *Antipater* saw nothing in this remoue, but the Kings disposition to send him after *Parmenio*, and the rest. With this *Antipater*, the King, notwithstanding his great courage, had no great appetite to grapple: Princes, though jealous, doe not stand in doubt of euery man ill-affected though valiant; but there is a kinde of Kingly courage, compounded of hardinesse and vnderstanding, which is many times so fearefull vnto them, as they take leaue both of Law and Religion, to free themselues thereof.

After hee had sent for *Antipater*, hee made a journie into *Media* to settle thinges there; where *Ephestion*, whom he fauoured most of all men, dies. The King according to the greatnesse of his loue, laments his losse; hangs his Phisition; and bestowes vpon his Monument twelue thousand talents: After which hee returnes to *Babylon*. Thither *Antipater* came not, but sent; and not to excuse himselfe, but to free himselfe. For if we beleeue *Curtius* (whom *Plutarch* and others gaine-say) *Antipater* by his Sonnes, *Cassander*, *Philip*, and *Iôlla*, who waited on *Alexanders* cup, gaue him poison, *Thessalus* (who was of the conspiracie) hauing inuited him to a drinking feast of purpose. For after he had taken a carouse in *Hercules* his cup, a draught of drinke stronger than *Hercules* himselfe, he quitted the World within a few daies.

Certainely the Princes of the World haue seldome found good by making their ministers ouer-great, and thereby suspitious to themselues. For he that doth not acknowledge fidelitie to bee a debt, but is perswaded that Kings ought to purchase it from their Vassalls, will neuer please himselfe with the price giuen. The only restoratiue, indeed, that strengthens it, is the goodnesse and vertue of the Prince, and his liberalitie makes it more diligent; so as proportion and distance be obserued. It may be that *Antipater* hauing commanded two or three Kingdomes twelue yeares, knew not now how to play any other part; no more than *Cæsar* did, after he had so long a time gouerned the *Gaules*, where he vtterly forgat the art of obedience. A most cruell and vngratefull traitor *Antipater* was, if *Curtius* doe not belie him: For though hee feared some ill measure vpon his remoue (the Tragedies of *Parmenio*, *Clytus*, and *Callisthenes*, hauing beene so lately acted) yet he knew nothing to the contrarie, but that the King had resolued to haue giuen him some other great gouernement in *Asia:* the old Souldiers thence returned, hauing perchance desired to be gouerned by *Craterus*, whom they had followed in all the former Warre.

§23. *Of* Alexanders *Person and qualities.*

Howsoeuer it were, *Alexanders* former cruelties cannot bee excused, no more than his vanitie to be esteemed the sonne

of *Iupiter*, with his excessiue delight in drinke and drunkennesse, which others make the cause of his feuer and death.
In that hee lamented his want of enterprising, and grieued
to consider what hee should doe when hee had conquered
the World, *Augustus Cæsar* found just cause to deride him,
as if the well gouerning of so many Nations and Kingdomes,
as he had alreadie conquered, could not haue offered him
matter more than aboundant, to busie his braines withall.
That he was both learned and a louer of learning, it cannot
be doubted. Sr *Francis Bacon*, in his first booke of the
aduancement of learning, hath proued it sufficiently. His
liberalitie I know not how to praise, because it exceeded
proportion. It is said, That when he gaue a whole Citie to
one of his Seruants, He, to whom it was giuen, did out of
modestie refuse it, as disproportionable to his fortune: to
whom *Alexander* replied, That hee did not enquire what
became him to accept, but the King to giue: of which
Seneca; . . . *It seemes a braue and royall speech, whereas
indeede it is very foolish. For nothing simply considered by it
selfe beseemes a man. We must regard what, to whom, when,
why, where, and the like; without which considerations no act
can be approued. Let honours bee proportioned vnto the persons:
for whereas vertue is euer limited by measure, the excesse is as
faultie as the defect.*

For his Person, it is very apparant, That he was as valiant
as any man, a disposition taken by it selfe, not much to be
admired; For I am resolued that hee had ten thousand in his
Armie as daring as himselfe. Surely, if aduenturous natures
were to be commended simply, wee should confound that
vertue with the hardinesse of Theeues, Ruffians, and mastife
Dogges. For certainely it is no way praise-worthie but in
daring good thinges, and in the performance of those lawfull
enterprises, in which we are imploied for the seruice of our
Kings and Common-weales.

If we compare this great Conquerour with other Troublers
of the World, who haue bought their glorie with so great
destruction, and effusion of bloud, I thinke him farre
inferiour to *Cæsar*, and many other that liued after him,
seeing hee neuer vndertooke any warlike Nation, the naked
Scythians excepted, nor was euer encountred with any

Armie of which he had not a most mastring aduantage, both
of weapons and of Commanders, euery one of his Fathers
old Captaines by farre exceeding the best of his Enemies.
But it seemeth, Fortune and Destinies (if we may vse those
termes) had found out and prepared for him, without any
care of his owne, both heapes of Men, that willingly offered
their necks to the yoke, and Kingdomes that inuited and
called in their owne Conquerours. For conclusion, wee will
agree with *Seneca*, who speaking of *Philip* the Father, and
Alexander the Sonne, giues this judgement of them. *Quod
non minores fuere pestes mortalium quàm inundatio, qua planum
omne perfusum est, quàm conflagratio qua magna pars ani-
mantium exaruit*; *That they were no lesse plagues to mankinde,
than an ouer-flow of waters, drowning all the leuell*; *or some
burning droughth, whereby a great part of liuing creatures is
scorched vp.*

Ch. III. *The raigne of* Aridævs

Ch. IV. *Of the great Lordship which* Antigonvs *got in Asia*

Ch. V. *Of the great ciuill Warre betweene* Alexanders Captaines ...

Ch. VI. *Of the warres betweene* ... Alexanders Princes ...

Ch. VII. *The growth of Rome: and setling of the Easterne Kingdomes*

THE FIRST PART OF THE HISTORIE OF THE WORLD:

Intreating of the times from the setled rule of Alexanders Successors in the East, vntill the Romans, preuailing ouer all, made Conquest of Asia and Macedon.

THE FIFTH BOOKE.

Ch. I. *Of the first Punick Warre*

§1. *A discussion of that probleme of* Livie; Whether the Romans could haue resisted the great Alexander. *That neither the Macedonian nor the Roman Souldier, was of equall valour to the English.*

That question handled by *Livie, Whether the great* Alexander *could haue preuailed against the Romans, if after his Easterne conquest, he had bent all his forces against them,* hath beene, and is, the subject of much dispute; which (as it seemes to me) the arguments on both sides do not so well explane, as doth the experience that *Pyrrhus* hath giuen, of the *Roman* power, in his daies. For if he, a Commander (in *Hannibals* judgement) inferior to *Alexander,* though to none else, could with small strength of men, and little store of monie, or of other needfull helps in warre, vanquish them in two battailes, and endanger their estate, when it was well setled, and held the best part of *Italie,* vnder a confirmed obedience: what would *Alexander* haue done, that was aboundantly prouided of all which is needfull to a Conquerour, wanting only matter of emploiment, comming vpon them before their Dominion was halfe so well setled. It is easie to say, that *Alexander* had no more, than thirtie thousand foot, and foure thousand horse (as indeede, at his first passage into *Asia,* he carried ouer, not many more) and that the rest of his followers were no better than base effeminate *Asiatiques.* But he that considers the Armies of *Perdiccas, Antipater, Craterus, Eumenes, Ptolomie, Antigonus,* and *Lysimachus,* with the actions by them performed, euery one of which (to omit others) commanded only some fragment of this dead Emperours power; shall easily finde, that such a reckoning is farre short of the truth.

It were needlesse to speake of Treasure, Horses, Elephants, Engines of batterie, and the like: of all which, the *Macedonian* had aboundance; the *Roman* hauing nought, saue men and armes. As for Sea-forces; he that shall consider after what sort the *Romans,* in their first *Punick* warre, were trained, in the rudiments of Nauigation; sitting vpon the shoare, and beating the sand with poles, to practise the stroke of the Oare, as not daring to lanch their ill-built vessels into the Sea; will easily conceiue, how farre too weake they would haue proued in such seruices.

Now for helpers in warre; I doe not see, why all *Greece* and *Macedon*, being absolutely commanded by *Alexander*, might not well deserue to be laid in ballance, against those parts of *Italie*, which the *Romans* held in ill-assured subjection. To omit therefore all benefit, that the Easterne world, more wealthie, indeede, than valiant, could haue affoorded vnto the *Macedonian*: let vs only conjecture, how the States of *Sicill* and *Carthage*, nearest neighbours, to such a quarrell (had it happened) would haue stood affected. The *Sicilians* were, for the most part, *Græcians*; neither is it to bee doubted, that they would readily haue submitted themselues vnto him, that ruled all *Greece* besides them. In what termes they commonly stood, and how ill they were able to defend themselues, it shall appeare anon. Sure it is, that *Alexanders* comming into those parts, would haue brought excessiue joy, to them that were faine to get the helpe of *Pyrrhus*, by offering to become his subjects. As for the *Carthaginians*; if *Agathocles*, the Tyrant of *Syracuse*, hated of his people, and ill able to defend his owne besieged Citie, could, by aduenturing to saile into *Affrick*, put their Dominion, yea and *Carthage* it selfe, in extreme hazard; shall wee thinke that they would haue beene able to withstand *Alexander?* But, why doe I question their abilitie, seeing that they sent Embassadours, with their submission, as farre as *Babylon*, ere the warre drew neare them? Wherefore it is manifest, that the *Romans* must, without other succour, than perhaps of some few *Italian* friends (of which yet there were none, that forsooke them not, at some time, both before and after this) haue opposed their valour, and good militarie discipline, against the power of all Countries, to them knowne, if they would haue made resistance. How they could haue sped well, in vndertaking such a match; it is vneasie to finde in discourse of humane reason. It is true; that vertue and fortune worke wonders: but it is against cowardly fooles, and the vnfortunate: for whosoeuer contends with one too mightie for him; either must excell in these, as much as his

enemie goes beyond him in power; or else must looke, both
to be ouer-come, and to bee cast downe so much the lower,
by how much the opinion of his fortune and vertue renders
him suspected, as likely to make head another time against
the vanquisher. Whether the *Roman*, or the *Macedonian*,
were in those daies the better Souldier, I will not take vpon
me to determine: though I might, without partialitie, deliuer
mine owne opinion, and preferre that Armie, which followed
not only *Philip* and *Alexander*, but also *Alexanders* Princes
after him, in the greatest dangers of all sorts of warre; before
any, that *Rome* either had, or in long time after did send
forth. Concerning fortune; who can giue a rule that shall
alwaies hold? *Alexander* was victorious in euery battaile that
he fought: and the *Romans* in the issue of euery warre. But
forasmuch as *Liuie* hath judged this a matter worthie of
consideration; I thinke it a great part of *Romes* good
fortune, that *Alexander* came not into *Italie:* where in three
yeares after his death, the two *Roman* Consulls, together with
all the power of that State, were surprized by the *Samnites*,
and enforced to yeeld vp their armes. We may therefore
permit *Liuie* to admire his owne *Romans*, and to compare
with *Alexander* those Captaines of theirs, which were
honoured sufficiently, in being thought equal to his followers:
that the same conceipt should blind our judgment, we
cannot permit without much vanitie.

Now in deciding such a controuersie, me thinks it were
not amisse, for an *Englishman*, to giue such a sentence
betweene the *Macedonians* and *Romans*, as the *Romans* once
did (being chosen Arbitrators) betweene the *Ardeates* and
Aricini, that stroue about a peece of land; saying, that it
belonged vnto neither of them, but vnto the *Romans* themselues.

If therefore it be demanded, whether the *Macedonian*, or
the *Roman*, were the best Warriour? I will answere: The
Englishmen. For it will soone appeare, to any that shall
examine the noble acts of our Nation in warre, that they
were performed by no aduantage of weapon; against no
sauage or vnmanlie people; the enemie being farre superiour
vnto vs in numbers, and all needfull prouisions, yea as well
trained as we, or commonly better, in the exercise of warre.

In what sort *Philip* wanne his Dominion in *Greece*; what manner of men the *Persians* and *Indians* were; whom *Alexander* vanquished; as likewise of what force the *Macedonian Phalanx* was, and how well appointed, against such armes as it commonly encountred: any man, that hath taken paines to reade the foregoing storie of them, doth sufficiently vnderstand. Yet was this *Phalanx* neuer, or very seldome, able to stand, against the *Roman* Armies: which were embattailed in so excellent a forme, as I know not, whether any Nation besides them haue vsed, either before or since. The *Roman* weapons likewise, both offensiue and defensiue, were of greater vse, than those with which any other Nation hath serued, before the fierie instruments of Gunne-powder were knowne. As for the enemies, with which *Rome* had to doe; we finde, that they, which did ouer-match her in numbers, were as farre ouer-matched by her, in weapons; and that they, of whom shee had little aduantage in armes, had as little aduantage of her in multitude. This also (as *Plutarch* well obserueth) was a part of her happinesse; that shee was neuer ouer-laied, with two great warres at once.

Hereby it came to passe, that hauing at first increased her strength, by accession of the *Sabines*; hauing wonne the State of *Alba*, against which shee aduentured her owne selfe, as it were in wager, vpon the heads of three Champions: and hauing thereby made her selfe Princesse of *Latium:* shee did afterwards, by long warre, in many ages, extend her Dominion ouer all *Italie.* The *Carthaginians* had well neare oppressed her: but their Souldiers were Mercinarie; so that for want of proper strength, they were easily beaten at their owne doores. The *Ætolians*, and with them all, or the most of *Greece*, assisted her against *Philip* the *Macedonian:* hee being beaten, did lend her his helpe, to beat the same *Ætolians.* The warres against *Antiochus*, and other *Asiatiques,* were such as gaue to *Rome* small cause of boast, though much of joy: for those opposites were as base of courage, as the lands which they held were aboundant of riches. *Sicil, Spaine,* and all *Greece,* fell into her hands by vsing her aide, to protect them against the *Carthaginians* and *Macedonians.*

I shall not neede to speake of her other conquests: it was easie to get more when shee had gotten all this. It is not my purpose to disgrace the *Roman* valour (which was very noble) or to blemish the reputation of so many famous victories: I am not so idle. This I say: that among all their warres, I finde not any, wherein their valour hath appeared, comparable to the *English*. If my judgement seeme ouerpartiall; our warres in *France* may helpe to make it good.

First, therefore it is well knowne; that *Rome* (or perhaps all the world besides) had neuer any so braue a Commander in warre, as *Iulius Cæsar:* and that no *Roman* armie, was comparable vnto that, which serued vnder the same *Cæsar*. Likewise, it is apparent, that this gallant Armie, which had giuen faire proofe of the *Roman* courage, in good performance of the *Heluetian* warre, when it first entred into *Gaule*; was neuerthelesse vtterly disheartened, when *Cæsar* led it against the *Germans*. So that we may justly impute, all that was extraordinarie in the valour of *Cæsars* men, to their long exercise, vnder so good a Leader, in so great a warre. Now let vs in generall, compare with the deedes done by these best of *Roman* Souldiers, in their principall seruice; the things performed in the same Countrie, by our common *English* Souldier, leauied in haste, from following the Cart, or sitting on the shop-stall: so shall we see the difference. Herein will we deale fairely, and beleeue *Cæsar*, in relating the acts of the *Romans:* but will call the *French* Historians to witnesse, what actions were performed by the *English*. In *Cæsars* time, *France* was inhabited by the *Gaules*, a stout people, but inferiour to the *French*, by whom they were subdued; euen when the *Romans* gaue them assistance. The Countrie of *Gaule* was rent in sunder (as *Cæsar* witnesseth) into many Lordships: some of which were gouerned by pettie Kings, others by the multitude, none ordered in such sort as might make it appliable to the nearest Neighbour. The factions were many, and violent: not only in generall through the whole Countrie, but betweene the pettie States, yea in euery Citie, and almost in euery house. What greater aduantage could a Conquerour desire? Yet there was a greater. *Ariouistus*, with his *Germans*, had ouer-runne the Countrie, and held much part of it in a subjection, little different from meere slauerie: yea, so often had the *Germans* preuailed in warre vpon the *Gaules*, that the *Gaules* (who had sometimes beene the better Souldiers) did hold themselues no way equall to those daily Inuaders. Had *France* beene so prepared vnto our *English* Kings, *Rome* it selfe, by this time, and long ere this time, would haue beene ours. But when King *Edward* the third beganne his warre vpon *France*, hee found the whole Countrie setled in obedience to one mightie King; a King whose reputation abroade, was no lesse, than his puissance at home; vnder whose Ensigne, the King of *Bohemia*, did serue in person; at whose call, the *Genowayes*,[1] and other Neighbour States, were readie to take armes: finally, a King vnto whom one Prince gaue away his Dominion, for loue; another sold away a goodly Citie and Territorie for monie. The Countrie lying so open to the *Roman*, and being so well fenced against the *English*; it is note-worthie, not who preuailed most therein (for it were meere vanitie, to match the *English* purchases, with the *Roman* conquest) but whether of the two gaue the greater proofe of militarie vertue. *Cæsar* himselfe doth witnesse, that the *Gaules* complained of their owne ignorance in the Art of warre, and that their owne hardinesse was ouer-mastered, by the skill of their enemies. Poore men, they admired the *Roman* Towers, and Engines of batterie, raised and planted against their walls, as more than humane workes. What greater wonder is it, that such a people was beaten by the *Roman*; than that the *Caribes*, a naked people, but valiant, as any vnder the skie, are commonly put to the worse, by small numbers of *Spaniards?* Besides all this, we are to haue regard, of the great difficultie that was found, in drawing all the *Gaules*, or any great part of them, to one head, that with joynt forces they might oppose their assailants: as also the much more difficultie, of holding them long together. For hereby it came to passe, that they were neuer able to make vse of oportunitie: but sometimes compelled to stay for their fellowes; and sometimes driuen, to giue or take battaile, vpon extreme disaduantages, for feare, least their Companies should fall a-sunder: as indeede, vpon any little disaster, they were readie to breake, and returne euery one to the defence of his owne. All this, and (which was little lesse than all this) great oddes in weapon, gaue to the *Romans*, the honour of

[1] i.e. Genoese.

many gallant victories. What such helpe? or what other worldly help, than the golden metall of their Souldiers, had our *English* Kings against the *French?* Were not the *French* as well experienced in feats of Warre? Yea, did they not thinke themselues therein our superiours? Were they not in armes, in horse, and in all prouision, exceedingly beyond vs? Let vs heare, what a *French* writer saith,[1] of the inequalitie that was betweene the *French* and *English,* when their King *Iohn* was readie to giue the on-set, vpon the *Black Prince,* at the battaile of *Poitiers.* Iohn *had all aduantages ouer* Edward, *both of number, force, shew, Countrie, and conceit (the which is commonly a consideration of no small importance in worldly affaires) and withall, the choise of all his horse-men (esteemed then the best in Europe) with the greatest and wisest Captaines of his whole Realme.* And what could he wish more?

I thinke, it would trouble a *Roman* antiquarie, to finde the like example in their Histories; the example, I say, of a King, brought prisoner to *Rome,* by an Armie of eight thousand, which he had surrounded with fortie thousand, better appointed, and no lesse expert warriours. This I am sure of; that neither *Syphax* the *Numidian,* followed by a rabble of halfe Scullions, as *Liuie* rightly tearmes them, nor those cowardly Kings *Perseus* and *Gentius,* are worthie patternes. All that haue read of *Cressie* and *Agincourt,* will beare me witnesse, that I doe not alleage the battaile of *Poitiers,* for lack of other, as good examples of the *English* vertue: the proofe whereof hath left many a hundred better marks, in all quarters of *France,* than euer did the valour of the *Romans.* If any man impute these victories of ours to the long Bow, as carrying farther, piercing more strongly, and quicker of discharge than the *French* Crosse-bow: my answere is readie; that in all these respects, it is also (being drawne with a strong arme) superiour to the Musket; yet is the Musket a weapon of more vse. The Gunne, and the Crosse-bow, are of like force, when discharged by a Boy or Woman, as when by a strong Man: weakenesse, or sicknesse, or a sore finger, makes the long Bow vnseruiceable. More particularly, I say, that it was the custome of our Ancestors, to shoot, for the

---

[1] Jean de Serres, in *Inventaire général de l'histoire de France* (1597); translated into English by E. Grimeston (1607).

most part, *point blanck:* and so shall hee perceiue, that will note the circumstances of almost any one battaile. This takes away all objection: for when two Armies are within the distance of a Butts length, one flight of arrowes, or two at the most, can be deliuered, before they close. Neither is it in generall true, that the long Bow reacheth farther, or that it pierceth more strongly than the Crosse-bow: But this is the rare effect, of an extraordinarie arme; whereupon can be grounded no common rule. If any man shall aske, How then came it to passe, that the *English* wanne so many great battailes, hauing no aduantage to helpe him? I may, with best commendation of modestie, referre him to the *French* Historian: who relating the victorie of our men at *Creuant,* where they passed a bridge, in face of the enemie, vseth these words; *The English comes with a conquering brauerie, as he, that was accustomed to gaine euery where, without any stay: hee forceth our garde, placed vpon the bridge, to keepe the passage.* Or I may cite another place of the same Authour, where hee tells, how the *Britons,* being inuaded by *Charles* the eight, King of *France,* thought it good policie, to apparell a thousand and two hundred of their owne men in *English* Cassacks; hoping that the very sight of the *English* red Crosse, would be enough to terrifie the *French.* But I will not stand to borrow of the *French* Historians (all which, excepting *De Serres,* and *Paulus Æmylius,* report wonders of our Nation) the proposition which first I vndertooke to maintaine; *That the militarie vertue of the English, preuailing against all manner of difficulties, ought to be preferred before that of Romans, which was assisted with all aduantages that could be desired.* If it be demanded; why then did not our Kings finish the conquest, as *Cæsar* had done? my answere may bee (I hope without offence) that our Kings were like to the race of the *Æacidæ,* of whom the old Poet *Ennius* gaue this note; *Belli potentes sunt magè quam sapienti potentes; They were more war-like than politique.* Who so notes their proceedings, may finde, that none of them went to worke like a Conquerour: saue only King *Henrie* the fift, the course of whose victories, it pleased God to interrupt by his death. But this question is the more easily answered, if another be first made. Why did not the *Romans* attempt the conquest of *Gaule,* before the time of *Cæsar?* why not after the *Macedonian* warre? why not after the third *Punick*, or after the *Numantian?* At all these times they had good leisure: and then especially had they both leisure, and fit oportunitie, when vnder the conduct of *Marius*, they had newly vanquished the *Cimbri*, and *Teutones*, by whom the Countrie of *Gaule* had beene piteously wasted. Surely, the words of *Tullie* were true; that with other Nations the *Romans* fought for Dominion; with the *Gaules*, for preseruation of their owne safetie.

Therefore they attempted not the conquest of *Gaule*, vntill they were Lords of all other Countries, to them knowne. We on the other side, held only the one halfe of our owne Iland; the other halfe being inhabited by a Nation (vnlesse perhaps in wealth and numbers of men somewhat inferiour) euery way equall to our selues; a Nation, anciently & strongly allied to our enemies the *French*, and in that regard, enemie to vs. So that our danger lay both before and behinde vs: and the greater danger at our backs; where comonly we felt, alwaies we feared, a stronger inuasion by land, than we could make vpon *France*, transporting our forces ouer Sea.

It is vsuall, with men, that haue pleased themselues, in admiring the matters which they finde in ancient Histories; to hold it a great injurie done to their judgment, if any take vpon him, by way of comparison, to extoll the things of later ages. But I am well perswaded, that as the diuided vertue of this our Iland, hath giuen more noble proofe of it selfe; than vnder so worthie a Leader, that *Roman* Armie could doe, which afterwards could win *Rome*, and all her Empire, making *Cæsar* a *Monarch;* so hereafter, by Gods blessing, who hath conuerted our greatest hindrance, into our greatest helpe, the enemie that shall dare to trie our forces, will finde cause to wish, that auoiding vs, hee had rather encountred as great a puissance, as was that of the *Roman* Empire. But it is now high time, that laying a-side comparisons, we returne to the rehearsall of deeds done: wherein we shall finde, how *Rome* began, after *Pyrrhus* had left *Italie*, to striue with *Carthage* for Dominion, in the first *Punick* warre.

§2. *The estate of Carthage, before it entred into warre with Rome.*

§3. *The beginning of the first Punick Warre . . .*

§4. *Of the Iland of Sicil.*

§5. *Of the recontinuation of the Roman warre in Sicil . . .*

§6. *How the Romans besiege and winne Agrigentum. Their beginning to maintaine a fleet. Their first losse, and first victorie by Sea. Of Sea-fight in generall.*

Hieron, hauing sided himselfe with the *Romans,* aided them with victualls, and other necessaries: so that they, presuming vpon his assistance, recall some part of their forces. The *Carthaginians* finde it high time to bestirre them; they send to the *Ligurians,* and to the troups they had in *Spaine,* to come to their aide; who being arriued, they made the Citie of *Agrigentum,* the seat of the warre, against the *Romans,* filling it with all manner of munition.

The *Roman* Consulls, hauing made peace with *Hieron,* returne into *Italie;* and, in their places, *Lucius Posthumius,* and *Quintus Mamilius,* arriue. They goe on towards *Agrigentum:*[1] and finding no enemie in the field, they besiege it,

[1] [Ralegh's marginal note:] *Agrigentum* was a goodly Citie, built by the *Geloi,* vnder conduct of *Ariston* and *Pystilus.* The compasse was ten miles about the walls; and it had sometimes in it eight hundred thousand Inhabitants. This Citie, by reason of the fertilitie of the soile, and the neighbourhood of *Carthage,* grew in a short space, from smal beginnings, to great glorie and riches. The plentie and luxurie thereof was so great, as it caused *Empedocles* to say, That the *Agrigentines* built *Palaces* of such sumptuositie, as if they meant to liue for euer; and made such feasts, as if they meant to die the next day. But their greatest pompe and magnificence, was in their goodly Temples, and Theaters, Water-conduits, and Fish-ponds: the ruines whereof at this day are sufficient argument, that *Rome* it selfe could neuer boast of the like. In the Porch of the Temple of *Iupiter Olympius,* (by which we may iudge of the Temple it selfe) there was set out on one side the full proportion of the Giants, fighting with the Gods, all cut out in polished marble of diuers colours; a worke the most magnificent and rare, that euer hath beene seene: on the other side, the warre of *Troy,* and the encounters which hapned at that siege; with the personages of the Heroes that were doers in that warre; all of the like beautifull stone, and of equall stature to the bodies of men in those ancient times: In comparison of which, the latter workes of that kinde, are but pettie things, and meere trifles. It would require a volume, to expresse the magnificence of the Temples of *Hercules, Æsculapius, Concord, Iuno Lacinia, Chastitie, Proserpina, Castor* and *Pollux;* wherein the Master-peeces of those

though it were stuffed with fiftie thousand Souldiers. After a while, the time of haruest being come, a part of the *Roman* armie range the Countrie to gather corne, and those at the siege grow negligent; the *Carthaginians* sallie furiously, and indanger the *Roman* Armie, but are in the end repelled into the towne with great losse: but by the smart felt on both sides, the Assailants redoubled their guards, & the besieged kept within their couert. Yet the *Romans*, the better to assure themselues, cut a deepe trench, betweene the walls of the Citie and their Campe: and another on the out-side thereof; that neither the *Carthaginians* might force any quarter suddenly, by a sallie, nor those of the Countrie without, breake vpon them unawares: which double defence kept the besieged also from the receiuing any reliefe of victualls, and munitions, whilest the *Syracusian* supplies the assailants with what they want. The besieged send for succour to *Carthage:* after they had beene in this sort pent vp fiue moneths. The *Carthaginians* imbarke an Armie, with certaine Elephants, vnder the command of *Hanno;* who arriues with it at *Heraclea*, to the West of *Agrigentum. Hanno* puts himselfe into the field, and surpriseth *Erbesus*, a Citie wherein the *Romans* had bestowed all their prouision. By meanes hereof, the famine without grew to be as great, as it was within *Agrigentum;* and the *Roman* campe no lesse streightly assieged by *Hanno*, than the Citie was by the *Romans:* insomuch, as if *Hieron* had not supplied them, they had beene forced to abandon the siege. But seeing that this distresse was not enough to make them rise; *Hanno* deter-mined to giue them battaile. To which end departing from *Heraclia*, he makes approch vnto the *Roman* campe. The *Romans* resolue to sustaine him, and put themselues in order. *Hanno* directs the *Numidian* horse-men to charge their Vantguard, to the end to draw them further on; which done, he commands them to returne, as broken, till they came to the body of the Armie, that lay shadowed behind some rising ground. The *Numidians* performe it accordingly; and while

---

exquisite Painters, and Caruers, *Phidias, Zeuxis, Myron,* and *Polycletus,* were to be seene. But in processe of time it ranne the same fortune that al other great Cities haue done, and was ruined by diuers calamities of warre; whereof this warre present brought vnto it not the least.

the *Romans* pursued the *Numidians*, *Hanno* giues vpon them, and hauing slaughtered many, beats the rest into their Trenches.

After this encounter, the *Carthaginians* made no other attempt for two moneths, but lay strongly incamped, waiting vntill some oportunitie should inuite them. But *Annibal*, that was besieged in *Agrigentum*, as well by signes as messengers, made *Hanno* know, how ill the extremitie which he indured, was able to brooke such dilatorie courses. *Hanno* thereupon, a second time, prouoked the Consulls to fight. But, his Elephants being disordered by his owne Vantguard, which was broken by the *Romans*, he lost the day: and with such as escaped, he recouered *Heraclea*. *Annibal* perceiuing this, and remayning hopelesse of succour, resolued to make his owne way. Finding therefore that the *Romans*, after this daies victorie, wearied with labour, and secured by their good fortune, kept negligent watch in the night, he rusht out of the Towne, with all the remainder of his armie, and past by the *Roman* campe without resistance. The Consulls pursue him in the morning, but in vaine: sure they were, that he could not carrie the Citie with him, which with little a-doe the *Romans* entred, and pittifully spoiled. The *Romans*, proud of this victorie, purpose henceforth rather to follow the direction of their present good fortunes, than their first determinations. They had resolued in the beginning of this Warre, only to succour the *Mamertines*, and to keepe the *Carthaginians* from their owne coasts: but now they determine, to make themselues Lords of all *Sicil*; and from thence, being fauoured with the winde of good successe, to saile ouer into *Africke*. It is the disease of Kings, of States, and of priuate men, to couet the greatest things, but not to enjoy the least; the desire of that which we neither haue nor neede, taking from vs the true vse and fruition of what we haue alreadie. This curse vpon mortall men, was neuer taken from them since the beginning of the World to this day.

To prosecute this Warre, *Lucius Valerius*, and *Titus Octacilius*, two new Consuls, are sent into *Sicil*. Whereupon, the *Romans* being Masters of the field, many inland Townes gaue themselues vnto them. On the contrarie, the *Cartha-*

ginians keeping still the Lordship of the Sea, many maritimate places became theirs. The *Romans* therefore, as well to secure their owne coasts, often inuaded by the *African* fleets, as also to equall themselues in euery kinde of warfare with their enemies, determine to make a fleet. And herein fortune fauored them with this accident, that being altogether ignorant in shipwrights-craft, a storme of winde thrust one of the *Carthaginian* Gallies, of fiue bankes, to the shore.

Now had the *Romans* a patterne, and by it they beganne to set vp an hundred *Quinqueremes,* which were Gallies, rowed by fiue on euery banke, and twentie, of three on a banke: and while these were in preparing, they exercised their men in the feat of rowing. This they did after a strange fashion. They placed vpon the Sea-sands many seates, in order of the bankes in Gallies, whereon they placed their water-men, and taught them to beat the sand with long poles, orderly, and as they were directed by the Master, that so they might learne the stroke of the Gallie, and how to mount and draw their Oares.

When their fleet was finished, some rigging and other implements excepted, *C. Cornelius,* one of the new Consulls (for they changed euery yeare) was made Admirall: who being more in loue with this new kinde of warfare, than well aduised, past ouer to *Messena* with seuenteene Gallies, leauing the rest to follow him. There he staid not, but would needes row alongst the coast to *Lipara,* hoping to doe some peece of seruice. *Hannibal,* a *Carthaginian,* was at the same time Gouernour in *Panormus;* who being aduertised of this new Sea-mans arriuall, sent forth one *Boodes,* a Senatour of *Carthage,* with twentie Gallies, to entertaine him. *Boodes,* falling vpon the Consull vnawares, tooke both him and the fleet he commanded. When *Hannibal* receiued this good newes, together with the *Roman* Gallies and their Consull; he grew no lesse foolish hardie than *Cornelius* had beene. For he, fancying to himselfe to surprise the rest of the *Roman* fleet, on their owne coast, ere they were yet in all points prouided; sought them out with a fleet of fiftie saile: wherewith falling among them, he was well beaten, and, leauing the greater number of his owne behinde him, made an hard escape with the rest: for of one hundred and twentie

SWR M

Gallies, the *Romans* vnder *Cornelius* had lost but seuenteene, so as one hundred and three remained, which were not easily beaten by fiftie.

The *Romans*, being aduertised of *Cornelius* his ouerthrow, make haste to redeeme him, but giue the charge of their fleet to his Colleague, *Duilius*. *Duilius*, considering that the *Roman* vessells were heauie and slow, the *African* Gallies hauing the speede of them, deuised a certaine engine in the prow of his Gallies, where-by they might fasten or grapple themselues with their enemies, when they were (as we call it) boord and boord, that is, when they brought the Gallies sides together. This done, the waightier ships had gotten the aduantage, and the *Africans* lost it. For neither did their swiftnesse serue them, nor their Marriners craft; the Vessells wherein both Nations fought, being open: so that all was to be carried by the aduantage of weapon, and valour of the men. Besides this, as the heauier Gallies were likely to crush and crack the sides of the lighter and weaker, so were they, by reason of their breadth, more steadie; and those that best kept their feet, could also best vse their hands. The example may be giuen betweene one of the long boates of his Majesties great ships, and a *London-barge*.

Certainely, he that will happily performe a fight at Sea, must be skilfull in making choice of Vessells to fight in: he must beleeue, that there is more belonging to a good man of warre, vpon the waters, than great during; and must know, that there is a great deale of difference, betweene fighting loose or at large, and grapling. The Gunnes of a slow ship pierce as well, and make as great holes, as those in a swift. To clap ships together, without consideration, belongs rather to a mad man, than to a man of warre: for by such an ignorant brauerie was *Peter Strossie* lost at the *Azores*, when he fought against the *Marquesse of Santa Cruz*. In like sort had the Lord *Charles Howard*, Admirall of *England*, been lost in the yeare 1588. if he had not beene better aduised, than a great many malignant fooles were, that found fault with his demeanour. The *Spaniards* had an Armie aboord them; and he had none: they had more ships than he had, and of higher building and charging; so that, had he intangled himselfe with those great and powerfull Vessells, he had greatly endangered this Kingdome of *England*. For twentie men vpon the defences, are equall to an hundred that boord and enter; whereas then, contrariwise, the *Spaniards* had an hundred, for twentie of ours, to defend themselues withall. But our Admirall knew his aduantage, and held it: which had he not done, he had not beene worthie to haue held his head. Here to speake in generall of Sea-fight (for particulars are fitter for priuate hands, than for the Presse) I say, That a fleet of twentie ships, all good sailers, and good ships, haue the aduantage, on the open Sea, of an hundred as good ships, and of slower sayling. For if the fleet of an hundred saile keepe themselues neare together, in a grosse squadron; the twentie ships, charging them vpon any angle, shall force them to giue ground, and to fall back vpon their next fellowes: of which so many as intangle, are made vnseruiceable, or lost. Force them they may easily, because the twentie ships, which giue themselues scope, after they haue giuen one broad side of Artillerie, by clapping into the winde, and staying, they may giue them the other: and so the twentie ships batter them in peeces with a perpetuall vollie; whereas those, that fight in a troupe, haue no roome to turn, and can alwaies vse but one and the same beaten side. If the fleet of an hundred saile giue themselues any distance, then shall the lesser fleet preuaile, either against those that are a-reare and hindmost, or against those, that by aduantage of ouer-sailing their fellowes keepe the winde: and if vpon a Lee-shore, the ships next the winde be constrained to fall back into their owne squadron, then it is all to nothing, that the whole fleet must suffer shipwrack, or render it selfe. That such aduantage may be taken vpon a fleet of vnequall speede, it hath beene well enough conceiued in old time; as by that Oration of *Hermocrates*, in *Thucydides*, which he made to the *Syracusians*, when the *Athenians* inuaded them, it may easily be obserued.

Of the Art of Warre by Sea, I had written a Treatise, for the Lord *Henrie, Prince of Wales*; a subject, to my knowledge, neuer handled by any man, ancient or moderne: but God hath spared me the labour of finishing it, by his losse; by the losse of that braue Prince; of which, like an Eclypse of the Sunne, wee shall finde the effects hereafter. Impossible it is to equall wordes and sorrowes; I will therefore leaue him in the hands of God that hath him. *Curæ leues loquuntur, ingentes stupent. . .*[1]

§7. . . . *The Romans prepare to inuade Africk . . .*

§8. *The Romans preuaile in Africk . . .*

§9. *How the affaires of Carthage prospered after the victorie against* Atilivs: *How the Romans hauing lost their fleet by tempest, resolue to forsake the Seas: The great aduantages of a good fleet in warre, between Nations diuided by the Sea.*

By the reputation of this late victorie, all places that had beene lost in *Africk*, returned to the obedience of *Carthage*. Only *Clypea* stands out; before which the *Carthaginians* sit downe, and assaile it, but in vaine: For the *Romans*, hearing of the losse of *Atilius* with their forces in *Africk*, and withall, that *Clypea* was besieged, make readie a grosse Armie, and transport it in a fleet of three hundred and fiftie Gallies, commanded by *M. Æmilius*, and *Ser. Fuluius*, their Consulls. At the *Promontorie* of *Mercurie*, two hundred *Carthaginian* Gallies, set out of purpose, vpon the bruit of their comming, encounter them: but greatly to their cost. For the *Romans* tooke by force an hundred and fourteene of their fleet, and drew them after them to *Clypea*; where they staid no longer, than to take in their owne men that had beene besieged: and this done, they made amaine toward *Sicil*, in hope to recouer all that the *Carthaginians* held therein. In this hastie voyage they despise the aduice of the Pilots, who pray them to finde harbour in time, for that the season threatned some violent stormes; which euer hapned betweene the rising of *Orion*, and of the *Dog-starre*.[2] Now although the Pilots of the

---

[1] Seneca: 'light griefs find utterance; deep griefs are dumb' (G. E. Hadow, 1917).

[2] [Ralegh's marginal note:] There is no Part of the World, which hath not some certaine times of outragious weather besides their accidentall stormes. We haue vpon our coast a Michaelmas flaw, that seldome or neuer failes: In the west *Indies*, in the moneths of *August* and *September*, those most forcible winds, which the *Spaniards* call the *Nortes*, or Northwindes, are very fearefull: and therefore they that Nauigate in those parts, take harbour till those

Roman Fleet had thus fore-warned them of the weather at hand, and certified them withall, that the South coast of *Sicil* had no good Ports, wherein to saue themselues vpon such an accident: yet this victorious Nation was perswaded, that the winde and seas feared them no lesse, than did the *Africans;* and that they were able to conquer the Elements themselues. So refusing to stay within some Port, as they were aduised, they would needes put out to Sea; thinking it a matter much helping their reputation, after this victorie against the *Carthaginian* fleet; to take a few worthlesse Townes vpon the coast. The mercilesse windes in the meane while ouertake them, and neare vnto *Camerina*, ouerturne and thrust headlong on the rocks, all but fourescore of three hundred and fortie ships: so as their former great victorie was deuoured by the Seas, before the same thereof recouered *Rome.*

The *Carthaginians,* hearing what had hapned, repaire all their warlike Vessells, hoping once againe to command the Seas: they are also as confident of their land-forces since the ouerthrow of *Atilius.* They send *Asdrubal* into *Sicil* with all their old Souldiers, and an hundred and fortie Elephants, imbarqued in two hundred Gallies. With this Armie and fleet he arriues at *Lilybæum;* where hee beginnes to vexe the *Partisans* of *Rome.* But aduersitie doth not discourage the *Romans:* They build in three moneths (a matter of great note) one hundred and twentie ships; with which, and the remainder of their late shipwrack, they row to *Panormus*, or *Palerma*, the chiefe Citie of the *Africans* in *Sicil,* and surround it by Land and Water: after a while they take it, and leauing a Garrison therein, returne to *Rome.*

Very desirous the *Romans* were to bee doing in *Africk:* to which purpose they imploied *C. Seruilius*, and *C. Sempronius*, their Consulls. But these wrought no wonders. Some

moneths take end. *Charles* the fift being as ill aduised, in passing the Seas towards *Algire*, in the Winter quarter, contrarie to the counsaile of *A. Doria*, as he was in like vnseasonable times to continue his siege before *Metz* in *Loraine*, lost an hundred and fortie ships by tempest, and fifteene Gallies, with all in effect in them of men, victuailes, horses, and munition: a losse no lesse great, than his retrait, both from before the one and the other, was extreme dishonourable.

spoile they made vpon the coasts of *Africa:* but Fortune robbed them of all their gettings. For in their returne, they were first set vpon the sands, and like to haue perished, neare vnto the lesser *Syrtes,* where they were faine to heaue all ouer-boord, that so they might get off: then, hauing with much a-doe doubled the Cape of *Lilybæum,* in their passage from *Panormus* towards *Italie,* they lost an hundred and fiftie of their ships by foule weather. A greater discouragement neuer Nation had; the God of the warres fauoured them no more, than the God of the waters afflicted them. Of all that *Mars* enricht them with vpon the Land, *Neptune* robbed them vpon the Seas. For they had now lost, besides what they lost in fight, foure hundred and sixe ships and gallies, with all the munition and Souldiers transported in them.

The exceeding damage hereby receiued, perswaded them to giue ouer their Nauigation, and their fight by Sea, and to send only a Land-armie into *Sicil,* vnder *L. Cæcilius,* and *C. Furius,* their Consulls. These they transported in some threescore ordinarie passage-boats, by the straights of *Messana,* that are not aboue a mile and an halfe broad from land to land. In like sort, the ouerthrow which *Atilius* receiued in *Africa,* occasioned chiefly by the Elephants, made them lesse cholerick against the *Carthaginians,* than before; so that for two yeares after they kept the high and woodie grounds, not daring to fight in the faire and champian Countries. But this late resolution of forsaking the Seas lasted not long. For it was impossible for them to succour those places which they held in *Sicil,* without a Nauie, much lesse to maintaine the warre in *Africa.* For whereas the *Romans* were to send forces from *Messana* to *Egesta,* to *Lilybæum,* and to other places in the extreme West parts of *Sicil,* making sometimes a march of aboue an hundred and fortie *English* miles by land, which could not be performed with an Armie, and the prouisions that follow it, in lesse than fourteene daies; the *Carthaginians* would passe it with their Gallies, in eight and fortie houres.

An old example we haue, of that great aduantage of transporting Armies by water, betweene *Canutus,* and *Edmond Ironside.* For *Canutus,* when he had entred the

Thames with his Nauie and Armie, and could not preuaile against *London*, suddenly imbarqued; and sailing to the West, landed in *Dorset-shire*, so drawing *Edmond* and his Armie thither. There finding ill entertainement, he againe shipt his men, and entred the *Seuerne*, making *Edmond* to march after him, to the succour of *Worcestershire*, by him greatly spoiled. But when he had *Edmond* there, he sailed back againe to *London:* by meanes whereof, he both wearied the King, and spoiled where he pleased, ere succour could arriue. And this was not the least helpe, which the *Netherlands* haue had against the *Spaniards*, in the defence of their libertie, that being Masters of the Sea, they could passe their Armie from place to place, vnwearied, and entire, with all the Munition and Artillerie belonging vnto it, in the tenth part of the time, wherein their enemies haue beene able to doe it. Of this, an instance or two. The Count *Maurice* of *Nassau*, now liuing, one of the greatest Captaines, and of the worthiest Princes, that either the present or preceding Ages haue brought forth, in the yeare 1590. carried his Armie by Sea, with fortie Canons, to *Breda:* making countenance either to besiege *Boisleduc*, or *Gertreuiden-Berg;* which the enemie (in preuention) filled with Souldiers, and victualls. But as soone as the winde serued, he suddenly set saile, and arriuing in the mouth of the *Meuze*, turned vp the *Rhine*, and thence to *Yssel*, and sate downe before *Zutphen*. So before the *Spaniards* could march ouer land round about *Holland*, aboue fourescore mile, and ouer many great Riuers, with their Cannon and carriage, *Zutphen* was taken. Againe, when the *Spanish* Armie had ouer-come this wearisome march, and were now farre from home, the Prince *Maurice*, making countenance to saile vp the *Rhine*, changed his course in the night; and sailing downe the streame, he was set downe before *Hulst* in *Brabant*, ere the *Spaniards* had knowledge what was become of him. So this Towne he also tooke, before the *Spanish* armie could returne. Lastly, the *Spanish* armie was no sooner arriued in *Brabant*, than the Prince *Maurice*, well attended by his good fleet, hauing fortified *Hulst*, set saile againe, and presented himselfe before *Nymegen* in *Gelders*, a Citie of notable importance, and mastred it.

And to say the truth, it is impossible for any maritime Countrie, not hauing the coasts admirably fortified, to defend it selfe against a powerfull enemie, that is master of the Sea. Hereof I had rather, that *Spaine* than *England* should be an example. Let it therefore be supposed, that King *Philip* the second, had fully resolued to hinder Sir *Iohn Norris* in the yeare 1589. from presenting *Don Antonio*, King of *Portugale*, before the gates of *Lysborne;* and that he would haue kept off the *English*, by power of his land-forces; as being too weake at Sea, through the great ouerthrow of his mightie *Armada*, by the fleet of Queene *Elizabeth*, in the yeare foregoing. Surely, it had not beene hard for him, to prepare an Armie, that should be able to resist our eleuen thousand. But where should this his Armie haue beene bestowed? If about *Lysborne;* then would it haue beene easie vnto the *English*, to take, ransack, and burne the Towne of *Groine*, and to waste the Countrie round about it. For the great and threatning preparations, of the Earle of *Altemira*, the Marquesse of *Seralba*, and others, did not hinder them from performing all this. Neither did the hastie leauie of eight thousand, vnder the Earle of *Andrada*, serue to more effect, than the increase of honour to S^r. *Iohn Norris*, and his Associates: considering, that the *English* charged these, at *Puente de Burgos*, and passing the great Bridge, behinde which they lay, that was flanked with shot, and barricadoed at the further end, routed them; tooke their campe; tooke their Generalls standard with the Kings Armes, and pursued them ouer all the Countrie, which they fired. If a roiall Armie, and not (as this was) a Companie of priuate aduen-turers, had thus begunne the warre in *Galicia;* I thinke it would haue made the *Spaniards* to quit the guard of *Portu-gale*, and make haste to the defence of their S^t. *Iago*, whose Temple was not farre from the danger. But, had they held their first resolution; as knowing, that Sir *Iohn Norris* his maine intent was, to bring *Don Antonio*, with an Armie, into his Kingdome, whither comming strong, he expected to be readily and joyfully welcomed: could they haue hindred his landing in *Portugale?* Did not he land at *Penicha,* and march ouer the Countrie to *Lysborne*, six daies journie? Did not he (when all *Don Antonio* his promises failed) passe along by

the Riuer of *Lysborne* to *Cascaliz*, and there, hauing wonne
the Fort, quietly imbarque his men, and depart? But these,
though no more than an handfull, yet were they *Englishmen*.
Let vs consider of the matter it selfe; what an other Nation
might doe, euen against *England*, in landing an Armie, by
aduantage of a fleet, if we had none. This question, *Whether
an inuading Armie be resisted at their landing vpon the coast of
England, were there no fleet of ours at the Sea to impeach it;*
is alreadie handled by a learned Gentleman of our Nation, in
his obseruations vpon *Cæsars* Commentaries,[1] that main-
taines the affirmatiue. This he holds only vpon supposition;
in absence of our shipping: and comparatiuely; as, that it is a
more safe and easie course, to defend all the coast of *England*,
than to suffer an enemie to land, and afterwards to fight with
him. Surely I hold with him, that it is the best way, to keepe
our enemie from treading vpon our ground: wherein, if we
faile, then must we seeke to make him wish, that he had
staied at his owne home. In such a case, if it should happen,
our judgements are to weigh many particular circumstances,
that belong not vnto this discourse. But making the question
generall, and positiue, *Whether England, without helpe of her
fleet, be able to debarre an enemie from landing;* I hold that it is
vnable so to doe: and therefore I thinke it most dangerous to
make the aduenture. For the incouragement of a first
victorie to an enemie, and the discourgement of being beaten
to the inuaded, may draw after it a most perilous consequence.

It is true, that the Marshall *Monluc,* in his Commentaries,
doth greatly complaine, that by his wanting forces, wherewith to haue kept the frontier of *Guienne*, they of the *Protestant* religion, after the battaile of *Moncounter*, entred that
Countrie, and gathered great strength and reliefe thence;
for if the King (saith he) would haue giuen me but reasonable meanes, *j eusebien garde a Monsieur l'Admiral, de faire
boire ses Cheuaux en la Garonne; I would haue kept the
Admiral from watering his horses in the Riuer of Garonne.
Monsieur de Langey,* on the contrarie side, preferres the
not fighting vpon a frontier with an inuading enemie, and

---

[1] Sir Clement Edmondes, in his *Obseruations upon Cæsars Commentaries*
(1600).

commends the delay; which course the Constable of *France* held, against the Emperour *Charles*, when he inuaded *Prouence*. Great difference I know there is, and a diuerse consideration to be had, betweene such a Countrie as *France* is, strengthned with many fortified places; and this of ours, where our Rampars are but of the bodies of men. And it was of inuasions vpon firme land, that these great Captaines spake: whose entrances cannot be vncertaine. But our question is, of an Armie to be transported ouer Sea, and to be landed againe in an enemies Countrie, and the place left to the choice of the Inuader. Hereunto I say, That such an Armie cannot be resisted on the coast of *England*, without a fleet to impeach it; no, nor on the coast of *France*, or any other Countrie: except euery Creeke, Port, or sandie Bay, had a powerfull Armie, in each of them, to make opposition. For let this whole supposition be granted; That *Kent* is able to furnish twelue thousand foot; and that those twelue thousand be laied in the three best landing places within that Countie, to wit, three thousand at *Margat*, three thousand at the *Nesse*, and sixe thousand at *Foulkston*, that is somewhat equally distant from them both; as also that two of these troups (vnlesse some other order be thought more fit) be directed to strengthen the third, when they shall see the enemies fleet to bend towards it: I say, that notwith-standing this prouision, if the enemie, setting saile from the Isle of *Wight*, in the first watch of the night, and towing their long boats at their sternes, shall arriue by dawne of day at the *Nesse*, and thrust their Armie on shore there; it will be hard for those three thousand that are at *Margat* (twentie and foure long miles from thence) to come time enough to re-enforce their fellowes at the *Nesse*. Nay, how shall they at *Foulkston* bee able to doe it, who are nearer by more than halfe the way? seeing that the enemie, at his first arriuall, will either make his entrance by force, with three or foure hundred shot of great Artillerie, and quickly put the first three thousand, that were intrenched at the *Nesse*, to runne; or else giue them so much to doe, that they shall be glad to send for helpe to *Foulkston*; and perhaps to *Margat*: wherby those places will be left bare. Now let vs suppose, that all the twelue thousand *Kentish* Souldiers arriue at the *Nesse*,

ere the enemie can be readie to disimbarque his Armie, so
that he shall finde it vnsafe, to land in the face of so many,
prepared to withstand him; yet must we beleeue, that he
will play the best of his owne game; and (hauing libertie to
goe which way he list) vnder couert of the night, set saile
towards the East, where what shall hinder him to take
ground, either at *Margat*, the *Downes*, or elsewhere, before
they at the *Nesse* can be well aware of his departure?
Certainely, there is nothing more easie than to doe it. Yea
the like may bee said of *Weymouth*, *Purbeck*, *Poole*, and of all
landing places on the South coast. For there is no man
ignorant, that ships, without putting themselues out of
breath, will easily out-runne the Souldiers that coast them.
*Les Armees ne volent poynt en poste; Armies neither flie, nor
runne post*, saith a Marshall of *France*. And I know it to be
true, that a fleet of ships may be seene at Sunne-set, and after
it, at the *Lisard*; yet by the next morning they may recouer
Portland, whereas an Armie of foot shall not bee able to
march it in sixe daies. Againe, when those troups, lodged on
the Sea-shores, shall be forced to runne from place to place,
in vaine, after a fleet of ships; they will at length sit downe
in the mid-way, and leaue all at aduenture. But say it were
otherwise; That the inuading enemie will offer to land in
some such place, where there shall be an Armie of ours
readie to receiue him; yet it cannot be doubted, but that
when the choice of all our trained bands, and the choice of our
Commanders and Captaines, shall be drawne together (as
they were at *Tilburie* in the yeare 1588) to attend the person
of the Prince, and for the defence of the Citie of *London:* they
that remaine to guard the coast, can be of no such force, as
to encounter an Armie like vnto that, wherewith it was
intended that the Prince of *Parma* should haue landed in
England.

The Ile of *Tercera* hath taught vs by experience, what to
thinke in such a case. There are not many Ilands in the
world better fenced by nature and strengthned by art: it
being euery where hard of accesse; hauing no good harbour
wherein to shelter a Nauie of friends; and vpon euery coue or
watering place a Fort erected, to forbid the approch of an
enemie boat. Yet when *Emanuel de Sylua*, and *Monsieur de*

Chattes, that held it to the vse of *Don Antonio*, with fiue or sixe thousand men, thought to haue kept the *Marquesse of Santa Cruz*, from setting foot on ground therin; the Marquesse hauing shewed himselfe in the Roade of *Angra*, did set saile, ere any was aware of it, and arriued at the *Port des Moles*, farre distant from thence, where hee wanne a Fort, and landed, ere *Monsieur de Chattes*, running thither in vaine, could come to hinder him. The example of *Philip Strossie*, slaine the yeare before, without all regard of his worth, and of three hundred *French* prisoners murdered in cold bloud, had instructed *de Chattes* and his followers, what they might expect at that Marquesse his hands: Therefore it is not like, that they were slow in carrying reliefe to *Port des Moles*. Whether our *English* would bee perswaded to make such diligent haste, from *Margat* to the *Nesse*, and back againe, it may bee doubted. Sure I am, that it were a greater march than all the length of *Tercera*; whereof the *French-men* had not measured the one halfe, when they found themselues preuented by the more nimble ships of *Spaine*.

This may suffice to proue, that a strong Armie, in a good fleet, which neither foot, nor horse, is able to follow, cannot be denied to land where it list, in *England*, *France*, or elsewhere, vnlesse it be hindred, encountred, and shuffled together, by a fleet of equall, or answerable strength.

The difficult landing of our *English*, at *Fayal*, in the yeare 1597.[1] is alleaged against this: which example moues me no way to thinke, that a large coast may bee defended against a strong fleet. I landed those *English* in *Fayal*, my selfe, and therefore ought to take notice of this instance. For whereas I finde an action of mine cited, with omission of my name; I may, by a ciuill interpretation, thinke, that there was no purpose to defraud me of any honour; but rather an opinion, that the enterprise was such, or so ill managed, as that no honour could be due vnto it. There were indeede some which were in that voiage, who aduised me not to vndertake it: and I hearkned vnto them, somewhat longer than was requisite, especially, whilest they desired me, to reserue the

---

[1] While preying on Spanish ships from the West Indies, Essex and Ralegh agreed to meet at Fayal in the Azores. Relegh arrived first and, to the intense irritation of Essex, stormed Fayal.

title of such an exploit (though it were not great) for a greater person. But when they began to tell me of difficultie: I gaue them to vnderstand, the same which I now maintaine, that it was more difficult to defend a coast, than to inuade it. The truth is, that I could haue landed my men with more ease than I did; yea without finding any resistance, if I would haue rowed to another place; yea euen there where I landed, if I would haue taken more companie to helpe me. But, without fearing any imputation of rashnesse, I may say, that I had more regard of reputation, in that businesse, than of safetie. For I thought it to belong vnto the honor of our Prince & Nation, that a few Ilanders should not thinke any aduantage great enough, against a fleet set forth by Q. *Elizabeth:* and further, I was vnwilling, that some *Low-Countrie* Captaines, and others, not of mine owne squadron, whose assistance I had refused, should please themselues with a sweet conceipt (though it would haue been short, when I had landed in some other place) *That for want of their helpe I was driuen to turne taile.* Therefore I tooke with me none, but men assured, Cōmanders of mine owne squadron, with some of their followers, and a few other Gentlemen, voluntaries, whom I could not refuse; as, Sir *William Brooke,* Sir *William Haruey,* Sir *Arthur Gorges,* Sir *Iohn Skot,* Sir *Thomas Ridgeway,* Sir *Henri Thinne,* Sir *Charles Morgan,* Sir *Walter Chute, Marcellus Throckmorton,* Captaine *Laurence Kemis,* Captaine *William Morgan,* and others, such as well vnderstood themselues and the enemie: by whose helpe, with Gods fauour, I made good the enterprise I vndertooke. As for the *working of the Sea, the steepnesse of the Cliffes,* and other troubles, that were not new to vs, we ouercame them well enough. And these (notwithstanding) made fiue or sixe Companies of the enemies, that sought to impeach our landing, abandon the wall, whereon their Musketiers lay on the rest for vs, and wonne the place of them without any great losse. This I could haue done with lesse danger, so that it should not haue serued for example of a rule, that failed euen in this example: but the reasons before alleaged, (together with other reasons well knowne to some of the Gentlemen aboue named, though more priuate, than to be here laid downe) made me rather follow the way

of brauerie, and take the shorter course; hauing it still in
mine owne power to fall off, when I should thinke it meet.
It is easily said, that *the Enemie was more than a Coward*;
(which yet was more than we knew) neither will I magnifie
such a small peece of seruice, by seeking to proue him better:
whom had I thought equall to mine owne followers, I would
otherwise haue dealt with. But for so much as concernes the
Proposition in hand; he that beheld this, may well remember,
that the same enemie troubled vs more in our march towards
Fayal, than in our taking the shore; that he sought how to
stop vs in place of his aduantage; that many of our men were
slaine or hurt by him, among whom Sir *Arthur Gorges* was
shot in that march; and that such, as (thinking all danger to
bee past, when wee had wonne good footing), would needes
follow vs to the Towne, were driuen by him, to forsake the
pace of a man of warre, and betake themselues to an hastie trot.

For end of this digression, I hope that this question shall
neuer come to triall; his Majesties many moueable Forts
will forbid the experience. And although the *English* will no
lesse disdaine, than any Nation vnder heauen can doe, to be
beaten vpon their owne ground, or elsewhere, by a forraigne
enemie; yet to entertaine those that shall assaile vs, with their
owne beefe in their bellies, and before they eate of our
Kentish Capons, I take to be the wisest way. To doe which,
his Majestie, after God, will imploy his good ships on the
Sea, and not trust to any intrenchment vpon the shore.

§10. *How the Romans attempt againe to get the mastrie of the
      Seas* . . .

§11. . . . *The condition of the peace between Rome and Carthage.*

Ch. II. *Of diuers actions passing betweene the first and second Punick Warres*

§1. *Of the cruell warre begunne betweene the Carthaginians and their owne Mercinaries.*

§2. *Diuerse obseruations vpon this warre with the mercinaries.*

†1. *Of Tyrannie, and how tyrants are driuen to vse helpe of mercinaries.*

Here let vs rest awhile, as in a conuenient breathing place: whence wee may take prospect of the subiect, ouer which wee trauaile. Behold a tyrannicall Citie, persecuted by her owne mercinaries with a deadlie warre. It is a common thing, as being almost necessarie, that a tyrannie should bee vpheld by mercinarie forces: it is common that mercinaries should be false: and it is common, that all warre, made against Tyrants, should be exceeding full of hate and crueltie. Yet wee seldome heare, that the ruine of a Tyrannie is procured or sought, by those that were hired to maintaine the power of it: and seldome or neuer doe we reade of any warre, that hath beene prosecuted with such inexpiable hatred, as this that is now in hand.

That which wee properly call Tyrannie, is *A violent forme of gouernment, not respecting the good of the subiect, but onely the pleasure of the Commander.* I purposely forbeare to say, that it is the vniust rule of one ouer many: for verie truely doth *Cleon* in *Thucydides* tell the *Athenians,* that their dominion ouer their subiects, was none other than a meere tyrannie; though it were so, that they themselues were a great Citie, and a Popular estate. Neither is it peraduenture greatly needfull, that I should call this forme of commanding, *violent:* since it may well and easily bee conceiued, that no man willingly performes obedience, to one regardlesse of his life and welfare; vnlesse himselfe bee either a mad man, or (which is little better) wholly possessed with some extreme passion of loue. The practise of tyrannie, is not alwaies of a like extremitie: for some Lords are more gentle, than others, to their very slaues; and he that is most cruell to some, is milde enough towards others, though it be but for his owne aduantage. Neuerthelesse, in large Dominions, wherein the Rulers discretion cannot extend itselfe, vnto notice of the difference which might bee found betweene the worth of seuerall men; it is commonly seene, that the taste of sweetnesse, drawne out of oppression, hath so good a rellish, as continually inflames the Tyrants appetite, and will not suffer it to be restrained with any limits of respect. Why should hee seeke out bounds, to prescribe vnto his desires, who cannot endure the face of one so honest, as may put him in remembrance of any moderation? It is much that hee hath gotten, by extorting from some few: by sparing none, hee should haue riches in goodly abundance. He hath taken a great deale from euery one: but euery one could haue spared more. He hath wrung all their purses, and now hee hath enough: but (as Couetousnesse is neuer satisfied) he thinkes that all this is too little for a stock, though it were indeede a good yearlie Income. Therefore he deuiseth new tricks of robberie, and is not better pleased with the gaines, than with the Art of getting. He is hated for this; and he knowes it well: but hee thinkes by crueltie to change hatred into feare. So he makes it his exercise, to torment and murder all, whom he suspecteth: in which course, if he suspect none vnjustly, he may be said to deale craftily; but if Innocencie be not safe, how can all this make any Conspiratour to stand in feare, since the Traitor is no worse rewarded, than the quiet man? Wherefore hee can thinke vpon none other securitie, than to disarme all his Subjects; to fortifie himselfe within some strong place; and for defence of his Person and state, to hire as many lustie Souldiers as shall bee thought sufficient. These must not bee of his owne Countrie: for if not euery one, yet some one or other, might chance to haue a feeling of the publique miserie. This considered, he allures vnto him a desperate rabble of strangers, the most vnhonest that can bee found; such as haue neither wealth nor credit at home, and will therefore be carefull to support him, by whose only fauour they are maintayned. Now lest any of these, either by detestation of his wickednesse, or (which in wicked men is most likely) by promise of greater reward, than he doth giue, should bee drawne to turne his sword against the Tyrant himselfe: they shall all be permitted to doe as hee doth; to robbe, to rauish, to murder, and to satisfie their owne appetites, in most outragious manner; being thought so much the more assured to their Master, by how much the more he sees them grow hatefull to all men else. Considering in what Age, and in what Language I write; I must be faine to say, that these are not dreames: though some *English-man* perhaps, that were vnacquainted with Historie, lighting vpon this leafe, might suppose this discourse to be little better. This is to shew, both how tyrannie growes to stand in neede of mercinarie Souldiers, and how those Mercinaries are, by mutuall obligation, firmely assured vnto the Tyrant.

†2. *That the tyrannie of a Citie ouer her Subiects is worse, than the tyrannie of one man: and that a tyrannicall Citie must likewise vse mercinarie Souldiers.*

Now concerning the tyrannie, wherewith a Citie or State oppresseth her Subjects; it may appeare some waies to be more moderate, than that of one man: but in many things it is more intolerable. A Citie is jealous of her Dominion; but not (as is one man) fearefull of her life: the lesse neede hath shee therefore, to secure her selfe by crueltie. A Citie is not luxurious in consuming her treasures; and therefore needes the lesse, to pluck from her Subjects. If warre, or any other great occasion, driue her to necessitie, of taking from her Subjects more than ordinarie summes of monie: the same necessitie makes either the contribution easie, or the taking excusable. Indeede, no wrongs are so grieuous and hatefull, as those that are insolent. *Remember* (saith *Caligula* the Emperor, to his Grand-mother *Antonia*) *that I may doe what I list, and to whom I list:* these wordes were accounted horrible, though he did her no harme. And *Iuuenal* reckons it, as the complement of all torments, inflicted by a cruell *Roman* Dame vpon her slaues; that whilest shee was whipping them, shee painted her face, talked with her Gossips, and vsed all signes of neglecting what those wretches felt. Now seeing that the greatest grieuances, wherwith a domineering State offendeth her Subjects, are free from all sense of indignitie: likely it is, that they will not extremely hate her, although desire of libertie make them wearie of her Empire. In these respects it is not needfull, that shee should

keepe a Guard of licentious cut-throts, and maintaine them
in all villanie, as a *Dionysius* or *Agathocles* must doe: her
owne Citizens are able to terrifie, and to hold perforce in
obedience, all male-contents. These things, considered alone
by themselues, may serue to proue, That a Citie is scarce able
to deserue the name of a Tyrannesse, in the proper signification.

   All this notwithstanding, it shall appeare, That the
miseries, wherewith a Tyrant lodeth his people, are not so
heauie, as the burdens imposed by a cruell Citie. Not without
some apparance of truth, it may bee said, that Lust, and
many other priuate passions, are no way incident to a Citie
or Corporation. But to make this good, wee shall haue neede
to vse the helpe of such distinctions, as the Argument in
hand doth not require. Was not *Rome* lasciuious, when *Cato*
was faine to rise and leaue the Theater, to the end, that the
reuerend regard of his grauitie, might not hinder the people
from calling for a shew of naked Courtisans, that were to
be brought vpon the open stage? By cõmon practise, and
generall approued custome, we are to censure the qualitie
of a whole State; not by the priuate vertue or vice, of any one
man; nor by metaphysicall abstraction, of *the vniuersall* from
the singular; or of *the Corporation*, from *those of whom it is
compounded*. I say therefore (as I haue said elsewhere) That
it were better to liue vnder one pernicious Tyrant, than
vnder many thousands. The reasons, prouing this, are too
many to set downe: but few may suffice. The desires of one
man, how inordinate soeuer, if they cannot be satisfied, yet
they may be wearied; hee is not able to search all corners;
his humour may be found, and soothed; age, or good aduice,
yea, or some vnexpected accident, may reforme him: all
which failing, yet is there hope, that his Successour may
proue better. Many Tyrants haue beene changed into
worthie Kings: and many haue ill vsed their ill-gotten
Dominion, which becomming hereditarie to their posteritie,
hath growne into the most excellent forme of Gouernement, euen a lawfull Monarchie. But they that liue vnder a
tyrannicall Citie, haue no such hope: their Mistresse is
immortall, and will not slacken the reines, vntill they bee
pulled out of her hands; and her owne mouth receiue the

bridle of a more mightie Chariotier. This is wofull: yet their
present sufferings make them lesse mindfull of the future.
New flies, and hungrie ones, fall vpon the same sore, out
of which, others had alreadie sucked their fill. A new
Gouernour comes yearly among them, attended by all his
poore kindred and friends, who meane not to returne home
emptie to their hiues, without a good lading of waxe and
honie. These flie into all quarters, and are quickly acquainted
with euery mans wealth, or whatsoeuer else, in all the
Prouince, is worthie to be desired. They know all a mans
enemies, and all his feares: becomming themselues, within a
little space, the enemies that he feareth most. To grow into
acquaintance with these masterfull guests, in hope to win
their friendship, were an endlesse labour (yet it must be
vnder-gone) and such as euery one hath not meanes to goe
about: but were this effected, what auaileth it? The loue of
one Gouernour is purchased with gifts: the Successour of
this man, he is more louing than could be wished, in respect
of a faire Wife or Daughter: then comes the third, perhaps of
the contrarie faction at home, a bitter enemie to both his
fore-goers, who seekes the ruine of all that haue beene
inward with them. So the miseries of this tyrannie are not
simple; but interlaced (as it were) with the calamities of
ciuill warre. The *Romans* had a Law *De Repetundis*, or *Of
Recouerie*, against extorting Magistrates: yet wee finde, that
it serued not wholly to restraine their Prouinciall Gouernours; who presuming on the fauour of their owne Citizens,
and of their kindred and friends at home, were bold in their
Prouinces, to worke all these enormities rehearsed; though
somewhat the more sparingly, for feare of judgement. If the
subjects of *Rome* groned vnder such oppressions; what must
we thinke of those, that were vassalls vnto *Carthage?* The
Romans imposed no burthensome tributes; they loued not to
heare, that their Empire was grieuous; they condemned
many noble Citizens, for hauing beene ill Gouernours. At
Carthage all went quite contrarie: the rapines newly deuised
by one Magistrate, serued as presidents[1] to instruct another;
euery man resolued to doe the like, when it should fall to his
turne; and he was held a notable statesman, whose robberies

[1] i.e. precedents.

had beene such, as might affoord a good share to the common treasure. Particular examples of this *Carthaginian* practise, are not extant: the gouernement of *Verres* the *Roman*, in *Sicil*, that is liuely set out by *Tullie*, may serue to informe vs, what was the demeanour of these *Punick Rulers*, who stood in feare of no such condemnation, as *Verres* vnder-went. By prosequuting this discourse, I might inferre a more generall Proposition; That a Citie cannot gouerne her subject Prouinces so mildly, as a King: but it is enough to haue shewed, That the tyrannie of a Citie is farre more intolerable, than that of any one most wicked man.

Suteable to the crueltie of such Lords, is the hatred of their subjects: and againe, suteable to the hatred of the subjects, is the jealousie of their Lords. Hence it followed, that, in warres abroad, the *Carthaginians* durst vse the seruice of *African* souldiers; in *Africk* it selfe, they had rather bee beholding to others, that were farther fetcht. For the same purpose did *Hannibal*, in the second *Punick Warre*, shift his mercinaries out of their owne Countries; . . . *That the Africans might serue in Spaine, the Spaniards in Africk, being each of them like to proue the better Souldiers, the farther they were from home, as if they were obliged by mutuall pledges.* It is disputable, I confesse, whether these *African*, and *Spanish* hirelings, could properly be termed *Mercinaries*: for they were subject vnto *Carthage*, and carried into the field, not only by reward, but by dutie. Yet seeing their dutie was no better than enforced, and that it was not any loue to the State, but meere desire of gaine, that made them fight, I will not nicely stand vpon proprietie of a word, but hold them, as *Polybius* also doth, no better than Mercinaries.

†3. *The dangers growing from the vse of mercinarie Souldiers, and forraigne Auxiliaries.*

The extreme danger, growing from the imploiment of such Souldiers, is well obserued by *Machiauel:* who sheweth, that they are more terrible to those whom they serue, than to those against whom they serue. They are seditious, vnfaith-full, disobedient, deuouers, and destroiers of all places and countries, whereinto they are drawne; as being held by no other bond, than their owne commoditie. Yea, that which is most fearefull among such hirelings, is, that they haue often, and in time of greatest extremitie, not only refused to fight, in their defence, who haue entertained them, but reuolted vnto the contrarie part; to the vtter ruine of those Princes and States, that haue trusted them. These Mercinaries (saith *Machiauel*) which filled all *Italie*, when *Charles* the eighth of *France* did passe the *Alpes*, were the cause that the said *French* King wonne the Realme of *Naples*, with his Buckler without a sword. Notable was the example of *Sforza*, the Father of *Francis Sforza*, Duke of *Millan*; who being entertained by Queene *Ioane* of *Naples*, abandoned her seruice on the sudden; and forced her to put her selfe into the hands of the King of *Arragon*. Like vnto his father was *Francis Sforza*, the first of that race Duke of *Millan:* who, being entertained by the *Millanois*, forced them to become his slaues; euen with the same Armie which themselues had leuied for their own defence. But *Lodouick Sforza*, the sonne of this *Francis*, by the just judgement of God, was made a memorable example vnto posteritie, in loosing his whole estate by the trecherie of such faithlesse Mercinaries, as his owne father had beene. For, hauing waged an Armie of *Switzers*, and committed his Duchie, together with his person, into their hands; he was by them deliuered vp vnto his enemie the *French* King, by whom he was inclosed in the Castle of *Loches* to his dying day.

The like inconuenience is found, in vsing the helpe of forraigne Auxiliaries. We see, that when the Emperor of *Constantinople* had hired ten thousand *Turkes*, against his neighbour Princes; he could neuer, either by perswasion or force, set them againe ouer Sea vpon *Asia* side: which gaue beginning to the *Christian* seruitude, that soone after followed. *Alexander*, the sonne of *Cassander*, sought aide of the great *Demetrius:* but *Demetrius*, being entred into his Kingdome, slue the same *Alexander* who had inuited him, and made himselfe King of *Macedon*. *Syracon* the *Turke* was called into *Ægypt* by *Sanar* the *Soldan*, against his Opposite: but this *Turke* did settle himselfe so surely in *Ægypt*, that *Saladine* his Successour became Lord thereof; and of all *the holy Land*, soone after. What neede we looke about for examples of this kinde? Euery Kingdome, in effect, can furnish vs. The *Britaines* drew the *Saxons* into this our

Countrie; and *Mac Murrough* drew the *English* into *Ireland*: but the one and the other soone became Lords of those two Kingdomes.

Against all this may be alleaged, the good successe of the vnited Prouinces of the *Netherlands*, vsing none other than such kinde of Souldiers, in their late warre. Indeede these *Low Countries* haue many goodly and strong Cities, filled with Inhabitants that are wealthie, industrious, and valiant in their kinde. They are stout Sea men, and therein is their excellencie; neither are they bad, at the defence of a place well fortified: but in open field they haue seldome beene able to stand against the *Spaniard*. Necessitie therefore compelled them to seeke helpe abroad: and the like necessitie made them forbeare to arme any great numbers of their owne. For, with monie raised by their Trade, they maintayned the warre: and therefore could ill spare, vnto the Pike and Musket, those hands, that were of more vse in helping to fill the common purse. Yet what of this? they sped well. Surely they sped as ill as might be, whilest they had none other than mercinarie Souldiers. Many fruitlesse attempts, made by the Prince of *Orange*, can witnesse it: and that braue Commander, Count *Lodowick of Nassau*, felt it to his griefe, in his retrait from *Groeninghen*; when in the very instant, that required their seruice in fight, his mercinaries cried out aloud for monie, and so ranne away. This was not the only time, when the hired souldiers of the *States*, haue either sought to hide their cowardize vnder a shew of greedinesse; or at least, by meere couetousnesse, haue ruined in one houre the labour of many moneths. I will not stand to proue this by many examples: for they themselues will not denie it. Neither would I touch the honour of *Monsieur* the Duke of *Aniou*, brother to the *French* King; saue that it is follie to conceale what all the world knowes. He that would lay open the danger of forraine Auxiliaries, needeth no better patterne. It is commonly found, that such Aiders make themselues Lords ouer those, to whom they lend their succour: but where shall we meet with such another as this *Monsieur*, who, for his protection promised, being rewarded with the Lordship of the Countrie, made it his first worke, to thrust by violence a galling yoke vpon the peoples neck?

Well, hee liued to repent it, with griefe enough. Euen whilest he was counterfeiting vnto those about him, that were ignorant of his plot, an imaginarie sorrow for the poore Burghers of *Antwerpe*, as verily beleeuing the Towne to bee surprised and wonne; the death of the Count S^t. *Aignan*, who fell ouer the wall, and the Cannon of the Citie, discharged against his owne troupes, informed him better what had hapned; shewing that they were his owne *French*, who stood in neede of pittie. Then was his fained passion changed, into a very bitter anguish of minde; wherein, smiting his breast, and wringing his hands, he exclaimed, *Helas, mon Dieu, que veulx tu faire de moy*; *Alas, my God, what wilt thou doe with me?* So the affaires of the *Netherlands* will not serue to proue, that there is litle danger in vsing mercinarie souldiers, or the helpe of forraine Auxiliaries. This not-withstanding they were obedient vnto necessitie, and sought helpe of the *English, Scots,* and *French:* wherein they did wisely, and prospered. For when there was in *France* a King, partaker with them in the same danger; when the Queen of *England* refused to accept the Soueraigntie of their Countrie, which they offered, yet being prouoked by the *Spaniard* their enemie, pursued him with continuall warre; when the heire of *England* raigned in *Scotland*, a King too just and wise (though not ingaged in any quarrell) either to make profit of his Neighbours miseries, or to helpe those that had attempted the conquest of his owne inheritance: then might the *Netherlanders* very safely repose confidence, in the forces of these their Neighbour-Countries. The souldiers that came vnto them from hence, were (to omit many other commendations) not only regardfull of the pay that they should receiue; but well affected vnto the cause that they tooke in hand: or if any were cold in his deuotion, to the side whereon he fought; yet was he kept in order, by remembrance of his owne home, where the *English* would haue rewarded him with death, if his faith had beene corrupted by the *Spaniard*. They were therefore trusted with the custodie of Cities; they were held as friends, and patrons; the necessitie of the poorer sort was relieued, before the pay-day came, with *lendings*, and other helps, as well as the abilitie of the States could permit. When three such Princes, raigning at one time, shall agree so well, to maintaine against the power of a fourth, injurious (or at least so seeming) to them all, a Neighbour-Countrie, of the same Religion, and to which they all are louingly affected: then may such a Countrie be secure of her Auxiliaries, and quietly intend her Trade, or other businesse, in hope of like successe. But these circumstances meet so seldome, as it may well hold true in generall, *That mercinarie, and forraigne auxiliarie forces, are no lesse dangerous, than the enemie, against whom they are entertained.*

†4. *That the moderate gouernment of the Romans gaue them assurance to vse the seruice of their owne subiects in their warres. That in mans nature there is an affection breeding tyrannie, which hindreth the vse and benefit of the like moderation.*

Here may it be demanded, whether also the *Romans* were not compelled to vse seruice of other souldiours in their many great warres, but performed all by their owne citizens? for if it were their manner to arme their owne subiects; how happened it, that they feared no rebellion? if strangers; how then could they auoide the inconueniences aboue rehearsed? The answere is; That their Armies were compounded vsuallie of their owne citizens, and of the *Latines*, in equall number: to which they added, as occasion required, some companies of the *Campanes*, *Hetrurians*, *Samnites*, or other of their subiects, as were either interested in the quarrell, or might best be trusted. They had, about these times, (though seldome they did implie so many,) tenne Roman Legions; a good strength, if all other helpe had beene wanting: which serue to keepe in good order their subiects, that were alwaies fewer in the Armie than themselues. As for the *Latines*, if consanguinitie were not a sufficient obligation; yet many priuiledges and immunities, which they enioyed, made them assured vnto the State of *Rome:* vnder which they liued almost at libertie, as being bound to little else, than to serue it in warre. It is true, that a yoke, how easie soeuer, seemes troublesome to the necke that hath beene accustomed to freedome. Therefore many people of *Italie* haue taken occasion of seuerall aduantages, to deliuer themselues from the *Roman* subiection. But still they haue beene reclaimed by warre; the Authors of rebellion haue sharpely punished; and the people, by degrees, haue obtained such libertie, as made them esteeme none otherwise of *Rome*, than as the common citie of all *Italie*. Yea, in processe of time it was granted vnto many cities, and those farre off remooued, euen to *Tarsus* in *Cilicia*, where Saint *Paul* was borne; That all the Burgesses should bee free of *Rome* it selfe. This fauour was conferred absolutlie vpon some; vpon some, with restraint of giuing voice in election of Magistrates, or with other such limitation, as was thought fit. Hereunto may be added, that it was their manner, after a great conquest, to release vnto their new subiects halfe of their tribute which they had beene wont to pay vnto their former Lords, which was a readie way, to bring the multitude into good liking of their present condition; when the reuiew of harder times past, should rather teach them to feare a relapse, than to hope for better in the future, by seeking innouation. Neither would it be forgotten, as a speciall note of the *Romans* good gouernment, That when some, for their well-deseruing, haue had the offer to be made citizens of *Rome*, they haue refused it, and held themselues better contented with their owne present estate. Wherefore it is no maruaile, that *Petellia*, a citie of the *Brutians* in *Italie*, chose rather to endure all extremitie of warre, than, vpon any condition, to forsake the *Romans*; euen when the *Romans* themselues had confessed, that they were vnable to helpe these their subiects, and therefore willed them to looke to their owne good, as hauing beene faithfull to the vtmost. Such loue purchased these milde Gouernours, without impairing their Maiestie thereby. The summe of all is: They had, of their owne, a strong Armie; they doubled it, by adioyning thereunto the *Latines*; and they further increased it, as neede required, with other helpe of their owne subiects: all, or the most of their followers, accounting the prosperitie of *Rome* to be the common good.

The moderate vse of souereigne power being so effectuall, in assuring the people vnto their Lords, and consequentlie, in the establishment or enlargement of Dominion: it may seeme strange, that the practise of tyrannie, whose effects are contrarie, hath beene so common in all ages. The like, I knowe, may bee saide, of all Vice, and Irregularitie whatsoeuer. For it is lesse difficult (whosoeuer thinke otherwise) and more safe, to keepe the way of Iustice and Honestie, than to turne aside from it; yet commonly our passions lead vs into by-pathes. But where Lust, Anger, Feare, or any the like Affection, seduceth our reason; the same vnrulie appetite either bringeth with it an excuse, or at least-wise taketh away all cause of wonder. In tyrannie it is not so: for as much as we can hardly descrie the passion, that is of force to insinuate it selfe into the whole tenour of a Gouernment. It must be confessed, that lawlesse desires haue bred many Tyrants: yet so, that these desires haue seldome beene hereditarie, or long-lasting; but haue ended commonly with the Tyrants life, sometimes before his death; by which meanes the Gouernment hath beene reduced to a better forme. In such cases, the saying of *Aristotle* holds, *That Tyrannies are of short continuance.* But this doth not satisfie the question in hand. Why did the *Carthaginians* exercise Tyrannie? why did the *Athenians?* why haue many other Cities done the like? If in respect of their generall good; how could they be ignorant, that this was an ill course for the safetie of the Weale publique? If they were led hereunto by any affection; what was that affection, wherin so many thousand citizens, diuided and subdiuided within themselues by factions, did all concurre, notwithstanding the much diuersitie of temper, and the vehemencie of priuate hatred among them? Doubtles, we must be faine to say, That Tyrannie is, by it selfe, a Vice distinct from others. A Man, we knowe, is *Animal politicum,* apt, euen by Nature, to command, or to obey; euery one in his proper degree. Other desires of Mankinde, are common likewise vnto bruit beastes; and some of them, to bodies wanting sense: but the desire of rule belongeth vnto the nobler part of reason; whereunto is also answerable an aptnesse to yeeld obedience. Now as hunger and thirst are giuen by nature, not onely to Man and Beast, but vnto all sorts of Vegetables, for the sustentation of their life: as Feare, Anger, Lust, and other Affections are likewise naturall, in conuenient measure, both vnto mankinde, and to all creatures that haue sense, for the shunning or repelling of harme, and seeking after that which is requisite: euen so is this desire of ruling or obaying, engrafted by Nature in the race of Man, and in Man onely as a reasonable creature, for the ordering of his life, in a ciuile forme of iustice. All these in-bred qualities are good and vsefull. Neuerthelesse, Hunger and Thirst are the Parents of Gluttonie and Drunkennesse, which, in reproach, are called beastlie, by an vnproper terme: since they grow from appetites, found in lesse worthie creatures than beastes, and are yet not so common in beastes, as in men. The effects of Anger, and of such other Passions as descend no lower than vnto bruit beastes, are held lesse vile; and perhaps not without good reason: yet are they more horrible, and punished more grieuously, by sharper Lawes, as being in generall more pernicious. But as no corruption is worse, than of that which is best; there is not any Passion, that nourisheth a vice more hurtfull vnto Mankinde, than that which issueth from the most noble roote, euen the depraued Affection of ruling. Hence arise those two great mischiefes, of which hath beene an old question in dispute, whether bee the worse; That all things, or That nothing, should be lawfull. Of these, a dull spirit, and ouer-loaden by fortune, with power, whereof it is not capable, occasioneth the one; the other proceedeth from a contrarie distemper, whose vehemencie the bounds of Reason cannot limit. Vnder the extremitie of either, no countrie is able to subsist: yet the defectiue dulnesse, that permitteth any thing, wil also permit the execution of Law, to which, meere necessitie doth enforce the ordinarie Magistrate; whereas Tyrannie is more actiue, and pleaseth it selfe in the excesse, with a false colour of iustice: Examples of stupiditie, and vnaptnes to rule, are not very frequent, though such natures are euery where found: for this qualitie troubles not it selfe in seeking Empire; or if by some errour of fortune, it encounter therewithall, (as when *Claudius*, hiding himselfe in a corner, found the Empire of *Rome*) some friend or else a wife, is it not wanting to supply the defect, which also crueltie doth helpe to shadow. Therefore this Vice, as a thing vnknowne, is without a name. Tyrannie is more bold, and feareth not to be knowen, but would be reputed honourable: for it is *prosperum & fœlix scelus, a fortunate mischief*, as long as it can subsist. *There is no reward or honour* (saith *Peter Charron*) *asigned to those, that knowe how to increase, or to preserue humane nature: all honours, greatnesse, riches, dignities, empires, triumphs, trophees, are appointed for those, that knowe how to afflict, trouble, or destroy it.* *Cæsar*, and *Alexander*, haue vn-made and slaine, each of them, more than a million of men: but they made none, nor left none behinde them. Such is the errour of Mans iudgement, in valuing things according to common opinion. But the true name of Tyrannie, when it growes to ripenesse, is none other, than *Feritie:* the same that *Aristotle* saith to be worse than any vice. It exceedeth indeed all other vices, issuing from the Passions incident both to Man, and Beast; no lesse than Periurie, Murder, Treason, and the like horrible crimes, exceede in villanie, the faults of Gluttonie and drunkennesse, that grow from more ignoble appetites. Hereof *Sciron*, *Procrustes*, and *Pityocamptes*, that vsed their bodily force to the destruction of Mankinde, are not better examples, than *Phalaris*, *Dionysius* and *Agathocles*, whose mischeiuous heades were assisted by the hands of detestable Ruffians. The same barbarous desire of Lordship, transported those old examples of *Feritie*, and these latter Tyrants, beyond the bounds of reason: neither of them knew the vse of Rule, nor the difference betweene Freemen, and slaues.

The rule of the husband ouer the wife, and of parents ouer their children, is naturall, and appointed by God himselfe; so that it is alwaies, and simplie, allowable and good. The former of these, is, as the dominion of Reason ouer Appetite; the latter is the whole authoritie, which one free man can haue ouer another. The rule of a King is no more, nor none other, than of a common Father ouer his whole countrie: which hee that knowes what the power of a Father is, or ought to bee, knowes to be enough. But there is a greater, and more Masterlie rule, which God gaue vnto *Adam*, when he said; *Haue dominion ouer the fish of the Sea, and ouer the fowle of the aire, and ouer euerie liuing thing that moueth vpon the earth:* which also hee confirmed vnto *Noah*, and his children, saying, *The feare of you, and the dread of you, shall be vpon euerie beast of the earth, and vpon euerie fowle of the aire, vpon all that moueth vpon the earth, and vpon all the fishes of the Sea*; *into your hands are they deliuered.* Hee who gaue this dominion to Man, gaue also an aptitude to vse it. The execution of this power hath since extended it selfe, ouer a great part of Mankinde. There are indeed no small numbers of men, whose disabilitie to gouerne themselues, proues them, according vnto *Aristotles* doctrine, to be naturallie slaues.

Yet finde I not in Scripture any warrant, to oppresse men with bondage: vnlesse the lawfulnesse thereof be sufficientlie intimated, where it is said, That a man shall not be punished for the death of a seruant, whom he hath slaine by correction, if the seruant liue a day or two, because *he is his monie*; or else by the captiuitie of the *Midianitish* girles, which were made bondslaues, and the Sanctuarie had a part of them for *the Lords tribute.* Doubtlesse the custome hath beene very ancient: for *Noah* laid this curse vpon *Canaan*, that he should be *a seruant of seruants*; and *Abraham* had of *Pharaoh*, among other gifts, *men-seruants, and maide-seruants,* which were none other than slaues. Christian Religion is said to haue abrogated this olde kinde of seruilitie: but surelie, they are deceiued, that thinke so. Saint *Paul* desired the libertie of *Onesimus*, whome he had wonne vnto *Christ*: yet wrote hee for this vnto *Philemon*, by way of request, crauing it as *a benefite*, not vrging it as a dutie. Agreeable hereto is the direction, which the same Saint *Paul* giueth vnto seruants: *Let euery man abide in the same calling wherein hee was called: art thou called, being a seruant? care not for it, but if thou maist be made free, vse it rather.* It is true, that Christian religion hath procured libertie vnto many; not onely in regard of pietie, but for that the Christian Masters stood in feare, of being discouered by their slaues, vnto the persecuters of religion. *Mahomet* likewise by giuing libertie to his followers, drewe many vnto his impietie: but whether he forbad it, as vnlawfull, vnto his sectatours, to hold one another of them in bondage, I cannot tell; saue that by the practise of the *Turks* and *Moores*, it seemes he did not. In *England* we had many bond-seruants, vntill the times of our last ciuile warres: and I thinke that the Lawes concerning *Villenage* are still in force, of which the latest are the sharpest. And now, since slaues were made free, which were of great vse and seruice, there are growne vp a rabble of Rogues, Cutpurses, and other the like Trades; slaues in Nature, though not in Lawe.

But whether this kind of dominion be lawfull, or not; *Aristotle* hath well proued, that it is naturall. And certainly we finde not such a latitude of difference, in any creature, as in the nature of man: wherein (to omit the infinite distance in estate, of the elect & reprobate) the wisest excell the most foolish, by far greater degree, than the most foolish of men doth surpasse the wisest of beasts. Therfore when Commiseration hath giuen way to Reason; we shall find, that Nature is the ground euen of Masterly power, and of seruile obedience, which is thereto correspondent. But it may be truly said, that some countries haue subsisted long, without the vse of any seruilitie: as also it is true that some countries haue not the vse of any tame cattaile. Indeed the affections which vphold ciuile rule, are (though more noble) not so simplie needfull, vnto the sustentation either of our kinde, as are Lust, and the like; or of euerie one, as are hunger and thirst; which notwithstanding are the lowest in degree. But where most vile, and seruile dispositions, haue libertie to shew themselues begging in the streetes; there may wee more iustly wonder, how the dangerous toile of sea-faring men can finde enough to vndertake them, than how the swarme of idle vagabonds should increase, by accesse of those, that are wearie of their owne more painefull condition. This may suffice to proue, that in Mankind there is found, ingrafted euen by Nature, a desire of absolute dominion: whereunto the generall custome of Nations doth subscribe; together with the pleasure which most men take in flatterers, that are the basest of slaues.

This being so, we finde no cause to meruaile, how Tyrannie hath beene so rife in all ages, and practised, not onely in the single rule of some vicious Prince, but euer by consent of whole Cities and Estates: since, other vices haue likewise gotten head, and borne a generall sway; notwithstanding that the way of vertue be more honourable, and commodious. Few there are that haue vsed well the inferiour Passions: how then can we expect, that the most noble affections should not bee disordered? In the gouernment of wife and children, some are vtterlie carelesse, and corrupt all by their dull conniuencie: others, by masterlie rigour, hold their owne blood vnder condition of slauerie. To be a good Gouernour is a rare commendation; and to preferre the Weale publicke aboue all respects whatsoeuer, is the Vertue iustly termed *Heroicall*. Of this Vertue, many ages affoord not many examples. *Hector* is named by *Aristotle*, as one of them; and deseruedlie, if this praise be due to extraordinarie heighth of fortitude, vsed in defence of a mans owne countrie. But if we consider, that a loue of the generall good cannot be perfect, without reference vnto *the fountaine of all goodnesse:* wee shall finde, that no Morall vertue, how great soeuer, can, by it selfe, deserue the commendation of *more than Vertue*, as the *Heroicall* doth. Wherefore we must search the Scriptures, for patterns hereof; such, as *Dauid, Iosaphat*, and *Iosias* were. Of Christian Kings if there were many such, the world would soone be happie. It is not my purpose to wrong the worth of any, by denying the praise where it is due; or by preferring a lesse excellent. But he that can finde a King, religious, and zealous in Gods cause, without enforcement either of aduersitie, or of some regard of state; a procurer of the generall peace and quiet; who not onely vseth his authoritie, but addes the trauaile of his eloquence, in admonishing his Iudges to doe iustice; by the vigorous influence of whose Gouernment, ciuilitie is infused, euen into those places, that had beene the dennes of sauage Robbers and Cutthrotes; one that hath quite abolished a slauish *Brehon* Law, by which an whole Nation of his subiects were held in bondage; and one, whose higher vertue and wisedome doth make the prayse, not onelie of Nobilitie and other ornaments, but of abstinence from the blood, the wiues, and the goods, of those that are vnder his power, together with a world of chiefe commendations belonging vnto some good Princes, to appeare lesse regardable: he, I say, that can finde such a King, findeth an example, worthie to adde vnto vertue an honourable title, if it were formerlie wanting. Vnder such a King, it is likelie by Gods blessing, that a land shall flourish, with increase of Trade, in countries before vnknowen; that Ciuilitie and Religion shall be propagated, into barbarous and heathen countries; and that the happinesse of his subiects, shall cause the Nations farre off remoued, to wish him their Souereigne.

I neede not adde hereunto, that all the actions of such a King, euen his bodilie exercises, doe partake of vertue: since all things tending to the preseruation of his life and health, or to the mollifying of his cares, (who, fixing his contemplation vpon God, seeketh how to imitate the vn-speakable goodnesse, rather than the inaccessible maiestie, with both of which himselfe is indued, as farre as humane nature is capable) doe also belong to the furtherance of that common good, which hee procureth. Least any man should thinke mee transported with admiration, or other affection, beyond the bounds of reason; I adde hereunto, that such a King is neuerthelesse a man, must die, and may erre: yet wisedome and fame shall set him free, from *errour*, and from *death*, both with and without the helpe of *time*. One thing I may not omit, as a singular benefite (though there be many other besides) redounding vnto this King, as the fruite of his goodnesse. The people that liue vnder a pleasant yoke, are not onelie louing to their Souereigne Lord, but free of courage, and no greater in muster of men, than of stout fighters, if neede require: whereas on the contrarie, he that ruleth as ouer slaues, shall bee attended, in time of necessitie, by slauish mindes, neither louing his person, nor regarding his or their owne honour. Cowards may bee furious, and slaues outragious, for a time: but among spirits that haue once yeelded vnto slauerie, vniuersallie it is found true, that *Homer* saith, *God bereaueth a man of halfe his vertue, that day when he casteth him into bondage.*

Of these things, I might perhaps more seasonablie haue spoken, in the generall discourse of Gouernment: but where so liuelie an example, of the calamitie following a tyrannicall rule, and the vse of Mercinaries, thereupon depending, did offer it selfe, as is this present businesse of the *Carthaginians*; I thought that the note would be more effectuall, than being barelie deliuered, as out of a common place.

Ch. III. *Of the second Punick Warre*

Ch. IV. *Of* Philip *the Father of* Persevs, *King of Macedon; His first Acts and warre with the Romans, by whom he was subdued*

Ch. V. *The Warres of the Romans with* Antiochvs *the great, and his adherents*

Ch. VI. *The second Macedonian Warre*

§8. *Of* L. Æmylivs Pavlvs *the Consvl . . . The Battaile of Pydna.* Persevs *his flight . . .*

§9. Gentivs, *King of the Illyrians, taken by the Romans.*

§10. *How the Romans behaued themselues in Greece and Macedon after their victorie ouer* Persevs.

Now began the *Romans* to swell with the pride of their fortune; and to looke tyrannically vpon those that had beene vnmannerly toward them before, whilest the Warre with *Perseus* seemed full of danger. The *Rhodian* Embassadours were still at *Rome*, when the tidings of these victories were brought thither. Wherefore it was thought good to call them

SWR N

into the Senate, and bid them doe their errand againe. This they performed with bad grace; saying, That they were sent from *Rhodes*, to make an ouerture of peace; forasmuch as it was thought, that this Warre was no lesse grieuous to the *Romans* themselues, than to the *Macedonians* and manie others: but that now they were verie glad, and in behalfe of the *Rhodians* did congratulate with the Senate and People of *Rome*, that it was ended much more happily than had beene expected. Hereto the Senate made answere, That the *Rhodians* had sent this Embassage to *Rome*, not for loue to *Rome*, but in fauour of the *Macedonian*; whose partizans they were, and should so be taken. By these threats, and the desire of some (couetous of the charge) to haue Warre proclaymed against *Rhodes*; the Embassadours were so affrighted, that in mourning apparell, as humble suppliants, they went about the Citie; beseeching all men, especially the great ones, to pardon their indiscretion, and not to prosecute them with vengeance for some foolish words. This danger of Warre from *Rome* being knowne at *Rhodes*, all that had beene anie whit auerse from the *Romans* in the late Warre of *Macedon*, were eyther taken and condemned, or sent prisoners to *Rome*; excepting some that slew themselues for feare, whose goods also were confiscated. Yet this procured little grace; and lesse would haue done, if olde *M. Cato*, a man by nature vehement, had not vttered a milde sentence, and aduertised the Senate, That in decreeing Warre against *Rhodes*, they should much dishonour themselues, and make it thought, that rather the wealth of that Citie, which they were greedie to ransacke, than anie just cause, had moued them thereto. This consideration, together with their good deserts in the Warres of *Philip* and *Antiochus*, helped well the *Rhodians:* among whome, none of anie marke remained aliue, saue those that had beene of the *Roman* Faction. All which notwithstanding, manie yeares passed, ere, by importunate suit, they could be admitted into the societie of the *Romans*: a fauour which, till now, they had not esteemed, but thought themselues better without it, as equall friends.

With the like, or greater seueritie, did the *Romans* make themselues terrible in all parts of *Greece*. *Æmylius* himselfe

made progresse through the Countrey; visiting all the
famous places therein, as for his pleasure: yet not forgetting
to make them vnderstand what power he had ouer them.
More than fiue hundred of the chiefe citizens in *Demetrias*
were slaine at one time by those of the *Roman* faction, and
with helpe of the *Roman* souldiors. Others fled, or were
banished, and their goods confiscated. Of which things,
when complaint was made to the Consul; the redresse was
such, as requited not the paines of making supplication. His
friends, that is to say, those which betrayed vnto the *Romans*
the libertie of their Countrey, he feasted like a King, with
excessiue cheare; yet so, that hee had all things verie cheape
in his Campe: an easie matter, since no man durst be back-
ward in sending prouisions, nor set on them the due price.
Embassadours likewise were sent from *Rome*; some, to giue
order for setling the estate of *Macedon*, towards which they
had more particular instruction from the Senate than was
vsuall in such cases; and some, to visit the affaires of *Greece*.
The Kingdome of *Macedon*, was set at libertie by *Æmylius*
and the Embassadours, his assistants, who had order therefore from the Senate. But this libertie was such as the
Romans vsed to bestow. The best part of it was, That the
Tribute which had been payed vnto the Kings, was lessened
by halfe. As for the rest; the Countrey was diuided into foure
parts, and they forbidden commerce one with the other. All
the Nobilitie were sent captiue into *Italie*, with their wiues
and children, as manie as were aboue fifteene yeares old.
The ancient Lawes of the Countrey were abrogated; and new
giuen by *Æmylius*. Such mischiefe the Senate thought it
better to doe, at the first alteration of things in this Prouince,
and in the time of Conquest, than otherwise to leaue anie
inconuenience that should be worse in the future. But concerning the *Greekes*, that were not subjects to *Rome*; the
things done to them could deserue no better name than
meere tyrannie, yea and shamelesse perjurie; were it not so,
that the familiar custome, among Princes and great Estates,
of violating Leagues, doth make the Oathes of confederation
seeme of no validitie. The Embassadors that were sent to visit
the *Greekes*, called before them all such men of note, from
euerie quarter, as had anie way discouered an vnseruiceable

disposition towards the *Romans*. These they sent to *Rome*; where they were made sure enough. Some of these had sent letters to *Perseus*, which fell at length into the *Romans* hands: and in that respect, though they were no subjects, yet wanted there not colour, for vsing them as traytors, or at least as enemies. But since onely two men were beheaded, for hauing beene openly on the *Macedonian* side; and since it is confessed, that the good *Patriotes* were no lesse afflicted in this inquisition, than they that had sold themselues to the King: this manner of proceeding was inexcusable Tyrannie. With the *Achæans* these Embassadors were to deale more formally: not so much because that Commonwealth was strong (though this were to be regarded by them, hauing no Commission to make or denounce Warre) and like to proue vntractable, if manifest wrong were offered; as for that there appeared no manner of signe, by letters, or otherwise, whereby anie one of the *Achæans* could be suspitiously charged to haue held correspondence with the *Macedonian*. It was also so, that neither *Callicrates*, nor anie of his adherents, had beene employed by the Nation, in doing or offering their seruice to the *Romans*, but onely such as were the best *Patriotes*. Yet would not therefore the Embassadours neglect to vse the benefit of the time: wherein, since all men trembled for feare of *Rome*, the season serued fitly to ranke the *Achæans* with the rest. And hereto *Callicrates* was verie vrgent: fearing, and procuring them to feare in behalfe of him and his friends, that if some sharpe order were not now taken, hee and his fellowes should be made to pay for their mischieuous deuices, ere long time passed. So the Embassadours came among the *Achæans:* where one of them, in open assemblie of the Nation, spake as *Callicrates* had before instructed him. Hee said, That some of the chiefe among them, had with money and other meanes befriended *Perseus*. This being so; he desired that all such men might be condemned, whom, after sentence giuen, he would name vnto them. After sentence giuen (cried out the whole assembly) what iustice were this? name them first, and let them answere; which if they cannot well doe, we will soone condemne them. Then said the *Roman* boldly, that all their Prætors, as many as had led their armies, were guiltie of this crime. If this were true, said *Xenon*, a temperate man, and confident in his innocence, then should I likewise haue beene friend to *Perseus:* whereof, if any man can accuse me, I shall throughly answere him, either here presently, or before the Senate at *Rome.* Vpon these words of *Xenon* the Embassador laid hold, and said that euen so it were the best way, for him and the rest to purge themselues before the Senate at *Rome.* Then began he to name others, and left not vntill he had cited aboue a thousand; willing them to appeare, and answere before the Senate. This might euen be tearmed the captiuitie of *Greece*; wherein so many of the honestest and worthiest men were carried from home, for none other cause than their loue vnto their Country; to be punished according to the will of those, who could not endure, that vertue, and regard of the publike libertie, should dwell together in any of the *Greekes.* At their comming to *Rome*, they were all cast into prison: as men already condemned by the *Achæans.* Many Embassages were sent from *Achaia* (where it is to be wondred, that any such honest care of these innocent men could be remaining: since honestie had beene thus punished as a vice, in so many of the worthiest among them) to informe the Senat, that these men were neither condemned by the *Achæans*, nor yet held to be offendours. But in stead of better answere it was pronounced; That the *Senate thought it not expedient for the Countrie, that these men should returne into Achaia.* Neither could any solicitation of the *Achæans*, who neuer ceased to importune the Senate for their libertie, preuaile at all; vntill after seuenteene yeeres, fewer than thirtie of them were enlarged, of whom that wise and vertuous man *Polybius*, the great Historian was one. All the rest were either dead in prison; or hauing made offer to escape, whether vpon the way before they came to *Rome*, or whether out of jayle, after that they were committed thereto, suffered death as malefactors.

This was a gentle correction, in regard of what was done vpon the *Epirots.* For the Senate being desirous to preserue the *Macedonian* Treasure whole; yet withall, to gratifie the souldiours, gaue order, That the whole Countrey of *Epirus* should be put to sacke. This was a barbarous and horrible crueltie; as also it was performed by *Æmylius* with mischieuous subtiltie. Hauing taken leaue of the *Greekes*, and of the *Macedonians*, with bidding them well to vse the libertie bestowed vpon them by the people of *Rome*; he sent vnto the *Epirots* for tenne of the principall men out of euerie Citie. These hee commaunded to deliuer vp all the gold and siluer which they had; and sent along with them, into euerie of their Townes, what companies of men he thought conuenient, as it were to fetch the money. But he gaue secret instruction to the Captaines, that vpon a certaine day by him appointed they should fall to sacke, euerie one the Towne whereinto hee was sent. Thus in one day were threescore and tenne Cities, all confederate with the *Romans*, spoyled by the *Roman* souldiors; and besides other acts of hostilitie in a time of peace, a hundred and fiftie thousand of that Nation made slaues. It may be granted, that some of the *Epirots* deserued punishment, as hauing fauoured *Perseus*. But since they, among this people, that were thought guiltie of this offence, yea, or but coldly affected to the *Romans*, had beene alreadie sent into *Italie*, there to receiue their due; and since this Nation, in generall, was not onely at the present in good obedience, but had, euen in this warre, done good seruice to the *Romans:* I hold this act so wicked, that I should not beleeue it, had anie one Writer deliuered the contrarie. But the truth being manifest by consent of all; it is the lesse meruailous, that God was pleased to make *Æmylius* childesse, euen in the glorie of his triumph, how great soeuer otherwise his vertues were.

In such manner dealt the *Romans*, after their victorie, with the *Greekes* and *Macedonians*. How terrible they were to other Kingdomes abroad; it will appeare by the efficacie of an Embassage sent from them to *Antiochus:* whereof before we speake, we must speake somewhat of *Antiochus* his foregoers, of himselfe, and of his affaires about which these Embassadors came.

§11. *The Warre of* Antiochvs *vpon Ægypt, brought to end by the Roman Embassadours.*

Antiochvs the Great, after his peace with the *Romans*, did nothing that was memorable in the short time following of his

raign and life. He died the six and thirtieth yeare after he
had worne a Crown, and in the seuenteenth or eighteenth of
Ptolemie Epiphanes: while he attempted to rob the Temple
of *Bel*, or (according to *Iustine*) of *Iupiter*. He left behinde
him three sonnes, *Seleucus Philopator*, *Antiochus Epiphanes*,
Demetrius Soter; and one daughter, *Cleopatra*, whom he had
giuen in marriage to *Ptolemie Epiphanes*, King of *Ægypt*.
Seleucus the fourth of that name, and the eldest of *Antiochus*
his sonnes; raigned in *Syria* twelue yeares, according to
Eusebius, *Appian*, and *Sulpitius:* though *Iosephus* giue him
but seuen. A Prince, who as hee was slouthful by nature, so
the great losse which his father *Antiochus* had receiued; tooke
from him the meanes of managing any great affaire. Of him,
about three hundred yeares before his birth, *Daniel* gaue
this judgement, *Et stabit in loco eius vilissimus & indignus
decore regio. And in his place* (speaking of *Antiochus* the father
of this man) *shall start vp a vilde person, vnworthy the honor
of a King.* Vnder this *Seleucus,* those things were done which
are spoken of *Onias* the High Priest, in these words, and
other to the same effect. *What time as the holy Citie was
inhabited with all peace, because of the godlinesse of* Onias *the
Priest, it came to passe, that euen the King did honor the place,
and garnished the Temple with great gifts.* And all that is
written in the third Chapter of the second of *Macchabees*, of
Simon of *Beniamin*, who by *Apollonius* betrayed the treasures
of the Temple: and of *Heliodorus* sent by the King to seize
them; of his miraculous striking by God; and his recouery at
the prayers of *Onias*; of the Kings death, and of his successor
Antiochus Epiphanes. It is therefore from the raigne of this
King, that the bookes of the *Macchabees* take beginning.
Which bookes seeme not to be deliuered by one and the
same hand. For the first booke, although it touch vpon
Alexander the Great, yet it hath nothing else of his storie,
nor of the acts of his successors, till the time of *Antiochus
Epiphanes*, the brother and successour of this *Seleucus*; from
whom downward to the death of *Simon Macchabeus* (who
died in the hundred threescore and seuenteenth yeare of the
Greekes in *Syria*) that first book treateth. The Author of the
second book, although he take the Storie somewhat further
off, by way of a Proæme, yet hee endeth with the hundred

and one and fiftieth yeare of the *Græcian* raigne, and with
the death of *Nicanor* slaine by *Iudas*: remembring in the fourth
Chapter, the practise of *Iason*, the brother of *Onias*, who
after the death of *Seleucus*, preuailed with *Antiochus Epiphanes*,
his successor for the Priesthood. It is also held by *Iansenius*
and other graue Writers, that it was in the time of this
Onias, that *Arius* King of the *Spartans* sent Embassadors to
the *Iewes*, as to their brothers and kinsmen. Which intelligence betweene them and the *Greekes*, *Ionathan* the brother
and successor of *Iudas*, remembreth in the Preamble of that
Epistle, which he himselfe directed to the people of *Sparta*
by *Numenius* and *Antipater* his Embassadors, whom hee
employed at the same time to the Senate of *Rome*; repeating
also the former Letters word by word, which *Arius* had sent
to *Onias* the High Priest, whereto *Iosephus* addes, that the
name of the *Lacedæmonian* Embassador was *Demoteles*, and
that the Letters had a square Volume, and were sealed with
an Eagle holding a Dragon in her clawes.

Now to this *Seleucus*, the fourth of that name, succeeded
Antiochus Epiphanes, in the hundred and seuen and thirtieth
yeare of the *Greekes* in *Syriæ*. Hee was the second sonne of
the Great *Antiochus:* and he obtained his Kingdome by
procuring the death of the King his brother; which also hee
vsurped from his brothers sonne.

Ptolemie Philometor, his Nephew by his sister *Cleopatra*,
being then very yong, had beene about seuen yeares King
of *Ægypt*.

Ptolemie Epiphanes, the father of this King *Philometor*, had
raigned in *Ægypt* foure and twentie yeares; in great quiet,
but doing little or nothing that was memorable. *Philip* of
Macedon, and the great *Antiochus*, had agreed to diuide his
Kingdome between them, whilest he was a childe. But they
found such other busines, ere long, with the *Romans*, as
made them giue ouer their vniust purpose; especially
Antiochus, who gaue, with his daughter in marriage, vnto this
Ptolemie, the Prouinces of *Cælesyria*, *Phænice*, and *Iudæa*,
which he had wonne by his victorie ouer *Scopas*, that was
Generall of the *Ægyptian* forces in those parts. Neuerthelesse, *Ptolemie* adhered to the *Romans:* whereby he liued in
the greater securitie. Hee left behind him two sons; this

Ptolemie Philometor, and *Ptolemie Physcon*, with a daughter, *Cleopatra*. *Cleopatra* was wife to the elder of her brethren, and after his death to the yonger, by whom she was cast off, and her daughter taken in her stead. Such were the marriages of these *Ægyptian* Kings.

Ptolemie Philometor, so called (that is, the louer of his mother) by a bitter nickname, because he slew her, fell into hatred with his subiects, and was like to be chased out of his kingdome: his yonger brother being set vp against him. *Physcon* hauing a strong partie, got possession of *Alexandria*; and *Philometor* held himselfe in *Memphis*, crauing succour of King *Antiochus* his vncle. Hereof *Antiochus* was glad: who vnder colour to take vpon him the protection of the yong Prince, sought by all meanes possible to possesse himselfe of that kingdome. He sent *Apollonius* the sonne of *Mnestheus* Embassador into *Ægypt*, and vnder colour to assist the Kings Coronation, hee gaue him instructions to perswade the Gouernours of the yong King *Philometor*, to deliuer the King his Nephew with the principall places of that kingdome into his hands; pretending an extraordinarie care and desire of his Nephewes safetie and well doing. And the better to answere all argument to the contrarie, he prepared a forcible armie to attend him. Thus came he alongst the coast of *Syria*, to *Ioppe*, and from thence on the sudden he turned himselfe towards *Ierusalem*, where by *Iason* the Priest (a Chaplin fit for such a Patron) hee was with all pompe and solemnitie receiued into the Citie. For though lately, in the time of *Seleucus*, the brother and predecessour of *Epiphanes*, that impious traytor *Simon* of the Tribe of *Beniamin*, ruler of the Temple, when he would haue deliuered the treasures thereof to *Apollonius* Gouernor of *Cœlesyria* and *Phœnicia*, was disappointed of his wicked purpose by miracle from heauen; the said *Apollonius* being stroken by the Angell of God, and recouering againe at the prayer of *Onias:* yet sufficed not this example to terrifie others from the like vngodly practises. Presently vpon the death of *Seleucus*, this *Iason*, the brother of *Onias*, seeking to supplant his brother, and to obtaine the Priesthood for himselfe, offered vnto the King three hundred and threescore talents of siluer, with other rents and summes of money. So he got his desire, though he not long enioyed it.

This naughtie dealing of *Iason*, and his being ouer-
reached by another, in the same kinde, calls to minde a
by-word taken vp among the *Achæans*, when as that mis-
chieuous *Callicrates*, who had beene too hard for all worthie
and vertuous men, was beaten at his owne weapon, by one
of his owne condition. It went thus.

> *One fire than other burnes more forcibly,*
> *One Wolfe than other Wolues does bite more sore;*
> *One Hawke than other Hawkes more swift does fly.*
> *So one most mischieuous of men before,*
> Callicrates, *false knaue as knaue might be,*
> *Met with* Menalcidas *more false than he.*[1]

And euen thus fell it out with *Iason:* who within three yeares
after, was betrayed, and ouerbidden by *Menelaus* the brother
of *Simon*, that for three hundred talents more obtained
the Priesthood for himselfe: *Iason* thereupon being forced
to flie from *Ierusalem*, and to hide himselfe among the
Ammonites.

From *Ierusalem*, *Antiochus* marched into *Phœnicia*, to
augment the numbers of his men of warre, and to prepare a
Fleet for his expedition into *Ægypt*; with which, and with a
mightie armie of land-forces, *Hee went about to raigne ouer*
Ægypt, *that he might haue the dominion of two Realmes, and*
entred Egypt *with a mightie companie, with* Chariots *and*
Elephants, *with* Horsemen, *and with a great* Nauie, *and moued*
warre against Ptolemævs *King of* Egypt, *but* Ptolemævs *was*
afraid of him and fled, and many were wounded to death. He
wanne many strong Cities, and took away the spoiles of the Land
of Egypt. Thus was fulfilled the Prophecie of *Daniel. He*
shall enter into the quiet and plentifull Prouinces, and he shall doe
that which his Fathers haue not done, nor his Fathers Fathers.
Neuer indeed had any of the Kings of *Syria* so great a
victorie ouer the *Ægyptians*, nor tooke from them so great
riches. For hee gaue a notable ouerthrow to the Captaines of
Ptolemie, between *Pelusium* and the hill *Cassius*, after which
he entered and sackt the greatest and richest of all the Cities
of *Ægypt*, *Alexandria* excepted, which he could not force.
In conclusion, after *that* Antiochvs *had smitten* Egypt, *he*
turned againe and went vp towards Israel *and* Ierusalem *with*

[1] Pausanias, *Description of Greece*, VII 12.

a mightie people, and entered proudly into the Sanctuarie, and
tooke away the golden Altar, and the Candlesticke for the light,
and all the Instruments thereof, and the table of the Shew-bread,
and the powring Vessels and the Bowles, and the golden Basons,
and the Vaile, and the Crownes, and the golden Apparell. He
tooke also the Siluer, and the Gold, and the precious Iewels, and
the secret Treasures: and when he had taken away all, he
departed into his owne Land, after he had murdered many men.

It was about the beginning of the *Macedonian* warre, that
Antiochus tooke in hand this *Egyptian* businesse. At what
time he first laid claime to *Cælesyria*; justifying his title by
the same allegations which his father had made; and stiffely
auerring, that this Prouince had not beene consigned ouer
to the *Egyptian*, or giuen in dowrie with *Cleopatra*. Easie it
was to approue his right vnto that which he had alreadie
gotten, when he was in a faire way to get all *Egypt*. The
Achæans, *Rhodians*, *Athenians*, and other of the *Greekes*,
pressed him, by seuerall Embassages, to some good conclusion. But his answere was; that if the *Alexandrians* could
be contented to receiue their King his Nephew *Philometor*,
the elder brother of the *Ptolemies*, then should the warre be
presently at an end; otherwise not. Yet when hee saw, that
it was an hard peece of worke to take *Alexandria* by force:
he thought it better to let the two brothers consume themselues with intestine warre, than by the terrour of his armes,
threatning destruction vnto both of them, to put into them
any desire of comming to agreement. He therefore withdrew
his forces for the present; leauing the *Ptolemies* in very weake
estate; the yonger, almost ruinated by his inuasion; the
elder hated and forsaken by his people.

But how weake soeuer these *Egyptians* were, their hatred
was thought to bee so strong, that *Antiochus* might leaue
them to the prosecution thereof; and follow, at good leasure
his other businesse at *Ierusalem* or elsewhere. So after the
sacke of *Ierusalem*, he rested him a while at *Antioch*; and
then made a journey into *Cilicia*, to suppresse the Rebellion
of the *Tharsians* and other in those parts, who had bin
giuen, as it were, by way of dowrie, to a Concubine of the
Kings, called *Antiochis*. For Gouernour of *Syria* in his absence,
he left one *Andronicus*, a man of great authoritie about him.

In the meane while *Menelaus* the brother of *Simon*, the same who had thrust *Iason* out of the Priesthood, and promised the King three hundred talents for an Income, comitting the charge of the Priesthood to his brother *Lysimachus*, stole certaine vessels of gold out of the Temple : whereof he presented a part to *Andronicus* the Kings Lieutenant, and sold the rest at *Tyre*, and other Cities adioyning. This he did, as it seemeth, to aduance the payment of the three hundred talents promised; the same being now by *Sostratus* eagerly demanded. Hereof when *Onias* the Priest (formerly dispossessed by *Iason*) had certaine knowledge, being moued with zeale, and detesting the sacriledge of *Menelaus*, he reproued him for it; and fearing his reuenge, he withdrew himselfe into a Sanctuarie at *Daphne*.

Daphne was a place of delight adjoyning as a suburb to *Antioch*. In compasse it had about ten miles : wherin were the Temples of *Apollo* and *Diana*, with a Groue, sweet Springs, banquetting places, and the like; which were wholly, in a manner, abused to lust, and other such voluptuousnesse. Whether it were well done of *Onias*, to commit himselfe to the protection of *Apollo* and *Diana*, or to claime priuiledge, from the holines of a ground consecrated to any of the Heathen gods, I will not stand to discourse. Only I say for mine owne opinion; that the inconuenience is far lesse, to hold this book as *Apocryphall*; than to judge this fearefull shift which *Onias* (though a vertuous man) made for his life, either commendable, or allowable, as the booke seemes to doe. As for this refuge, it could not saue the life of the poore old man : for Menelavs *taking* Andronicvs *apart, prayed him to slay* Onias. *So when he came to* Onias, *he counselled him craftily, giuing him his right hand with an oath, and perswading him to come out of the Sanctuarie; so he slew him incontinently, without any regard of righteousnesse.* Hereof when complaint was made to *Antiochus* after his returne out of *Cilicia*, *Hee tooke away* Andronicvs *his garment of purple, and rent his cloathes, and commanded him to be led throughout the City, and in the same place where hee had committed the wickednesse against* Onias, *hee was slaine as a murderer.* In taking reuenge of this innocent mans death, I should haue thought that this wicked King had once in his life-time done Iustice.

But presently after this, at the suite of one *Ptolemie*, a traytor to *Ptolemie Philometor*, he condemned innocent men to death; who justly complained against *Menelaus*, and his brother *Lysimachus*, for a second robbing of the Temple, and carrying thence the Vessels of gold remaining. Hereby it is manifest, that he was guided by his owne outragious will, and not by any regard of justice: since he reuenged the death of *Onias*, yet slew those that were in the same cause with *Onias*, *Who had they told their cause, yea, before the* Scythians, *they should haue beene heard as innocent.* By reason of such his vnsteadinesse, this king was commonly tearmed *Epimanes*, that is, madde, in stead of *Epiphanes*, which signifieth Noble or Illustrious.

After this, *Antiochus* made preparation for a second voyage into *Ægypt, and then were there seen throughout all the Citie of* Ierusalem, *fortie dayes long, horsemen running in the aire with Robes of gold, and as bands of Spearemen, and as troopes of Horsemen set in aray, incountring and coursing one against another.* Of these prodigious signes, or rather forewarnings of God, all Histories haue deliuered vs, some more, some lesse. Before the destruction of *Ierusalem* by *Vespasian*, a starre in the forme of a sword appeared in the Heauens directly ouer the Citie, after which there followed a slaughter like vnto this of *Epiphanes*, though farre greater. In the *Cymbrian* warres, *Pliny* tells vs that Armies were seene fighting in the aire from the morning till the euening.

In the time of Pope *Iohn* the eleuenth, a fountaine powred out bloud in stead of water, in or neare the Citie of *Genoa*; soone after which the Citie was taken by the *Saracens*, with great slaughter. Of these and the like prodigious signes, *Vipera* hath collected many, and very remarkable. But this one seemeth to me the most memorable, because the most notorious. All men know that in the Emperour *Nero*, the Off-spring of the *Cæsars*, as well naturall as adopted, tooke end; whereof this notable signe gaue warning.

When *Liuia* was first married to *Augustus*, an Eagle let fall into her armes a white Henne, holding a Lawrell braunch in her mouth. *Liuia* caused this Henne to be carefully nourished, and the Lawrell braunch to be planted: Of the Henne came a faire encrease of white Poultrie, and from the little braunch there sprang vp in time a Groue of Lawrell: so that afterwards, in all Triumphs, the Conquerors did vse to carrie in their hands a braunch of Bayes taken out of this Groue; and after the Triumphs ended, to set it againe in the same ground: which braunches were obserued, when they happened to wither, to foreshew the death of those persons who carried them in triumph. And in the last yeare of *Nero*, all the broodes of the white Hennes died, and the whole Groue of Bayes withered at once. Moreouer, the heads of all the *Cæsars* Statues, and the Scepter placed in *Augustus* his hand, were stricken downe with lightning. That the *Iewes* did not thinke such strange signes to be vn-worthie of regard; it appeares by their calling vpon God, and praying, that these tokens might turne to good.

Now, as the first voyage of *Antiochus* into *Ægypt* was occasioned by discord of the two brethren therein raigning: so was his second Expedition caused by their good agree-ment. For the elder *Ptolemie* being left in *Memphis*, not strong enough to force his brother, who had defended *Alexandria* against all the power of their vncle; thought it the best way to seeke entrance into that royall Citie, rather by persuasion than by armes. *Physcon* had not as yet forgotten the terrour of the former siege: the *Alexandrines* though they loued not *Philometor*, yet loued they worse to liue in scarcitie of victuals (which was alreadie great among them, and like to grow extreame) since nothing was brought in from the Countrey; and the friends of the younger brother saw no likelyhood of good issue to be hoped for without reconcilia-tion. These good helpes, and aboue all these, the louing disposition of *Cleopatra*, who then was in *Alexandria*, en-couraged *Philometor* in his purpose. But that which made him earnestly desirous to accomplish it, was the feare wherein he stood of his vncle. For though *Antiochus* were gone out of *Ægypt* with his armie; yet had he left behinde him a strong garrison in *Pelusium*; retaining that Citie, which was the Key of *Ægypt*, to his owne vse. This consideration wrought also with *Physcon*, and with those that were about him; so as by the vehement mediation of *Cleopatra* their sister, the two brethren made an end of all quarrels.

When the newes of this accord was brought to *Antiochus*,

hee was greatly enraged: for notwithstanding that hee had pretended no other thing than the establishment of the King *Philometor* his nephew, and a meaning to subject his yonger brother vnto him, which he gaue in answere to all Embassadours; yet he now prepared to make sharpe warre vpon them both. And to that end hee presently furnished and sent out his Nauie towards *Cyprus*, and drew his Land Armie into *Cælesyria*, readie to enter *Ægypt* the Spring following. When he was on his way as farre as *Rhinocorura*, he met with Embassadors sent from *Ptolemie*. Their errand was partly to yeeld thankes to *Antiochus* for the establishing of *Philometor* in his Kingdome; partly to beseech him, That he would rather be pleased to signifie what hee required to haue done in *Ægypt*, which should be performed, than to enter it as an enemie with so puissant an Armie. But *Antiochus* returned this short answere, That he would neither call backe his Fleet, nor withdraw his Armie, vpon anie other condition, than that *Ptolemie* should surrender into his hands, together with the Citie of *Pelusium*, the whole Territorie thereto belonging: and that hee should also abandon and leaue vnto him the Isle of *Cyprus*, with all the right that he had vnto either of them for euer. For answere vnto these demaunds, hee set downe a day certaine, and a short one. Which being come and past, without anie accord made, the *Syrian* Fleet entred *Nilus*, and recouered as well those places which appertained to *Ptolemie* in *Arabia*, as in *Ægypt* it selfe; for *Memphis* and all about it receiued *Antiochus*, being vnable to resist him. The King hauing now no stoppe in his way to *Alexandria*; passed on thitherwards by easie journeyes.

Of all these troubles past, as well as of the present danger wherein *Ægypt* stood; the *Romans* had notice long agoe. But they found, or were contented to finde, little reason for them to entermeddle therein. For it was a ciuill warre: and wherein *Antiochus* seemed to take part with the juster cause. Yet they gaue signification, that it would be much displeasing vnto them, to haue the Kingdome of *Ægypt* taken from the rightfull owners. More they could not, or would not doe; being troubled with *Perseus*; and therefore loath to prouoke *Antiochus* too farre. Neuerthelesse, the *Ægyptian* Kings being reconciled, and standing joyntly in neede of helpe against their *Vncle*, who prepared and made open warre against them both: it was to bee expected, that not onely the *Romans*, but many of the *Greekes*, as being thereto obliged by notable benefits, should arme in defence of their Kingdome. *Rome* had beene sustained with food from *Ægypt* in the warre of *Hannibal*; when *Italy* lying waste, had neither corne, nor money wherewith to buy sufficient store. By helpe of the *Ægyptian*, had *Aratus* laid the foundation of that greatnesse, whereto the *Achæans* attained. And by the like helpe, had *Rhodes* beene defended against *Demetrius Poliorcetes*. Neither were these friendly turnes, which that bountifull house of the *Ptolemies* had done for sundrie people abroad, ill followed or seconded, by other as bad in requitall: but with continuance of sutable beneficence, from time to time encreased. Wherefore the two brothers sent abroad confidently for ayde: especially to the *Rhodians* and *Achæans*, who seemed most able to giue it effectually. To the *Romans*, *Physcon* and *Cleopatra* had sent, a yeare since: but their Embassadours lay still in *Rome*. Of the *Achæans* they desired in particular, that *Lycortas* the braue warriour might be sent to them as Generall of all the *Auxiliaries*, and his sonne *Polybius* Generall of the Horse. Hereunto the *Achæans* readily condescended: and would immediately haue made performance; if *Callicrates* had not interposed his mis-chieuous arte. Hee, whether seeking occasion to vaunte his obsequiousnesse to the *Romans*; or much rather enuying those Noble Captaines, whose seruice the Kings desired; withstood the common voice; which was, That their Nation should, not with such small numbers as were requested, but with all their power, be aiding vnto the *Ptolemies*. For it was not now (hee said) conuenient time to entangle themselues in any such businesse, as might make them the lesse able to yeeld vnto the *Romans* what helpe soeuer should be required in the *Macedonian* warre. And in this sentence, hee with those of his faction obstinately persisted; terrifying others with bigge words, as it were in behalfe of the *Romans*. But *Polybius* affirmed, that *Martius* the late Consul had signified vnto him, that the *Romans* were past all need of helpe: adding further, that a thousand foote, and two hundred horse, might well bee spared, to the ayde of their benefactours, the *Ægyptian*

Kings, without disabling their Nation to performe any seruice to the *Romans*; for as much as the *Achæans* could, without trouble, raise thirtie or fortie thousand souldiours. All this not withstanding, the resolution was deferred from one meeting to another; and finally broken, by the violence of *Callicrates*. For when it was thought that the Decree should haue passed; he brought into the Theater where the assembly was held, a Messenger with letters from *Martius*; whereby the *Achæans* were desired to conforme themselues to the *Roman* Senate, and to labour, as the Senate had done, by sending Embassadors, to set *Ægypt* in peace. This was an aduice against all reason. For the Senate had indeed sent Embassadours to make peace; but as in a time of greater businesse elsewhere, with such milde words, that nothing was effected. Wherefore it was not likely, that the *Achæans* should doe any good in the same kinde. Yet *Polybius* and his friends durst not gaine-say the *Roman* Councell; which had force of an iniunction. So the Kings were left in much distresse; disappointed of their expectation. But within a while was *Perseus* ouercome: and then might the Embassador sent from the *Roman* Senate, performe as much as any Armie could haue done.

Audience had beene lately giuen by the Senate, vnto those Embassadors of *Physcon* and *Cleopatra*; which hauing stayed more then a whole yeare in the Citie, brought nothing of their businesse to effect vntill now. The Embassadours deliuered their message in the name of those that had sent them: though it concerned (which perhaps they knew not) *Philometor*, no lesse than his brother and sister.

In this Embassage of *Ptolemie*, now requesting helpe from *Rome*; appeared a notable change of his fortune, from such as it had bin before three or foure yeares last past. For in the beginning of these his troubles, which began with the *Macedonian* warre; either he, or *Eulæus* and *Lenæus* (vpon whom the blame was afterwards laid) which had the gouernment of him, thought his affaires in such good estate, that not only he determined to set vpon *Antiochus*, for *Cælesyria*; but would haue interposed himselfe betweene the *Romans* and *Perseus*, as a competent Arbitrator; though it fell out well, that his Embassador was by a friend perswaded, to forget that point of his errand. From these high thoughts, he fell on the sudden, by the rebellion of his brother and subiects, to liue vnder protection of the same *Antiochus*. And now at such time as by attonement with his brother and subiects, hee might haue seemed to stand in no need of such protection; he hath remaining none other helpe whereby to saue both his Kingdome and life, than what can be obtained by their intercession which were employed against him. This miserable condition of him, his brother and sister, shewed it selfe euen in the habit of those Embassadors. They were poorely cladde; the haire of their heads and beards ouergrowne, as was their manner in time of affliction; and they carried in their hands, branches of Oliue. Thus they entered into the Senate; and there fell groueling and prostrate vpon the floare. Their garments were not so meane and mournefull, nor their lookes and countenances so sad and deiected, but that their speech was than either of the other farre more lamentable. For hauing told in what danger their King and Countrey stood; they made a pitifull and grieuous complaint vnto the Senate, beseeching them to haue compassion of their estate, and of their Princes, who had alwayes remained friendly and faithfull to the *Romans*. They said that the people of *Rome* had so much heretofore fauoured this *Antiochus* in particular, and were of such account and authoritie, with all other Kings and Nations; as if they pleased but to send their Embassadours, and let *Antiochus* know, that the Senate was offended with his vndertaking vpon the King their Confederate; then would he presently raise his siege from before *Alexandria*, and withdraw his Armie out of *Ægypt* into *Syria*. But that if the Senate protracted any time or vsed any delay; then should *Ptolemie* and *Cleopatra* be shortly driuen out of their Realmes, and make repaire to *Rome*, with shamefull dishonor to the Senate and people thereof, in that, in the extreame dangers of all their fortunes, they had not vouchsafed to relieue them.

The Lords of the Senate moued with compassion, sent incontinently *C. Popilius Lenus*, *C. Decimius*, and *A. Hostilius*, as Embassadours, to determine and end the warre betweene those Kings. In commission they had first to finde King *Ptolemie*, and then *Antiochus*, and to let them both vnderstand, that vnlesse they surceassed and gaue ouer Armes, they would take that King no more for a friend to the Senate and people of *Rome*, whom they found obstinate or vsing delay. So these *Romans*, together with the *Alexandrine* Embassadours, tooke their leaue, and went onward their way within three dayes after.

Whilest *Popilius* and his fellowes were on their way toward *Ægypt*, *Antiochus* had transported his Armie ouer *Lusine*, some fortie myles from *Alexandria*. So neare was hee to the end of his journey, when the *Roman* Embassadors met him. After greeting and salutations at their first en-counter, *Antiochus* offered his right hand to *Popilius:* but *Popilius* filled it with a Role of paper; willing him to reade those *Mandates* of the Senate, before hee did anie thing else. *Antiochus* did so; and hauing a little while considered of the businesse, hee tolde *Popilius*, That hee would aduise with his friends, and then giue the Embassadours their answere. But *Popilius*, according to his ordinarie blunt manner of speech, which hee had by nature, made a Circle about the King with a Rodde which he held in his hand, willing him to make him such an answere as hee might report to the Senate, before hee moued out of that Circle. The King astonished at this so rude and violent a Commaundement, after hee had stayed and pawsed a while, I will be content (quoth he) to doe whatsoeuer the Senate shall ordaine. Then *Popilius* gaue vnto the King his hand, as to a Friend and Allie of the *Romans*.

Thus *Antiochus* departed out of *Ægypt*, without anie good issue of his costly Expedition; euen in such manner as *Daniel* had prophesied long before:[1] yea, fulfilling euerie particular circumstance, both of returning, and of doing mischiefe to *Ierusalem* after his returne; like as if these things had rather beene historified than fore-told by the Prophet. As for the *Roman* Embassadours, they stayed a while, and setled the Kingdome of *Ægypt*, leauing it vnto the elder brother, and appointing the younger to raigne ouer

[1] Daniel 11.29 ff.: 'At the time appointed he [the king of the north] shall return, and come toward the south . . .', etc. Ralegh's allusion is typical of the common interpretation of historical events in the light of apocalyptic books such as Daniel and Revelation.

Cyrene. This done, they departed towards *Cyprus*; which they left, as it had beene, in the power of the *Ægyptian*, hauing first sent away *Antiochus* Fleet, which had alreadie giuen an ouerthrow to the *Ægyptian* shippes.

§12. *How the Romans were dreadfull to all Kings. Their demeanour towards* Evmenes, Prvsias, Masanissa, *and* Cotys. *The end of* Persevs *and his children. The instabilitie of Kingly Estates. The Triumphs of* Pavlvs, Anicivs, *and* Octavivs. *With the Conclusion of the Worke.*

By this peremptorie demeanour of *Popilius*, in doing his Message, and by the readie obedience of King *Antiochus* to the will of the Senate; wee may perceiue how terrible the *Romans* were growne, through their conquest of *Macedon*. The same *Popilius* had beene well contented, a yeare before this, to lay aside the roughnesse of his naturall condition, and to giue good language to the *Achæans* and *Ætolians*, when hee went Embassadour to those people of *Greece*, that were of farre lesse power than the King *Antiochus*. Likewise, *Antiochus* had with good wordes, and no more than good wordes, dismissed other Embassadours which came from *Rome*, in such sort, as they complained not, much lesse vsed anie menacing tearmes, though hee performed nothing of their request. But now the case was altered. So found other Kings as well as *Antiochus*.

Eumenes sent to *Rome* his brother *Attalus*, to gratulate the victorie ouer *Perseus*, and to craue helpe or countenance of the Senate against the *Gallogreekes*, which molested him. Verie welcome was *Attalus*, and louingly entertained by most of the Senatours: who bad him be confident, and request of the Senate his brothers Kingdome for himselfe; for it should surely be giuen him. These hopefull promises tickled *Attalus* with such ambition, that hee eyther approued, or seemed to approue the motion. But his honest nature was soone reclaymed by the faithfull counsaile of *Stratius* a Physician; whome *Eumenes* had sent to *Rome* of purpose to keepe his brother vpright. So, when hee came into the Senate, hee deliuered the errand about which hee had beene sent; recounted his owne seruices done to the *Romans* in

the late Warre, wherewithall he forgat not to make of his
brother as good mention as he could: and finally requested,
That the Townes of *Ænus* and *Maronea* might be bestowed
vpon himselfe. By his omitting to sue for his brothers
Kingdome, the Senate conceiued opinion, that he meant to
craue another day of audience for that businesse alone.
Wherefore, to make him vnderstand how gracious hee was,
they not onely graunted all his desire; but in the presents
which they gaue to him (as was their custome to Embassadours that came with an acceptable message) they vsed
singular magnificence. Neuerthelesse, *Attalus* tooke no
notice of their meaning; but went his way, contented with
what they had alreadie graunted. This did so highly dis-
please the Senate, that whilest hee was yet in *Italie*, they
gaue order for the libertie of *Ænus* and *Maronea:* thereby
making vneffectuall their promise; which otherwise they
could not, without shame, reuoke. And as for the *Gallogreekes*, which were about to inuade the Kingdome of
Pergamus; they sent Embassadours to them, with such
instructions, as rather encouraged than hindered them in their
purpose. The displeasure of the Senate being so manifest;
Eumenes thought it worthie of his labour to make another
voyage to *Rome*. Hee might well blame the follie of his
second voyage thither, for this necessitie of the third: since,
by his malice to *Perseus*, hee had layed open vnto these
ambitious Potentates the way to his owne dores. No sooner
was he come into *Italie*, than the Senate was readie to send
him going. It was not thought expedient to vse him as an
enemie, that came to visit them in loue: neyther could they,
in so doing, haue auoided the note of singular inconstancie:
and to entertaine him as a friend, was more than their
hatred to him, for his ingratitude, as they deemed it, would
permit. Wherefore they made a Decree, That no King
should be suffered to come to *Rome*; and by vertue thereof
sent him home, without expence of much further complement.

Prusias King of *Bithynia* had beene at *Rome* somewhat
before; where he was welcommed after a better fashion. Hee
had learned to behaue himselfe as humbly as the proud
Romans could expect or desire. For entring into the Senate,

hee lay downe, and kissed the threshold, calling the *Fathers* his gods and sauiours: as also hee vsed to weare a Cappe, after the manner of slaues newly manumised,[1] professing himselfe an enfranchised bondman of the People of *Rome*. He was indeede naturally a slaue, and one that by such abject flatterie kept himselfe safe; though doing otherwise greater mischiefe than anie wherewith *Perseus* had beene charged. His errand was, besides matter of complement, to commend vnto the Senate the care of his sonne *Nicomedes*, whom he brought with him to *Rome*, there to receiue education. Further petition he made, to haue some Townes added to his Kingdome: whereto, because the graunt would haue beene vnjust, hee receiued a cold answere. But concerning the Wardship of his sonne, it was vndertaken by the Senate: which, vaunting of the pleasure lately done to *Ægypt*, in freeing it from *Antiochus*, willed him thereby to consider, what effectuall protection the *Romans* gaue vnto the children of Kings, that were to their patronage commended.

But aboue all other Kings, *Masanissa* held his credit with the *Romans* good. His quarrels were endlesse with the *Carthaginians*; which made the friendship of the *Romans* to him the more assured. In all controuersies they gaue judgement on his side: and whereas hee had inuaded the Countrey of *Emporia*, holding the Lands, but vnable to winne the Townes; the *Romans* (though at first they could finde no pretext, whereby to countenance him in this oppression) compelled finally the *Carthaginians* both to let goe all their hold, and to pay fiue hundred Talents to the *Numidian*, for hauing hindered him of his due so long. Now indeede had *Rome* good leysure to deuise vpon the ruine of *Carthage*: after which, the race of *Masanissa* himselfe was shortly by them rooted vp. But heereof the olde King neuer dreamed. Hee sent to *Rome* one of his sonnes, to congratulate the victorie ouer *Perseus*; and offered to come thither himselfe, there to sacrifice for joy vnto *Iupiter* in the *Capitol*. His good will was louingly accepted; his sonne rewarded; and hee entreated to stay at home.

Cotys the *Thracian* sent Embassadours, to excuse himselfe

[1] freed.

touching the aide by him giuen to *Perseus*, for that the *Macedonian* had him bound by hostages; and to entreat, That his sonne, which was taken with the children of *Perseus*, might be set at libertie for conuenient ransome. His excuse was not taken; since hee had voluntarily obliged him-selfe to *Perseus*, by giuing hostages, without necessitie: Yet was his sonne giuen backe to him ransome-free; with admonition, to carrie himselfe better toward the *Romans* in time following. His Kingdome lay betweene *Macedon* and some barbarous Nations; in which respect, it was good to hold him in faire tearmes.

As for those vnhappie Kings, *Perseus* and *Gentius*, they were ledde through *Rome*, with their children and friends, in the Triumphs of *Æmylius* and *Anicius*. *Perseus* had often made suite to *Æmylius*, that hee might not be put to such disgrace: but hee still receiued one skornefull answere, That it lay in his owne power to preuent it; whereby was meant, that hee might kill himselfe. And surely, had hee not hoped for greater mercie than hee found, hee would rather haue sought his death in *Macedon*, than haue beene beholding to the courtesie of his insolent enemies for a wretched life. The issue of the *Roman* clemencie, whereof *Æmylius* had giuen him hope, was no better than this: After that hee, and his fellow King, had beene ledde in chaynes through the streetes, before the Chariots of their triumphing Victors, they were committed to prison, wherein they remayned without hope of release. It was the manner, that when the Triumpher turned his Chariot vp towards the *Capitol*, there to doe sacrifice, hee should command the captiues to be had away to prison, and there put to death: so as the honour of the Vanquisher, and miserie of those that were ouercome, might be both together at the vtmost. This last sentence of death was remitted vnto *Perseus:* yet so, that hee had little joy of his life; but eyther famished himselfe, or (for it is diuersly reported) was kept watching perforce by those that had him in custodie; and so died for want of sleepe. Of his sonnes, two died; it is vncertaine how. The youngest called *Alexander* (onely in name like vnto the Great, though destined sometimes perhaps by his father, vnto the fortunes of the Great) became a Ioyner, or Turner, or, at his best preferment, a Scribe vnder the *Roman* Officers. In such pouertie ended the Royall House of *Macedon:* and it ended on the suddaine; though some eightscore yeares after the death of that Monarch, vnto whose ambition this whole Earth seemed too narrow.

If *Perseus* had knowne it before, that his owne sonne should one day bee compelled to earne his liuing by handie-worke, in a painefull Occupation; it is like, that he would not, as in a wantonnesse of Soueraignetie, haue commaunded those poore men to be slaine, which had recouered his treasures out of the sea, by their skill in the feat of diuing. He would rather haue been verie gentle, and would haue considered, that the greatest oppressors, and the most vndertroden wretches, are all subject vnto One high Power, gouerning all alike with absolute command. But such is our vnhappinesse; in stead of that blessed counsaile, *Do as yee would be done vnto,* a sentence teaching all moderation, and pointing out the way to felicitie; wee entertaine that arrogant thought, *I will be like to the Most High:* that is, I will doe what shall please my selfe. One hath said truly:

> *Et qui nolunt occidere quenquam*
> *Posse volunt.*

> *Euen they that haue no murdrous will,*
> *Would haue it in their power to kill.*[1]

All, or the most, haue a vaine desire of abilitie to doe euill without controule: which is a dangerous temptation vnto the performance. God, who best can judge what is expedient, hath graunted such power to verie few: among whome also, verie few there are, that vse it not to their owne hurt. For who sees not, that a Prince, by racking his Soueraigne authoritie to the vtmost extent, enableth (besides the danger to his owne person) some one of his owne sonnes or nephewes to root vp all his progenie? Shall not manie excellent Princes, notwithstanding their brotherhood, or other nearenesse in bloud, be driuen to flatter the Wife, the Minion, or perhaps the Harlot, that gouernes one, the most vnworthie of his whole house, yet raigning ouer all? The vntimely death of

[1] Juvenal, x 96–97.

manie Princes, which could not humble themselues to such flatterie; and the common practise of the *Turkish* Emperours, to murder all their brethren, without expecting till they offend; are too good proofes hereof. Hereto may be added, That the heire of the same *Roger Mortimer*, who murdered most traiterously and barbarously King *Edward* the second; was, by reason of a marriage, proclaimed, in time not long after following, heire apparent to the Crowne of *England:* which had he obtained, then had all the power of *Edward* fallen into the race of his mortall enemie, to exercise the same vpon the Line of that vnhappie King. Such examples of the instabilitie whereto all mortall affaires are subject; as they teach moderation, and admonish the transitorie Gods of Kingdomes, not to authorize, by wicked precedents, the euill that may fall on their owne posteritie: so doe they necessarily make vs vnderstand, how happie that Countrie is, which hath obtained a King able to conceiue and teach, That God *is the sorest and sharpest Schoolemaister, that can be deuised, for such Kings, as thinke this world ordained for them, without controlment to turne it vpside-downe at their pleasure*.[1]

Now, concerning the Triumph of *L. Æmylius Paulus*; it was in all points like vnto that of *T. Quintius Flaminius:* though farre more glorious, in regard of the Kings owne person, that was ledde along therein, as part of his owne spoyles; and in regard likewise both of the Conquest and of the Bootie. So great was the quantitie of Gold and Siluer carried by *Paulus* into the *Roman* Treasurie, that from thenceforth, vntill the ciuile Warres, which followed vpon the death of *Iulius Cæsar*, the Estate had no need to burthen it selfe with anie Tribute. Yet was this noble Triumph likely to haue beene hindered by the souldiors; who grudged at their Generall, for not hauing dealt more bountifully with them. But the Princes of the Senate ouer-ruled the People and Souldiors herein, and brought them to reason by seuere exhortations. Thus *Paulus* enjoyed as much honour of his victorie as men could giue. Neuerthelesse, it pleased God to take away from him his two remayning sonnes, that were not

[1] In a marginal note Ralegh describes this statement as 'The true Law of free Monarchies'.

giuen in adoption: of which, the one died fiue dayes before
the Triumph; the other, three dayes after it. This losse hee
bore wisely: and told the People, That hee hoped to see the
Commonwealth flourish in a continuance of prosperitie;
since the joy of his victorie was requited with his owne
priuate calamitie, in stead of the publike.

About the same time, *Octauius* the Admirall, who had
brought *Perseus* out of *Samothrace:* and *Anicius* the Prætor,
who had conquered *Illyria*, and taken King *Gentius* prisoner;
made their seuerall triumphs. The glory of which magnificent spectacles; together with the confluence of Embassages
from all parts; and Kings, either visiting the Imperiall Citie,
or offering to visit her, and doe their duties in person; were
enough to say vnto *Rome, Sume superbiam, Take vpon thee
the Maiestie, that thy deserts haue purchased.*

By this which we haue alreadie set downe, is seene the
beginning and end of the three first Monarchies of the
world; whereof the Founders and Erectours thought, that
they could neuer haue ended. That of *Rome* which made the
fourth, was also at this time almost at the highest. We haue
left it flourishing in the middle of the field; hauing rooted
vp, or cut down, all that kept it from the eyes and admiration
of the world. But after some continuance, it shall begin to
lose the beauty it had; the stormes of ambition shal beat her
great boughes and branches one against another; her leaues
shall fall off, her limbes wither, and a rabble of barbarous
Nations enter the field, and cut her downe.

Now these great Kings, and conquering Nations, haue bin
the subiect of those ancient Histories, which haue beene
preserued, and yet remaine among vs; and withall of so
many tragicall Poets, as in the persons of powerfull Princes,
and other mightie men haue complained against Infidelitie,
Time, Destinie, and most of all against the Variable successe
of worldly things, and Instabilitie of Fortune. To these
vndertakings, the greatest Lords of the world haue beene
stirred vp, rather by the desire of *Fame*, which ploweth vp
the Aire, and soweth in the Winde; than by the affection of
bearing rule, which draweth after it so much vexation, and
so many cares. And that this is true, the good aduice of

Cineas to *Pyrrhus* proues. And certainly, as Fame hath often beene dangerous to the liuing, so is it to the dead of no vse at all; because separate from knowledge. Which were it otherwise, and the extreame ill bargaine of buying this lasting discourse, vnderstood by them which are dissolued; they themselues would then rather haue wished, to haue stolne out of the world without noise; than to be put in minde, that they haue purchased the report of their actions in the world, by rapine, oppression and crueltie, by giuing in spoile the innocent and labouring soule to the idle and insolent, and by hauing emptied the Cities of the world of their ancient Inhabitants, and filled them againe with so many and so variable sorts of sorrowes.

Since the fall of the *Roman* Empire (omitting that of the *Germaines*, which had neither greatnesse nor continuance) there hath beene no State fearefull in the East, but that of the *Turke*; nor in the West any Prince that hath spred his wings farre ouer his nest, but the *Spaniard*; who since the time that *Ferdinand* expelled the *Moores* out of *Granado*, haue made many attempts to make themselues Masters of all *Europe*. And it is true, that by the treasures of both *Indies*, and by the many Kingdomes which they possesse in *Europe*, they are at this day the most powerfull. But as the *Turke* is now counterpoised by the *Persian*, so in stead of so many Millions as haue beene spent by the *English*, *French*, and *Neatherlands* in a defensiue war, and in diuersions against them, it is easie to demonstrate, that with the charge of two hundred thousand pound continued but for two yeares or three at the most, they may not only be perswaded to liue in peace, but all their swelling and ouerflowing streames may be brought backe into their naturall channels and old bankes. These two Nations, I say, are at this day the most eminent, and to be regarded; the one seeking to roote out the Christian Religion altogether, the other the truth and sincere profession thereof, the one to joyne all *Europe* to *Asia*, the other the rest of all *Europe* to *Spaine*.

For the rest, if we seeke a reason of the succession and continuance of this boundlesse ambition in mortall men, we may adde to that which hath been already said; That the Kings and Princes of the world haue alwayes laid before them, the actions, but not the ends, of those great Ones which præceded them. They are alwayes transported with the glorie of the one, but they neuer minde the miserie of the other, till they finde the experience in themselues. They neglect the aduice of God, while they enioy life, or hope it; but they follow the counsell of Death, vpon his first approach. It is he that puts into man all the wisdome of the world, without speaking a word; which God with all the words of his Law, promises, or threats, doth not infuse. *Death* which hateth and destroyeth man, is beleeued; God which hath made him and loues him, is alwayes deferred. *I haue considered* (saith *Salomon*) *all the workes that are vnder the Sunne, and behold, all is vanitie and vexation of spirit*: but who beleeues it, till Death tells it vs. It was Death, which opening the conscience of *Charles* the fift, made him enjoyne his sonne *Philip* to restore *Nauarre*; and King *Francis* the first of *France*, to command that justice should be done vpon the Murderers of the Protestants in *Merindol* and *Cabrieres*, which till then he neglected. It is therfore Death alone that can suddenly make man to know himselfe. He tells the proud and insolent, that they are but Abiects, and humbles them at the instant; makes them crie, complaine, and repent, yea, euen to hate their forepassed happinesse. He takes the account of the rich, and proues him a begger; a naked begger, which hath interest in nothing, but in the grauell that filles his mouth. He holds a Glasse before the eyes of the most beautifull, and makes them see therein, their deformitie and rottennesse; and they acknowledge it.

O eloquent, just and mightie Death! whom none could aduise, thou hast perswaded; what none hath dared, thou hast done; and whom all the world hath flattered, thou only hast cast out of the world and despised: thou hast drawne together all the farre stretched greatnesse, all the pride, crueltie, and ambition of man, and couered it all ouer with these two narrow words, *Hic iacet*.

Lastly, whereas this Booke, by the title it hath, calles it selfe, The first part of the *Generall Historie* of the *World*, implying a *Second*, and *Third* Volume; which I also intended, and haue hewen out; besides many other discouragements, perswading my silence; it hath pleased God to take that glorious *Prince* out of the world, to whom they were directed; whose vnspeakable and neuer enough lamented losse, hath taught mee to say with Iob, *Versa est in Luctum Cithara mea, & Organum meum in vocem flentium.*[1]

FINIS.

---

[1] 'My harp also is turned to mourning, and my organ into the voice of them that weep.' – Job 30.31 (AV).

A Dictionary of Names

Dates are 'A.D.' unless otherwise stated; they also conform to modern usage, not to the elaborate chronological scheme which Ralegh had to construct in the light of the accepted short age of the world (see entry under 'Adam'). The entries on the kings of Israel and Judah are clarified in the table given below, p. 415.

Abel: 2nd son of Adam (q.v.)

Abia: *see* next entry

Abijah: King of Judah (see Table, p. 415)

Abraham (21st cent. B.C.?): Hebrew patriarch, led his family from Chaldea to Canaan, then Egypt

'Academics': adherents of Plato's philosophy

Achilles: the Greek hero of the Trojan war

Adam: according to tradition, the first man (estimated by Ralegh to have been created in 4031 B.C.)

Adonis: beloved of Venus, killed by a boar

Aelian (3rd cent. or earlier): Roman historian

Aemilius Paulus: *see* Paulus Aemilius

Aemilius, Paulus (d. 1529): Italian chronicler of French history

Agar: *see* Hagar

Agathocles: tyrant of Syracuse (316–304 B.C.) and king (304–289)

Agathon (late 5th cent. B.C.): Athenian tragic poet

Agesilaus II (445–361 B.C.): Spartan king and general

Agricola, G. Julius (37–93): Roman general and statesman

Ahab: King of Israel (see Table, p. 415), personification of wickedness

Ahaz: King of Judah (see Table, p. 415)

Ahaziah: King of Israel (see Table, p. 415)

Ahaziah (also Jehoahaz): King of Judah (see Table, p. 415)

Alba: *see* Alva

Albinovanus Pedo (1st cent.): Roman poet

Alcinous: in the *Odyssey*, king of the Phaeacians

Alcuin (*c.* 735–804): English scholar

Alexander III the Great: King of Macedon (336–323 B.C.)

Alexander V: King of Macedon with his brother Antipater (297–294 B.C.)

Alva, Duke of (1508?–83): commander of the Spanish forces in the Netherlands

Amaziah: King of Judah (see Table, p. 415)

Ambrose, St (*c.* 339–97): Bishop of Milan, Doctor of the Church

Ammianus Marcellinus (fl. *c.* 390): Roman soldier and historian

Ammon: an Egyptian god, identified by Greeks with Zeus
Amphiaraus: mythical Argive hero and seer
Anaxagoras (500?–428 B.C.): Greek philosopher
Anaxandrides (fl. 376–347 B.C.): Greek comic poet
Anaximenes of Miletus (6th cent. B.C.): Greek philosopher
Anicius: Roman praetor, conqueror of Illyricum (168 B.C.)
Anjou: French noble family (from 9th cent.)
Annibal: *see* Hannibal
Antaeus: son of Neptune, wrestled with Hercules
Antigonus I: King of Macedon (306–301 B.C.), initially general under Alexander the Great
Antiochus III the Great: King of Syria (223–187 B.C.)
Antiochus IV Epiphanes: King of Syria (175–163 B.C.)
Antipater (398?–319 B.C.): Macedonian general, regent of Macedon
Antipater (fl. 125 B.C.): Roman historian
Antoninus, St: Antonio Pierozzi (1389–1459), Italian Dominican theologian and chronicler
Antônio, Dom (1531–94): claimant to the Portuguese throne (1580)
Apocalypsis: i.e., Book of Revelation
Apollo: Olympian god of music and poetry
Apollonius Dyscolus (fl. 2nd cent.): Alexandrian grammarian
Apollonius Rhodius (237?–186 B.C.): Greek epic poet and grammarian
Apollonius of Tyana (1st cent.): Greek Neopythagorean philosopher
Appian (2nd cent.): Roman historian from Alexandria
Apuleius (2nd cent.): Roman philosopher and rhetorician
Aquinas: *see* Thomas A.
Aratus of Sicyon: strategos of the Achæan League from 245 B.C.
Aratus of Soli (*c.* 315–*c.* 245 B.C.): Greek physician and poet, quoted by St Paul (Acts 17.28)
Arianus: *see* Arrian
Arias Montanus, Benedictus (1527–98): Spanish theologian and Orientalist
Aridaeus: *see* Arrhidaeus
Ariobarzanes II: King of Pontus (363–337 B.C.)
Ariovistus (fl. 71?–58 B.C.): Germanic tribal chief
Aristobulus (4th cent. B.C.): Greek historian of Alexander's campaigns
Aristotle (384–322 B.C.): Greek philosopher
Armagnac: noble French house (from 10th cent.)
Armaignac: *see* previous entry
Arminius, Jacobus (1560–1609): Dutch anti-Calvinist theologian
Arnobius (fl. 300): Christian apologist
Arrhidaeus: Macedonian general, regent after death of Perdiccas (q.v.)
Arrian (fl. 2nd cent.): Greek historian and biographer of Alexander the Great
Artabazus: Persian general under Darius III (q.v.)
Artaxerxes II Mnemon: King of Persia (404–359 B.C.)
Artemisia: regent of Halicarnassus, ally of Xerxes at Salamis
Asclepius: god of medicine
Asdrubal: *see* Hasdrubal
Astraea: goddess of justice

Atabalipa (Atahualpa): last Inca king of Peru (1525–33)
Athaliah: Queen of Judah (see Table, p. 415), daughter of Ahab and Jezebel (q.v.)
Athenaeus (late 2nd/early 3rd cent.): Greek scholar
Atossa: wife of Darius I, mother of Xerxes I (q.v.)
Attalus II Philadelphus: King of Pergamum (160?–38 B.C.), brother of Eumenes II (q.v.)
Augustine, St (354–430): the greatest theologian of the early Latin Church
Augustus: 1st Roman emperor (27 B.C.–A.D. 14)
Aventinus, Johannes (1477–1534): Bavarian historian
Avicenna (980–1037): Arabian philosopher
Bacchus (Dionysus): Olympian god of wine and revelry, son of Jupiter and Semele
Bacon, Sir Francis (1561–1626): philosopher and essayist
Bajazet I: Sultan of the Ottoman Empire (1389–1403), captured by Timur (q.v.)
Bardisanists: Gnostic dualists (?), disciples of the Syrian Bardesanes (154–222)
Baruch: a book of the Apocrypha
Basil the Great, St (c. 330–79): Bishop of Caesarea, Father of the Church
Bathsheba: mistress and then wife of David (q.v.), mother of Solomon (q.v.)
Becanus, Martinus (1550–1624): Jesuit from Brabant, theologian and exegete
Bede, St (c. 673–735): English scholar, 'Father of English History'
Bel: i.e., Baal, a great Babylonian deity
Belisarius (505?–65): general of the Eastern Roman Empire
Bellay, Guillaume du, seigneur de Langey (1491–1543): French soldier, diplomat, author
Bellisarius: see Belisarius
Ben Sira: the author of Ecclesiasticus
Bernard, St (1090–1153): Abbot of Clairvaux, theologian and mystic
Berosus (3rd cent. B.C.): Babylonian historian
Bessus: satrap under Darius III (q.v.)
Bevis of Southampton, Sir: hero of a medieval tale, avenged his father's murder
Beza, Theodore (1519–1608): French Calvinist theologian
Black Prince: see Edward
Boethius (c. 480–c. 524): Roman philosopher and statesman
Buchanus = Buchanan, George (1506–82): Scottish historian and scholar
Bunting, Heinrich (1545–1606): German theologian and chronologer
Busiris: son of Neptune, mythical king of Egypt
Cabalists: adherents of the cabala, the occult Jewish philosophy
Caesar, G. Julius: Roman dictator (49–44 B.C.)
Cain: eldest son of Adam and Eve
Cajetan, Tomasso de Vio (1470–1534): Italian-Spanish cardinal and theologian
Caligula: Roman emperor (37–41)
Calisthenes: see Callisthenes

SWR O

Callicrates (d. 149 B.C.): general of the Achaean League

Callisthenes (360?–328? B.C.): Greek philosopher and historian with Alexander

Calvin, John (1509–64): French Reformer and theologian

Canute II the Great: King of England (1016–35) and Denmark (1018–35)

Carion, Johann (1499–1538): German scholar and chronicler

Casaubon, Isaac (1559–1614): Swiss classical scholar

Cassander: King of Macedon (316–297 B.C.)

Cato, Marcus Porcius (234–149 B.C.): Roman statesman

Catullus (84–54 B.C.): Roman lyric poet

Cecil, Sir Robert, 1st Earl of Salisbury (1563–1612): Secretary of State to Elizabeth I and James I

Ceres (Demeter): Olympian goddess of agriculture

'Chaldean Paraphrast': i.e., commentator on Bible in Aramaic ('Targum)

Cham: *see* Ham

Charlemagne: Charles I the Great, King of the Franks (768–814) and Emperor of the West (800–814)

Charles V: Holy Roman Emperor (1519–56), and King of Spain as Charles I (1516–56)

Charles VIII: King of France (1483–98)

Charles the Great: *see* Charlemagne

Charron, Pierre (1541–1603): French philosopher and theologian

Chrysippus of Soli (*c.* 280–207 B.C.): Stoic, continued work of Cleanthes (q.v.)

Chrysostom: *see* John C.

Cicero (106–43 B.C.): Roman orator, philosopher and statesman

Claudian (d. *c.* 395): Latin poet

Claudius I: Roman Emperor (9 B.C.–A.D. 54)

Cleanthes of Assos (331–232 B.C.): Stoic, pupil of Zeno (q.v.)

Cleon (d. 422 B.C.): Athenian demagogue during the Peloponnesian War

Cleopatra I: wife of Ptolemy V (q.v.)

Clitus (d. 328 B.C.): commander under Alexander the Great, killed by him

Clitus (d. 318 B.C.): commander under Alexander the Great, defeated by Antigonus

Clytus: *see* previous entries

Codrus: last king of Athens, said to have reigned *c.* 1068 B.C.

Coke, Sir Edward (1552–1634): Lord Chief Justice, writer on law

Coligni or Coligny, Gaspar de (1519–72): French admiral, leader of Huguenots

Comestor: *see* Peter C.

Comines, Philip de (1447?–1511?): French chronicler

Constantine the Great: Roman Emperor (306–337)

Cornutus, Lucius Annaeus (1st cent.): Roman Stoic philosopher

Cotys (d. *c.* 356 B.C.): King of Thrace

Craterus (d. 321 B.C.): Macedonian general, ruled with Antipater, killed by Eumenes (q.v.)

Cratippus (4th cent. B.C.): Greek historian

Ctesias (5th cent. B.C.): Greek historian of Persia

Cumaean Sibyl: prophetess from whom Rome's last king bought oracular utterances

Curtius Rufus (fl. 1st cent.): Latin biographer of Alexander the Great

Cusanus: *see* Nicholas of Cusa

Cybele: the goddess of nature; sometimes 'the mother of the gods' Rhea

Cyprian, St (d. 258): Bishop of Carthage, pastoral theologian

Cyril, St (376–444): Archbishop of Alexandria, Father of the Church

Cyrus the Great: King of Persia (550–529 B.C.), founder of Persian Empire

Cyrus the Younger (*c*. 424–401 B.C.): Persian satrap whose defeat occasioned retreat of Xenophon (q.v.)

Daedalus: mythical inventor, built Labyrinth for Minos (q.v.)

Dagon: a Philistine deity

Damascene: *see* John of Damascus

Danaeus (Daneau), Lambertus (1530–95): French divine and theologian

Danett, Thomas (fl. 1566–1601): English chronicler, translator of chronicles of Comines (q.v.)

Daniel: i.e., Book of the 'prophet' Daniel

Dannet, Thomas: *see* Danett

Darius I the Great: King of Persia (521–486 B.C.), defeated at Marathon (490)

Darius III Codomannus: King of Persia (336–330 B.C.), defeated at Issus (333), etc.

David: the 2nd king of Israel (see Table, p. 415), accepted as author of Psalms

Deborah: a 'judge' of Israel

Decemviri: Roman board of ten commissioners

Demetrius I Poliorcetes: King of Macedon (294–283 B.C.)

Demetrius I Soter: King of Syria (162–150 B.C.)

Democritus (late 5th/early 4th cent. B.C.): Greek philosopher, developed atomistic doctrine of Leucippus (q.v.)

Demogorgon: a terrifying underworld demon; sometimes, a primeval creator

Demosthenes (*c*. 385–322 B.C.): Athenian statesman, the greatest of Greek orators

Dercillus: *see* next entry

Dercyllus (3rd cent. B.C.); Greek historian

Deucalion: the only survivor, with his wife Pyrrha, of the flood sent by Jupiter

Diana (Artemis): Olympian goddess of hunting and virginity

Diodor(e): *see* next entry

Diodorus Siculus (late 1st cent. B.C.): Greek historian

Dionysius the Elder: tyrant of Syracuse (405–367 B.C.)

Dionysius the Younger: tyrant of Syracuse (367–356, 347–344 B.C.)

Dionysius the Pseudo-Areopagite (*c*. 500): mystical theologian, often confused with St Paul's convert in Athens

Doria, Andrea (1468?–1560): Genoese admiral and statesman

Duilius Nepos (fl. 3rd cent. B.C.): Roman general

Ecclesiastes: *see* Solomon

Ecclesiasticus: *see* Ben Sira

Edmondes, Sir Clement (1564?–1622): English writer on military art
Edmund II Ironside (980?–1016): King of the English
Edward II: King of England (1307–27)
Edward III: King of England (1327–77)
Edward IV: King of England (1461–70, 1471–83)
Edward the Black Prince (1330–76): Prince of Wales, eldest son of Edward III
Ehud: a 'judge' of Israel
Eli: high priest and 'judge' of Israel
Eliah: *see* Elijah
Elianus: *see* Aelian
Elijah (9th cent. B.C.): Hebrew prophet
Elizabeth I: Queen of England (1558–1603)
Empedocles (5th cent. B.C.): Greek philosopher and statesman
Ennius (236–169? B.C.): Roman poet
Enoch: Hebrew patriarch, 'translated' to Heaven
Epaminondas (*c.* 418–362 B.C.): Theban statesman and general
Ephestion: *see* Hephaistion
Epicurus (342?–270 B.C.): Greek philosopher
Epimenides (7th cent. B.C.): Cretan philosopher and poet-prophet
Epiphanes: *see* Antiochus IV
Epiphanes: *see* Ptolemy V
Erasmus, Desiderius (1467–1536): Dutch scholar and humanist
Esay: *see* Isaiah
Esdras: title of two books of the Septuagint (four of the Vulgate)
Eugubinus: *see* Steuco
Eumenes (360?–316 B.C.): Macedonian general, allotted Cappadocia and Paphlagonia
Eumenes II: King of Pergamum (197–160? B.C.)
Euripides (*c.* 480–406 B.C.): the last of the three greatest Attic tragedians
Eurybiades: Spartan commander of the Greek fleet at Artemisium and Salamis (480 B.C.)
Eusebius (*c.* 260–340): Bishop of Caesarea, 'Father of Church History'
Evan Vasilowich: *see* Ivan III
Evaristus, St: Pope (*c.* 99–*c.* 107)
Ezechia: *see* Hezekiah
Farnese, Alessandro: Duke of Parma (1586–92), head of the Spanish armies in Netherlands
Ferdinand V: King of Aragon and Castile (1479–1516), and of Naples as Ferdinand III (1504–16)
Ficino, Marsilio (1433–99): Florentine Neoplatonist and humanist
Foix, Gaston de, Duc de Nemours (1489–1512): commander of French army in Italy
Francis I: King of France (1515–47)
Galen (fl. 2nd cent.): Greek physician and writer
Gentius (fl. 180–167 B.C.): King of Illyricum
Gideon: a 'judge' of Israel
Gilbert, Sir Humphrey (1539–83): soldier, navigator and colonist

Gog: a people (Ezek. 38.2), later a power under Satan's dominion (cf. Rev. 20.8)

Gómara, Francisco Lopez de (1510?–60): Spanish author of early history of America

Gomer: son of Japheth (q.v.)

Gondomar, Diego Sarmiento de Acuña, Count of (1567–1626): Spanish diplomatist, ambassador to London (1613–18, 1620–22)

Gorges, Sir Arthur (d. 1625): poet, translator, naval commander

Goropius: see Becanus

Gregoire, Pierre, Tholosain (1540?–97?): French jurist

Gregory of Nazianzus, St (c. 329–389): Bishop of Constantinople, Father of the Church

Gregory of Nyssa, St (c. 330–c. 395): Bishop of Nyssa, Father of the Church

Gregory the Great, St: Pope (590–604), Doctor of the Church

Grotius, Hugo (1583–1645): Dutch statesman and humanist

Guicciardini, Francesco (1483–1540): Florentine historian and statesman

Guichardine: see previous entry

Hagar: servant of Sarah, and wife of Abraham (q.v.)

Hakluyt, Richard (1552?–1616): English geographer

Ham: son of Noah (q.v.)

Hammon: see Ammon

Hannibal (247–183 B.C.): the Carthaginian general who invaded Italy

Hanno the Great (270–190 B.C.): Carthaginian general

Hasdrubal (d. 207 B.C.): Carthaginian general, brother of Hannibal (q.v.)

Hazael: King of Syria, anointed by Elijah (q.v.)

Hector: the foremost Trojan warrior, killed by Achilles (q.v.)

Hellen: the fabled ancestor of the Hellenic race, son of Deucalion (q.v.)

Henry I: King of England (1100–35)

Henry III: King of France (1574–89)

Henry IV: King of England (1399–1413)

Henry V: King of England (1413–22)

Henry VI: King of England (1422–61, 1470–71)

Henry VII: King of England (1485–1509)

Henry VIII: King of England (1509–47)

Henry Prince of Wales: heir apparent to James I, died aged 18 (1612)

Hephaistion (d. 324 B.C.): Macedonian general, intimate friend of Alexander the Great

Heraclitus (6th/5th cent. B.C.): Greek philosopher

Hérauld, Didier (c. 1579–1649): French scholar

Hercules (Heracles): the son of Jupiter and Alcmene, completed the 12 'labours' imposed by Juno (q.v.)

Hermes surnamed Trismegistus ('the thrice-greatest'): legendary author of Greek and Latin religious and philosophical writings

Herodotus (484–425 B.C.): Greek historian

Herrault: see Hérauld

Hesiod (8th cent. B.C.): Greek poet, author of *Theogony*

Hezekiah: King of Judah (see Table, p. 415)

Hieremie: *see* Jeremiah
Hierome: *see* Jerome
Hieron II: tyrant of Syracuse (270/265?–215 B.C.)
Hierusalem: i.e., Jerusalem
Higinus: *see* Hyginus
Homer: understood as author of the two epics and the 'Homeric' hymns
Hooker, Richard (1554?–1600): Anglican theologian, author of *Laws of Ecclesiastical Polity*
Hopkins: i.e. Joannes Hopkinsonus, author of *Synopis paradisi sive paradisi descriptio* (Leyden, 1593)
Horace (65–8 B.C.): Roman poet
Howard, Charles (1536–1624): Lord High Admiral, chief commander against the Spanish Armada
Hugh of St Victor (*c.* 1096–1141): theologian and mystic
Hugo: *see* previous entry
Hyginus, Gaius Julius (1st cent. B.C.): Roman miscellaneous author
Ironside: *see* Edmund II
Isaiah (8th cent. B.C.): Hebrew prophet
Isidore, St (*c.* 560–636): Archbishop of Seville, encyclopedic scholar
Ivan III Vasilievich, the Great: grand duke of Moscow (1462–1505)
Jaddus: high priest at the time of Alexander the Great
James I: King of Great Britain (1603–25) and of Scotland as James VI (from 1567)
James V: King of Scotland (1513–42)
Jansenius, Cornelius (1510–76): Flemish biblical scholar
Janus: the patron god of beginnings and endings
Japheth: son of Noah (q.v.)
Jason: leader of the Argonauts
Jason (Joshua) I: high priest (174–171 B.C.), brother of Onias (q.v.)
Jehoahaz: King of Israel (see Table, p. 415)
Jehoahaz: King of Judah (see Table, p. 415)
Jehoash: King of Israel: *see* Joash
Jehoash: King of Judah (see Table, p. 415)
Jehoram: King of Israel: *see* Joram
Jehoram: King of Judah (see Table, p. 415)
Jehoshaphat: King of Judah (see Table, p. 415)
Jehu: King of Israel (see Table, p. 415)
Jephthah: a 'judge' of Israel
Jeremiah (7th cent. B.C.): Hebrew prophet
Jeroboam (I): King of Israel (see Table, p. 415)
Jeroboam (II): King of Israel (see Table, p. 415)
Jerome, St (*c.* 342–420): scholar, translator of the Bible (Vulgate), Doctor of the Church
Jethro: father-in-law of Moses (q.v.)
Jezebel: the idolatrous wife of Ahab (q.v.)
Joane of Naples: *see* next entry
Joanna II: Queen of Naples (1414–35)
Joash: King of Israel (see Table, p. 415)

Joash: a son of King Ahab (q.v.)

John Chrysostom, St (*c.* 347–407): Patriarch of Constantinople, Father of the Church

John of Damascus, St (*c.* 675–*c.* 749): Eastern encyclopedic theologian and scholar

John II the Good: King of France (1350–64)

John XI: Pope (931–36)

Jonson, Ben (1573–1637): poet and dramatist

Joram: King of Israel (see Table, p. 415)

Josaphat: *see* Jehoshaphat

Josephus, Flavius (38?–100?): Jewish historian

Joshua: the successor of Moses (q.v.), conqueror of Palestine

Josiah: King of Judah (see Table, p. 415)

Jove: *see* Jupiter

Jubal: son of Lamech (Gen. 4.21)

Julian 'the Apostate': Roman Emperor (361–363)

Julius Agricola: *see* Agricola

Julius Solinus: *see* Solinus

Junius (Du Jon), Franciscus (1545–1602): French theologian and biblical scholar

Juno (Hera): queen of the Olympian gods, wife of Jupiter

Jupiter (Zeus): the supreme Olympian god

Jupiter Hammon: *see* Ammon

Justin Martyr, St (*c.* 100–*c.* 165): Christian apologist

Justine: *see* next entry

Justinus (3rd cent.?): Roman historian

Juvenal (*c.* 60–*c.* 140): Roman lawyer and satirist

Kemis, Laurence: *see* next entry

Keymis, Lawrence (d. 1618): naval commander with Ralegh, committed suicide after last abortive expedition

Lactantius (*c.* 240–*c.* 320): Christian apologist

Langey: *see* Bellay

La Trimouille, Louis de (1460–1525): French military commander

Lessius, Leonardus (1554–1623): Flemish Jesuit theologian

Leucippus (5th cent. B.C.): Greek founder of atomistic philosophy

Lewis: *see* Louis

Linus: son of Apollo, considered an inventor of poetry

Linus, St: Pope (*c.* 67–*c.* 79)

Livia Drusilla: wife of Augustus (q.v.)

Livy (59 B.C.–A.D. 17): Roman historian

Lodowick of Nassau: *see* Louis of N.

Lombard, Peter: *see* Peter L.

Lopes, Eduardo (late 16th cent.): Spanish (or Portuguese) explorer, author on the Congo

Lopez, Francisco: *see* Gómara

Louis I le Débonnaire: King of Aquitaine (from 781), and Emperor (813–33, 835–40)

Louis XI: King of France (1461–83)

Louis XII: King of France (1498–1515)

Louis of Nassau (1538–74): brother of William of Orange (q.v.), defeated by Alva (q.v.)

Loys: *see* Louis

Lucan (39–65): Roman poet

Lucilius (180–102 B.C.): Roman poet, creator of satire

Lycurgus: according to tradition, the foremost Spartan lawgiver

Lyranus: *see* Nicholas of Lyra

Lysborne: i.e., Lisbon

Lysimachus: King of Thrace (306–281 B.C.), initially general under Alexander the Great

Maccabees (Hasmonaeans): family of Jewish patriots, 2nd–1st cent. B.C.

Macchabees: *see* previous entry

Machiavelli, Niccolò (1469–1527): Florentine statesman and political philosopher

MacMurrough, Dermot: Irish ruler, king of Leinster (1126–71)

Magog: a land (Ezek. 38.2), later a power under Satan's dominion (cf. Rev. 20.8)

Mahomet: *see* Mohammed

Manasseh (Greek form, Manasses): King of Judah (see Table, p. 415)

Mandeville, Sir John: presumed author of 14th-cent. book of travels

Manetho (3rd cent. B.C.): Egyptian historian

Manichaeans: 3rd–4th cent. dualists, disciples of the Persian Manes (*c.* 215–275)

Mardonius (d. 479 B.C.): commander of Persian army at the time of Salamis (480) and at Plataea (479)

Marius Gaius (155?–86 B.C.): Roman general and political leader

Mars (Ares): Olympian god of war

Mary: Queen of England (1553–58)

Masanissa: *see* next entry

Masinissa: King of Numidia which he conquered with Roman help (201 B.C.)

Masius, Andreas (1515?–73): Belgian Orientalist

Maurice of Nassau (1567–1625): Dutch military leader, defeated Spaniards

Medea: sorceress who helped Jason (q.v.) obtain the Golden Fleece

Mela, Pomponius (1st cent.): Latin geographer

Melanchthon, Philipp (1497–1560): German Reformer and humanist

Melissus (5th cent. B.C.): Greek philosopher, disciple of Parmenides (q.v.)

Memnon (d. 333 B.C.): Greek general in the service of Darius III (q.v.)

Menander (*c.* 343–*c.* 291 B.C.): Athenian writer of comedies

Menedemus (350?—276? B.C.): Greek philosopher of Eretria

Mercer, John: *see* next entry

Mercerus (Mercier), Joannes (d. 1570): French biblical scholar

Mercurius Trismegistus: *see* Hermes T.

Mercury (Hermes): Olympian god of commerce, eloquence, etc.

Midas: legendary king of Phrygia, turned everything he touched into gold

Minerva (Athena): Olympian goddess of wisdom

Minos: legendary king of Crete; cf. Daedalus

Mirandula: *see* Pico

Mnemon: *see* Artaxerxes II

Mohammed (570–632): Arabian prophet, founder of Islam

Monluc(t): *see* Montluc

Montanus, Arias: *see* Arias M.

Montezuma I (1390?–1464?): Aztec ruler of Mexico

Montluc, Blaise de Lasseran-Massencome, Seigneur de (1501?–77): marshal of France and military author

Moses: the founder and lawgiver of Israel

Moses Bar-Cepha (*c.* 813–903): Syrian bishop, biblical scholar

Musaeus: legendary pre-Homeric Greek poet, pupil of Orpheus (q.v.)

Myron (fl. 460–440 B.C.): one of the greatest of ancient Greek sculptors

Nabonassar: King of Babylon (747–734 B.C.)

Naboth: refusing to yield to Ahab (q.v.), was put to death (I Kings 21.1–24)

Nabuchodonosor: *see* Nebuchadnezzar

Nauclerus, Johannes (d. 1510): German chronicler and jurist

Nazianzenus: *see* Gregory of Nazianzus

Nearchus: officer under Alexander the Great, commander of fleet (325/4 B.C.)

Nebuchadnezzar II: King of Babylon (605–562 B.C.)

Nemures (Nemours): *see* Foix

Neptune (Poseidon): Olympian god of the sea

Nero: Roman emperor (54–68)

Nicholas of Cusa (*c.* 1400–64): German cardinal and philosopher

Nicholas of Lyra (1270?–1340?): Franciscan biblical scholar, professor at the Sorbonne

Nimrod: legendary founder of Assyrian Empire

Ninias: successor of Semiramis (q.v.)

Ninus: legendary founder of Nineveh, husband of Semiramis (q.v.)

Noah: 10th in descent from Adam, father of Shem, Ham and Japheth

Nonius Marcellus (4th cent.): Latin grammarian and lexicographer

Norris, Sir John (1547?–97): English military commander, with Drake ravaged the Iberian coast (1589).

Octavius: *see* Augustus

Ogyges: legendary 1st king of Thebes; the deluge in his time preceded Deucalion's (q.v.)

Olympias (d. 316 B.C.): mother of Alexander the Great

Onesicritus (fl. 335–323 B.C.): Greek historian, accompanied Alexander the Great

Onesimus: the slave of Philemon (q.v.)

Onias III: high priest (*c.* 180 B.C.)

Orange, Prince of: *see* William I

Origen (*c.* 185–*c.* 254): Alexandrian biblical scholar and theologian

Orithyia: the nymph beloved of Boreas

Orosius, Paulus (5th cent.): Spanish author of popular universal history

Orpheus: legendary pre-Homeric poet, founder of the mystic Greek cult Orphism

Othoniel: a 'judge' of Israel

Otto of Freising (1114?–58): German bishop and historian

Ovid (43 B.C.–*c.* A.D. 17): Roman poet

Pagninus, Santes (d. 1541): Spanish Dominican biblical scholar
Palladius (c. 368–c. 341): Greek Christian prelate and writer
Pallas: see Minerva
Papirius, Lucius (late 4th cent. B.C.): Roman general and politician
Papyrius: see previous entry
Pareus, David (1548–1622): German theologian and biblical exegete
Paris, Matthew (1200?–59): English historian
Parma: see Farnese
Parmenides (5th cent. B.C.): Greek philosopher, head of Eleatic school
Parmenio (d. 330 B.C.): Macedonian general under Philip and Alexander
Patricius: see Patrizzi
Patritius: see next entry
Patrizzi, Francisco (1529–97): Italian philosopher and scholar
Paulus, L. Aemilius (229?–160 B.C.): Roman general, defeated Perseus (q.v.)
Pausanias: regent of Sparta, commander of Greek forces at Plataea (479 B.C.)
Pausanias (2nd cent.): Greek traveller and geographer
Pazaro, Francisco: see Pizarro
Pedro III the Great: King of Aragon (1276–85)
Pedro el Cruel: King of Castile and León (1350–69)
Penthesilea: daughter of Mars and the Queen of the Amazons
Perdiccas (d. 321 B.C.): Macedonian general under Alexander, later regent
Pereira, Bento (1535–1610): Spanish theologian and biblical scholar
Pererius: see previous entry
'Peripatetics': philosophers of the school of Aristotle
Perondinus, Petrus (early 16th cent.): Italian scholar and historian
Perseus: the son of Jupiter and Danaë, slayer of Medusa
Perseus (d. 167 B.C.): last king of Macedon, defeated at Pydna (168)
Peter Comestor (d. c. 1179): French biblical scholar
Peter Lombard (c. 1100–60): author of the standard textbook of medieval theology, the 'Sentences'
Petrarch (Petrarca), Francesco (1304–74): Italian poet and humanist
Phalaris: tyrant of Agrigento (570–554 B.C.)
Pherecydes of Leros (5th cent. B.C.): Greek philosopher
Phidias (b. c. 500 B.C.): the most celebrated sculptor of ancient Greece
Philemon: the recipient of St Paul's letter requesting forgiveness of Onesimus (q.v.)
Philip II: King of Macedon (359–336 B.C.)
Philip II: King of Spain (1556–98)
Philo (c. 20 B.C.–c. A.D. 50): Jewish thinker and exegete
Philometor: see Ptolemy VI
Philostratus (170?–245): Greek biographer and philosopher
Philotas (d. 330 B.C.): Macedonian general, son of Parmenio (q.v.)
Philoxenus (d. 523): Bishop of Hierapolis, scholar
Phoebus: see Apollo
Phornutus: see Cornutus
Phylostratus: see Philostratus
Physcon: see Ptolemy VII

Piccolominy: *see* Pius II

Pico della Mirandola, Giovanni (1463–94): Florentine scholar and mystic

Pindar (*c.* 522–443 B.C.): Greek lyric poet

Pineda, Juan de (1558–1637): Spanish theologian and biblical exegete

Pityocamptes: a mythical murderer of travellers

Pius II (Enea Silvio de Piccolomini): Pope (1458–64), historian and patron of letters

Pizarro, Francisco (1470?–1541): Spanish conqueror of Peru, overthrew Atabalipa (q.v.)

Plato (427–347 B.C.): the foremost Greek philosopher

'Platonics': the Neoplatonists generally, disciples of Plotinus (q.v.), Ficino (q.v.), *et al.*

Pliny (23–79): Roman scholar, author of encyclopedic *Historia naturalis*

Plotinus (*c.* 205–270): Neoplatonist philosopher and mystic

Plutarch (*c.* 46–*c.* 120): Greek biographer

Polybius (*c.* 202–120 B.C.): Greek historian

Polyclitus (fl. 450–420 B.C.): the most celebrated sculptor of antiquity after Phidias (q.v.)

Pompey the Great (106–48 B.C.): Roman general and statesman

Pomponius Mela: *see* Mela

Priamus: i.e. King Priam of Troy

Priscillianists: 4th–5th cent. Manichaean dualists, disciples of Priscillian (*c.* 370)

Proclus (*c.* 410–485): Greek Neoplatonist

Procopius of Gaza (*c.* 475–*c.* 538): Biblical scholar and rhetorician

Procrustes: a mythical robber who mutilated his captives, killed by Theseus (q.v.)

Proserpina (Persephone): daughter of Ceres (q.v.), wife of Pluto

Prusias II: King of Bithynia (192–148 B.C.)

Psellus, Michael (*c.* 1019–*c.* 1078): Byzantine historian and philosopher

Ptolemy (2nd cent.): Alexandrian astronomer and geographer

Ptolemy I Soter: general under Alexander, later king of Egypt (323–285 B.C.)

Ptolemy V Epiphanes: King of Egypt (203–181 B.C.)

Ptolemy VI Philometor: King of Egypt (181–145 B.C.)

Ptolemy VII Physcon: King of Egypt (145–116 B.C.)

Ptolomie: *see* previous entries

Pyrrhus: King of Epirus (306–272 B.C.), defeated Romans at Asculum (279)

Pythagoras (6th cent. B.C.): Greek philosopher and mathematician

Rehoboam: son of Solomon (q.v.), 1st King of Judah (see Table, p. 415)

Reineck, Reinerus (1541–95): German historian

Reinerius *or* Reynerius: *see* previous entry

Rhodius Anaxandrides: *see* Anaxandrides

Richard II: King of England (1377–99)

Richard III: King of England (1483–85)

Roger of Wendover (d. 1236): English chronicler

Romulus: a son of Mars, founder of Rome

Roxane (d. 310 B.C.): Bactrian princess, wife of Alexander the Great
Rupertus = Rupert of Deutz (*c.* 1070–1129): scholastic theologian
Saladin: Sultan of Egypt and Syria (1174–93), fought against Crusaders
Salomon: *see* Solomon
Samson: Hebrew hero, the last of the great 'judges'
Samuel: the first of the great Hebrew prophets
Santa Cruz, Marquis of (1526–88): Spanish admiral, defeated Turks at Lepanto (1571)
Sapores: *see* Shapur
Sarah: wife of Abraham (q.v.)
Sarmiento: *see* Gondomar
Saul: the 1st King of Israel (see Table, p. 415)
Schmidl, Ulrich (1511–79): German historian and traveller in America
'Schoolmen': teachers of philosophy and theology at medieval European universities ('schools')
Sciron: a mythical robber, killed by Theseus (q.v.)
Seld(ius), Georg Sigismund (1516–65): German statesman
Seleucus IV Philopator: King of Syria (187–175 B.C.)
Sem: *see* Shem
Semiramis: legendary queen of Assyria, wife of Ninus (q.v.)
Seneca (*c.* 4 B.C.–A.D. 65): Roman statesman, philosopher and playwright
Senensis, S.: *see* Sixtus of Siena
Septuagint: the translation of the Old Testament into Greek (3rd cent. B.C.)
Serres, Jean de (1540–98): French historian
Sesac: *see* Shishak
Seth: 3rd son of Adam (q.v.)
'Seventy Interpreters': the reputed translators of the Septuagint (q.v.)
Sforza, Francesco (1401–66): Milanese soldier, ruler of Lombardy
Sforza, Lodovico: Duke of Milan (1481–99)
Shapur I: King of Persia (241–272)
Shem: son of Noah (q.v.)
Shishak: King of Egypt, invaded Judah under Rehoboam (q.v.)
Sibyl: any inspired prophetess. Cf. Cumaean S.
Sidney, Sir Philip (1554–86): poet, statesman and soldier
Simon Maccabee: leader (143–134 B.C.) of the Maccabees (q.v.)
Siracides: *see* Ben Sira
Sixtus V: Pope (1585–90)
Sixtus of Siena (1520–69): theologian
Sleidanus, Johannes Philippson (1506–?56): German historian
Solinus, G. Julius (early 3rd cent.): Latin grammarian and encyclopedic author
Solomon: the 3rd king of Israel (see Table, p. 415), accepted as author of Ecclesiastes, Proverbs, and Wisdom of S.
Sophonisba (d. 204 B.C.): daughter of Hasdrubal, wife of Syphax (q.v.)
Sphinx: a winged monster perched outside Thebes
Statira: daughter of Darius III, wife of Alexander the Great
Stephanus (6th cent. ?): Byzantine author of geographical dictionary
Steuchius Eugubinus: *see* next entry

Steuco, Agostino (1497–1548): Italian formulator of concept of 'perennial philosophy'

Stoics: followers of the Graeco-Roman school of philosophy founded by Zeno (q.v.)

Strabo (c. 63 B.C.–c. A.D. 24): Greek geographer

Strossi, Philip: see next entry

Strozzi, Filippo (1488–1538): Florentine statesman, opponent of Cosimo de' Medici

Suidas: traditionally author of an encyclopedic Lexicon (c. 1000)

Sulpicius Severus (360?–410?): chronicler from Aquitaine

Sybilla: see Sibyl

Syphax (d. c. 201 B.C.): King of Numidia, rival of Masinissa (q.v.)

Syracides: see Ben Sira

Tacitus, Cornelius (52?–after 117): Roman orator, politician, historian

Tamerlane: see Timur

Tantalus: son of Jupiter; his punishment: eternal hunger and thirst

Tereus: legendary king of Thrace

Tertullian (c. 160–c. 220): theologian, Father of the Latin Church

Thais (late 4th cent. B.C.): Greek haetera, mistress of Alexander the Great

Thales of Miletus (c. 640–546 B.C.): Greek philosopher and scientist

Thalestris: a mythical queen of the Amazons at the time of Alexander the Great

Themistocles (527?–460? B.C.): Athenian statesman and commander of the fleet at Salamis (480)

Theodoret (c. 393–c. 458): Bishop of Cyrrhus, prolific exegete, historian, etc.

Theophrastus (d. c. 287 B.C.): Greek philosopher and author of 'characters'

Theseus: the chief mythical hero of pre-classical Attica

Tholosanus: see Gregoire, P.

Thomas: see next entry

Thomas Aquinas, St (c. 1225–74): Italian Dominican philosopher and theologian

Thucydides (471?–400? B.C.): the greatest historian of antiquity

Tiberius: 2nd emperor of Rome (14–37)

Timur (1336–1405): the celebrated Turkic conqueror

Tostado, Alonso (d. 1455): Spanish theologian and biblical exegete

Tostatus: see previous entry

Trajan: Roman emperor (98–117)

Tremouille: see La Trimouille

Triumviri: Roman board of three rulers (e.g. Mark Antony, Octavian and Lepidus)

Trivulzi, Gian Giac. (1448–1518): Italian marshal of France

Trogus, G. Pompeius (fl. 1st cent. B.C.–1st cent. A.D.): Roman historian

Trophonius: legendary architect of Apollo's temple at Delphi, later consulted as an oracle

Tubal: 5th son of Japheth (q.v.)

Tubalcain: son of Lamech (Gen. 4.22)

Tully: see Cicero

Ulpian (c. 170–228): Roman jurist and author

Urban V: Pope (1362–70)
Uriah: 1st husband of Bathsheba (q.v.)
Uzziah: King of Judah (see Table, p. 415)
Vadianus: *see* Watt, J.
Valentia, Gregorio de (1550?–1603): Spanish theologian
Valerian: Roman emperor (253–260)
Varro, Marcus Terentius (116–27 B.C.): Roman scholar
Vatablus, Francescus (d. 1547): French classical and biblical scholar
Vegetius (4th cent.): Roman writer on military science
Venus (Aphrodite): Olympian goddess of love, beauty, etc.
Verres, Gaius (d. 43 B.C.): tyrannical governor of Sicily from 74 B.C.
Victorinus, St (d. *c.* 304): Bishop of Pettau, the 1st exegete of the Western
    Church
Vincent of Beauvais (d. before 1264): French Dominican encyclopedic
    scholar
Vipera: *see* next entry
Viperano, Giovanni Antonio (1535–1610): Italian scholar
Virgil (70–19 B.C.): the greatest Roman poet
Vives, Juan Luis (1492–1540): Spanish humanist and philosopher
Vulcan (Hephaestus): Olympian god of fire
Vulgate: *see* Jerome
Watt, Joachim von (1484–1551): Swiss humanist, author, commentator
Willet, Andrew (1562–1621): English divine and biblical scholar
William I the Silent, Prince of Orange (1533–84): Dutch leader against
    Alva (q.v.)
Xenophon (*c.* 434–*c.* 355 B.C.): Greek historian and essayist, led retreating
    mercenaries through Asia Minor
Xerxes I: King of Persia (486–465 B.C.), defeated at Salamis (480)
Zameis: *see* Ninias
Zeno of Citium (335–263 B.C.): founder of Stoicism
Zerxes: *see* Xerxes
Zeus: *see* Jupiter
Zeuxis (fl. late 5th cent. B.C.): one of the most famous painters of ancient
    Greece
Zoroaster (fl. prob. 6th cent. B.C.): founder of Zoroastrianism, the religion
    of the ancient Persian peoples

Sequence of the Kings of Israel and Judah

The United Israel (1028–933 *B.C.*)
Saul
David
Solomon

JUDAH (*the Southern Kingdom;* *capital: Jerusalem*)	ISRAEL (*the Northern Kingdom;* *capital: Samaria*)
Rehoboam	Jeroboam I
Abijah	
Asa	Nadab
	Baasha
	Elah
	Zimri
	Omri
Jehoshaphat	Ahab
	Ahaziah
Jehoram	Joram
Ahaziah	
Athaliah	Jehu
Jehoash	
	Jehoahaz
Amaziah	Joash
Uzziah	Jeroboam II
	Zechariah
	Shallum
Jotham	Menahem
	Pekahiah
	Pekah
Ahaz	Hoshea
	(*Fall of Samaria,* 722 *B.C.*)
Hezekiah	
Manasseh	
Amon	
Josiah	
Jehoahaz	
Jehoiakim	
Jehoiachin	
Zedekiah	
(*Fall of Jerusalem,* 586 *B.C.*)	

A Bibliographical Note

The place of publication is given only if it is other than London or New York.

Quotations from Ralegh's prose in my Introduction are from the original editions, except where the quoted passages are also available in the present edition. His poetry is quoted from *The Poems of Sir Walter Ralegh*, ed. Agnes M. C. Latham (1951). A new edition of the complete works, commissioned by the Clarendon Press with Pierre Lefranc as general editor, will be published by 1980 in eight or more volumes.

In addition to the bibliographical information provided in the notes to the Introduction, the following studies are expressly concerned with *The History of the World*:

J. H. Adamson and H. F. Folland, *The Shepherd of the Ocean: An Account of Sir Walter Ralegh and his Times* (1969) pp. 385–401.

J. W. Allen, 'Raleigh', in his *English Political Thought*, vol. 1: *1603–1644* (1938) pp. 63–67.

Anon., 'Sir Walter Ralegh's Prose', *The Times Literary Supplement*, 31 Jan 1935 (pp. 53–54).

C. F. Tucker Brooke, 'Sir Walter Ralegh as Poet and Philosopher', in *Essays on Shakespeare and other Elizabethans* (New Haven, 1948) ch. xiv; reprinted from *ELH: A Journal of English Literary History*, v (1938) 93–112.

T. N. Brushfield, *A Bibliography of Sir Walter Ralegh*, 2nd rev. ed. (Exeter, 1908) Pts x–xi. Cf. Racin, below.

T. N. Brushfield, 'Sir Walter Ralegh and his *History of the World*', *Transactions of the Devonshire Association for the Advancement of Science, Literature, and Art*, xix (1887) 389–418; also issued separately with new pagination.

T. N. Brushfield, 'Raleghana. Part VI. *The History of the World*, by Sir Walter Ralegh. A Bibliographical Study', *Transactions of the Devonshire Association for the Advancement of Science, Literature, and Art*, xxxvi (1904) 181–218; also issued separately with new pagination.

Lily B. Campbell, *Shakespeare's 'Histories': Mirrors of Elizabethan Policy* (San Marino, Calif., 1947) pp. 79–84.

Leonard F. Dean, *Tudor Theories of History Writing*, University of Michigan Contributions in Modern Philology, No. 1 (1947) pp. 17–22.

Edward Edwards, *The Life of Sir Walter Ralegh* (1868) vol. 1, ch. xxiii.

Sir Charles Firth, 'Sir Walter Raleigh's *History of the World*', in *Essays*

Historical & Literary (Oxford, 1938) pp. 34–60; reprinted from *Proceedings of the British Academy*, VIII (1917–18) 427–46.

F. Smith Fussner, *The Historical Revolution: English Historical Writing and Thought 1580–1640* (1962) ch. vii, 'Sir Walter Ralegh and Universal History'.

Christopher Hill, *Intellectual Origins of the English Revolution* (Oxford, 1965) ch. iv, 'Ralegh – Science, History, and Politics'.

Jean Jacquot, 'L'élément platonicien dans *L'Histoire du Monde* de Sir Walter Ralegh', in *Mélanges d'Histoire littéraire de la Renaissance offerts à Henri Chamard* (Paris, 1951), pp. 347-53.

Pierre Lefranc, *Sir Walter Ralegh écrivain: l'œuvre et les idées* (Paris, 1968), ch. x–xi, and *passim*; with the fullest up-to-date bibliography, pp. 693–712.

John I. McCollum, Jr, 'Ralegh's *The History of the World*', *The Carrell: Journal of the Friends of the University of Miami [Fla.] Library*, v (1964) i 1–6.

Walter Oakeshott, 'Sir Walter Ralegh's Library', *The Library*, 5th series, XXIII (1968) 285–327. On part of the contents of Ralegh's commonplace book whose discovery was first announced in 'An Unknown Ralegh MS.: The Working Papers of *The History of the World*', *The Times*, 29 Nov 1952 (p. 7).

C. A. Patrides, *The Phoenix and the Ladder: The Rise and Decline of the Christian View of History* (Berkeley and Los Angeles, 1964) pp. 45–47.

John Racin, Jr, 'The Early Editions of Ralegh's *History of the World*', *Studies in Bibliography: Papers of the Bibliographical Society of the University of Virginia*, XVII (1964) 199–209.

Newman T. Reed, 'The Philosophical Background of Sir Walter Ralegh's *History of the World*', *Northwestern University Summaries of Dissertations*, II (1934) 12–19.

William Stebbing, *Sir Walter Ralegh: A Biography* (Oxford, 1891; reissued 1899) pp. 270–84.

Ernest A. Strathmann, *Sir Walter Ralegh: A Study in Elizabethan Skepticism* (1951) *passim*.

Edward Thompson, *Sir Walter Ralegh: The Last of the Elizabethans* (1935) pp. 233–40.

Arnold Williams, 'Commentaries on Genesis as a basis for Hexaemeral Material in the Literature of the late Renaissance', *Studies in Philology*, XXXIV (1937) esp. pp. 200–4; cf. *The Common Expositor* (Chapel Hill, N.C., 1948).

On Ralegh's portraits, see Roy Strong, *Tudor and Jacobean Portraits* (1969) i 254–59; with further references.